GOVERNING
PEOPLES AND
TERRITORIES

GOVERNING PEOPLES AND TERRITORIES

Edited by
Daniel J. Elazar

ISHI A Publication of the
Institute for the Study of Human Issues
Philadelphia

Typeset in Israel
Printed in the United States of America

1 2 3 4 5 6 7 8 9 10 90 89 88 87 86 85 84 83 82

Library of Congress Cataloging in Publication Data

Main entry under title:

Governing peoples and territories.

   Based on the 3rd annual Paterson Conference on
Federal Responses to Current Political Problems,
held in Jerusalem, May 27-30, 1979.
   Includes bibliographical references.
   1. Federal government—Congresses. 2. Federal
government—Palestine—Congresses. 3. Jordan
(Territory under Israeli occupation, 1967-   )—
Politics and government—Congresses. 4. Gaza
Strip—Politics and government—Congresses.
5. Jewish-Arab relations—1973-   —Con-
gresses. I. Elazar, Daniel Judah. II. Paterson Con-
ference on Federal Responses to Current Political
Problems (3rd : 1979 : Jerusalem).
JC355.G68   321.02   81-20298
ISBN 0-89727-034-7   AACR2

For information, write:

Director of Publications
ISHI
3401 Science Center
Philadelphia, Pennsylvania 19104
U.S.A.

Part Three: Realities

Part Four: Directions

Appendices

Acknowledgements

I would like to thank Senator Norman M. Paterson of Ottawa, Ontario, Canada, for his support of the conference from which this volume emerged and the American Enterprise Institute of Washington, D.C., for its assistance in bringing the project to fruition. Carol Clapsaddle and Harriet Elazar undertook copy-editing and proofreading responsibilities while Sarah Lederhendler, Tsipi Stein, and Judy Ann Cohen handled the many tasks which must be done to make an assembly of people into a true conference and a "finished" manuscript into a book—all with the high competence we have all come to expect from them.

This book is dedicated to Aileen and Gerson Epstein, good friends and warm supporters of our efforts.

Daniel J. Elazar
Jerusalem

Introduction
Autonomy in a Post-Statist World
Daniel J. Elazar

I: The Changing Character of the Contemporary Polity

The focus of this volume, the product of the third Paterson Conference on Federal Responses to Current Political Problems, is on
autonomy arrangements, solutions for the problem of governing
peoples and territories and, specifically, the utility of such arrangements in the case of Israel and the Palestinian Arabs. Its title,
"Governing Peoples and Territories," embraces the three key
words that describe what classically are considered the three elements of a polity: *people, government,* and *territory.* The classic
definition of the modern nation-state demands the combination of
all three within an integrated whole.

For well over 300 years, at least since the beginning of the
modern era, the major political efforts of European civilization as
well as those peoples and countries influenced by European civilization, have been directed to building reified, politically sovereign
states which force the peoples in their respective territories into
the procrustean or sodomian jurisdiction of a single central
government. In other words their goal has been "one people, one
government and one territory." In some cases, this goal has been
linked to revolutionary radicalism, in others to reaction; in some it
has been liberal in content, in others conservative. But whatever
the form or content, statism has been the common denominator of
the age.

In all too many cases, the centralized sovereign state became
the procrustean state at the very least. Indeed, the term that was
invented to describe this new creature, "nation-state" was, in itself,
an ideal projection or a sleight of hand. We now are far enough
removed from the process to recognize that usually no homogeneous nation preceded the creation of a given state embracing
a given territory, a state whose boundaries were often established
by violent means. The creation of the nation came afterward,
when the central authority subdued all the dissident elements
within the territory to make the self-defined nation-state a reality. In
the nation-state a reality. In the course of its development, the
nation-state often became a citizen state, where each person was

1

This combination has been challenged in the post-modern era which began in the late 1940s principally because the homogeneous state polity with so close a linkage between people, government and territory in every respect simply has not come to pass, even in those countries where it seemed to be farthest along the road. One major characteristic of the post-modern era is the ethnic revival, the reemergence of the sense of primordial ties as central to individual identity. This development is reflected politically in the world-wide movement from class-based to ethnic-based politics.[1]

A second new relationship is the linkage of peoples or nations across state borders. Inter-regional arrangements such as those in the Upper Rhine Valley offer one example of such linkages. There people of Allemanian background living in three different nation-states—France, Germany, and Switzerland—a number of Swiss cantons and the German *land* of Baden-Wurtemberg are linked together through a variety of devices.[2] State-diaspora arrangements of the kind that are characteristic of the Jewish people offer another example. Yet another is reflected in the inter-state relations which are characteristic of the Arab world, which perceives itself as one Arab nation divided into a number of states but with trans-state linkages.

A third characteristic is the development of new governmental arrangements—at least new to the modern era (some have classic antecendents)—to accomodate post-modern trends. There are common markets which transcend the boundaries of the older nation-states. There are federacies or associated-state arrangements through which a great power and a small polity are linked together in what might be called an asymmetrical federal arrangement for their mutual advantage.[3] Mini-states of a few thousand population have emerged which can exist because of the overall security shield provided by the great powers and the general predisposition on the part of the larger nations of the world to tolerate such entities and to protect them even though they could not protect or sustain themselves under the state system of the modern era. Among the new developments are entities within polities which possess autonomy or home-rule in one form or another. These new governmental arrangements have moved in two directions simultaneously, to create both larger and smaller political units for different purposes, to gain the economic or strategic advantages of larger size while at the same time maintaining smaller scale structures to secure kinds of indigenous community or to better accommodate ethnic diversity.

A fourth characteristic of the post–modern era is the creation of new relationships between governments and territories, most of which flow out of these new governmental arrangements. The idea of more than one government exercising powers over the same territory was anathema to the European fathers of the modern nation-state. The 20th century, on the other hand, is the same territory was anathema to the European fathers of the modern nation-state. The 20th century, on the other hand, is the age of federalism, hence the existence of more than one government over the same territory each with its special powers, competences, or tasks, is becoming an increasingly common phenomenon.[5]

A fifth characteristic in these new relationships is the growing reality of the limitations on sovereignty. No state today is as sovereign as any state thought it was 100 years ago, if only because even the great powers recognize their limits in a nuclear age when it comes to making unilateral decisions about war and peace. Many states are accepting these increased limitations and trading them off, as it were, for advantages. The European Common Market is a major example of how the acceptance of limitations on sovereignty in the economic sphere can be "traded off" for greater economic benefits. It is not the only such example. At the other end of the Eurasian land mass, the members of ASEAN, the Association of Southeast Asian Nations, have taken substantial steps in the direction of limiting their freedom of action in many matters, while not formally limiting their political sovereignty, to attain greater military security and economic development.

Finally, the revival of religious fundamentalism as a political factor seems to be increasingly characteristic of the post-modern age. Its political implications are not yet fully apparent. In the Middle East at the present time, at least three states—Iran, Afghanistan, and Pakistan—are being greatly affected by Muslim fundamentalists while many of the others in the region are trying to reach some accommodation with them.

A New Theory of Political Relationships

The efforts to come to grips intellectually with all of these phenomena have been much slower than developments in the real world. The accepted intellectual models of state-building in particular have tended to lag behind these new realities. Only recently is there beginning to be a recognition that new thinking and other models are needed to deal with them. More specifically, the dominant center-periphery model of statehood is being challenged by the champions of a new model which views the polity as a matrix of overlapping, interlocking units, powers, and relationships.[6] A separate theory of federal relations is developing to replace the notion that such arrangements simply represent points on a centralization-decentralization continuum. This theory is not confined to the definition of intergovernmental relations but is related to a larger understanding of politics, a federalist understanding which is challenging the dominant Jacobin-Marxian view on a number of fronts.

Jacobinism is a European invention given form in the French revolution and subsequently extended and reshaped by Marx center-periphery model, whereby power is concentrated in a single center which may or may not be signifiantly influenced by its periphery (Figure 1), is almost inevitably Jacobin in its contemporary expression. This model is derived from the organic theory of the polity and represents an effort to democratize monarchic and aristocratic, polities by conquering and transforming the center of power in each. While its democratic expressions are Jacobin, its modern political sources are to be found in Bourbon France, in the works of French political theorists exemplified by Jean Bodin, and in Rousseau's statist interpretation of the general will. Lenin and Laski were perhaps the most articulate 20th century proponents of Jacobinism, Lenin in its totalitarian collectivist manifestation and Laski in its social democratic form. Centralization is the organizational expression of Jacobinism, which distrusts dispersed power because of the historical experience out of which it grew, in which localism was synonymous with support for the pre-revolutionary power-holders.

Figure 1
The Jacobin Model

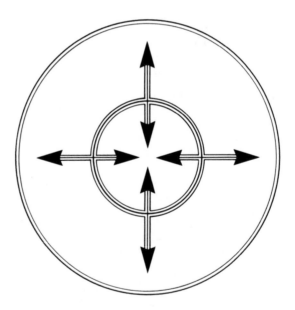

The matrix model, whereby authority and power are dispersed among a network of arenas within arenas, is inevitably federalist in its origins. Federalism is derived from covenant and compact theories of the polity and, in its modern form, represents the effort to democratize republicanism. For moderns, its immediate political sources were the Puritans, Reformed and Calvinist theologians, Hobbes, Locke, and Montesquieu. The foundations of modern federalism are to be found in the American revolutionary experience, including its constitution-making phase. The most articulate expressions of this model are to found in *The Federalist* and Alexis de Tocqueville's *Democracy in America.* Its organizational expression is non-centralization, the constitutional diffusion and sharing of powers among many centers (Figure 2 overleaf). Its logical outcome is the construction of the body politic out of diverse entities that retain their respective integrities within the common framework.

Forms of Autonomy or Self-Rule

In *Varieties of Autonomy Arrangements,* a working paper published by the Jerusalem Institute for Federal Studies in anticipation of the autonomy talks, 91 currently functioning examples of autonomy or self-rule, ranging from classic federation to various forms of cultural home-rule were identified in 52 different polities. Since then, several others have come to the Institute's attention, bringing the total to over a hundred.

Figure 2
The Federal Matrix
Interacting Power-Centers of General,
State, and Local Government

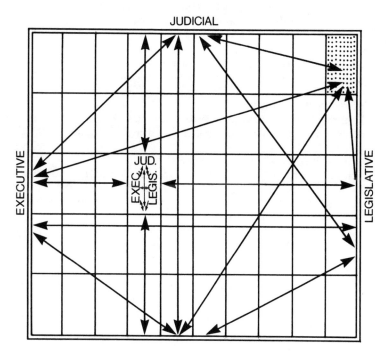

The variety of arrangements extant includes:

- Federations: there are 17 formally federal systems in the world today.
- Confederations: the European Community is the prime example.
- Decentralized unions in which there is regional or local functional autonomy or which are divided into historic provinces with autonomous municipal powers (e.g., the Netherlands).
- Feudal arrangements transformed (e.g., Jersey, Guernsey, the Isle of Man, Monaco, and San Marino).
- Federacies such as Puerto Rico and the United States or Bhutan and India.
- Home-rule, of which there are at least two kinds—that which is unilaterally granted with local consent, as in ex-colonial situations; or constitutional home-rule by charter.
- Cultural home-rule, designed to preserve a minority language or religion.
- Autonomous provinces or national districts (which the Communist world has developed extensively but which also exist in countries like Nigeria).
- Regional arrangements, both intra-national where there is regional decentralization as in Italy and Spain, or trans-national, such as the kind of regional functional arrangements in the upper Rhine valley.
- Customs unions, an old-fashioned device which has taken on new meaning, particularly in southern Africa.
- Leagues based upon common national or cultural ties, such as the Benelux, the Nordic Union, or the Arab League.
- State-diaspora ties,such as those which link the Jewish people the world over or those in India which link the Union's constituent states and their diaspora communities in other parts of the country.
- Extra-territorial arrangements or enclaves: Egypt and the Sudan have a fairly elaborate system of enclaves on their borders.
- Condominiums, such as Andorra.
- Special central government arrangements for specific regions or groups: even Greece, which stays faithfully with the old model of the centralized state has a minister of Macedonian affairs located in Salonica.
- State structures imposed upon autonomous tribes: Afghanistan has such a two-tier system. Recently one party captured the state structure but has not been able to deal with the autonomous tribes and consequently is in trouble.
- Consociational arrangements of two kinds: equal pillars (e.g., Belgium) or ethno-religious communities in rank order, some of which are dominant and others subordinate (e.g., Lebanon).

Where such arrangements exist, they usually exist in multiples. The United States is a good example of this with its federal system, constitutional home rule within the states, federacy arrangements with Puerto Rico and the Northern Marianas, and the special status of Indian tribal areas. Or take the United Kingdom with its different special relationships with Scotland, Wales, Ulster, the Isle of Man, Jersey and Guernsey, growing out of its pre-modern constitutional history, not to speak of its home-rule colonies and its tradition of decolonization through federal arrangements. In short, where there is a turning from the reified state-exclusive sovereignty-centralism syndrome toward a self rule-shared rule syndrome, it manifests itself more or less across the board.

Political Solutions and the Problem of Consent

In any case, the problem of dealing with ethnic diversity is essentially political and institutional. All too often in considering these issues, there is a tendency to emphasize the legal aspects of the problem when what counts are the political solutions. The law can be adapted to fit virtually every situation. Thus it is the political problem that must be confronted first and foremost.

In most situations calling for shared rule solutions, there are multiple political problems to be considered, both external and internal in character. One major problem that must be considered in every circumstance is that of consent. Government with the consent of the governed is characteristic of modern and post-modern societies. What such consent involves and how it is obtained and maintained is a complex matter, requiring various levels of initiative and response on the part of the parties involved or their representatives. There may be stages or levels of consent in a particular situation, which, after some initially narrow commitments evolve into broader based consensus. However it is developed, the problem of consent cannot be ignored.

II. Governing Peoples and Territories in the Middle East[7]

The two great peoples who stand at the center of our concern, the Jews and the Arabs, never fit easily into the mould of the reified state, although both have made very real efforts to do so in this century, each in its own way. The Jewish people with its long diaspora tradition, longed to return to its ancient homeland and to reestablish its corporate presence there within an appropriate political framework. However, even the Zionist movement did not formally opt for statehood in the modern sense as its goal until 1942, after the failure of the British mandate and the Nazi holocaust had made it apparent that only a fully independent state could protect and advance Jewish interests, including the sheer survival of Jews.

Jews everywhere hailed the achievement of statehood in 1948 and since then have been fully committed to the maintenance of Israel's independence. At the same time, hand in hand with the Zionist victory came a general revival of the sense of Jewish peoplehood and the development of institutions linking state and diaspora, where some 80 percent of the Jews continued to reside. The continued existence of a Jewish people with political interests which embrace and transcend those of the State of Israel has kept the state from taking on the characteristics of an ordinary nation-state, while the existence of a long-standing Jewish political tradition which rejects the reification of the state has made Israelis very hesitant about *etatism* (*mamlachtiut*, in Hebrew) when it has been advocated in one quarter or another.

The emergence of modern Arab nationalism at the same time as Zionism was closely linked with the pan-Arab idea. The political realities of late colonialism re-enforced certain historic divisions in the Arab world and led to the division of the Arab nation into several states, each of which acquired its own identity in the process but without losing its commitment to pan-Arabism. This has led to a certain ambivalence in identity in the Arab world with Egyptians, Syrians, Iraqis, etc., viewing themselves as both Arabs and nationals of their respective states. Thus the Arabs, too, remain somewhat uncomfortable with the European-originated state system which they have embraced, and have tried a variety of means to institutionalize the links between their states. It is this ambivalence which has made the issue of the Palestinians' claim to separate peoplehood so cloudy. On one hand, the Palestinian Arabs seem to have found a sense of collective identity which is real enough; on the other, a reading of the internal discussions within the Arab world as a whole, in which the Palestinian Arabs and others strongly reaffirm their undiluted ties to the Arab Nation, gives the strong impression that "Palestinian nationalism" exists primarily as a means to pursue the Arab attack against Israel.

Permanent and Transient Elements in the Search for Middle East Peace

The problem of the Palestinians that has surfaced as the major stumbling block in the present peace negotiations should indicate to all those involved that what is needed are new ideas that break through the barriers of conventional thinking regarding the principal points at issue in the Israel–Arab conflict. Such new thinking is not only desirable but possible, provided it is based upon the recognition of certain constants in the Middle East situation which seem to have been ignored by most if not all of the parties involved.

Four points stand out:

1. The most permanent elements in the Middle East are not the territorial states as they presently exist in the region but its peoples, those ethno-religious communities which, in their most comprehensive form, reflect a common kinship manifested through a common creed. In the long history of this, the most ancient historical region in the world, empires, states, provinces, even cities have come and gone but the peoples of the region have had an amazing persistence. Not only the Jews have a recorded presence in the region continuously for well over three thousand years, but other peoples—the Armenians, the Copts, the Arabs, the Kurds, the Maronites to mention only a few—have histories stretching back two thousand years or more. Even such relative latecomers as the Turks have been in the region for a millenium or more. These peoples have made their adjustments to different political structures, sometimes being their creators, sometimes their subjects, but as peoples they have persisted while states have come and gone. In fact, the Middle East is a mosaic of long-lived peoples who have used various political devices over time to achieve as much political self-determination as possible.

Precisely because of the ancient character of the peoples of the Middle East, "instant peoplehood"—as has been touted in the case of the Palestinian Arabs—is suspect. The Palestinian Arabs have, indeed, come to constitute a "public" within the Arab nation, an extended group sharing a common interest and affected by a common set of externalities. But peoples in the Middle East take form over centuries, not in a decade or two, and the truly legitimate structures, whether states or churches, are those created by these ancient peoples.

All the evidence points to the fact that modernization has not eliminated the primacy of ethno-religious identity but has only sharpened certain aspects of it. Those who thought that the imposition of new categories of statehood would undermine the old order have discovered how mistaken they were, often learning of their error through bloody civil war or massacre. Iran is only the latest Middle Eastern state to confront this reality. The various peoples in Iran, suppressed under the Pahlevi regime, have taken the first opportunity to surface with their claims for autonomy. Thus, any settlement must take into consideration the permanence of ancient peoples and the precedence of their rights while remaining duly skeptical about these claims based on situations of fifteen or thirty or even fifty years duration.

2. Even more than states, boundaries in the Middle East have been highly impermanent, rarely lasting more than a generation or two under the best conditions. The Middle East essentially consists of oasis areas surrounded by deserts, with the struggle between the desert and the sown one of its few constants. The carving up of those oasis heartlands which are of such continuous geographic identity as exists in the region and the division of the

territories in between has been a regularly recurring effort.

There is not a single boundary in the Middle East today that is as much as a hundred years old. To take the Israeli case, the oldest boundary is that between Israel and Sinai which was drawn in 1906. Israel's northern boundaries were only established in the early 1920s while its eastern boundaries have never been formally established except on an interim basis. The same is true for the boundaries between Syria or Egypt and their neighbors, not to speak of Jordan which does not even have an historic heartland known by that name.

Nor is this simply a phenomenon of modern nation-building in the region. It is a recurring pattern. Even during the days of imperial rule, the imperial boundaries changed regularly as a result of external and internal wars and the imperial powers were constantly redividing the territories within their domain. The Ottoman Turks redrew the provincial boundaries in what was known as Syria and Palestine on the average of twice every century. The whole purpose of boundaries in the Middle East has not been to encompass geographically fixed nations but to provide security for the peoples of the various heartlands or for the powers able to make their needs felt at any given time. To repeat, in this region peoples, not boundaries, are constant.

3. Not only are peoples more persistent than political structures and boundaries but the peoples are so situated that homogeneous states have been rarely if ever attainable in the region. Excluding Egypt, at best one can identify homogeneous areas the size of relatively small provinces or medium size American counties. In urban areas, peoples usually have been substantially intermixed, at most separated into neighborhood groupings. In rural areas, the division has often been on a village by village basis which leads to great complications when trying to draw boundaries on a more than local level. History has demonstrated that every successful political arrangement in the region must involve the satisfaction of some majority people along with the maintenance of the communal rights of the minority peoples within the same jurisdiction. Thus every polity in the region is, in some respects at least, a compound one, with no possibility of becoming an ethnically unitary nation-state as called for in European theories of nationalism, without resorting to expulsion or genocide.

4. As a consequence of the foregoing, peace has existed in the Middle East only under conditions when now-conventional notions of sovereignty have been drastically limited and principles of shared power have operated in their place. The various empires that have succeeded in bringing peace to the region, particularly the ancient Persian Empire and the more recent Ottoman Empire, were built on principles of local autonomy, at times ethnic, at times a combination of ethnic and territorial, whereby each of the peoples within the imperial system were

granted or guaranteed some significant measure of cultural, religious and even political self-determination or home rule within the imperial framework. The rulers of these empires recognized the aforementioned "constants" or "facts of life" in the Middle East for what they were. Unfortunately, the historical record shows that only where there have been dominant empires have these peaceful relations obtained, albeit at some cost to all but the imperial rulers. In those periods—which have come at repeated intervals—when the region has broken up into separate states or small empires, consistent interstate warfare has generally been the rule, with all that such warfare has meant for peace and stability of populations and, most particularly, of boundaries.

Today, we are once again in a period in which the region is divided among many states. The result is once again as heretofore, not only with regard to the conflict between Israel and its Arab neighbors. During the post-World War II generation—the first of independent statehood for most of the states in the region—there have been civil wars in Cyprus, Ethiopia, Iraq, Iran, Lebanon, Sudan and Yemen; revolutions based on ethno-religious differences in Lebanon and Syria; interstate conflicts or border clashes between Egypt and Libya, Iraq and Iran, Ethiopia and Somalia (not to mention Eritrea), Syria and Turkey, Syria and Jordan; and such foreign interventions as the Egyptian war in Yemen of the mid-1960s which added a new twist to the general pattern of regional conflict through the use of poison gas.

None of the peoples in the region would wish for a return of imperialism, even in the name of peace. Nor would any of the states in the area wish to sacrifice their independence for that reason. However, the record has once again demonstrated that the system of fully sovereign states as developed in modern Europe is not appropriate to the Middle East. Thus new inventions are necessary to achieve peace within the framework of modern nationalism and, hopefully, democracy. Such inventions must be in the spirit of the region, not foreign transplants likely to be rejected by the region's bodies politic. In the development of these new inventions, it is even possible to learn from old imperial solutions, even if these cannot be applied as they were in imperial times.

Two particular arrangements stand out as having had recurring success in imperial peace systems of the past. One is the principle of ethnic autonomy or home rule, what in the Ottoman period was known as the millet system, and the other is the principle of extra-territorial arrangements whereby particular groups can be protected by external powers with which they have an affinity, what were known in Ottoman times as capitulations.

While both the millet and capitulation systems have been roundly rejected by newly sovereign states jealous of their sovereign prerogatives, in fact serious remnants of the millet system persist in every one of those states and the outside intervention of brethren or great powers has been tacitly reaffirmed. Even the most extreme among them have discovered that, unless they are willing to exterminate minority populations or drive them out—the pattern followed by the first new states in the region early in the twentieth century—it is necessary to come to some accommodation with them. All but the most extreme rulers have found that it costs less to do so by giving them formal or informal cultural and religious autonomy in some spheres and even legal powers in matters of personal status (marriage, divorce, and inheritance are the most common of these) rather than to try to force them to give up ways of life that stretch back in continuous form to antiquity.

With a few exceptions, these accomodations have not been constitutionalized in writing because of the reluctance of the new states to formally limit their sovereignty but, for all intents and purposes, they cannot be changed without civil war or great upheaval. To the extent that they become constitutionalized over time, it will mean that, while not every group that has an identity of its own can have a state in the complex pattern of the Middle East, each can have the wherewithal to preserve its own integrity.

Extra-territorial arrangements are in greater disfavor in the newly established states of the Middle East, principally because they smell of colonialism. Indeed, were they to involve overt intervention from outside the region, they would be just that. Extra-territorial arrangements among neighbors are another matter, however. Even now, a number of such arrangements prevail on the Egyptian-Sudanese border, where they have been formally incorporated into the settlement between the two states.

The Israeli government's proposal to grant autonomy to the Arab inhabitants of the administered territories of the West Bank reflects a perception, perhaps only intuitive, perhaps more, of the limitations of the sovereignty concept in the Middle East. While no state in the area wishes to give up the essence of its sovereignty, it is quite proper to think of Israel's recommendation as a first step towards creating shared arrangements on the peripheries of sovereignty which can foster peace, in part because they overcome the jurisdictional problems that have always arisen on the peripheries of the many oases that comprise the region and in part because the problems can be solved by so intertwining the various parties that war becomes difficult and unprofitable for all.

Moving Toward a Solution

Nearly a decade ago, Moshe Dayan stated a simple truth: "We must recognize the fact that we have two peoples living in the same land, each desirous of preserving its own national and cultural integrity." However Eretz Israel/Palestine and the peoples within it are defined, few thoughtful people disagree with such a statement. In essence, this is the problem whose solution is the key to peace in the area. How can both peoples who are fated to live in physical proximity create a life together that will enable them to preserve their respective national and cultural integrities?

Israel's security needs rule out simply returning the territories to Jordanian (or Egyptian) rule. The existence of a substantial Arab population with nationalistic aspirations rules out any unilateral Israeli action to simply incorporate the territories into the Jewish state. Nor is a separate Palestinian state west of the Jordan River a reasonable option. First of all, the creation of a second Arab state within the historic Land of Israel/Palestine ignores the Palestinian character of Jordan. Today at least half of the Palestinians live in Jordan and more than half of Jordan's population is of Palestinian origin so that such a plan would actually permanently divide rather than unite them. Demographically and socially, Jordan is already a Palestinian state.

Even disregarding Israel's own need for secure borders, a separate West Bank state would be extremely vulnerable to extremist control. Under the best of circumstances, it could not help but be a nest for continued terrorist activity. One need only consider the situation in Ireland to understand why. The Irish Republic has no interest in encouraging trouble in Northern Ireland. Quite to the contrary, the Irish government would like to avoid trouble. Even so, with all the good will in the world, it cannot prevent the IRA from using Republic territory as a staging ground for terrorist activities in Ulster and a haven afterward, except perhaps through draconian measures that would be intolerable for its own citizens. Even if it were responsibly led, a small Palestinian state could not be expected to have nearly the same desire for peace as Eire and would be even less able to control its "crazies."

The conventional response to the problem has been a repartition of the land west of the Jordan River, whether through a complete Israeli withdrawal to the pre-1967 lines (the Arab position), a withdrawal with "minor territorial adjustments" (the American position), or a major redrawing of the boundaries along the lines of the Allon Plan (the position of the Israeli Labour Party). It is this response which has proved to be inadequate—a "non-starter" in one way or another—and which Camp David has effectively jettisoned.

From Partition to Sharing

The framework of peace signed by Carter, Begin and Sadat in the final dramatic moment of the Camp David summit marks a turning point in the direction of Israel-Arab accommodation in more ways than one. Not only does it put both parties on the road to a peace settlement but it changes the basis for making peace within the Land of Israel/Palestine that has prevailed for the past two generations by necessitating some combination of self-rule and shard rule for Jews and Arabs (or Israel, the Palestinian Arabs and Jordan) within the land.

Since the Churchill White paper of 1922 which detached Trans-Jordan from the Jewish national home in Palestine provided for by the League of Nations Mandate, precisely in order to guarantee an Arab share in the common land, the whole thrust of efforts to achieve accommodation between Jews and Arabs has been based upon partition of the land among them. The Peel Commission report of 1937 carried the partition idea a step further with a plan to divide Cis-Jordan (Western Palestine) as well. While it was never implemented, the idea was revived in the 1947 United Nations partition plan which was adopted as the basis for establishing Jewish and Arab states in Western Palestine. In fact, the Israel War of Liberation restored the connection between Arab-occupied Cis-Jordan and Trans-Jordan and the armistice agreements signed between Israel and the Hashemite Kingdom of Jordan in 1949 ratified a partition status quo between the two, encompassing all but a fraction of the historic land of Israel, which held until 1967.

The Six Day War destroyed that status quo by placing Israel along the Jordan and removing Jordanian rule west of the river (and, for that matter, Egyptian rule in the Gaza Strip). However, it did not solve the problems of peace in the land because the Arabs, settled in the territories formerly occupied by Egypt and Jordan, were not prepared to be annexed by Israel. Rather, the war stimulated a sense of Palestinian identity which had hitherto been relatively dormant. Had the Palestinian Arabs been willing to acquiesce to citizenship in an enlarged Israel, then the partition solution of 1922 would have been restored. This, indeed, became the goal of certain substantial elements on the Israeli political scene including Menachem Begin's Likud which was to gain power in the May 1977 elections.

On the other hand, the then ruling Labor Party, while unable to fully crystallize its position, leaned to a repartition of the territory west of the Jordan on terms more advantageous to Israel from a security point of view. This position was embodied in the Allon Plan, which was based on the premise that the heavily populated hill country in the heart of the West Bank, with its large concentration of Arabs, would be returned to Jordan in some way while Israel would annex a wider band of territory along the western foothills plus the Jordan valley. In fact, the proponents of this plan had no more success in persuading the Arabs or, for that matter, Israel's own friends, of the acceptability of this more modest repartition than those who espoused the Likud position had with regard to their plan. The Arabs insisted on a return to the pre-Six Day War borders, and even the Americans supported that demand for all intents and purposes. Stalemate ensued.

The events since 1977 have broken that stalemate, substantially with regard to relations between Israel and Egypt and now at least potentially with regard to relations between Jews and Arabs within the Land of Israel/Palestine. A major element in breaking that stalemate is a shift away from partition as the basis for a settlement and a search for other alternatives. Simply put, partition has reached a dead end. None of the three partition schemes on the table are acceptable to more than one of the parties involved. In current diplomatic slang, they have become "non-starters."

The first formal break in partitionist thinking came with Begin's announcement of his autonomy plan in December 1977. That plan, although purposely limited, for the first time formally suggested that the solution to the problem did not lie in partition but in some combination of self-rule and shared rule. Rejected at first by the Arabs, it was accepted by the Americans as a possible basis for an interim arrangement and, with some significant modifications, became the basis for the interim arrangement agreed upon for a five year period at Camp David. Each of the two parties to the conflict accepted this new framework for its own reasons, reasons which are still to a great extent virtually contradictory in their expectations.

It is precisely because of these contradictory expectations and the impossibility of satisfying them through partition that a shift of direction toward federative solutions has begun. It remains to be seen whether this initial shift can be utilised to achieve a peace that sufficiently reconciles the contradictory expectations to bring peace. But the framework does provide a basis for moving toward achievement of the classic goal of federative arrangements, namely to enable the several parties to the arrangement to have enough of their cake and to eat enough of it as well.

Autonomy: The Revival of the Federative Option

The shift from the pursuit of partition to the pursuit of federative arrangements raises a theme that has been played in a minor key throughout the history of the Israel-Arab conflict to new importance. Between 1917 and 1978 some 60 proposals for federative solutions were advanced. None had any serious impact because they were all based upon expectations of Jewish-Arab cooperation which were unrealistic at the time. Between 1948 and 1967, voices for federative solutions were muted although they did not entirely disappear. A few remained to build their paper castles in the sky.[8]

After the Six Day War, the search for federative solutions received a new impetus. The idealists reemerged with beautiful plans that continued to ignore stubborn realities, but even more cautious realists began to suggest that the federative option was the only one that offered any promise of movement at all. Shimon Peres endorsed the pursuit of federative options in a vague way within two years after the war, later elaborating a plan for a redivision of the entire Cis-Jordanian area into multiple Jewish and Arab cantons. Moshe Dayan suggested a functional solution for the administered territories which would involve shared rule by Israel and Jordan. Even Yigal Allon suggested that the West Bank areas to be returned to Jordan be linked with that state in a federation, with the whole confederated with Israel.[9]

Unfortunately, none of these plans nor those put forward by others outside of political life, such as this writer, produced any echoes in the Arab camp. As has been said, Israel found no partners. Now, for the first time, there is a very slim but still real possibility that partners will appear on the scene.

A detailed look at the text of the framework for peace in the Middle East, with all its ambiguities and opportunities for interpretation in one direction or another, indicates how this is so. On one hand, the framework provides for "a self-governing authority freely elected by the inhabitants" of the West Bank and Gaza on a transitional basis under the supervision of Israel, Jordan and Egypt. What is suggested here and for the future final settlement is a Palestinian entity that will not be a sovereign state, and hence will have to be linked with some state—which is a question that is left open. The provision for Jordan's entry into joint arrangements with Israel leaves the possibility open for a link to Jordan, Israel or both.

Knowing Israel's position about full evacuation of the territories and the Arabs' position about full relinquishment of any part of them, only one option remains, namely some kind of shared arrangement. This is further enhanced by the specific involvement of Jordan, Egypt and Israel in any decision involving the Palestinians' future along with the representatives of the Palestinian inhabitants of the territories. The provision for joint committees and security forces is a first step in the direction of some kind of shared rule arrangement, even though they are to be established on a five year interim basis only at this point.

All told, the Camp David agreement is a major step toward some combination of self-rule and shared rule provided that the parties to the agreement recognize the possibilities inherent in such arrangements and the severe limitations if not impossibility of any other approach.

This Volume

The first step in this process is the establishment of Palestinian Arab autonomy within the territories west of the Jordan River beyond the 1949 "Green Line." This volume is devoted to exploring this possibility in light of certain current trends in world affairs, the respective political traditions of Jews and Arabs, the results of experiments with autonomy in other polities, the experience of the military occupation and its impact on the residents of the territories, and the policies of the states involved in the peace negotiations. Most of its chapters emphasize the need to seek solutions that combine self rule and shared rule for the long term as well as for the next five years.

The idea of combining self-rule and shared rule, which was either ridiculed as utterly impractical or rejected as "unthinkable" when it was first enunciated by the Jerusalem Institute for Federal Studies in 1976 (not to mention the fact that at least one of its Fellows put forth a range of options to that end beginning in 1969), has now become the common coin of the realm among Israelis. Today the principal argument within Israel is over how to implement this combination, not over its validity or utility. This new common ground does not dispose of the operational problems of achieving a settlement with the Palestinians—as this book amply documents—but does offer a basis for dealing with it. As we have emphasized from the first, our land and its peoples need a unique solution. This volume is designed to contribute in at least a modest way to the development of the groundwork for such a solution.

Notes

1.   See Nathan Glazer, "From Class-Based to Ethnic-Based Politics" below, pp. 35–45.

2.   See Susan Koch, "Toward a Europe of Regions: Trans-national Political Activities in Alsace," in *Publius*, Vol. 4, No. 3 (Summer 1974) and Stephen Schechter, "Sharing Jurisdiction Across Frontiers," in *Self-Rule/Shared Rule*, Daniel J. Elazar, ed. (Ramat Gan, Israel: Turtledove Publishing, 1979).

3.   See R. Michael Stevens, "Asymmetrical Federalism: The Federal Principle and the Survival of the Small Republic," in *Publius*, Vol. 7, No. 4 (Fall 1977).

4.   This subject is treated more fully in Daniel J. Elazar, ed., *Federalism and Political Integration* (Ramat Gan, Israel: Turtledove Publishing, 1979), particularly the Introduction and Chapter I.

5.   *Federalism and Political Integration, passim.*

6.   Daniel J. Elazar, *Varieties of Autonomy Arrangements* (Jerusalem: Jerusalem Institute for Federal Studies, 1979), 2nd ed.

7.   This section draws heavily on Daniel J. Elazar, *The Camp David Framework for Peace: A Shift in the Direction of Federal Solutions* (Washington: American Enterprise Institute, 1979).

8.   Meir Nitzan, *Proposed Federative Arrangements in the Land of Israel, 1917–1977* (Jerusalem: Jerusalem Institute for Federal Studies, 1978). Hebrew only.

9.   In a conversation with this author in August 1979, shortly before his death, Allon moved even closer toward embracing a federal solution as the key to peace, suggesting that his proposal included confederation between the Jewish and Arab states from the first.

Part One
Perspectives

People, Land, and State in Israel

Daniel J. Elazar

For all its striving for normality, Israel remains a state with few contemporary parallels. Formally, Israel is built upon the modern European model of statehood which sees states as reified polities, existing apart from their citizens and sovereign in all things, the cornerstones of all political life and the primary focus of human loyalty (or at least that human loyalty which is not transcendent in character). Yet the Jews of Israel are ambivalent in their reaction to that conception of statehood insofar as they see Israel as a Jewish state (that is, one in which Jewish ways and values are dominant) and wish it to be true to itself and the purposes for which it was founded. Aside from the weight of the Jewish political tradition —which, though hardly recognized for what it is, still animates the attitudes and behavior of Jews toward their political institutions including states—three principal factors have led to the rejection of European conceptions of statehood in practice, if not yet in theory, and to a search, just beginning in Israel, for a conception more appropriate to the Israeli condition. They are: 1) the fact that Israel is the only state of the Jewish people; 2) the fact that Israel is one of two states in the land of Israel; and 3) the fact that Israel as a state is a compound polity.

Statehood and the Jewish Political Tradition

Before closer examination of the aforementioned three factors, a word is in order about the idea of statehood in the Jewish political tradition. There can be no doubt that the idea of the Jewish people living independently in their own land stands at the heart of the Jewish political tradition; no matter how reckoned in the various traditional sources, the fulfillment of the *mitzvot* (Divine command-ments) in their completeness depends upon the existence of a Jewish polity in Eretz Israel (the land of Israel). To the extent that Zionism represents a secularization of that tradition, it also represents an intensification of contemporary Jewry's attachment to Eretz Israel—which is seen as vital to the survival of the Jewish people from any of several perspectives current among Jews. At the same time, important as it is to enable the Jewish people to fulfill the tasks for which, according to believing Jews, they were commissioned by God, and, according to others, are those which can lead to the good life for the Jewish people, the polity is not an

21

end in itself. It is clearly a means to that end, but no more.

Classical Hebrew reflects this understanding. There is no generic term for state in the Bible or the Talmud. The term *medina* occurs in both; in the former it refers to an autonomous jurisdiction, like a state in the American federal system, that is to say a territory whose identity is marked by the existence of political institutions but which is not independent and certainly not sovereign, even in the modern sense of the term. It first appears in the Book of Kings in connection with Ahab's division of the Northern Kingdom of Israel; there the *medinot* are clearly no more than provinces, administrative districts with a minimum of autonomy. In the Scroll of Esther, the term is used to describe what today would be termed autonomous provinces, within the Persian Empire, of the kind being discussed in this volume. In the Talmud, the term is used in a similar way that often is even more vague from a political perspective, as in the case of *medinat hayam* ("somewhere in another jurisdiction"). It is only in modern times that *medina* is adapted as the term for a "sovereign state," parallel to the transformation of the term "estate" in the European languages.

In part, this terminological difference is reflective of the Jewish avoidance of the kind of abstract conceptualization for which Greek thought is noted. Thus, while much of the Bible is devoted to discussion of political ideas and activity, there is no generic term for politics in classical Hebrew. One consequence of this is that Jewish political thought does not fall into the error of suggesting that there is only one right political order. Hebrew, and therefore the Jewish political tradition, has a variety of terms for different kinds of political systems. What is characteristic of them all is that each focuses on a particular relationship between governors and governed. Thus, the rich political terminology of Biblical Hebrew describes relationships rather than "states," using terms such as *edah* (the assembled people in their constitutional capacity or a partnership in which the whole people have a voice or an interest—a commonwealth); *malchut* (kingship); *mamlacha* (dominion, perhaps empire); and *kahal* (the assembled people in their ordinary legislative capacity)—terms which primarily imply certain kinds of actions or relationships and regimes or polities by derivation.

In the Biblical view, peoples, nations and languages have the kind of permanent character as entities which states have in modern European political thought. What is not fixed for them is the form of regime or political structure under which they operate, or the boundaries of the territories they rule. Peoples, nations and languages are concrete, hence they are permanent; states are abstractions, hence they are identified only as they manifest themselves as regimes.

The basic reason for the classic Jewish rejection of reified state sovereignty in its European form rests with the strong Jewish conception that sovereignty reposes in God alone and that humans merely exercise delegated powers. Moreover, the Jewish political tradition has consistently held that, under the terms of the partnership established with God under the covenant, the primary delegatee of the power to govern the Jewish people is the Jewish people, either in its entirety or in conjunction with special delegatees such as an *Eved Adonai* (minister — in political sense—of the Lord; e.g., Moses and Joshua); *shofet* (Judge); *navi* (prophet); *melech* (king) or *sanhedrin* (assembly). These delega-tees, in turn, establish regimes through covenants among the principal powerholders (and their delegatees) within the terms established in the original covenant between God and Israel as embodied in the Torah. Under such a system there can be no reified state. What there is, is a people which exists as body politic as a result of powers delegated to it, and which in turn establishes regimes by further delegating those powers. Secularized, this approach leads to the idea that sovereignty resides in the people as a whole and the state is simply one of delegated authority (even a complex of authorities).

Under such conditions, a state is a receptacle through which the true exercisers of sovereignty can establish political order but which has no life apart from them—something closer to a *medina* in the Biblical sense. Perhaps the most accurate term for describing the classic Jewish polity is *edah*, the term used to describe the polity established by Moses and Jewish communities in every subsequent age (until the present when the term was distorted to acquire the new and misleading meaning of "ethnic" group). This is further reflected in the expression *am v'edah* which combines the dual bonds linking the Jewish people—kinship and consent.

This political framework and orientation, which has its roots in the Bible itself, continued to be the dominant one in the Jewish political tradition, even during the years of exile. Even when outside authorities attempted to impose patterns of rule upon the Jewish people or some segments of it, as in Babylonia, the Jews found ways to at least redefine these patterns in terms of the set of relationships that is in accord with the Jewish political tradition. In the Middle Ages, when local Jewish communities had more autonomy in such matters, this framework and orientation was made crystal clear in literally hundreds, if not thousands of *has-kamot* (articles of agreement establishing local communities) and *takanot* (ordinances adopted by those communities). The great debate of medieval Jewry as to whether communities can rule by majority decision or require unanimity for their decisions to take effect is a clear reflection of this conception of the polity as *edah*.

It was only after Spinoza that the Jews began to grapple with the idea of the reified state, under the influence of modern European political thought. And until the rise of Zionism the concept found little place among those Jews concerned with political matters. Even within Zionist theory, there was a great hesitancy to opt for statehood in that sense. Some Zionist theorists, such as Ahad Ha'am in the secular camp and various religious Zionists, sought to avoid statehood in any case, seeing it as being dangerous or improper for Jews. Others, such as Martin Buber, who could see the necessity for political independence, developed a concept of statehood far more in keeping with the Jewish political tradition. Buber, indeed, drew heavily upon that tradition to express his own radical conception of what a Jewish polity properly should be.

Whatever Zionist theorists may have desired, events created a general consensus among Jews that political independence was not only desirable but was only achievable through statehood. In a world of states, only a Jewish state would have the requisite authority and power to save Jewish lives and rebuild the Jewish people. No Jew in the mainstream of Jewish life today regrets that turn in the pursuit of the Zionist goal. The only question is what kind of statehood? Under what view or conception of the state?

Israel as a State of the Jewish People

All the evidence points to the fact that a very large majority of the Jews of Israel view Israel as the state of the Jewish people. Recently, the head of the Israeli government reaffirmed this view as the official policy of his government and of the state. True, there is a small but vocal minority among the Jews (not to speak of a rising chorus among the Arabs) that rejects this understanding of Israel as a state. But no matter how vocal, it is small and appears to be growing smaller, having reached its high point (at least to date) in the late 1950s and early 1960s when "*Mamlachtiut*"—the principle of strengthening the institutions of the state even at the expense of all others was also at its apex. In those days, the trend toward the separation of Israel from the Jewish people was quite pronounced and had at least latent sympathy even in segments of the establishment.

Within the ranks of that very large majority who view Israel as the state of the Jewish people, there are two basic orientations: those who see the Jewish people of Israel as practically coterminous with the Jewish people and those who see the state as one unit, albeit the central one, within a larger Jewish people. The first group is mindful of the existence of a Jewish diaspora, but considers the diaspora to be merely an appendix of the state, probably transitory in character, either because diaspora Jews will be compelled to move to Israel as a result of local pressures or because they will assimilate sooner or later into the general society in which they are located. From this perspective, practically speaking, the Jews who count are the Jews of Israel, hence they represent the Jewish people.

Those in the second camp not only argue that the diaspora is likely to be in existence for the foreseeable future but are prepared to reckon with the fact that the Jews of Israel constitute less than one-fourth of the total number of Jews in the world and that the largest Jewish community, that of the United States, has almost twice as many Jews as Israel. They argue that, since Israel is the only independent Jewish state and is, in addition, the focal point of Jewish tradition, it is necessarily central to Jewish existence and certainly far more important than mere numbers would indicate. However, they are also prepared to see it as one unit within a Jewish polity that has other elements as well.

To this observer, the latter view seems more correct. Not only is the diaspora likely to continue to exist for the foreseeable future, but at least certain diaspora communities will continue to exist as organized and powerful ones in their own right. To suggest this is not to suggest that such communities will exist independently of Israel; quite to the contrary, they are strengthened by virtue of the existence of Israel (just as the reverse is true). The Jewish world is too interdependent for any other course but, as a body politic, its parts also interact to strengthen each other. Moreover the most articulate elements among the Jews of Israel see the fostering of those relationships as one of the tasks of the state in all of its organs.

The principal institutional manifestations of this special relationship between Israel and the Jewish people are to be found in the "national institutions" functioning within the Land of Israel. These institutions are so named because they are considered to belong to the entire Jewish people (in Zionist terminology—nation) and not to the State of Israel, although their major purpose may be to carry out projects or perform certain functions within the state. Among them are the Jewish Agency and the World Zionist Organization (WZO), which are responsible for settlement of the land, absorption of immigrants, and the Zionist education of Jews in Israel and outside, and the Jewish National Fund (JNF), which is responsible for land purchases and development throughout the country wherever the Israel Lands Authority is not empowered to act.

The Hebrew University is formally designated a national institution, as is its library—which also serves as the national library and is so named. The reality of this is manifested in the university's board of governors, which is drawn from the Jewish community worldwide, and the fact that some two-thirds of its budget comes from world Jewish sources and only ten percent from the funds of the State of Israel. While the Hebrew University is the only one formally designated by law as a national institution, all the other universities in the country have the same status, *de facto*, since they have the same arrangements for governance and funding, with the added factor that at least two of them, the Universities of Tel-Aviv and Haifa, were founded by their respective municipalities which continue to make their contributions as well. The others also get some support from the budgets of the local governments in whose jurisdictions they are located.

The relationship between the Jewish Agency and the State of Israel was formalized in the covenant between the state and the World Zionist Organization adopted in 1952 through an Act of the Knesset. since then, the Jewish Agency itself has been reconstituted to make it more broadly representative of the Jewish diaspora and, in 1979, a new covenant was signed between it and the state to recognize the changes. The relationship between the state and the universities has been formalized through the Council for Higher Education. It is noteworthy that budgeting and policy-making powers are shared by the state's Council for Higher Education, the universities' "national" governing boards, and each university's senate. These are roughly the equivalent of state, federal and local bodies, if one were to translate them into conventional political terminology.

Through the Jewish Agency and its related organizations, the Jewish people as a whole undertakes numerous settlement, social and educational projects throughout the Land of Israel, in both rural and urban areas, and often in cooperation with the local authorities. The various bodies have regional offices in different parts of the country and, in some cases, local ones as well which serve local populations in their spheres of authority as if they were governmental agencies. The Jewish Agency is principally responsible for the construction of such local facilities as high schools and community centers with funds raised outside of Israel and recently inaugurated a program for neighborhood redevelopment in cooperation with the government of Israel and local diaspora communities.

In addition to these highly structured institutions, the Israeli government seeks to institutionalize the relationship between Israel and the diaspora Jewish communities through common organizations and associations structured along functional, professional, ideological, social and interest lines; encourages study programs in Israel; and send emissaries to Jewish communities overseas to work with them in strengthening Jewish life.

Finally, the Law of Return, which guarantees virtually every Jew (except those fleeing criminal prosecution of one kind or another) the right of entry into Israel and more rapid naturalization than non-Jewish immigrants, in effect obligates the state and local governments of Israel to provide all services to every Jewish immigrant from the moment of his or her settlement in the country.[1] In fact, because of the dominant political culture, virtually all such services and benefits are extended immediately to all those accepted as residents of the state, Jewish or non-Jewish.

In the meantime, Israelis have acquired representation on a number of other world Jewish bodies through a network of voluntary organizations functioning within the state, such as the Israeli section of the World Jewish Congress, the Israel Branch of the World Zionist Organization and the like. While there has been talk from time to time of creating some overarching body to speak in the name of the entire Jewish people, the realities of Jewish existence have prevented any such development, nor is any likely to take place. Certainly the State of Israel would not surrender any of its prerogatives to such a body, while diaspora communities have a certain hesitancy about committing them-selves to any such arrangements. Instead, they have developed numerous "authorities" (in contemporary governmental terminol-ogy) designed to undertake the special tasks which world Jewry seeks to undertake as a body. Many of these authorities focus on Israel. Others, such as ORT, do not, even though they may have activities in Israel. Israel's participation in such bodies and in such meetings as the Brussels conferences on behalf of Soviet Jewry, often through official delegations, is another indication of how the state sees itself as part of the larger entity known as the Jewish people.

Israel as a State in Eretz Israel

Regardless of one's stand on the political issues of the day, it is possible to agree that the State of Israel as we know it, with or without the "territories," does not encompass the entire land referred to in Hebrew as Eretz Israel, or what Aryeh Eliav (a noted dove) has referred to as "the land of the 12 tribes," which includes both banks of the Jordan from the Mediterranean Sea to the eastern desert. To recognize this does not mean that one has to espouse an irredentist position with regard to the land. The historical record shows that, even in the heyday of Jewish national existence in the land, it was more common than not for the land to be divided among several states, only one (or, at one time, two) of which was Jewish. Moreover, the two exceptions to this rule (the brief Davidic and Hasmonean empires) came at a price that not many Israelis would wish to pay. Thus, while reestablishing Jewish national existence in the land can be seen as an exercise of the Jewish people's religious and historical rights, total redemp-tion of the land is not a necessary political goal but can be considered a matter of "forcing the end."[2]

The reality that the State of Israel is less than the Land of Israel has several important implications. In the first place, it means that there is a difference between the religious commitment to the land and loyalty to the state; the two are not identical. It is possible to love the land of Israel in its entirety apart from one's commit-ment to the State of Israel or to any particular set of boundaries to which the state is entitled. The Jewish state must be in the land but need not embrace all of the land. Similarly, it is possible for Jews to accept the reality that another people also lives in the land, which they even have given another name.

Many secular Jews have emphasized, mistakenly, love of

state as the equivalent of love of country, or have certainly been tempted to do so. Religious Jews have not had that problem to the same extent, though some have also been susceptible to it from time to time. At the same time, recognition of the reality that Eretz Israel is to be shared with another people does not require Jews to give up their love for all of it. It may be that the day will come when peace permits the settlement of Jews in all parts of the land of Israel, even outside of territories embraced by the State of Israel. Even if those Jews are citizens of that state, the difference will be there. In sum, it is politically and morally salutary to maintain the distinction between land and state, for the sake of all parties involved.

Israel as a Compound Polity

The State of Israel itself is also compounded of several different ethno-religious minorities in addition to the Jewish majority: Muslim Arabs; Christians, mostly Arab, divided into various churches; Druse, Bahai, Circassians and Samaritans, each with its own socio-religious structure and legal status. Following the Middle Eastern pattern, all of these groups seek to preserve their corporate identity and Israel has granted them legal status, institutional frameworks, and government support through which to do so. In this respect, Israel is but a more enlightened example of a general phenomenon among Middle Eastern governments, all of which have ethnic minorities which must be accomodated in this way (as was true in Lebanon) or severely repressed (as in the case of the Kurds in Iraq and the Copts in Egypt at one time). In a sense, this represents a partial adaptation to the realities of what in the period of the Ottoman Empire was known as the millet system, whereby every such group was constituted as a millet with its own internal autonomy.

As a consequence of all this, Israel is also a republic compounded of different religious groups, each recognized and supported by the state, yet claiming its own higher source of authority. Among the minorities, religious belief and practice is quite high, and even among the Jewish majority it is significant, with perhaps one-third of the population quite religious in practice and another 40 percent selective observers of Jewish tradition. Even most of the so-called "secular" Jews have very definite expectations with regard to the public observance of Jewish religion which they see as befitting a Jewish state. Hence there are very few people in any community who are opposed to the present arrangements.

It should be recalled that there is no established religion in Israel, only government-recognized and supported religious communities ("Jewish state" in Zionist parlance refers to nationality, first and foremost). As a result, the various religious communities have substantial institutional structures of their own, recognized in law, in some cases governed by bodies chosen under state law because they provide state-supported services and thus must follow certain standard procedures with regard to selection and representation (not to speak of accountability and proper administrative procedures). Thus each religious community has its own religious courts whose judges, in the case of most, hold commissions from the state on the basis of qualifications determined by each religious community, and are selected by the appropriate bodies of each religious community under procedures provided for under state law. These courts administer the religious laws of their community, each of which has its own legal system for matters within its competence, which stands in relationship to the secular legal system of Israel roughly as state law stands in relationship to federal law in a federation with a dual legal system.

While from the point of view of the state these religious groups obtain their powers through state law, from the perspective of each of the religious communities their powers flow directly from Heaven and their law represents the Divine will. As far as they are concerned (and this goes for the Jewish religious authorities as much as for any of the others), the state should have only a minimal role in determining their existence and certainly no legitimate role in determining their powers other than that to which they are willing to acquiesce.[3]

Each of the several communities represents a further compound within its ranks. Every Arab locality is a compound of extended families—really clans—so much so that voting and political office-holding, not to speak of decision-making and the distribution of political rewards, is dependent upon the competition or cooperation among the extended families in each locality. Every so often a group of young people emerge to challenge this arrangement and there is talk in the land that the Arabs are modernizing and will no longer be bound by this kind of familial loyalty, but every time all but the most radical of the youth end up following the lead of their families in these matters.

The Jewish community in Israel is a compound of a different sort. Rather than being based upon the organic connections of extended families, it was originally based upon federal connections between groups from different countries of origin or between different Zionist movements. In effect, the Jewish community of Israel is compounded of communities of culture and communities of interest, both of which manifest themselves through ideological movements and territorial settlements.

There are two kinds of communities of interest, those with a religious or ideological base, usually referred to as movements, and those whose concerns are primarily with the management of power or the securing of special economic or social goals. These communities of interest are reasonably well known to all, although perhaps too little attention has been paid to the way in which they relate to one another and have since the beginning of the Zionist enterprise. Thus the various groups of socialist Zionists, each with its own ideology, began to erect their own settlements and institutions in the country. Paralleling them were Zionists with a liberal (in the European sense) ideology and others whose primary ideology was derived from traditional religion, ranging from religious socialists—who based what was, after all, a modern collectivist ideology on ancient religious sources—to the religious right which saw no reason to allow any kinds of secular thinking or behavior in the state to be.

. Each of these movements sought to create as comprehensive a range of institutions as it could, a kind of a non-territorial state of its own, but within the framework of the overall Zionist effort. Since they also wanted the overall effort to succeed, they federated together through various roof organizations and institutions through which they could pursue the common objective, even while contesting with one another with regard to the shape of the state to come and the vision that would inform it. This federation of movements became the basis of the present party system which organizes and informs Israel's political system. As such it has persisted after the establishment of the state. As a result of the transition from the settlement stage when ideological democracy was dominant to a stage of rootedness when territoriality asserts itself, it may now be weakening. Nevertheless, the state's institutional infrastructure continues to reflect these prestate federal arrangements through the party system and the Histadruth (General Federation of Labor), so much so that the arrangements inform even the ostensibly neutral governmental, cooperative and private bodies shared in common.

Today, as in the past, the country fairly well divides into three "camps": Labor, Liberal or "Civil" (known in Hebrew as *Ezrachi*), and Religious. The voting patterns in Israel since 1948 (and in reality since the 1920s when the elections to the governing bodies of the pre-state Jewish community are included) reflect of this basic division. Such electoral shifts as have taken place rarely have crossed the boundaries of the camps, reflecting only changes within each. Even the masses of post-1948 immigrants who tripled the population of the state were settled, employed, educated and politically absorbed on the basis of the "party key" through which the relative strength of the various parties within the three camps was maintained. Since the 1930s, Israel's governing coalitions have been based on alliances between the major parties of two of the three camps which represent a kind of concurrent majority system in Israeli politics. The results of the 1977 elections reflect a break in the party pattern of the Labor camp and a resulting cross-camp coalition different from previous ones rather than any break in the camps themselves.

At one time, virtually all services provided Jewish citizens were provided through the parties, or in the case of Labor through the Histadruth, which united several of the different labor parties for certain purposes. Again, the analogy to a federal system is apt. Just as in a federal territorial polity one has to be a resident of a state to avail oneself of the services of the polity as a whole, so too in pre-state Israel was it necessary to be linked to a party or camp. With the establishment of the state, the government took over more and more of the services, beginning with the military services (before 1948, the movements actually had separate para-military formations), continuing with the schools (which are subdivided into trends to accomodate the different religious attitudes within the Jewish community) and most social services. The parties or camps, however, still retain control of sports (the football leagues, for example, are organized on the basis of party teams although the divisions have become meaningless since the players are recruited on the basis of their ability without any regard to their party orientation—if indeed they have any), health insurance and ordinary medical facilities, and, to some extent, banking. Even those functions that have been absorbed by the formal institutions of government maintain an informal division by party key for employment purposes.

The importance of the compound of parties is such that even the most casual student of Israeli affairs is aware of it. In fact, however, many manifestations of the old divisions are disappearing. More and more services are provided neutrally by the state or local governments or, as is more often the case, through cooperative arrangements involving both. Party influence exists in the government structure and primarily touches those who pursue governmental careers rather than the public at large, although in a government-permeated society this is by no means an insignificant bastion of party strength. The expectation is that, aside from the division between the strictly religious and non- or not-so-religious, the division themselves will continue to grow weaker (but not necessarily disappear), unless there is a strong upsurge of secular ideology. The raison d'etre for many of the divisions has so weakened that only in the religious camp do the ideological justifications remain sufficiently strong to create demands of pre-state intensity and they are accomodated by allowing for parallel institutions in many fields.

Similarly, those communities which have acquired a primarily territorial identity are becoming increasingly important as the country makes the transition from the days of its ideologically rooted founding to a more settled character. Whatever the criticism sometimes raised against territorially based communities, it is generally recognized that the expression of interest on a territorial basis is natural enough to any society and certainly not foreign to Israel. While the political parties may seem to oppose the shift to territorially based representation on ideological grounds, in fact they do so primarily because their own self-interest demands that they protect their present bases. At best they can argue that such interest supports parochialism, an argument which is countered by the strong desire on the part of Israelis to achieve greater rootedness in the country—rootedness which includes local patriotism.

Circumstances have led to the emergence of a state that is more or less organized to accommodate certain of the complexities of its population but within a formal structure borrowed whole from another context altogether. In fact, that structure goes against the grain of most of the realities of Israeli society and politics and has had to be accommodated to those realities by a heavy reliance on extra-legal methods. While there is something to be said for having allowed the system to just evolve on a pragmatic basis, as it has, focusing on the relationships desired in each case rather than on the formalities of structure, there does come a point where structure itself is crucial, if only because of the way it influences relationships. Many Israelis have begun to perceive, perhaps dimly, that the structure of their governing institutions, derived as it is from nineteenth century European models, does not square with their expectations as citizens. Nor are Israelis particularly aware of the compound character of their polity. Even those who would be, for the most part look at the system through glasses colored by non-indigenous ideologies or methodologies that lead them away from a proper perception of the reality in which they live. At the same time, as Israeli Jews become more settled into their new state, they are beginning to rediscover the Jewish dimension of their political tradition that, in itself, is likely to make possible the political transformations that are necessary to bring about a new era of peace.

Notes

1.   There is a great deal of misunderstanding regarding the Law of Return. Israel has immigration laws similar to those of other Western countries, with permits issued upon application and naturalization following in due course. However, since Israel is considered the state of the Jewish people, Jews enter almost as if they were engaging in interstate migration in the American manner. It should be noted that similar laws hold true in other countries with regard to those considered their nationals even if born outside their borders.

2.   According to the prophecies for the end of days, the land will be restored to the Jews in their capacity as members of the same people divided into 12 tribes, each of which will have its own tribal government within the common federation.

3.   It would not be incorrect to estimate that as many as one-third of all Israelis hold the religious law of their respective communities in equal or higher regard than the law of the state, including a small group of Jews (perhaps several hundred) who reject state law altogether.

Definitions of the Political Community in Islam

Leonard Binder

Islamic political thought is primarily concerned with relating political realities to a theological ideal. All bodies of political thought are
similarly centrally concerned with understanding and perhaps
affecting the relationship between the real and the ideal, hence
the unique aspect of Islamic political thought is to be found in its
concept of the ideal, its notion of the remoteness of that ideal from
realization, and the ideational and institutional devices employed
in an effort to reduce or justify the moral and political hiatus. These
aspects of Islamic thought have attained their special characteristics from Quranic revelation, from the historical circumstances
which have attended the diffusion of Islam, its attainment of
worldly dominion and its subsequent political decline, and from
the intellectual and political institutions which were largely the
inventions of Muslim scholars, judges, and statesmen.

While it is important to establish the unique bases of Islamic
political thought, it is also indispensable to understanding to know
that, with the expansion of Islam in space and time, Muslims came
into contact with all of the higher civilizations of the world. Islamic
thought is, consequently, partially the heir of ancient Greek
thought, as well as of the ideas of imperial Iran and India, and of
the dualisms of Iran in moral doctrine and of the Christian West in
social and political doctrine. Non-Islamic influences had their
affect on Islamic thought at various times in history, but never
were any so decisive as to obliterate earlier tendencies and particularly not the fundamentally shaping force of the earliest period of
Islam.

The Islamic community was founded as a political and a religious community, or as it is sometimes loosely put, as a state and a
church simultaneously. Not only were these two aspects of social
life joined, but it is apparent that their unification presented no
difficulty of a religious or philosophical sort. Islam was a theocracy,
ruled by Allah through his prophet. If Allah could not be thought of
as directly ruling the Islamic community, which might rather be
thought of as "submitting" to the eternally existing will of Allah,
then it is equally true that the prophet was thought to know and to
act in accordance with the will of Allah in all particulars.

33

Muhammad neither struck the rock nor was he buried on Mount Nebo. The due of Caesar and the due of God were not differentiated. Hence, the ineradicable Muslim tendency to seek the political absolute of the establishment of the kingdom of God on earth.

Within 25 years of the death of the prophet, the fundamental problem of politics was intruded into the consciousness of Muslims through the controversial reign of Uthman as third Caliph and his shocking assassination. From this time forward a major tension dominates Islamic political thought; the tension between "legitimist" groups of schismatics on the one hand, and the exponents of Sunni orthodoxy on the other. The legitimist groups, and particularly the Shiite groups, claimed that the political absolute was in principle attainable, but that it had not been attained historically because the wrong persons had been installed as rulers. The legitimate ruler was either a designated descendant of Ali, son-in-law of the prophet, or someone qualified by a particular sort of wisdom or gnosis. The orthodox ideology which was counterposed to these utopian doctrines held that opposition to the established Caliphate (esp. the Abbasid Cali-phate A.D. 750–A.D. 1258) was sinful so long as the Community (in the sense of religious community or "church," the *ummah*) remained united (in belief?), retained its continuity (the link with the interpretations of the prophet and his companions), and was divinely guided (as manifested in the consensus of the commu-nity rather than in its political leadership).

The essential elements of the Islamic concept of the political community may be compressed into a discussion of a few key concepts, after the manner of the orientalists. This approach has many dangers in it, though, because it treats a number of bits of language as though they were not only eidetic truths but as though they expressed ontological absolutes invested by divine speech with eternal, unequivocal and inevitable moral signifi-cance. Consequently, there is a tendency toward the view that there is, or ought to be, one and only one Islamic position on the issue evoked by each word. There is a further tendency when using *paired*, dichotomous, concepts, to draw more extremely uni-vocal conclusions than are warranted by what is known histori-cally. Hence these concepts are to be taken as contraries rather than contradictories, in the Aristotelian sense—or they may be taken as the opposites which when united bring out the logical unity of the idea of which they are both a part.

The concepts which we shall briefly discuss are the following:

ummah and *millah*
khilafah and *mulk*
dar al-islam and *dar al-harb*
al-adalah and *et-Tughyan*
shari'a and *'urf*

siyasa and *ahkam*
dunya and *din*

Throughout the following discussion a number of themes will reappear in slightly different form, but it is well to realize that there are a few fundamental intellectual, even epistemological issues which link together these concepts which are usually found in diverse contexts and which are rarely if ever discussed in terms of the problem of the political community in Islam. The most important themes may be stated as follows: (1)does the polity determine determine the community or does the community determine the polity? (2) is the polity an historical entity or a moral entity? (3) what is the weight to be given historical, social and economic conditions in determining the application of divine law? (4) can the kingdom of God be realized here on earth?

Essentially, the question of definition of the political community asks who are the human beings who are members of a given polity, who are to be ruled by a given government within the moral framework of a particular regime? Another way of posing this question is to ask which is the terminal group to which a set of individuals owe political allegiance, or even what set of human beings define the limits of the sovereignty of a given state? These questions may be answered in an empirical fashion regarding particular historical entities, but when normative judgements are entered regarding those historical entities these issues become much more complicated. We are concerned with Islamic normative judgements concerning these matters, but it is well to remember that, for some Muslims, at least, history too has a normative character. That normative character is no more absolute for devout Muslims than for Jews, but history and nature, too, may not be ignored.

The words ummah and millah have overlapping meanings. Both may be used to refer to a religious community, a confessional group, a church, or the collection of individuals who hold the same religious belief or who, having been born of parents so identified, have not denied that belief. Usually ummah is used to refer to the Muslim community. Millah invokes the attribution to the Ottoman government of an administrative and legal policy of dealing with various religious communities known as the millet system. Millah has been used for Muslims and Ummah has been used to refer to non-Muslims. Millah in modern Persian means simply nation. There is, however, reasonably good hermeneutical sense for regarding the word ummah as representing the special characteristics which one attributed to the Muslim community as opposed to the general characteristics of all religious communities which may be conveyed by the word millah. The word ta'ifah, often used to describe confessional communities in Lebanon, retains the connotation of faction which is relevant both to Lebanese politics and to the widely held view that Lebanon contains only fragments of millal—a view which the Maronites have difficulty in accepting.

The relevance of these linguistic nominations emerges when we consider whether the Islamic state is constituted by the Islamic ummah, or whether parts of the ummah are properly found as the Islamic millah in a number of states? Part of the answer to this question turns on the weight given to the notion of community. Usually community implies some sort of social order rather than a simple commonality of religious identity and no more than a Durkheimian organic solidarity. Presumably there is some sort of legitimating link between the Islamic state and the Islamic community, although clearly the existence of the Islamic state may be necessary in the sense of religious obligation but not in the sense of a law of nature or even as an essential rather than an accidental precondition of salvation. Thus it may be argued that the Ottoman empire was not an Islamic state and that the position of the Islamic ummah within that empire was similar to that of other millal, except that various Muslim factions, or tawa'if, provided the ruling elite or constituted the ruling class—if that terminology is preferred.

From the foregoing it may be argued that if the state is invested with religious legitimacy, that legitimacy may be drawn in part from the Islamic ummah, but if the state is not itself Islamic it may be legitimated by religious communities on certain conditions and on ground other than the sacredness of the state itself. Clearly the most extreme position, taken by some funda- mentalists, and more recently by Khomeini, is that the Islamic ummah is ideally a sacred community and can only achieve its obligatory character through the activities of a similarly sacred political order. Within this general framework, non-Muslim mono- theists may live in religious communities, under the protection of the Islamic state, enjoying rights and duties proper to their status but not identical to those of the ummah.

When we come to the notions of the Caliphate and kingship the emphasis changes from that of the political, or religious community to what the state does and to the character of its institutions. The literature on the Caliphate is quite extensive since it is one of the very few topics in Islamic political thought that has received reasonably adequate attention. Consequently, I am only going to raise one or two of the issues most relevant to our present discussion rather than offer a comprehensive interpretation. The term Caliphate refers to both the institution and its function. The institution came to be very carefully defined in Sunni law, which holds that the Caliphate is the successorship to the Prophet, that is, the continuation of the role played by Muhammed in all public spheres except that of prophecy itself. But the institution was also defined in terms of dynastic continuity, the physical and mental capacities of the incumbent, his piety and the method of his appointment. The function of the office is essentially legal, administrative, political, military and economic. All of these activities are directed at religious goals in the sense that they facilitate the pursuit of religious goals by the ummah, or that some particular acts or policies are specifically required or forbidden by texts of the Quran, or in the sense that all acts of government in a sacred polity are invested with religious meaning.

Some western writers have been at pains to point out that the Caliphate was a political rather than a religious office. Others insist on the unity of the two spheres in Islam as though such distinctions were of no import. And yet others, like my own teacher, Sir Hamilton Gibb, were inclined to emphasize the secular character of the Caliphate at one time and what Gibb called the totalitarian character of Islam at another time. The essential points are, I think, that the Caliph could not alter the Shari'a although he could interpret it, he did not prophesy, he was considered fallible, he was to take counsel and was not considered inspired by God, and he was not chosed by God but by men.

Hence, while it may not make much sense to say that the Caliphate is not a religious office, it makes perfectly good sense to say that it is not a divinely ordained office. The shi'ite view of the highest political office, usually referred to as the Imamate, differs fundamentally in that most Shi'ite theorists hold that it is a divinely ordained office and, consequently, when the divinely designated and divinely inspired Imam holds that supreme office, the Islamic state may be said to be a reality and its sacred character manifest. Such a situation prevailed only briefly during the Caliphate of Ali ibn Abu Talib.

We have now established that there is some difference of opinion regarding the sacred character of the Islamic state, even in its ideal form. Sunni theorists have, moreover, agreed that the Caliphate no longer exists. Some have even claimed that the Caliphate was valid for only the first four Caliphs and since then Muslims have been governed by ordinary monarchies. The Shi'ite theorists similarly hold that the true Imam has been occulted for centuries and his messianic return is awaited. Until that time, Muslims must order their affairs in accordance with their own devices. The significance of these doctrines for our inquiry is that, even if the ideal Islamic state defined the Islamic political community, it is doubtful that a similar function may be attributed to the less than ideal. If it is held that there is a reciprocal relationship between the community and the state, each constituting or defining the other, and thus together constituting the Islamic state, then we must ask whether a less than ideal Islamic state can do the same thing.

is clear that when Ibn Khaldun writes of the transformation of the Caliphate into monarchy, after the manner of Aristotle's discussion of the corruption of just regimes, as an historical or natural process, he does not invest the resultant monarchy with any residual sacral, legitimacy. Religious legitimacy depends on the determination of the ruler to uphold the Shari'a, and there will be certain natural or historical as well as spiritual consequences of his policies. But for Ibn Khaldun, the limits of the political community are set by natural and historical forces—as they were for the exponents of Greek philosophy in Islam—and in this sense there will necessarily be more than one Muslim state. Even the orthodox Sunni legists could not quite bring themselves to insist that there could never be more than one Caliph at a time and, hence, more than one Islamic community.

Following Ibn Khaldun's view, it would appear that it is the Islamic community which determines the degree to which its government will be Islamic by means of the response of the community to the ruling elite. Moreover, it is an important part of post-Abbasid doctrine to argue that the salvation of individual Muslims does not depend upon the nature of the regime under which they live, because the alternative position would render salvation unattainable for all members of the ummah. In late Abbasid times, by contrast, al-Ghazzali argued that the Caliphate was necessary, even though the reigning Abbasids were obviously unqualified except by descent, because there are certain social and legal arrangements which must be sustained on behalf of the Muslim community.

There are then three general categories of state to which the Muslim community may be related: the Islamic state, the pious sultanate, and the naturally determined or accidental state, which may be either neutral or hostile to Islam. In recent times both Sunni and Shi'i fundamentalists have argued that it is obligatory to establish one or more Islamic states whose sacred character will be determined by the institutions and policies of the state rather than by the imput of Muslims into any given historically evolved institutional arrangement. Some liberal theorists have argued that an Islamic state will be the result of democratic process when and where the majority of Muslims have been properly educated and are individually motivated to act as pious Muslims.

The classic legal terminology for distinguishing between the Islamic political community and anything else employs the words dar al-Islam or the place where Islam prevails for the former, and dar al-harb or the place where war prevails for the latter. This seems a simple, dichotomous, distinction but in fact the matter is a little more complicated. For one thing, two "abodes" are actually dynamically and historically related, and for another thing there are some situations which are unclear and about which the legists disagree.

Dar al-Islam is in the first instance the territory within which the Shari'a is in force. In this sense it does not merely mean the place where individual Muslims fulfill their religious obligations. In this primary sense dar al-Islam refers to the historical process by which Islam was spread by the force of arms. I do not mean to argue that Islam was spread only by the force of arms, or that those who converted to Islam did so only because of the pressure of conquest or because of the material benefits accruing from joining the ruling millah. This terminology explicitly refers to the *futah al-buldan*, or the "conquest of the countries" and the rulings of the Shari'a regarding how war and peace are made and what sort of conditions might be offered to those who have been defeated in war, who have surrendered without fighting, or who have bargained for a measure of autonomy. Obviously the crucial concept is dar al-harb in this instance, since it defines that part of the world which has not yet come to any arrangement with the Muslims. In the classic and fundamentalist versions, this process of the expansion of Islam is still continuing despite temporary historical and psychological difficulties. It is the special task of those Muslim rulers over the Muslim territories bordering on dar al-harb to continue the jihad, on an annual basis, if possible, and thus to maintain constant military and political pressure on the unbelievers' state. Manifestly, dar al-Islam may include more than a single political entity, but the differences among the Muslim ruled polities are secondary from the point of view of whether the shari'a prevails. Theoretically it is possible to declare a state ruled by Muslims to be dar al-harb if the shari'a is not upheld by the rulers, but usually dar al-harb refers to territory ruled by unbelie-vers. Note especially that dar al-Islam and dar al-harb have a very strong territorial rather than a personal referrent. Further implica-tions of this conceptual scheme are that Muslim arms are in the long run successful, that treaties between Muslims and non-Muslims follow Muslim conquests, and that treaties which do not follow wars generally reflect the acceptance of Muslim terms by non-Muslims. not all of these conditions result in the same sort of regime and some legists were inclined to make fine distinctions between the more general dar al-Islam on the one hand and dar al-sulfi (where a ﺻﻠﺢ peace treaty follows warfare) and dar al-ahd (where terms are accepted) on the other.

This rather one-sided or non-reciprocal scheme has been modified by various scholars on two grounds: one, the historical facts of the defeat of Muslims, the loss of territory to dar al-harb, and the residence of large numbers of Muslims under non-Muslim rulers under a variety of conditions, some not so bad and some not so good; and two, the desire to develop a doctrine of international law founded on Islamic principles which would justify recriprocity, equality, non-intervention, international comity, and legitimating the general international law of treaties.

The question of whether a state ruled by non-Muslims is necessarily dar al-harb, even if a majority of Muslims resided within it was raised regarding imperialist regimes, most notably in the Dutch East Indies. A similar question arose in India after the "Mutiny" and during the course of the Wahhabi movement, as a consequence of the replacement of a not very strong Muslim government over a country in which Muslims were not a majority.

The issue was even more complicated in Indonesia after independence when the Dar al-Islam revolution opposed the nationalist government of Sukarno. The extremist *takfir wal-hijra* movement in Egypt has declared that country to be ruled by unbelievers who have turned it into dar al-harb whereupon it is incumbent on all believing Muslims to emigrate and to undertake the jihad against the Egyptian government.

There are, however, many more liberal Muslim scholars who, on the basis of quite valid earlier sources, argue that dar al-harb is restricted to those territories which are contiguous to dar al-Islam, which have broken a treaty with dar al-Islam, in which none of the Islamic laws is upheld so that it is impossible for a Muslim to practice Islam in any meaningful measure, and where the guarantees to the protected monotheists are not upheld. As might be expected, some legists and scholars insist that all of these conditions together must prevail before a territory can be declared dar al-harb, and some say that any one is enough. Some argue that Israel is dar al-harb simply because it was once Muslim ruled and others because Muslims do not rule or because the shari'a is not generally in force. Some argue that the so-called territories are dar al-harb because of the political and legal circumstances of Muslims or the regime for the holy places. Obviously, one criterion that religious critics will bring to bear on the autonomy talks now in progress is whether the resultant arrangement will allow the territories of the West Bank and of Gaza to be called dar al-Islam rather than dar al-harb.

Muhammad Hamidullah and Majid Khadduri are probably the two best known scholars who have attempted to elaborate what they call an Islamic system of international law parallel to the Western system, which is based on religious doctrine, historical precedent, and generally thought to have been first coherently expressed by Hugo Grotius. Each of these scholars is in the position of a Muslim Grotius. Their arguments generally accord with the widespread practice of most Muslim governments today of participating fully in the now universalized European system of international law, although some may reserve to themselves their own interpretation of the legal status and obligation or binding character of each international engagement which they undertake. That is to say, the government of Saudi Arabia may or may not consider that in signing an agreement with the United States it is doing the same thing as when signing an agreement with Morocco, Iraq, or Pakistan. Furthermore, where one is dealing with non-contiguous countries, the doctrines of dar al-Islam and dar al-harb need not be affected. Nevertheless, the entry of modern Muslim states into the comity of nations has greatly weakened the applicability of the doctrine, and the important migrations of Muslims from Algeria to France, from Pakistan to England, from Turkey to Germany, and from Palestine to America, has produced anomalous situations in which it seems inappropriate to apply any of the classical terms, although some might, for example, be willing to argue that the UK is now dar al-Islam. Despite the potential relevance of this issue in the present autonomy talks, I think that the issue will attain real political significance when it is once again vigorously applied to the Muslim majority territories of the Soviet Union. The doctrine has the most relevance, or at least seems to make sense, where it has some application in its classic terms, and that is in traditionally Muslim lands in the sense that Muslims were both the majority of the population and the rulers. In such areas there is a tendency to apply this doctrine regardless of whether Muslims are allowed to practice their religion freely, and regardless of whether the shari'a is upheld in the public domain. Still, it should not be forgotten that many ulama held British India to be dar al-Islam, and dissociated themselves from the adventurism of those they thought to be too ready to disrupt public order and endanger Muslims in a project in which they might not succeed, or wherein if they did succeed they might be misled into some fanatically distorted interpretation of Islam.

The related notions of al-adalah w'at-tughyan, justice and tyranny, may be applied to non-Muslim government as well as to Muslim government, but the most usual application in Islamic political thought is to Muslim government. In general, government based on Islamic law, the Caliphate or the Imamate is just government, and government which is not so based may be called tyranny. More precisely, however, a government which does not function by means of Islamic institutions, but which does not prevent Muslims from acting in accordance with divine commands may be a just government if it is concerned with the welfare of its subjects. Such a government can be considered legitimate only if it is agreed that a government of Islamic institutions specifically dedicated to upholding the shari'a is historically impossible, even though clearly desirable. Consequently, if Muslims are not to be condemned to a sinful existence or to eternal damnation, the government under which they live must be able to be taken in a religiously neutral sense. In spite of this condition, tyranny is not condoned by Islam. The doctrine of revolution is complex, however, since it is generally assumed that the grave disruption of public order is a greater detriment to the realization of the social and individual virtues of Islam than the tyranny of the rulers. Resistance is justified when tyranny exceeds those bounds where Islamic practice is possible and in particular when resistance has a chance of succeeding. Few indeed are the ulama who would follow Khomeini's simplistic view that Muslims must resist tyranny by force without qualification as to circumstance, method, or degree. Generally it is those who believe that Islam is fundamentally incomplete when there is no Islamic state who subordinate all other values to the achievement of a sacred polity, whether they are Shi'ite or Sunni fundamentalists.

Where al-adalah is not simply equated with the shari'a, it may be given different content by diverse thinkers. Often the content of just government will vary from historical period to historical period reflecting the standards of justice and morality of the day. For the most part just government maintains order and sustains social control, it provides security from foreign enemies, maintains the infrastructure of transport, communications, agriculture and exchange, it does not impose ruinous taxes and it provides for the indigent. A just government maintains the order of society, treating all citizens as equals in some regards and distinguishing among them with regard to their differences of status.

In modern times, it is apparent that political justice cannot be understood, apart from the democratic participation of the political community in its own governance. The issue arose in Iran, and the fact that Khomeini rejected the word democratic aroused a quite sensational response throughout the world. Khomeini's explana-tion of his position was not a rejection of democracy so much as a reflection of the kind of logic used to justify burning the library at Alexandria. Since Islamic government is by definition just govern-ment, and since Islamic government reflects the will of God, it cannot be subject to democratic whim, but should rather reflect the commitment of a whole people united in their dedication to living in accordance with divine command.

For those who do not believe that it is possible to realize the kingdom of God on earth, who believe that an Islamic state must be an historical phenomenon, then the secular content of adalah as reflected in the regime, its institutions and its relation to the governed is a crucial matter of concern. It is, of course, in this sense that a regime which does not allow Palestinian Arab participation in the determination of their own affairs and which denies that the Palestinian Arabs comprise a political community, may be called tyrannical without direct reference to the concept of the Islamic state. In other words, a refutation of the fundamentalist Islamic position and the rejection of the dar al-Islam and dar al-harb doctrine as anachronistic, do not exhaust the range of Islamic political thought and the grounds for the Islamic critique of regimes.

In the recognition that other sources of legislation may coexist with the Shari'a, Islam also recognizes alternative, non-sacred bases of legitimating historical political communities. In addition to the Shari'a—and especially where it allows a range of choice—cus-tom, common opinion, administrative convenience, technical requirements, and other bases of legislation are acceptable. Custom and common opinion or cultural preference of a given community seems to be especially relevant to legitimating nationalism as a ground for determining the political community. Islam does not require nation states, and many ulama have even argued that nationalism is a form of *shirk*. Nevertheless for many others there is nothing in Islam which opposes nationalism and it may even be possible to find some ambiguous religious valida-

tion of Arab nationalism. Arab and Turkish fundamentalists tend
to be more suspicious of nationalism than are the Iranians, but
even so, it is possible to find passages which support a nationalist
definition of the political community as a proper framework for
establishing an Islamic state in the works of Hasan al-Banna as
well as in the writings of Khomeini. In these cases it is easy to
recognize the great emphasis placed upon anti-imperialism, on
the challenge of Western Christianity to Islam, and on the rejection
of Western social practice.

The word *ahkam* has virtually the same referrent in Islam as
does the word *mitzvot* in Judaism. Both words, it seems to me,
point to direct, unequivocal commands from God which man may
readily understand, which he may disobey only at great peril to
his soul, and which may not be subverted by casuistic reasoning.
From certain points of view the content of these religions is ideally
a comprehensive set of such commands sufficient for every
situation in which human beings find themselves. But since
revelation has a primarily narrative form and since there are many
historical elements in revelation, the ahkam, which are the
clearest expression of God's will are not comprehensive. Some
theorists hold that there is no need for more explicit rules, and that
wherever there is no explicit rule we may conclude that it was not
God's intention that we act in accordance with a strict rule. Others
argue that all rules, even the ahkam, have to be understood in the
twin contexts of the whole revelation and the social situation in
which the issue arises. Yet others, in the moderate manner of
Sunni and Shi'i orthodoxy follow a middle path, allowing the
extension of the force of ahkam in some areas, and also
recognizing that there are some spheres in which there is neither a
hukm nor an equivocal method of extending by analogy or
reason an established hukm of an apparently different
application.

The main idea here is not so much what to do about areas
where we have no ahkam, but rather what are the consequences
for the political community of the ahkam we do have. There is a
strong tradition stretching from al-Ghazzali to Khomeini, of all
people, which insists that certain ahkam, referring to the whole
Islamic community, require the existence of a government in
order to be carried out. Al-Ghazzali is of the opinion that such a
government need not enjoy constitutive or institutional legitimacy.
Its legitimacy may stem only from its performance of these public
functions required by the ahkam. Khomeini may appear more
liberal here in that he seems to define a government as Islamic if it
carries out these functions, but, of course, al-Ghazzali was writing
during Abbasid times and Khomeini's views are premised by the
assumption that the great occultation continues in our day. From
this general position it follows that the great majority, at least, of
Muslims should be ruled by a government which is not merely
persuasive but which actively engages in carrying out the

relevant ahkam. There may, of course, be more than one such government, according to most theorists, but, clearly, the Islamic political community is constituted by obedience to the ahkam, which require public action. Khomeini tends to argue that there are a larger number of such ahkam than some other religious leaders might accept but the principle is pretty much the same for all.

The word siyasa is generally used for politics in modern Arabic and it suggests management of affairs, accomodating oneself to circumstances, making choices and selecting strategies, dealing with the human element, in more classical language, applying practical wisdom. Obviously siyasa is not based on ahkam, but the more important issue is whether siyasa plays any role in the fulfillment of ahkam bearing on the public domain. The answer of Ibn Taiymiyya, generally regarded as a representative of a school of strict interpretation is surprisingly affirmative.

The principle which is expressed in the phrase siyasa shari'a, the title of Ibn Taiymiyya's political treatise, is that the application of the shari'a in matters of public concern entails siyasa or practical wisdom. This principle does not subordinate the shari'a to siyasa, but renders siyasa the instrument or the auxiliary of shari'a. Manifestly, this view takes the applicability of the shari'a in specific situations to be possibly problematic. Siyasa would not be relevant where the ahkam are thought to be applicable entirely independently of circumstances.

It seems to me that it follows from the standpoint of siyasa shari'a that the definition of the political community may be a matter of political prudence or of historical accident to which no moral considerations need apply so long as that political community is ruled by Muslims, whether as a consequence of their majority of the population or for some other reason not excluding the success of Muslim arms.The point is that while the definition of the political community is not necessarily a matter of the shari'a, if it is defined in such a manner as to make the application of the shari'a difficult then some alternative siyasa is required.

It is not the intention of siyasa shari'a to mundanize the transcendant but rather to exalt the mundane. These two concepts, the religiously transcendant and the mundane are often rendered as din and dunya in Arabic. Most commentators on Islam are at pains to emphasize the monistic tendency in Islam in contrast to the dualism which is so frequently a feature of ancient philosophy. The dualistic posture of ancient philosophy poses the central question of human life as contradiction and suggests that the answer is a resolution of conflicting opposites, usually by means of a balance in the selection of a moderate or middle path. An alternative metaphysical pattern conceives of the solution as a merger, blending or a union of the opposites in a process which may or may not have dialectical aspects. The Islamic perspective is deeply influenced by this ancient dualistic frame of reference.

The dualistic paradigm is ubiquitous in Islamic theology and political thought. The resolution of the dualistic tension is the result of the proper practice of Islam. That is to say, Islam does not propose an alternate monistic metaphysics. It accepts the classical dualism as the context of thought and deed which defines the peculiar excellence of Islam and the necessity of revelation. Order can be brought to the affairs of communities if the revealed will of God can be obeyed as the practice of governments. Islam does not hold that the religious and the earthly are one, nor even that church and state or millah and dawlah are one. Islam rather holds that they can be made one, or coordinated, or that the contradiction can be diminished by means of the practice of Islam.

There is, of course, a considerable difference in whether one believes that dunya and din can be totally reconciled or whether one holds that governments may achieve greater or lesser degrees of success in coping with the tensions between the two. Even the exaggerated phrasing which states that dunya wa-din are twins does not identify the two, but, it seems to me, sets up a goal to be sought by those who hold political power. Hence the bringing together of dunya and din does not necessarily require abandoning the notions of siyasa, of urf, of mulk and of millah. There are, however, some who firmly believe that practical wisdom has little to do with the decisive deductive linkage that defines al-adalah in terms of the shari'a, the shari'a in terms of ahkam, the ahkam in terms of the union of din and dunya, and that union in terms of dar al-Islam, and dar al-Islam in terms of the government of the caliphate over the Islamic ummah.

The theoretical analysis and critique of these ideas runs the risk of artificiality and alienation because they have been abstracted from their historical context. It is not that Islamic thought takes no notice of the world because as we have seen that is far from the truth. Rather, Islamic doctrine was and is overwhelmingly practical and attuned to the problems of the day. As a consequence, situations which are highly unlikely to occur are ignored, and those situations which were unlikely to change in the short run are often taken for granted.

Most of the world Muslim population lives in a belt of contiguous territories within which they constitute the overwhelming majority. As a consequence much of the problematics of defining the political community is irrelevant and has been for most Muslims for most of Muslim history. The issue is precisely important on the periphery, away from the heartland and in territories which are not contiguous to the largest Muslim majority. By the same token, of course, one has the impression that this secondary importance has left the issue somewhat obscure. The basic doctrinal framework exists but one hardly knows how to proceed in particular cases, all of which seem to be difficult when we approach them from the point of view of abstract doctrine. When they are approached in historical and political context, the consensual Muslim position often appears to be obvious, although it may not be easy to explicate Islamic political theory in a manner that unequivocally upholds that consensual position. Thus the broad outlines of the political position on the West Bank, Gaza and parts of Jerusalem are fairly clear to most Muslims. When and if that position requires doctrinal support, the materials we have dis- cussed will be put together by different theorists in ways which they think will best express what the majority of Muslims feel is the case. If the doctrinal statements turn out to be faulty, that will not change political realities very much. It simply means that efforts to improve the doctrinal characterization of the consensual grasp of the contemporary historical situation will have to be intensified. Changing the consensual understanding is more difficult and it may require changing the situation itself, either by the creation of really new facts, or merely by the proliferation of more facts such as those which have already constituted the existing situation.

From Class-Based to Ethnic-Based Politics

Nathan Glazer

For some years there has been a growing sense among political analysts that ethnicity is taking a larger place as against class as a basis for political mobilization and action. The consciousness of this development is not limited to one country or a few, to the Western World or the Eastern, to the developed countries or the undeveloped, to the rich North or the poor South. It probably first became evident in the 1950s and 1960s, as tribalism or some equivalent (language-based politics in India) seemed, surprisingly to some, to supersede the near universal opposition to colonialism that had preceded independence. The 1960s saw the rise of the black issue to a dominant position in American domestic politics, and in its wake the growing significance of the Mexican American population in the politics of the Southwest, and in national politics. The 1960s also saw the increasing gravity of the Francophone-Anglophone conflict in Canada, now moving to a climax.

One could argue that these were all exceptional cases, to be explained by early and imperfect modernization, superimposed on artificial boundaries, in developing countries, and by the special immigration history of the United States and Canada. But then there were ethnic-based movements for autonomy in the oldest national states of Europe—France and the United Kingdom. We became more aware of ethnic strains and potential conflicts in Russia and China. Ethnicity began to appear as a universal force, with a power to move people that was putting class—"rational" interest, if one uses an oversimple distinction, as against the "irrational" traditional forces of peoplehood, language and religion—in the shade.[1]

I do not intend to exaggerate this development: class—income, occupation, status, or, if you will, relation to the means of production—is clearly a crucial and common basis for understanding how people organize themselves, vote, participate in politics. It is particularly important, I think, in Western Europe, in Japan, and in the United States—states that are for the most part either homogeneous or highly developed. But there are parts of the world where it seems illusory and self-deceptive to take any great account of class if one is to explain what is happening. Just to our north, where a terrible civil war and its aftermath still rends

47

Lebanon, it is an act of obstinate blindness to explain the conflict by reference to "left-wing" and "right-wing" forces. Christians may be better off than Muslims in Lebanon, but it would be as ridiculous to ascribe the destruction of that country to class bitterness as to explain the Holocaust by the middle-class position of most German Jews in the early 1930s. There are forces that transcend class and rational economic interest, and in the developing world, and in particular in the Mideast, only perverse ideological commitments unconnected to empirical fact would lead anyone to place class factors over ethnic factors in explaining the current situation.

I am using ethnic in a very broad sense. Jews are different from Arabs in religion and language, as well as in the vaguer sense of peoplehood—yet who is to say what in this complex is most significant? Kurds, sharing the same religion as Iraqis, Turks, and Iranians, remain a subjugated and rebellious minority. I do not wish to give any primacy to ethnicity as against language—gener-ally a feature of any ethnic group—or religion, for they form an indissoluble mix, with different weights in different situations, yet for convenience I use ethnicity to describe those features of any groups that derive from *birth* in a recognized community with some self-consciousness, and this may include a community defined primarily by religion or language.

Now it is true those of us interested in an working on ethnicity may be tempted to see more of it in any situation than actually exists, and to make more of what exists than we should. We should lean over backwards and maintain our skepticism in judg-ing the power of ethnic attachments in any given situation. Never-theless, it is true that the role that ethnicity has taken in politics in the last two decades has been unexpected and surprising. As Moynihan and I argued in *Ethnicity*, the "liberal expectancy" has been to some degree belied. We may include in the "liberal expec-tancy" the "socialist" and "radical" expectancy, as well. After all, for Marx, it was not only religion that was the opium of the masses —national attachments were equally ridiculed as superstitious remnants by that cosmopolitan. and his heirs in 1914 were unanimously agreed that for workers to fight against their capital-ist oppressors because of their class was a primary example of false consciousness, one that would hopefully fall away as workers developed a stronger sense of their own interests under the modernizing discipline of work in alienated settings. It is thus not the absolute significance of ethnicity in determining political action that has led to so much attention and analysis, but the increase of its relative weight at a time all accepted analysis, lib-eral and radical, called for this to decline.

We now have a whole litany of cases in which ethnicity has become *the* problem and the key political dividing line, rather than class. I will not review the litany. The weight of ethnicity is particularly impressive when it emerges in situations where it was not expected to be important, and where class, or something like it, was expected to play the dominant role in politics. Two contemporary examples. It was expected that the great problem for democracy in Spain would be either communism representing or claiming to represent the workers, and the army, representing not only itself, of course, but a group of class interests that had prospered under Franco. This may still turn out to be the great challenge to Spanish democracy. But at the moment, the great problem of Spanish democracy is the Basques, and it is the terrorism of Basque extremists that may well lead to or provide an excuse for the great class actors, communists and army, who were expected to dominate the scene to do so.

Or—to come closer to the Middle East—one recalls all the arguments that it was lower classes of peasants and workers who would rise up against the autocratic rule of the Shah, under whom the business and commercial classes flourished. It certainly seemed like a reasonable expectation. It may still come to pass. But in the Iranian revolution—an authentic revolution, to my mind, but I will not go into the argument as to the proper signs of a true revolution—it was a strange cross-class alliance of mullahs, bazaar merchants, the intellectuals, students and workers, too, who overthrew the Shah: whatever explains this almost universal uprising, it could hardly have been class. The dominating element, it appears, is a commitment to traditional Shi'ism—the national religion of the Iranian people, and thus to some degree an ethnic commitment. Certainly the conflicts that have emerged in the aftermath of the Shah's overthrow, with Iranian Kurds and Arabs, and the fears of other minorities, suggest that what occurred was a national and xenophobic uprising that had almost nothing to do with class, except insofar as the most prosperous inevitably had more foreign connections.

Of course we have recent examples on the other side, too, of the *declining* significance of ethnicity. We have—again to draw from very recent events—the case of the sudden decline of the Scottish Nationalists in the last British elections, and the return of many Scots to the Labour fold.

There is no "law," of course. The tendency for ethnicity to become a more potent base for mobilization than class is partial, to be found here and there, dependent on specific circumstances, and only surprising because it was unexpected. And there are always class factors involved in any ethnic conflict. Those Basques who do not go along with the terrorists are probably (I speak from ignorance, and only hypothetically) those whose economic interests are best advanced through a fuller association with the rest of Spain; and those apparently few Iranians who supported the Shah were very likely those whose economic interests were advanced by his government. In Canada, I would guess it is those Quebecers in the modern economic sectors who will vote against a full separation in the plebiscite that is promised there. And yet, maybe not.

But what we can agree on is that the tendency of ethnic and ethnic-type factors to prevail over class factors in ethnically divided societies is one of the unexpected features of the politics of the last twenty years. Radicals and Marxists still hope for something else. They hope, for example, that the Chinese and Malay poor in Malaysia will unite against the Chinese and Malay middle and upper classes. A vain hope. Noam Chomsky and other sectarians still hope that Arab and Jewish workers will combine against the privileged classes, regardless of ethnicity, religion, and language. An even vainer hope.

● ● ● ●

All this is I believe familiar. But having engaged in an analytical battle with the "liberal" and "radical" expectancies, I believe it is time to pause, and for those of us who have been sympathetic to ethnicity as a legitimate basis for political action to ask ourselves whether the class basis for politics is not *safer* than an ethnic basis? I believe defense of a culture, a religion, or a language is no less decent an objective, and I would so argue, than the defense of an economic interest, but I have chosen the word "safer" with a certain care. What I have in mind is that among the chief aims of politics is to achieve an acceptance of a society as decent and legitimate by the largest numbers of those affected by its decisions, to prevent the isolation and exploitation—or, at the extremes, the destruction by expulsion or killing—of any element of the population, and to do this with a level of conflict that does not become unmanageable, approaching dissolution and civil war. But if this is so, do we not have a better chance to achieve these goals if people act more on their economic interests and less on their ethnic connections? I think so, and would like to give a number of reasons why I consider class-based politics "safer" than ethnic-based politics.

First, I believe—as do other analysts of the rise of ethnic-based politics—that a greater emotional weight attaches to ethnic connections than to class connections. Daniel Bell, in an interesting essay, argues that it is easier to attach affect to ethnic elements of identity as against class elements.[2] Ethnicity after all refers to a community linked by blood, actual in terms of relatedness, or mythical in terms of belief. Class comrades may be addressed as "brothers" but fellow ethnics are brothers in a sense closer to actual brothers. Where blood is concerned, one is expected to act without calculation, spontaneously. It may be argued whether (1) in every case ethnic connectedness bears more emotional weight than class connectedness, and (2) whether this is a bad thing. But it would seem to follow from the greater emotional load on ethnic connections that actions would be less calculated, more spontaneous, and it follows, more violent.

At any rate, I am struck by the fact that we have had to invent a word for the wiping out by killing of an ethnic group — "genocide"—but we have found no need to invent a similar word for the wiping out of a class by killing. Undoubtedly we have seen cases of class murder, partial (Russia and China) and perhaps even more complete (Cambodia). Nevertheless, it may be argued that violence would be somewhat moderated if it were grounded on class difference rather than ethnic difference. It is the Chinese—not only the middle-classes—who are now being forced out into the open sea by the Vietnamese Communists. Their fate would be less grim if they differed only in class.

There is a second difference between class and ethnicity: people can change their class position, or be expected to change their class position, rather more easily than they can change their ethnicity. This should moderate antagonism. One may someday be a member of the class one opposes. I do not want to underestimate the stiffness of class in many societies, and the difficulty of persons of lower classes rising to higher classes, or of higher descending to lower. But the upper classes—Chinese, Russian, or Cambodian—can be converted by revolutionaries. When they are stripped of their possessions and undergo brain-washing, they may, while still subject to suspicion and penalties because of class origin, be accepted into the new revolutionary community. If the community is itself based on ethnicity, it is much harder to accept those who by definition are outside it, and to make a place for them.

A third difference emerges when we leave aside the rigors of revolutionary class war, and consider less extreme forms of politics. The fact is that a class in a minority may hope to become a majority by modifying its politics so as to include those close to it in class position. In the Marxist perspective, with its rigorous commitment to the definition of class by relations to the means of production, this kind of management of class politics may be difficult. But in other views of class, where it is seen as more of a continuum defined by degrees of income and status, this is possible. Indeed, empirically, we often see the case of a socialist or labor party trying to appeal to the more prosperous by modifying its policies, and of conservative parties trying to appeal to the less prosperous by modifying theirs. The ethnic minority has no hope of becoming a majority, except in the long run perhaps by outbreeding—or by annexing adjacent territory inhabited by the same ethnic group. The ethnic majority similarly has no fears of becoming a minority. This key difference should lead to a more calculating—measuring and reasoning—approach by a class in politics than by an ethnic group. In a majority, an ethnic group can be indifferent to the pain it inflicts on a minority. As a minority, it may become desperate because it cannot hope to see, within the bounds of an existing state, its views triumph. An ethnic majority does fear because a minority may act with even greater extremism than it might otherwise, to prevent such a damaging change in its status.

Fourth, the very forms of argument of class-based politics permit slicing the pie, and rational discussions as to who will get how much under which circumstances. Class-based demands by their nature are economic demands, raised with concrete expectation that the economic circumstances of a group will improve. This is a matter that can then be subjected to analysis—not that both sides in a class-based conflict will agree with any given analysis. Demands based on ethnicity, for autonomy or independence or special status, may be supported with the argument that this will improve the economic circumstances of the group, and in some circumstances they do have directly economic objectives (more jobs for us, more contracts for us), but economic interest is not the basic ground of ethnic demands—there is always a deeper ground, the maintenance and interest of the ethnic group. And many ethnic demands are non-economic, and not argued on economic grounds, but on grounds of justice, of self-evident rightness, whether or not the economic circumstances of the group are thereby improved. Thus, Quebec may be better off independent, but that is highly unlikely. This will not give many of the proponents of independence pause. Zionists used to argue —perhaps some still do— that Arabs were economically better off because of the Jewish immigration and building up of Palestine. We now realize that kind of argument cuts no ice when ethnic interests are involved. They are, in Clifford Geertz's term, considered "primal"—before reason, before analysis, and in the face of a rational analysis that most people will be worse off if they are implemented. When ethnicity is the ground of political conflict what is considered right replaces what is to the members of the group their immediate economic advantage.

●   ●   ●   ●

I have been arguing that class interests are more "rational" than ethnic interests, and for that reason, less murderous, ultimately. In the marketplace one can always split the difference. But I realize this argument rests on somewhat tenuous grounds. Philosophers and political scientists could have a field day with any definition of the rational, and history demonstrates that an "irrational" ethnic interest may have been in the end far more "rational" than the "rational" class interest. It would have been to the interests of all Jews, whatever their class position and economic losses, to get out of Germany and Eastern Europe—even for the then impossible dream of a Jewish state in the Middle East.

But whatever is decided by history and by heaven as to the ultimate rationality, in the last analysis, of depending on economic interests rather than ethnic connection, it is a fact that liberals and political scientists, who are generally liberal, have a fundamental suspicion of ethnicity as not contributing to a harmonious, efficient, and rational society. They are less suspicious of class—indeed, they accept that as the natural basis or the most natural basis for the forming of coalition and faction.

I have not taken a poll, but one may give many examples of the bias. Consider the general liberal response to an overemphasis on ethnic factors in selecting nominees to office. The classical liberal position has been to oppose even so mild a response to ethnic realities as the balanced ticket, in which nominees are selected on the basis of race, creed, and national origin. Liberalism says the best man should be selected, as the *New York Times* insisted, in vain, for decades. American liberals, despite the recent split in their ranks on the issue of affirmative action, agree that ethnic and racial criteria are inappropriate in public and private action: the disagreement is only whether these criteria should be eliminated now, or later, after some ethnic and racial groups have achieved a stronger position in the economy and professions. There was no more classic liberal than Supreme Court Justice William O. Douglas, and in his opinion on the DeFunis case—the first major case in which a white student challenged preference for minorities in admission to professional school—he argued that race and ethnicity could not, but class criteria could be a legitimate ground for preference. One could take into account the fact that a candidate was poor, or had suffered hardship. One should not take into account the fact that he or she was black, or Italian. Justice Douglas argued on constitutional grounds. But who can deny these are preeminently liberal grounds?

Almost all political scientists share the same bias against secession and division that rulers of nations do. This generally means they approve of states in which different ethnic groups are brought together within common boundaries, and in which some, inevitably, have the power to dominate others, and they fear the unloosing of the ethnic element. Thus, if Nigeria is to be divided into states, they would agree with its present rulers that it is best for the states not to coincide with ethnic lines of division. Let us not accentuate the ethnic divisions, and let us try to cross-cut them with other interests—a regional interest, an economic interest. If the appeal of Scottish nationalism declines, most political scientists would see that as a good thing—good for Britain, good for common sense in British politics. And of course what rises when Scottish nationalism declines is class interest, in the Scottish case a return to Labour.

In the United States, we are considered blessed because the political boundaries of our federal units do not coincide with concentrations of ethnic groups. In any case, this would be difficult in the United States because of its settlement history. And yet different historical choices might have made it possible for some states, for example, to be predominantly German, and in fantasy one can envisage a Union in which Massachussetts is Irish, Rhode

Island Italian, New York Jewish, Minnesota Norwegian, New Mexico Mexican, Mississippi Black, and so on. The mere statement of that possibility would lead most Americans, and most political scientists, to breathe a sigh of relief: "Thank Heaven it didn't happen that way."[3]

I have made my case by a pastiche of examples, and by forays into generalization, but I hope I have made it. Whatever the situation during the French or Russian revolutions, or in the nineteenth century, today class is seen by informed analysts as a better basis for political division than ethnicity: because it is rational, because deals can be made, because differences can be more easily compromised, because the passions aroused are not as deep and thus more manageable. It is for this reason that the liberal and democratic Israeli state is in a dilemma in appealing and holding liberal opinion—for liberal and democratic as it is, it is clearly a state based on ethnicity and religion, and liberal opinion will by very troubled by that.

• • • •

But whatever our bias—as modern men, as liberals, as political scientists—in favor of a class basis of politics, what is one to do when ethnic divisions are so deep, so strongly felt, so long-standing that there is no hope for blurring the lines of ethnicity by other interest, when class or income or status or region simply pales before the vigor and primacy of the ethnic connection? When this happens, it is folly to insist that class interests, because they are so powerful and rational, will or must blur the ethnic lines of division. The Chinese and Malay workers will not join together against their upper classes, nor the Muslim and Hindu, nor the Jewish and Arab. Ethnicity is sometimes mildly felt, lightly put on or off. In this case, statesmen are careful not to give it more importance than it deserves. In the United States, for example, it is folly to accentuate through public action and policy the relatively mild ethnic identities of Pole, Italian, Slovak and the like. There is point to trying to reduce the tendency of Black or Spanish-surnamed Americans to act on an ethnic rather than a class basis. It will reduce conflict, it will further integration. Sometimes it seems as if public policy stands at a crossroad. It can strengthen ethnic identity by some actions, weaken it or make it irrelevant by others. When one stands at such a crossroads, I think it is wisdom not to strengthen the forces of ethnicity. This is why I oppose the development of affirmative action in the United States—the program under which employers report to government the numbers of their employees in given ethnic categories, and are required to develop plans so that their work force mirrors the ethnic and racial composition of the labor force. This accentuates the role of ethnicity in the fate of any individual. It leads to conflicts between groups as to whether they should or should not receive the protection of affirmative action. Better, I would say with Justice Douglas, to give out benefits, if one has reason to shift from using sheer ability or merit, on non-ethnic grounds, for example, on the basis of some past deprivation.

But when the lines of division have already been driven deep, there is no alternative to division. Division is then argued for on many grounds: that it is necessary to protect the economic rights of the group, that it is necessary to protect the cultural integrity of the group, and finally, as against any specific reason, on the ground that the group wants a place of its own, and a place where it decides whatever is in the power of a politically sovereign power to decide, without the need for accommodation of the interests and desires of other groups. One can regret such decisions, and the multiplicity of states and statelets and conflicts between them that must inevitably follow, but there may be no alternative to accepting them.

But there is an art even in division to overcoming divisiveness. The history of the Mandate shows many schemes proposed to permit Arabs and Jews to live separate lives which were nevertheless to be joined together at some points. And we are now at the stage in the development of the Middle East conflict where new schemes are proposed that recognize the distinctive-ness of each group and its desires for a separate life, while recognizing they must be bound nevertheless by common interests. However this matter of "autonomy" or the recognition of the national rights of the Arabs of former Palestine is to be managed, one's hope is that even though one must go through division, a form of division may be found that offers hope of overcoming it. Not that the two peoples will ever be merged into one. That is not what either of them want—and in this sense, the Arab-Jewish division is very different from the division, let us say, between black and white in the United States, neither of whom wish to give up the benefits of a common country and a common citizenship, and both of whom are already parts of an integrated, if only partially integrated, society, which takes the other as an integral part of that society.

In the Middle East—and elsewhere in the world—the aim of integration is not the same as in the United States, and in other countries of immigration, such as Australia or Brazil, and one must recognize these differences. But even in the Middle East, an exclusive and total division cannot be the answer. One's hope is that through a division that recognizes and ensures security and the fundamental right to a decent existence and to political and cultural expression for both groups, the possibility will still be retained that some day other forms of political action on other bases than ethnicity will bring together the divided groups. And these other bases will have to be economic interests, whether we call it class or something else.

Isn't it something like this that is finally happening in Europe?

What would have been the point of electing a European parliament if it was not generally expected that some breakup of national blocs on the basis of interest would occur, whether this interest was defined as regional (poor versus prosperous), or as an agricultural or industrial interest, or a class interest? This is what most of us consider for the best, as against exclusively national identification, in which the French have to fear, as they did for a hundred years, the greater size and economic power of Germany.

It has taken a long time for Europe to get to this point, and there is no telling how long it will take the Middle East, if it ever does come to this point. Now ethnicity dominates identity totally, to the exclusion of common regional or economic or class interests that might operate across ethnic lines. The political mechanisms that will define the degree of separateness and protection for each group, now being negotiated for the Arabs of the occupied territories, are crucial here. If they are properly constructed, they should permit the emergence in time of interests that transcend Arabness and Jewishness, that is, of class interests.

Notes

1. Many volumes could now be listed analyzing this phenomenon. For convenience, I refer only to *Ethnicity: Theory and Experience*, edited by the author and Daniel P. Moynihan, Harvard University Press, 1975, and references therein (particularly in the introduction), for this article is a speculative and initial sketch of one problem in this development, rather than a finished essay.

2. See "Ethnicity and Social Change," in *Ethnicity*, op. cit.

3. See Nathan Glazer, "Federalism and Ethnicity: The Experience of the United States," in *Publius*, Fall 1977, Vol. 7, No. 4, pp. 71-87.

Part Two
Parallels

Kosovo and Vojvodina
One Yugoslav Solution to Autonomy in a Multiethnic State
Francine Friedman

Yugoslavia has long been a subject of study for scholars interested in either its simultaneous position as a socialist state outside the Soviet bloc, a nonaligned state, and a Balkan state of geo-strategic importance to both superpowers,[1] or its unique political as well as socio-economic structures.[2] With the advent of a new decade and the imminent change in the influence wielded by 86-year old Josip Broz-Tito, thus far the major unifying and stabilizing factor in the country, the issue of Yugoslavia's viability in regard to each of these facets is of interest. In an attempt to fill a noticeable gap in the literature in regard to Yugoslavia's federal political structure, this study addresses a subject which has become increasingly important for Yugoslavia itself: the Autonomous Provinces of Kosovo and Vojvodina.

The Socialist Federal Republic of Yugoslavia is widely considered to be a federation in the sense described by Carl J. Friedrich: "a federation is a union of groups, united by one or more common objectives, rooted in common values, interests, or beliefs, but retaining their distinctive group character for other purposes."[3] In the case of Yugoslavia, the federation was formed in order to "unify separate peoples for important but limited purposes, without disrupting their primary ties to the individual polities that constitute the basic units of federation."[4] Under such circumstances, it follows that the locus of power would be relatively localized. That is, in keeping with the wide distribution of differing values within various segments of the population, the federal government would retain only those powers necessary to preserve unity of the federation in respect to internal or external threats to that cohesion. It is thus to be expected that most of the governmental powers would remain in the hands of sub-federal or constituent units which would be the ones maintaining closest contact with the people.[5]

In order for the federation of a multiethnic state like Yugoslavia to retain the loyalty of the people, the federal government must promise—and deliver—some degree of regional self-rule or autonomy to its constituent units. The word "autonomy" is derived from the Greek *autos* meaning "self" and *nomos* meaning "law."

59

Autonomy in the psychological sense is defined as the "mainte-nance of the integrity of the self."[6] Extrapolating from the individual to societal units, autonomy may be viewed as the ability of a political collectivity to preserve its integrity by determin-ing its own laws or, more formally, as the "power and authority, as well as the legitimate capacity to govern oneself in those matters which form the basis of the community."[7]

Autonomy may be examined from two points of view: how much autonomy is legally granted to a governmental or adminis-trative unit and how much autonomy is actually permitted to be implemented. In this paper we will be discussing whether the legal grant of autonomy is allowed to be fulfilled in reality in the case of two of Yugoslavia's constituent units, the Autonomous Provinces of Vojvodina and Kosovo.

The 1946 Constitution of the Federative People's Republic of Yugoslavia created a federation[8] composed of six republics, which corresponded to the traditional national divisions of the country: Serbia, Croatia, Slovenia, Montenegro, Macedonia and Bosnia-Herzegovina.[9] The Yugoslav Constitution was modeled on the 1936 Stalin Constitution of the Soviet Union, which had bowed to the realities of being a multiethnic empire and had, in form if not in substance, contravened the Leninist warning against federal-ism.[10] Like the Soviet Union, Yugoslavia did not follow the prescription for federalism in a multiethnic country; instead of keeping for the central gevernment only those powers which would unify the various peoples of the country, both the Soviet Union and postwar Yugoslavia opted for highly centralized states. This decision was made, in both cases, in response to the Marxist belief that history was marching toward the eventual merger of nations into larger, homogeneous units, but that, in the transitional stage to that era, certain concessions to national feelings in multinational units would have to be made—i.e., a federal state in form but a highly centralized state in content.

In further emulation of the Soviet Union, Yugoslavia adopted the device of "autonomous province." Within the Socialist Repub-lic of Serbia were two regions which, although belonging to it by historical and geographical claim, nevertheless had been histori-cally constituted communities with unique national, cultural, demographic and political features: Vojvodina and Kosovo-Metohija. It was partially as a result of this fact that Serbia was divided into three administrative regions: Serbia proper, the Autonomous Province (*pokrajna*) of Vojvodina, and the Autonom-ous Region (*oblast*) of Kosovo-Metohija.

This division of the Serbian Republic into three areas is thus in some ways a present-day reflection and result of historical circumstances. It is perhaps opportune at this time, therefore, to review briefly the development of pre-modern Serbia, including its relationship with Kosovo-Metohija and Vojvodina, remembering that much of Yugoslavia's modern political history has been shaped by the reactions of the other South Slavs to threats posed by the possible resurgence of the historical Greater Serbia.

Pre-Modern Serbia

The first major South Slav political entity was the Kingdom of Serbia established in the early thirteenth century. Although the South Slavs first penetrated the Balkan peninsula at the beginning of the sixth century and, by the mid-seventh century, had conquered the lands "from the Danube to the Maritza, from the Adriatic to the Black Sea... broken only by Albania and Southern Thrace,"[11] the various Slavic tribes (Bulgars, Serbs, Croats, Slovenes) coexisted on the Balkan Peninsula without much political unity. They preferred to form themselves into "free communities of peasant owners," rather than kingdoms of theocracies.[12] This initial lack of political coherence was reflected in the fact that between the ninth and twelfth centuries the Serbs were at various times part of the Bulgarian and the Byzantine Empires, while the Croats were subjects of Hungary or of Venice. Ecclesiastical matters, too, mirrored this absence of cohesion among the South Slavic tribes: while the Serbs followed Constantinople, the Croats adhered to Rome.

The Serbian kingdom was formed by the conquest of Serbia proper, Montenegro and Herzegovina under the banner of the Nemanja dynasty. During the thirteenth century Serbia acquired both civil independence and an antocephalous church. In the fourteenth century, Tsar Stephen VIII (Dushan) further extended the Serbian Empire by conquering Albania, Southern Dalmatia, Bosnia, Northern Macedonia and a large portion of Greece.

Ottoman penetration into Europe meant the end of the independent Kingdom of Serbia. On June 15, 1389, the historic Battle of Kosovo was won by Ottoman forces, and the Serbian empire was obliterated. Serbia became a vassal principality under Ottoman rule and for the next five hundred years ceased to be an independent political entity.

Nevertheless, the Ottoman Empire did not extend its civil jurisdiction to many parts of Serbia. Instead, the descendants of those Serbian nobles who had managed to obtain the good will of the Sultan and thus to retain control of their lands, ruled the area independently,[13] subject only to the approval of the Pasha in Belgrade. Approval was generally forthcoming as long as the Serbian vassal principalities supplied men for the army and tribute for the Pasha and the Sultan. In fact, "so long as they got their soldiers and their money and protected Mussulmans against the infidel dogs, the Turks cared very little about civil government."[14]

Turkish conquests in the sixteenth century sent many Serbs into exile in South Hungary, Slavonia, Dalmatia and various parts of Central Croatia. These Serbian exiles, called *prechani* by the

Serbs in Serbia, continued to dream of reunion with their co-nationals still under Ottoman rule. The Serbs who remained in Serbia meanwhile staged a series of revolts against Turkish rule aided by the restored Serbian national church, which vigorously assumed leadership in Serbia's ecclesiastic as well as civil affairs. It was not until the eighteenth century, however, that the Serbs of the Habsburg Empire and the Serbs of Serbia were again united by the momentary rout (1718-1739) of Ottoman forces at the hands of the Austrians.

Long used to *de facto* civil self-government and an independent national church,[15] the Serbs were the first of the Balkan peoples to achieve independence. The fact that the Serbian borders within the Ottoman Empire did not encompass all Serbs had been the major factor in the rise of a Serbian political patriotism as far back as the mid-1840s.[16] But even earlier their armed revolts against the Turks gained Serbia a measure of freedom. In 1804, the Serbs rose up and successfully challenged the Ottoman Empire, with some Russian and Austrian aid, until 1813, when their leader Karadjordje mysteriously and ignominiously disappeared into exile.[17]

The second Serbian insurrection, led by Milos Obrenovic, was more successful than the first. During a struggle of fifteen years, the Serbs gradually won autonomy within the Ottoman Empire, with the material help and direction of the intellectually awakened and nationalistic *prechani*. In 1836 Obrenovic was made prince of the self-governing principality of Serbia. Serbia's independent status was guaranteed from then on by Turkish fear of Russia, which had promised to come to Serbian aid if necessary.

When Serbian autonomy within the Ottoman Empire was assured, the Serbs began to develop their version of "Yugoslavism" more fully, the major premise being that all South Slavs should be united within one political unit. This became the rationale behind the Serbian desire for destruction of the Ottoman and Habsburg Empires. If these empires disappeared, all South Slavs would be liberated and unified under the already autonomous Serbia. Of greatest initial importance to the Serbs, however, was the liberation of their fellow Serbs; the primary targets were the Vojvodina area, ruled by the Habsburg Empire, and Bosnia and Herzegovina, held by the Ottoman Empire (after 1878 by Austria).

The Serbs had particular historic ties with Vojvodina. Serb refugees from the Ottoman Empire had filled the academies, the Orthodox monasteries, and the cultural societies which arose there in an attempt to inspire and keep alive the Serbian national culture even under adverse conditions. In fact, Harold Temperley has argued that the influence which the Serbs in Serbia wielded over the Serbs in Hungary and in Austro-Hungary's newly acquired Bosnia frightened the Habsburgs into refusing many of the territorial claims raised by Serbia as a victor in the Russo-

Turkish War of 1877–78.[18] The two constituent parts of present-day Serbia thus remained separated from the autonomous Serbia of the nineteenth century. Kosovo, which was primarily inhabited by Moslem Albanians who had replaced the Kosovar Serbs that had migrated to Habsburg territory, remained under Ottoman control until 1912, and Vojvodina stayed under direct Magyar administration. Bosnia and Herzegovina were still to be administered by the Austro-Hungarian Empire.

Such a state of affairs served to intensify Serbia's anti-Habsburg feelings. Increased sympathies for the idea of a union of South Slavs appeared among the Croats and Slovenes, as well as among the Serbs still living under Habsburg rule. The assassination of the Austrian Archduke Francis Ferdinand by a Bosnian nationalist, Gavrilo Princep, thus "represented both a continuation and the culmination of a process that fed on political and social grievances and nationalist passions."[19]

Kingdom of the Serbs, Croats, and Slovenes

In 1917, by the pact of Corfu, the Serbs, Croats and Slovenes pledged that they would unite into a democratic kingdom led by the Serbian Karadjordjevic dynasty. Bosnia-Herzegovina and Montenegro joined the other South Slavs, and on December 1, 1918, the Kingdom of the Serbs, Croats and Slovenes (officially named Yugoslavia after 1929) was declared.

Hungary awarded to the new state Vojvodina, with its mixture of Serbs, Magyars, Germans, Romanians and Slovaks. And that historical province of medieval Serbia in which Serbia had been so badly defeated by the Ottoman forces, Kosovo-Metohija, also became part of Yugoslavia. Both Vojvodina and Kosovo-Metohija were considered integral parts of Serbia and were permitted no autonomy whatsoever within the kingdom.

The form of government of the new state was a major bone of contention. The Serbs, who still possessed an army and the remnants of a civil service, desired a centralized state along the lines of pre-war Serbia. Other nationalities, however, fearing that they would then be subjected to intensified pan-Serbian pressures, argued for regional autonomy within a federal state so that the central government would have only limited powers.

In fact, no real compromise was achieved during the interwar period. The autocratic King Alexander insured that the governments which served under the 1921 Constitution were always mainly Serbian in composition, as were all high offices in the army, banking and finance. Later, as a result of the crisis in 1928 ensuing from the shooting of the leader of the opposition (Croat Peasant Party), and the subsequent withdrawal of the Croats from political life until their demand for an almost anarchically loose federation should be instituted, a dictatorship was declared and the constitution suspended. New provinces (called *banovinas*) cutting across historical regions were created in an attempt to produce a true Yugoslav nation, albeit with a Serb complexion. Only in 1939, a day before the signing of the German-Soviet pact, was a compromise (the *Sporazum*) worked out between the central government and the Croats. Under the provisions of the *Sporazum*, Croatia-Dalmatia was to become an autonomous administrative unit with its own governor. Its legislature would be located in the regional capital of Zagreb, and Croatia would have its own budget. All other affairs, such as foreign trade and affairs, national defense, internal security, transportation, religion, education policy, etc., would still be the province of the central government.

The compromise had no chance to work during wartime. In the wake of the German invasion in April 1941, Yugoslavia was dismembered: Slovenia was partitioned by Germany and Italy; Dalmatia went to Italy as did military control of nominally independent Montenegro; Albania as well as parts of western Macedonia and Serbian Kosovo-Metohija also were given to Italy; Bulgaria received the rest of Macedonia and parts of South Serbia; Hungary received portions of Vojvodina; the remaining parts of Croatia were joined with Bosnia-Herzegovina to form the Independent State of Croatia, ruled in theory by an Italian duke but in practice by the Croatian Fascists; the remainder of Serbia was administered by Germany.

Many non-Slavs welcomed the disintegration of Yugoslavia. This was so particularly in the case of the Albanians of Kosovo-Metohija, who were joined with their co-nationals under the Italian rule of "Greater Albania."[20] The German-speaking minorities in both Slovenia and Vojvodina and the Magyars of Vojvodina were also pleased with the World War II dispersal of their territories.

Yugoslav Federalism and the Autonomous Provinces

During World II, modern-day Yugoslav federalism first emerged as the Communist Party's solution to the national question when military operations were divided into separate geographic zones under regional partisan command. Furthermore, a generally autonomous Peoples' Liberation Committee was formed to handle the civil administration in each area liberated from foreign rule by Tito's partisans. Such provisions created during wartime a *de facto* federal structure which recognized the different nationalities, utilized the various South Slavic languages for command, and gave symbolic representation to all the national minorities.[21] Even though the Communist Party retained full leadership of partisan activities within the country, this, too, was of a multiethnic character.

The wartime government of Yugoslavia, represented by the partisans' Anti-Fascist Council of Peoples' Liberation of Yugoslavia

(AVNOJ), was formed in 1942. Among the first declarations issued by this body was the resolution that postwar Yugoslavia would be constituted on a federal basis. The question of the monarchy's role would be settled by plebiscite after liberation

Postwar Yugoslavia's first Constitution recognized the wartime legal status of the Peoples' Liberation Committees (Article 6) and thus implicitly the contributions of the various nationalities and national groups to the liberation of Yugoslavia. The 1946 Constitution was deliberately modeled on Stalin's 1936 Constitution (in its provisions, but, even more importantly, in its interpretation by Yugoslav leaders) and thus created a state which was federal in name only. Nevertheless, "to many, especially to the non-Serbs, who stood to lose from a victory of the Serbian Cetniks (the Yugoslav Monarchy's pan-Serbian representative in wartime Yugoslavia), let alone of the Axis powers, even this limited solution represented an advance."[22]

A major exception to this generalization was the Albanian minority located mainly in Kosovo-Metohija. Many Kosovar Albanians (although not those fighting in the Albanian guerilla forces set up and dominated by the Yugoslavs[23]) had feared during World War II that their Albanian nationalist aspirations would be suppressed by an Allied victory which would return Kosovo-Metohija to Yugoslav hands. Even before the end of World War II, therefore, a civil war was being fought simultaneously with the anti-fascist conflict within Albania. As in Yugoslavia (which also suffered a civil war parallel to fighting the fascists), future political rivals were trying to eliminate each other, sometimes to the benefit of the fascist invaders.

The non-Communist Albanians resisted the return of Kosovo-Metohija to Yugoslav control at the end of World War II (and, as we shall see later, the Albanian Communists also came to turn on Yugoslavia).[24] They staged an uprising in 1944–45 which was ruthlessly suppressed, and Kosovo-Metohija was reintegrated into Yugoslavia.[25]

Nevertheless, for a long time, the development of Kosovo-Metohija was given a low priority by Yugoslav officials.[26] Politically, too, the region suffered from neglect. Thus, the distinction between autonomous province and autonomous region was not explicitly defined in the 1946 Yugoslav Constitution, although a lower status for the Autonomous Region of Kosovo-Metohija than for the Autonomous Province of Vojvodina was implied by the differences in organization of the two units (see Chapter XL of the 1946 Constitution).[27] This was possibly another imitation of the Soviet system, which would symbolize the difference in social and economic development between the backward Kosovo-Metohija and the more advanced Vojvodina.[28]

It is informative to note, however, that there are certain other factors which may have influenced the decision to create autonomous areas in Serbia in the first place, aside from a

Yugoslav desire to emulate as closely as possible the federal system of the Soviet Union. For example, the creation of the sub-units within Serbia constituted a recognition of the mixed population of the areas. The units were historically tied to Serbia; after World War II, however, Vojvodina contained a large number of Magyars aside from its Serbian population, and Kosovo-Metohija had the numerically preponderant Albanians. Neither of these groups, it was felt, would submit quietly to being subsumed within the Serb population without some special recognition of their particular problems.

Furthermore, Dennison L. Rusinow suggested that the creation of these two units within Serbia had additional significance. The recognition of some autonomy for Vojvodina within Serbia was also a compromise between Serbia's historic claims due to Vojvodina's large number of Serbs and Croatia's historic and ethnic claims to the Syrmia area which Serbia was not likely to honor. Therefore, although Vojvodina was considered part of the Serbian Republic, it was called an autonomous province so that the spectre of pan-Serbianism should not be raised on this issue. The Autonomous Region of Kosovo-Metohija, on the other hand, argued Rusinow, was established in recognition of the possibility that one day it might become the nucleus of another Yugoslav republic when joined with Albania,[29] which was in the immediate postwar era in effect a Yugoslav satellite.

Frits Hondius has conjectured that the Yugoslav leaders believed that the affairs of both Kosovo-Metohija and Vojvodina...

> concerned Yugoslavia as a whole. Economically and so-cially, Kosmet (Kosovo-Metohija) was a backward region, and its uplift was considered a challenge for the Federation. The device of autonomy enabled the Federation to stake off Kosmet as a problem area and to make special allocations for its economic development and for the cultural awakening of the people. Vojvodina, on the other hand, was one of the advanced regions of Yugoslavia. It was the only part of the country where collectivization had been successful. Auto-nomy was applied here in order to give the region a direct link to the Federation and also in order to overcome the risk of failing loyalty of the minority groups.[30]

If any or all of these factors were indeed important in recommending the formation of autonomous areas within Serbia, it would be easier to understand why the status of the autonom-ous areas and their relations to the various other units of government and administration in Yugoslavia remained ill-defined in the early postwar years. If the Yugoslav leaders were trying to deal successfully with such potentially touchy and contradictory situations, they may have wished to postpone as long as possible any definitive characterization of the position of the autonomous areas in Yugoslavia possibly hoping that time and circumstances would resolve the problems felicitously.

Post-War Yugoslavia and the Status of the Autonomous Provinces

Article 103 of the 1946 Constitution provided that "the rights and the scope of the autonomy of autonomous provinces and autonomous regions are determined by the constitution of the republic," i.e., the Serbian Republic, since in no other republic then or since has there been created a new autonomous region or autonomous province. The Serbian Constitution of 1947 set some guidelines for the autonomous province and autonomous region, but, nevertheless, the status of both the Autonomous Province of Vojvodina and the Autonomous Region of Kosovo-Metohija in relation to Serbia and in relation to the federation remained vague, although whatever the connection was appears to have been equal for both autonomous areas.

Hondius suggested that the grant of autonomy for Kosovo-Metohija and Vojvodina was clearly meant to be an important element of the federal formula in Yugoslavia since that status was provided for in the federal Constitution with both units mentioned by name (Article 2). It was intended, he argued, to prevent the predominance of Serbia over all other republics by removing at least a little of its territory from direct rule.[31] In actuality, however, autonomy as previously defined was absent. True, both autonomous units were permitted to send their own delegations to the Federal People's Assembly, the federal law-enacting body, but this institution was, during the early postwar years, merely a rubber-stamp for policies put forward by the Communist-dominated government. Otherwise, the autonomous units had only that authority which was expressly delegated to them by the Federal Constitution (which in fact conferred upon them no specific authority or rights) or by the Constitution of the People's Republic of Serbia. This relationship was reaffirmed in 1948 by the statutes of the autonomous areas promulgated by their assemblies. The powers of the autonomous areas, particularly those of Kosovo-Metohija, did not differ greatly from those of the local units of government, i.e., setting prices, founding schools, and rubber-stamping budget and economic plans. There was thus some amount of executory autonomy but no autonomy in policy initiative.[32]

During the initial postwar period, what was called later the "administrative" period in Yugoslavia, the Yugoslav Communist Party initiated most policies and directly administered their execution at all levels of government and administration, even down to the level of the enterprise. On paper, however, the People's Assembly of the Autonomous Province of Vojvodina was vested with the power to enact provincial statutes, social plans, budgets, etc., to elect and recall its Central Executive Committee, to enact general legislation for the province, and to elect judges of the Supreme Court of the Autonomous Province of Vojvodina, which in status and jurisdiction resembled the republican supreme courts.[33] Kosovo-Metohija was ruled by the Regional People's Committee, which was a unicameral representative body entrusted with the "general management of the entire activity of the People's Committees on the territory of the Region."[34] A Regional Executive Committee, elected by and responsible to the Regional People's Committee, managed executive-administrative functions for the Autonomous Region of Kosovo-Metohija. There was no separate supreme court of Kosovo-Metohija, so presumably judicial matters were settled by the courts of the Serbian Republic.

Cultural autonomy was another matter entirely. Since the end of World War II, the autonomous areas were accorded a large measure of freedom in dealing with their minorities, possibly since one of their major functions was to provide for and protect the rights of their constituent minority populations. Official use of the various minority languages was permitted as was whatever else within reason was deemed important to aid the cultural and social survival of the national minorities.[35] Schools were provided for all nations and minorities, and cultural organizations were formed under communist supervision. State aid was provided for publications in the various languages as well as for the maintenance of theaters, libraries, etc.

Economically, the country was centralized after World War II, so that no constituent unit had much autonomy.[36] All planning was controlled by the state, which owned and managed most of Yugoslavia's economic sectors, including actual management of most economic enterprises. At this point, there was little of the overt antagonism and jealousy between various sub-federal units that would later appear. The war had left all regions in severe hardship and all were dependent to some extent upon the central government for rehabilitative aid. Unity, not autonomy, was the necessity of that era at every level.

The 1948 expulsion of Yugoslavia from the Soviet bloc, and the subsequent economic boycott, had a profound effect upon all levels of Yugoslav society, including the autonomous areas. A new set of ideological guidelines had to be formulated in response to the perceived Soviet threat to the country and to the Yugoslav system. First of all, in regard to the autonomous areas, it became clear that they now bordered upon highly hostile areas and thus would no longer serve as possible nuclei for enlarging the Yugoslav federation. In fact, they now became targets for irredentist pressures by previously quiescent neighbors whenever the Soviet Union wanted to create more tension in Yugoslavia. Secondly, the economic orientation of Yugoslavia had to be shifted from almost complete dependence upon trade with the

Soviet Union to the initiation of large-scale trade with the West. This necessitated not only a change in attitude toward the West but also a modification in industrial output to include products which would attract Western currency.[37]

What followed was an alteration of the basic formulation of Yugoslavia's economic principles. In the immediate postwar era the emphasis had been upon equalization of development among the various regions in Yugoslavia. Now national survival dictated that investment funds be directed to productive enterprises that could supply Western markets more easily and efficiently, i.e., to the already more-developed areas.[38] Vojvodina, one of the more advanced areas in Yugoslavia, thus gained from the exigencies of the moment while the development of backward Kosovo-Metohija was sacrificed, at least temporarily.

The increasing importance of profitability forced Yugoslav leaders to alter the ideological underpinnings of Yugoslav socialism. The resulting theory was workers' self-management.[39] Institution of this new form of economic self-management called for some amount of economic decentralization. The local and republican governments and parties particularly were the beneficiaries of greater planning power as a result of these reforms. Nevertheless, the federal government still largely controlled enterprise earnings and was able to continue to redistribute some investment capital from the more developed republics which earned it to the less-developed areas which needed it for economic advancement. The difference between this practice in the immediate postwar era and that of the post-1948 era was that the decentralization formula allowed the receiving regions to determine the use of the capital. This was the genesis of the so-called "political factories," those enterprises built with federally-authorized funds for political reasons and without necessarily being economically rational investment.

During this period of the introduction of workers' self-management, the status of the autonomous areas was but little improved and still remained relatively unspecified in terms of their relationship to the federal and republican levels. With the promulgation of the Constitutional Law of 1953, the organization of power within the autonomous areas paralleled that within the republics (i.e., bicameralism). Both of the autonomous areas were represented in the Federal Council[40] and the Council of Nationalities, so that, to the extent of the powers of these bodies, the autonomous areas did have some input into federal law enactment.

The change in status of the autonomous areas dictated by the promulgation of the 1963 Constitution was very small. In fact, it has been argued that, in some ways, the status of the autonomous areas was downgraded by the constitutional provisions.[41]

One change, which showed some little progress in the attitudes toward the autonomous areas, was the fact that Kosovo-Metohija was upgraded in status from an autonomous region to an autonomous province so that it now had the same rights and obligations as the Autonomous Province of Vojvodina.[42] Both would now send an equal number of representatives to the Federal Chamber of Nationalities. Furthermore, the representative organ of Kosovo-Metohija, which had previously been on the format of the local government organs, was transformed into the assembly model like that in Vojvodina, which followed closely the organization of power and administration in the Socialist Republic of Serbia.

Another alteration in the status of the autonomous provinces was the fact that the Serbian Constitution defined more precisely than previously the functions of the autonomous provinces and the relationship which was to exist between republican agencies and provincial agencies. For example, all provincial organs were to be set up in the manner defined by the republican constitution. The autonomous provinces were to have statutes of their own by which to regulate their functions (although the guidelines were all there already in the Serbian Constitution).

On the negative side was the fact that the 1963 Federal Constitution no longer specified the position of the autonomous provinces as being federal creations. Robert W. King quoted a leading Yugoslav authority on the federal system as saying that "unlike the 1953 constitutional law the present (1963) constitution is no longer the legal document which created the autonomous units."[43] The constitution specified that the republics could "found autonomous provinces in accordance with the constitution in areas with distinctive national characteristics or in areas with other distinguishing features, on the basis of the express will of the population of these areas" (Article 111). The only limitation on the republics was that a constitutional amendment or constitutional law approving the republic's action had to be passed. This rule applied for the creation and the dissolution of an autonomous province. The rights, duties, and organizational principles of the autonomous units were thus still to be determined by the republican constitution and laws.

In the judicial branch, a rather significant change was recorded. Whereas Vojvodina previously had possessed its own Supreme Court, now that organ was abolished. Its place was taken, in both autonomous provinces, by newly created departments of the Supreme Court of Serbia located in the provincial capitals. The peculiarity of this system was that, although the courts were branches of the Serbian Supreme Court, their judges were elected by the provincial assemblies and the departments were to keep these assemblies apprised of their operations. It was the opinion of Frits Hondius that these departments "were for all intents and purposes the own supreme court of the Province."[44] On the other hand, King reported an interview with Iliaz Kurtesi, an Albanian leader in Kosovo-Metohija, who saw this provision, and others of the 1963 Constitution,as eliminating "the provinces' state judiciary, autonomy, and sovereignty."[45]

Also deserving of mention is the fact that the separate delegations to the Federal Assembly were abolished. The five delegates from each autonomous province became part of Serbia's republican delegation, and, as such, we may suppose, were more subject to pressure for conformity from the republic than they had previously been.

A close reading of the relevant provisions of the Serbian Constitution (particularly Chapter VI entitled "The Autonomous Province") will reveal that the autonomous provinces were completely dependent upon the republic for all their rights and privileges and could take only rare initiatives. For example, although the autonomous provinces were given the right to organize provincial education (Article 129 of the Constitution of the Socialist Republic of Serbia), in Chapter VII ("The Rights and Duties of the Republic") the Serbian Republic reserved for itself under Article 141 the right to "determine a system or organization of education and directly attend to the development of high schools." One may thus question whether the autonomous provinces, even in this area, had in fact the authority which they possessed in theory.

Furthermore, if one accepts Henry Teune's proposition that "a traditional criterion of autonomy is the capability to raise and spend money independent of the decisions of other governmental units,"[46] one could only conclude that, as a result of the 1963 Yugoslav Constitution and the 1963 Serbian Constitution, the autonomous areas of Yugoslavia were autonomous in name only and not in ability to regulate their own affairs. The autonomous provinces were given the right to "decide about the utilization of provincial revenues" (Article 129 of the Serbian Constitution), but they had no ability to raise their own revenues. Instead, they were dependent upon republican grants or voluntary grants from their own constituent units, i.e., the districts and communes (Article 130 of the Serbian Constitution).

There was, however, one area in which the autonomous provinces did have a certain amount of autonomy. The Serbian Constitution in Article 84 gave to the autonomous provinces (as well as to the districts and communes involved) the right to determine by statute or decision the "details and the procedure for the implementation of the rights of the members of the nationalities...in conformity with law." As previously, the decisions about maintaining cultural and social survival of the national minorities were to be taken by those bodies which were closest to the people and could thus most easily determine the exigencies of the moment.

The Transition Period

It is clear that there was no appreciable change in the status of the

autonomous provinces as a result of the adoption of the 1963 Con-
itution. No substantial alteration actually occurred until the mid-
1960s when, in an attempt to invigorate Yugoslavia's economy
which had suffered from resistance to the decentralizing innova-
tions begun in the 1950s, a new economic reform was promul-
ted in 1965. A major aim of the reform was to weaken the
influence of the political elites who supported the continued functioning of unproductive enterprises (political factories). Politics was
to be removed from economic decision-making, and the League
of Communists of Yugoslavia would guide and control the economy through "broad indicative plans."[47]

In regard to the status and authority of the autonomous areas,
two separate tendencies appeared. The controversy which ensued as a result of the reforms was described in an article in
Yugoslav Survey by three officials—a deputy of the Serbian
Assembly, the Vice President of the Assembly of the Autonomous
Province of Kosovo, and the director of the Social Planning Office
of the Autonomous Province of Kosovo. They reported the conflict
between "a bureaucratic-centralistic approach according to which
nothing was to be changed in the status of the Autonomous
Provinces, or only minor changes should be made, a view which
spread mistrust and stirred up nationalistic feelings," and "a
separatistic approach which, proceeding from particularistic positions, negating the results achieved, and resorting to demagogic
slogans, was in fact aimed at undermining the brotherhood and
unity of the nations and national minorities in the Socialist
Republic of Serbia and the Socialist Federal Republic of Yugoslavia."[48] One may thus deduce that the Serbs were attempting
to hold onto their disproportionate amount of influence within
the federal government and over the autonomous provinces
against the increasing demands for greater autonomy by the
national minorities.

The prototype of the anti-reformists was Aleksandar Rankovic,
Yugoslav Vice-President, head of state security, and head of
cadres policy, and, significantly, a close friend and possible
successor of Tito. Rankovic, a Serb, represented those who
opposed the economic reforms as well as the accompanying
political-social reforms that the reformers in the League of
Communists had been trying to implement since the 1950s.
Rankovic's secret police had been accused of violating the civil
rights of Yugoslavia's national minorities, particularly of the
Albanians, as part of a Rankovic-Tito attempt in the 1950s and
early 1960s to foster "supranational Yugoslav nationalism."[49] The
non-Serb minorities, therefore, were especially pleased at Rankovic's political demise in the summer of 1966 and the shift in
federal policy away from the assimilationist emphasis of "Yugoslavism," which appeared to threaten a revival of Serbian
domination ("Greater Serbia").

Many of the obstacles to the economic and socio-political

reforms disappeared and the reforms were now vigorously applied. At this point, the national minorities began to assert their rights more forcefully than previously. Those areas containing many minorities, especially Vojvodina and Kosovo, began to press for greater autonomy. Some people, particularly in Kosovo, even began to demand republican status for their province.

And, in fact, the aspirations of the national minorities for greater autonomy began to be satisfied. Already in June 1967, a seminar concerned with reforms recommended alterations in the status of the autonomous provinces. By early 1968 proposals were being formulated to amend the constitutions of the Yugoslav federation and the Serbian Republic and the statutes of the autonomous provinces in order to increase the self-governing powers of the latter. After more than twenty years of serving, in the main, as paper devices to maintain the passivity of otherwise potentially assertive groups of people, it seemed that the autonomous provinces were finally to be given some of the tools which would allow them to become effective centers of interest articulation and aggregation as well as rule-making and enforcement.

The Current Legal Status of the Autonomous Provinces

Two sets of amendments to the 1963 Yugoslav Constitution and the Serbian Constitution were promulgated—in 1968–1969 and 1971–1972. These amendments served to redefine and make more precise the status and authority of the autonomous provinces, giving them in many instances almost the same powers as those wielded by the republics, except in name.

First of all, the autonomous provinces were raised to the level of socialist democratic socio-political communities (previously only socio-political communities) and, as such, attained the name of Socialist Autonomous Province.[50] They were still basically constituent parts of Serbia, but their supreme law became a constitution, rather than a statute. They acquired independent court systems and people's assemblies, which could pass laws, rather than by-laws only. Serbia was restricted from abolishing or changing the borders of the autonomous provinces without approval of the assembly of that autonomous province. Delegations to the Federal Chamber of Nationalities from the provinces were to be selected by the provincial assembly, rather than by the Serbian Assembly. And the autonomous provinces were authorized "to determine the sources and kinds of their revenue within the framework of the unified financial system."[51]

Under Amendments XVIII and XIX to the Federal Constitution and Amendments IV and V to the Serbian Constitution, the legislative powers of the autonomous provinces were separated from those of the republic. Henceforth, the Serbian Republic would be responsible for those matters which necessarily had to be uniformly regulated throughout the entire republic, while provincial authorities would deal with all other questions of importance to the autonomous provinces. Furthermore, the areas of competence of the republic were now specified individually so that the delineation between jurisdictions was much more precise than previously.

The caveat which existed in all of this was that although on paper the provincial assemblies had a relatively broad area of legislative autonomy, most· of these powers devolved to the autonomous provinces only by virtue of the legislative policy of either the Federation or the Serbian Republic. That is, in certain areas, namely in regard to comprehensive, basic, and general laws,[52] provincial abilities to legislate depended upon whether the federal government or the republican government permitted them to pass laws on these subjects. Thus, "in the spheres of exclusive and comprehensive federal legislation, the autonomous provinces could regulate individual questions by provincial legislation only if they were so authorized by republican statute. Although the provinces could, in principle, regulate matters in the spheres of basic and general federal legislation, this right was not exclusive, because the Republic could also regulate matters and questions falling within these spheres uniformly for its entire territory by its own laws passed by a special procedure."[53]

The Serbian Republic utilized its power to supersede autonomous provincial powers only rarely. In fact, out of seventeen republican statutes using this principle, only ten may be viewed as denying the autonomous provinces the ability to pass their own legislation, and these ten regulated questions most of which the autonomous provinces agreed should be standardly regulated for the entire republic.[54] Nevertheless, these qualifications to the provincial powers still existed and denied in fact that authority that had in theory been granted to the autonomous provinces.

The 1971 constitutional amendments, on the other hand, strengthened the autonomy of the republics and concurrently that of the autonomous provinces, "and in all but a few relatively minor instances treated the autonomous provinces in the same manner as they did the republics."[55] The autonomous provinces would now be independently represented in all basic federal agencies and would participate directly in the formulation and implementation of federal policy in the same manner as the republics.[56] Furthermore, the economic functions of the Federation would be confined to two fields: insuring the unity of the Yugoslav market and providing "common functions for social-economic relationships based on self-management."[57]

As a result particularly of the new, far more decentralized economic scheme precipitated by the 1971 Constitutional Amendments, a multiple economic system was, in effect, set up. The degree of change initiated by these amendments was so significant, in fact, that one Yugoslav observer was led to comment that "in view of the constitutional powers given the republics and provinces, some parts of the economic system are certain to differ from one republic and province to another. . . different conditions of economic activity may emerge within individual regions, branches and sectors of the economy. This represents a partial danger to the functioning of the integral Yugoslav market."[58]

The succeeding 1974 Constitution represented an attempt to eliminate these differences and also to regularize the other relationships and competences first set out in the 1968–1969 and 1971–1972 amendments. The almost confederal structure of the Yugoslav state was thus retained. The federal government's role remained that of "an apparatus for agreement" among the various competing power centers.

The autonomous provinces retained their status of quasi-republic, and in practically every article of the constitution were mentioned as having the same rights, privileges, and responsibilites as the republics. The only significant difference appeared to be in name, or, more precisely, in the specific grant of territorial autonomy. And in that difference appeared to lie, at least for militant Albanian nationalists in Kosovo, the major weakness of the new system initiated in the mid-1960s.

The Nationalities Question in the Autonomous Provinces

The restlessness of the Albanian minority was first manifested in violent demonstrations which broke out in various cities of Kosovo, coinciding with neighboring Albania's celebrations of its own National Day. A proclamation appeared which demanded that Kosovo receive republic status, its own constitution and the right of self-determination. Albanians living in the Macedonian Republic joined the demonstrations and demanded that Albanian areas of Macedonia be annexed to Kosovo in order to create an Albanian national republic in Yugoslavia.[59]

The demands for a constitution and greater self-determination were met by the ensuing constitutional amendments and the 1974 Constitution. But formal republican status was not forthcoming for either of the autonomous provinces. As a matter of fact, however, during all the turmoil, Vojvodina did not press for republican status. This fact provokes the obvious question—what is the difference between the two provinces that makes their aspirations different?

A number of reasons could be suggested as to why the inhabitants of Vojvodina appear to be satisfied with the concessions to their autonomy made by the Federation and by Serbia, whereas many inhabitants of Kosovo are not yet reconciled to non-republican status. One reason is the demographic differences in the two autonomous provinces. Although Vojvodina contains most of Yugoslavia's Hungarian population, the majority population is Serbian. Since the Serbs in Vojvodina actively participate in the affairs of that province, their influence is large there. In Kosovo, on the other hand, the Albanians are predominant in the population and continue to grow at a faster rate than that of almost any other group in Yugoslavia, due to natural increase as well as to the increasing migration of Serbs and Montenegrins from Kosovo. The Albanian majority in Kosovo may therefore be expected to grow both in numbers and in influence while it appears that the Hungarian percentage of the population in Vojvodina will continue to decline.

Economic factors also play a role in differentiating between the situations of Vojvodina and Kosovo. Vojvodina inherited from the Austro-Hungarian Empire modern forms of agriculture and industry as well as modern administrative techniques. Vojvodina thus came into Yugoslavia as a relatively advanced and productive area and has maintained a high level of development. Kosovo, on the other hand, suffered from the neglect and impoverishment to which the non-Moslem areas of the Ottoman Empire were subjected. The gap between Kosovo's economic development and that of the more developed areas in Yugoslavia has, if anything, widened. The Albanian nationality in Yugoslavia may thus have seen themselves caught up in a vicious circle of unemployment, population explosion and poverty which their lowly status as autonomous province (i.e., a constituent part of the Serbian Republic) would not help them escape. The Albanians may have figured that republican status would equalize them a bit in the struggle waged by the republics for scarce resources. Kosovo had fallen victim to the decrease in federal subsidies when profitability became the rule instead of equalization of productivity in all the regions in Yugoslavia. It seemed to many Kosovar Albanians that only with republican status could they command the resources they needed for rapid development and modernization on an equal level with the republics. Serbia, it appeared, was not representing their interests forcefully enough. Vojvodina, on the other hand, sides with the Slovenian and Croatian republics on economic matters and seeks as much decentralization and federal noninterference as possible so that it can continue to attempt to narrow the gap between its production capability and that of Central Europe.

Kosovo and Vojvodina thus appear to have different interests, and yet their fates are linked together. Until now, they have received equally whatever greater autonomy and self-determination the federal government and Serbia have chosen to confer upon them. Their political organizations are similar, and, most significantly, the Serbs consider both areas historically and geographically Serbian.

Serbian reluctance to permit any decrease in its territory, for whatever reason, is notable. Aside from their own development needs which became harder to realize after the institution of the reforms of the 1960s, the Serbs probably feel that it is enough that they have lost all but nominal control over the autonomous territories without having physically to be separated from them. This is particularly so as a result of the fact that much of the progress made by the minorities in the autonomous provinces has been in the context of anti-Serbianism.

In Vojvodina the specter of pan-Serbianization of the area has always been a real one because of the overwhelming majority of Serbs living there. Few overt attempts to change the character of the provinces have been recorded. Nevertheless, it must still be a potentially thorny problem, although less so after the supreme defender of Serbia's rights, Rankovic, left the political stage. But it must be remembered that Croatia still claims that it has rights to part of Vojvodina. One wonders what the Serbian response might be to Croatia's pressing of these historical and ethnic claims to the Syrmia region of Vojvodina. Would the Serbs respond with an attempt to unify, even homogenize the area? Despite the possibility of these potentially disrupting problems, the inhabitants of Vojvodina have been thus far quiet about any republican aspirations they might have.[60]

Serbia's relations with Kosovo, on the other hand, have been more troublesome. To begin with, as already mentioned, the population of Albanians is far larger than that of Serbs in Kosovo. This has led to much concern among Serbs that the Albanians are attempting to supplant Serbian control over the province and will then begin to discriminate against them.

The Serbs also may fear irredentist tendencies within the two provinces, although more in Kosovo than in Vojvodina. The Hungarians in Yugoslavia seem to have been fairly successfully assimilated into the Yugoslav society. And Hungary does not appear to be too concerned over the treatment of the Magyar minority in Yugoslavia. No real trouble has appeared on this question.

The problem of the relationship between Albania and Kosovo is another matter, however. Since 1948 Albania's relations with Yugoslavia have been almost purely hostile. It is not surprising, since the 1948 Cominform Resolution extricated Albania from a position of near-satellite status and possible future incorporation as an integral part of Yugoslavia. Ever since that near thing, the Albanians have seized every opportunity to create problems for Yugoslavia by helping to stir up trouble in Kosovo. Possibly the Albanians still have some residue of fear that Yugoslavia may again try to annex Albania and for that reason circulate an anti-Yugoslav line to create anti-Yugoslav feelings within Albania and to keep Yugoslavia busy with managing its own Albanian minority. Even as relations gradually improve between Yugoslavia and Albania there is still that bone of contention, the Kosovar Albanians, between them.

The Serbs might also fear that the Yugoslav Albanians yearn to be reunited with their brothers across the border in a Greater Albanian state, and that granting Kosovo the status of republic and thus the ability to secede, in theory if not in practice,[61] from the Yugoslav Federation, might prove too much of a temptation for the Yugoslav Albanians to resist. A further interesting factor here which could add to the seriousness of this temptation is the fact that the Albanian minority "accounts for 40 per cent of the numerical strength of the entire Albanian nation (which) lends a crucial importance" to Yugoslavia's Kosovo region.[62] And, in fact, after the 1968 demonstrations in Kosovo, "the fear was expressed that the Albanians in Yugoslavia were attempting to become the new center of the Albanian nation."[63]

We may thus ask, if the Kosovar Albanians continue to demand republican status as in the past, and if it is refused, might we expect that they will be more responsive to the idea of separation from Yugoslavia in the future? In speculating upon this question, which is of great importance to the Yugoslavs, it might be instructive to consider it from the point of view of relative deprivation theory. Ted Robert Gurr presented a composite typology of values which he considered to be "most relevant to a theory of political violence."[64] He telescoped the "general categories of conditions valued by many men" into three groups: welfare values, "those that contribute directly to physical well-being and self-realization"; power values, "those that determine the extent to which men can influence the actions of others and avoid unwanted interference by others in their own actions"; and interpersonal values, "the psychological satisfactions we seek in nonauthoritative interaction with other individuals and groups," including the desire for status.

In Kosovo, as already mentioned, achievement of the "welfare values" is a subject of much discontent. Kosovo remains the least developed area in Yugoslavia. Mahmut Bakali, President of Kosovo's Provincial Committee of the League of Communists, asserted in 1976 that the League of Communists realized the problem and "has opted, as was specifically reiterated at the Tenth Congress, in favour of special measures to be undertaken by the whole of society to accelerate the development of the Province of Kosovo, and thus to reduce as soon as possible the differences in the level of development."[65] Nevertheless, when discussing utilization of one of Kosovo's most promising avenues for development, exploitation of the minerals in its mountainous areas, Fred Singleton pointed out that "even with the most up-to-date techniques of civil engineering, the problems of providing this core area (Kosovo, eastern Bosnia, and southern Serbia) with an adequate infrastructure are almost insuperable."[66] Having been subjected for many years to the ideological arguments of communism as being the best way to satisfy the economic needs of modern man, and yet living daily with the problems of

unemployment, population explosion, and all those other problems associated with underdevelopment and lack of modernization, the Kosovar Albanians must feel particularly frustrated at
their lack of advancement.

This may also tie in with the category of "interpersonal values,"
i.e., the status considerations through which the Kosovar Albanians may view themselves as the "poor cousins" in Yugoslavia. On
one hand, if the socio-economic status of the Kosovar Albanians
were compared with that of Albania's population, it would be
obvious that "life in Yugoslav Kosovo is easier than in Hoxha's
Albania."[67] On the other hand, however, the feelings of self-
deprecation which may accompany the expressions of contempt
coming from the wealthier republics when called upon to sacrifice
some of their growth in order to help in the development of
Kosovo have further exacerbated Albanian resentment of their
status within Yugoslavia. When making their demands for more
federal aid for development and modernization, the reference
group against which the Yugoslav Albanians measure their
well-being, and conclude that they are being short-changed, is that
of other inhabitants of Yugoslavia and not that of their brother
Albanians across the border. And, in fact, Dennison Rusinow
reported that:

> as for emotional links with their kinsmen in Albania across
> the mountains, or irredentist sentiments which would prefer
> the rule of their own kind in Tirana to the rule of Slavs in
> Belgrade, President Ali Sukri was probably being candid and
> a true representative of the attitude of his people when he
> confessed to the former but denied the latter. "We definitely
> have a feeling of relationship with the Albanians of Albania,"
> he told us in Pristina, "but Yugoslavia is our homeland."[68]

What, then, about the third set of values, the "power values?"
In discussing contemporary civil strife, Gurr presented cross-
national survey evidence which "suggested that people in the
1950s and 1960s have been considerably more concerned about
and dissatisfied with their economic lot than political issues."[69]
Since, however, participants in contemporary civil strife very often
"have political motives and direct their demands at political
targets,"[70] Gurr suggested that "the implication is that most
discontents in the modern world are not political but politicized."
This he considered to be the result of two characteristics of
contemporary societies: "the ambiguity of origin of many deprivations in increasingly complex societies, and the widening scope of
governmental responsibility in fact and in popular expectation for
resolving value-distribution conflicts and generating new
values."[71]

Without straining the analogy too far, this analysis may in
some part apply to the case of the Kosovar Albanians. As

mentioned above, the Albanians in Kosovo may be expected to harbor resentment at their low socio-economic status in reference to many of the other inhabitants of Yugoslavia. The problem is exacerbated by the ideology promulgated by the ruling elite of the relative well-being through self-management and non-exploitation of labor that accrues to the inhabitants of a country following the Yugoslav socialist model. If, as Gurr suggested, contemporary society is characterized by an ambiguity of the origin of deprivations and a parallel widening of popular expectation that the government is assuming an ever-growing role in resolving value-distribution conflicts, it stands to reason that the Kosovar Albanians may respond to their feelings of deprivation by attacking the way the decision-making apparatus which seemingly has denied them their desired values is constructed. And in fact, the Kosovar Albanians have been demanding a greater role in decision-making at the highest governmental levels through an upgrading of their status to that of republic so that they might have an equal share with the other republics in value (resource) distribution.

The feeling of relative deprivation in regard to all three value categories may thus have been at least partially defused with the enlargement of the powers and rights of the autonomous provinces by the 1974 Constitution. Some of the urgency may have been removed from the desire for republican status among the Albanian nationality in Yugoslavia since they have received most of the rights and privileges accruing to the republics. It is unlikely that Serbia would willingly and easily allow the autonomous provinces to be detached from even the nominal status that they hold now as constituent parts of Serbia; the Kosovar Albanians would therefore have to take drastic steps and risk the loss of the relative independence they have now. Possibly some of the more enterprising Albanian nationalists have decided to work with their new powers for the present while they set their sights on the post-Tito era, figuring that after Tito, the major unifying element of the nationalities, has left the scene, they might have a better chance to capitalize on the anticipated chaos. In the meantime, Kosovar communists must continue to battle against periodic manifestations of tendencies of ethnic separatism even while they avoid the threat of Serbian hegemony.

We may conclude our survey of the utility and viability of the Yugoslav autonomous provinces as a device for defusing tensions in a multiethnic nation by observing that as a result of the formal institutionalization of an equal role in all the affairs of government and governing for the autonomous provinces with the republics, it is apparent that what was once merely a mechanism useful for demonstrating to the minorities of Serbia that their rights would be respected in Yugslavia has recently become a relatively mutually satisfying arrangement. The largest minorities in Yugoslavia may make their wishes and concerns known in the governmental chanbers while the Serbian Republic is not threatened by a loss of some of its territory. How the autonomous provinces emerge from the imminent turmoil of the post-Tito succession crisis will be an interesting study of their actual viability under stress. For now, however, in Yugoslavia, the device of autonomous province seems to have evolved from a powerless and mostly showcase type of governmental unit into a relatively vibrant federal mechanism.

Notes

I would like to thank Daniel J. Elazar of the Jerusalem Institute for Federal Studies and Galia Golan of Hebrew University for their critical readings and useful suggestions on earlier drafts of this paper.

1.   See, for example, Alvin Z. Rubinstein, *Yugoslavia and the Nonaligned World* (Princeton, N.J.: Princeton University Press, 1970); Francine Friedman, "Yugoslav Foreign Policy's Ambivalence Towards *Detente*," *International Perspectives* (January-February 1979), pp. 19-24; John C. Campbell, "Insecurity and Cooperation: Yugoslavia and the Balkans," *Foreign Affairs* 51 (July 1973), pp. 778-93; Robin Alison Remington, "Yugoslavia and European Security," *Orbis* 17 (Spring 1973), pp. 197-226.

2.   See, for example, Fred Singleton, *Twentieth-Century Yugoslavia* (New York: Columbia University Press, 1976); George Macesich, *Yugoslavia: The Theory and Practice of Development Planning* (Charlottesville: University of Virginia Press, 1964); Dennison I.Rusinow, *The Yugoslav Experiment 1948-1974* (Berkeley: University of California Press, 1977).

3.   *Trends of Federalism in Theory and Practice* (New York: Praeger, 1968), p. 177. For more on Yugoslav federalism, see Bogdan Denitch, "The Evolution of Yugoslav Federalism," *Publius* 7 (Fall 1977), pp. 107-17, and Stephen L. Burg, "Ethnic Conflict and the Federalization of Socialist Yugoslavia," *Publius* 7 (Fall 1977), pp. 119-43.

4.   Daniel J. Elazar, "The Principles and Practices of Federalism: A Comparative Historical Approach," Working Paper No. 8, Center for the Study of Federalism, Temple University (Philadelphia, 1972), p. 5.

5.   In another form of federalism, on the other hand, the initial unity in background or origin of the peoples involved would not militate against a strong federal government sharing with constituent units close contact with the people, as illustrated, for example, in the case of the United States. Ibid.

6.   Hubert Bonner, "Autonomy," in Julius Gould and William L. Kolb, eds., *A Dictionary of the Social Sciences* (New York: Free Press of Glencoe, 1964), p. 46.

7.   Carl J. Friedrich, "New Tendencies in Federal Theory and Practice: General Report," Paper delivered at the Sixth World Congress of the International Political Science Association, Geneva, September 21-5, 1964, pp. 4-5.

8.   Why a federation for Yugoslavia? Peter Jambrek observed that the Yugoslav Communist Party early recognized that political consensus and integration failed to appear in Yugoslavia as a result of "the suppression of the overlapping ethnic and regional interests in the political centralised

and Serbian-ruled pre-war Yugoslav Monarchy." The Communist leaders responded to this problem by creating a federation which "amounted to the legal and political recognition of the processes which already took place during the Partisan war against the Germans." *Development and Social Change in Yugoslavia: Crises and Perspectives of Building a Nation* (Lexington, Mass.: Lexington Books, 1975), p. 114.

9.   Wartime planning about the establishment of postwar Yugoslavia had envisaged that Bosnia-Herzegovina would be classified as an autonomous province and not as a republic because of the extreme heterogeneity of its population. Rodoljub Colakovic described the reasons for the abandonment of this view and the eventual designation of Bosnia-Herzegovina as the sixth Yugoslav republic in "Solving the National Question (With Special Reference to Bosnia and Herzegovina)," *Socialist Thought and Practice* 14 (March 1974), pp. 3–16. Paul Shoup claimed that at one time during the war promises of autonomy had also been made to the Italians and to the inhabitants of the Sandjak (neither of which materialized). "Yugoslavia's National Minorities under Communism," *Slavic Review* 22 (March 1963), p. 75, note 42.

10.   See, for example, Vladimir Ilich Lenin, *Collected Works* (Moscow: Foreign Languages Publishing House, 1961), Vol. 6, p. 328.

11.   J.A.R. Marriott, *The Eastern Question: An Historical Study ·in European Diplomacy* (Oxford: Clarendon Press, 1958), p. 51.

12.   Ibid., p. 57.

13.   It appears that this practice was a source of instability in the fifteenth-century Ottoman Empire. Stanford Shaw cited this as one of a number of factors which led to the fall of the first Ottoman Empire in 1402: "Tamerlane's invasion was so successful because the Ottoman Empire built during the fourteenth century contained important seeds of instability, particularly the vassal system, which left Christian princes in a position to assert their independence whenever the central authority was troubled or weak." *History of the Ottoman Empire and Modern Turkey*, Vol. 1 (Cambridge: Cambridge University Press, 1976), p. 35.

14.   Harold W.V. Temperley, *History of Serbia* (New York: Fertig, 1969), p. 119. See also Shaw, *History of the Ottoman Empire and Modern Turkey*, Vol. 1, pp. 24–25.

15.   "It was oppression that was new in Serbia, it was the feeling of nationality that was old." Temperley, *History of Serbia*, p. 167.

16.   Ivo J. Lederer, "Nationalism and the Yugoslavs," in Peter F. Sugar and Ivo J. Lederer, eds., *Nationalism in Eastern Europe* (Seattle: University of Washington Press, 1969), p. 405.

17.   From 1809 to 1813, Napoleon's victory over Austria gave to France parts of Croatia and Dalmatia which were brought together into a common political-administrative framework known as the "Illyrian Provinces." This union, together with the armed alliance of Serbia and a Montenegro struggling to retain its independence from the Ottoman Empire, were the first manifestations of South Slav unity in the Balkans.

18.   *History of Serbia*, p. 270.

19.   Lederer, "Nationalism and the Yugoslavs," p. 428.

20.   Singleton reported that the Yugoslav Communist Party early recognized the kindred feelings between the Albanians in Kosovo-Metohija and Albania and had voted at its fifth Conference in 1940 to reaffirm a 1928 resolution that Kosovo should be given to Albania. *Twentieth-Century Yugoslavia*, p. 91.

21.   Aside from the Partisan appeal to all ethnic groups, Jambrek

emphasized that the large amount of regional autonomy in wartime Yugoslavia was also a result of the "German occupation of the whole territory (and) their control of all major means of communication and transportation." *Development and Social Change in Yugoslavia*, p. 114.

22. K.F. Cviic, "The Missing Historical Dimension in Yugoslavia," *International Affairs* (London) 48 (July 1972), p. 417.

23. For more on the genesis and evolution of the Albanian Communist Party and guerilla forces, see Paul Lendvai, *Eagles in Cobwebs: Nationalism and Communism in the Balkans* (London: Macdonald, 1969), pp. 182–205.

24. For a more detailed account of the positions taken by the various groups in Albania regarding Kosovo and of the Yugoslav involvement in the issue, see Robert Lee Wolff, *The Balkans in Our Time* (Cambridge, Mass.: Harvard University Press, 1956), pp. 220–2.

25. Presumably the official Yugoslav view of Kosovo's reintegration into Yugoslavia was expressed by Stanoje Aksic, Bozidar Dimitrijevic and Neset Zubi, who maintained that the resolution passed by the Yugoslav Provisional People's Assembly by which Kosovo-Metohija became a constituent part of the Serbian Republic "was adopted at the wish of the population of Kosovo and Metohija, expressed in a resolution of the Second Session of the Regional People's Committee passed at an assembly held in Prizren from July 8-10, 1945." "Socialist Autonomous Province of Kosovo," *Yugoslav Survey* 11 (May 1970), p. 15.

26. For instance, Mahmut Bakali, President of Kosovo's Provincial Committee of the League of Communists, admitted that in Kosovo "until 1957 there had been no dynamic investment and growth." "Thirty Years of the Socialist Development of Kosovo," *Socialist Thought and Practice* 16 (January 1976), p. 16. This could possibly be explained as a policy aiming toward the pacification of an area which had struggled against incorporation into Yugoslavia.

27. Thus, for example, Vojvodina was entitled to send twenty delegates to the Federal Assembly while Kosovo-Metohija could send only fifteen. For a further description of the difference in governmental arrangements between the Autonomous Province of Vojvodina and the Autonomous Region of Kosovo-Metohija in this initial period, see Aleksander Fira, "Autonomous Provinces," *Yugoslav Survey* 6 (July-September 1965), p. 3187, and Frits W. Hondius, *The Yugoslav Community of Nations* (The Hague: Mouton, 1968), p. 160.

28. Dennison I. Rusinow, "The Other Albanians: Some Notes on the Yugoslav Kosmet Today," *American Universities Field Staff* (Southeast Europe Series) 12 (November 1965), p. 22; see also Robert R. King, *Minorities Under Communism: Nationalities as a Source of Tension among Balkan Communist States* (Cambridge, Mass.: Harvard University Press, 1973), p. 134.

29. *The Yugoslav Experiment 1948-1974*, p. 47. For more on Tito's territorial expansion aspirations, see William H. Riker, *Federalism: Origin, Operation, Significance* (Boston: Little, Brown, 1964), pp. 40-41, and King, *Minorities under Communism*,, pp. 61—68.

30. *The Yugoslav Community of Nations*, pp. 158-9.

31. Hondius further stated that there was no evidence that the autonomous areas were created by popular self-determination as was assumed in most official or semi-official descriptions of the genesis of these areas. (See, for example, above note 25). Ibid., p. 159.

32. Ibid., p. 160.

33. Fira, "Autonomous Provinces," p. 3190.

34. Aksic, Dimitrijevic, and Zubi,"Socialist Autonomous Province of Kosovo," p. 18.

35. The caveat, of course, was that, particularly for the relatively backward national minorities such as the Albanians, social equality and equality of opportunity were not so easily obtainable since the required social and economic development to achieve these goals would not be attained by the poorer minorities for quite a long time. Rusinow, "The Other Albanians," p. 23.

36. Hondius pointed out, for example, that the chapters of the general economic plan were divided according to industrial sector rather than geography. *The Yugoslav Community of Nations*, p. 172.

37. Nicholas R. Lang, "The Dialectics of Decentralization: Economic Reform and Regional Inequality in Yugoslavia," *World Politics* 27 (April 1975), p. 316.

38. Lang pointed out a further consideration favoring larger investment in the more developed areas—namely, that the fear of Soviet military intervention in Yugoslavia put a premium upon choosing as sites for defense industry the western-most regions, which, coincidentally, also happened to be the more advanced economically. Ibid.

39. For a description of the origins and application of workers' self-management, see Macesich, *Yugoslavia*; Deborah D. Milenkovitch, *Plan and Market in Yugoslav Economic Thought* (New Haven: Yale University Press, 1971); Branko Horvat, *An Essay on Yugoslav Society* (New York: International Arts and Sciences Press, 1969).

40. Ten delegates per republic, six for the Autonomous Province of Vojvodina and four for the Autonomous Region of Kosovo-Metohija.

41. King, *Minorities under Communism*, p. 135.

42 An exception to this equality mentioned by Aleksandar Fira was that "because of the high level of its economic development and the complexity of prevailing economic relations, the Autonomous Province of Vojvodina also has a High Commercial court." "Autonomous Provinces," p. 3191.

43. Jovan Djordjevic, *Novi Ustavni Sistem* (Belgrade: Savremena Administracija, 1964), p. 599, cited in *Minorities under Communism*, p. 135.

44. *The Yugoslav Community of Nations*, p. 307. See Article 227 of the Constitution of the Socialist Republic of Serbia.

45. Cited in *Minorities under Communism*, p. 135.

46. "The Future of Federalism: Federalism and Political Integration," in Valerie Earle, ed., *Federalism: Infinite Variety in Theory and Practice* (Itasca, Ill.: Peacock, 1968), p. 222.

47. Lang, "The Dialectics of Decentralization," pp. 324–5.

48. Aksic, Dimitrijevic, and Zubi, "Socialist Autonomous Province of Kosovo," p.19.

49. Lendvai, *Eagles in Cobwebs*, p. 203. Lendvai also described some of Rankovic's methods for maintaining control over the minority populations, p. 158. See also Shoup, "Yugoslavia's National Minorities under Communism," pp. 77–8, for more on Yugoslavia's policy of "Yugoslavism" during this period. Shoup is also the author of *Communism and the Yugoslav National Question* (New York: Columbia University Press, 1968) which contains an excellent analysis of the evolution of Yugoslavia's nationalities policies.

50. Kosovo-Metohija was newly designated just Kosovo. The removal

of the Serbian geographic designation Metohija was a concession to Albanian national sentiment.

51.   Milan Cukovic, Nikola Stefanovic, Savin Jogan, "Constitutional Changes in Yugoslavia," *Yugoslav Survey* 10 (August 1969), p. 7.

52.   Comprehensive laws are federal statutes in an area of exclusive federal legislative jurisdiction; basic laws are federal statutes containing principles and major rules of law in a certain field, the specific rules of which may be legislated by the constituent governments; general laws are federal statutes which outline general guidelines for republican legislation which do not take effect without implementing republic legislation. See Aksic, Dimitrijevic, Zubi, "Socialist Autonomous Province of Kosovo," p. 22, notes 6, 7, 8.

53.   Radovan Temerinac and Abedin Ferovic, "Legislative Powers of the Socialist Autonomous Provinces," *Yugoslav Survey* 15 (February 1974), pp. 40-1.

54.   Ibid., p. 41.

55.   King,*Minorities under Communism*, p. 142.

56.   Dorde Miljevic, Nikola Stefanovic, Dusan Marinkovic,"The Latest Changes (1971) in the Constitution of the Socialist Federal Republic of Yugoslavia," *Yugoslav Survey* 12 (November 1971), p. 5. For a discussion of some of the provisions of the 1971 Constitutional Amendments, see Paul Shoup, "The National Question in Yugoslavia," *Problems of Communism* 21 (January-February 1972), pp. 25-27.

57.   Milivoje Jelicic, "The Economic Functions of the Repubics Within the Federation," *Socialist Thought and Practice* 14 (January 1974), p. 41.

58.   Ibid., p. 43.

59.   King, *Minorities under Communism*, p. 140. King also recorded Tito's answer: "The Autonomous Province must enjoy all the rights provided by the system of self-government. These rights must be complete, and they must be assured through constitutional changes. Republican status alone will not solve all the problems. If the rights under autonomous status are properly expanded, for which maximum efforts must be made, then this status too can solve all the social, economic, and cultural problems of the territory in question." p. 139, from *Rilindja* (November 4, 1968). For a discussion concerning the reasons why the heavily Albanian portions of Macedonia were separated from those of Kosovo, see ibid., p. 132.

60.   This quiescent attitude was shaken somewhat by factional problems in Vojvodina in the early 1970s. See a description by Dusan Alimpic, "Through Its Own Emancipation, The Working Class Emancipates the Whole of Society," *Socialist Thought and Practice* 14 (May 1974), pp. 115-9.

61.   Every Yugoslav constitution since, and including, the 1946 Constitution has conferred upon the Yugoslav nations the (theoretical!) right to secede.

62.   Lendvai, *Eagles in Cobwebs*, p. 204.

63.   King, *Minorities under Communism*, p. 138.

64.   The following discussion of relative deprivation relies heavily on Gurr's presentation of relative deprivation theory in *Why Men Rebel* (Princeton, N.J.: Princeton University Press, 1970), especially pp. 24-30.

65.   "Thirty Years of the Socialist Development of Kosovo," p. 36.

66.   *Twentieth-Century Yugoslavia*, p. 27.

67.   F.B. Singleton, "Albania and Her Neighbours: The End of Isolation," *World Today* 31 (September 1975), p. 385.

68. "The Other Albanians," p. 23.
69. *Why Men Rebel*, p. 179.
70. Ibid., p. 177.
71. Ibid., p. 179.

Selected Bibliography

Aksic, Stanoje, Dimitrijevic, Bozidar, and Zubi, Neset. "Socialist Autonomous Province of Kosovo," *Yugoslav Survey* 11 (May 1970), pp. 15–48.

Alimpic, Dusan. "Through its own Emancipation, the Working Class Emancipates the Whole of Society," *Socialist Thought and Practice* 14 (May 1974), pp. 114–20.

Bakali, Mahmut. "Thirty Years of the Socialist Development of Kosovo," *Socialist Thought and Practice* 16 (January 1976), pp. 14–40.

Bonner, Hubert. "Autonomy," in Julius Gould and William L. Kolb, eds. *A Dictionary of the Social Sciences*. New York: Free Press of Glencoe, 1964, pp. 46–7.

Burg, Steven L. "Ethnic Conflict and the Federalization of Socialist Yugoslavia: The Serbo-Croat Conflict," *Publius* 7 (Fall 1977), pp. 119–43.

Campbell, John C. "Insecurity and Cooperation: Yugoslavia and the Balkans," *Foreign Affairs* 51 (July 1973), pp. 778–93.

Colakovic, Rodoljub. "Solving the National Question (With Special Reference to Bosnia and Herzegovina)," *Socialist Thought and Practice* 14 (March 1974), pp. 3–16.

Cukovic, Milan, Stefanovic, Nikola, Jogan, Savin. "Constitutional Changes in Yugoslavia," *Yugoslav Survey* 10 (August 1969), pp. 1–22.

Cviic, K.F. "The Missing Historical Dimension In Yugoslavia," *International Affairs* (London) 48 (July 1972), pp. 414–23.

Denitch, Bogdan. "The Evolution of Yugoslav Federalism," *Publius* 7 (Fall 1977), pp. 107–17.

Elazar, Daniel J. "The Principles and Practices of Federalism: A Comparative Historical Approach,"Working Paper No. 8, Center for the Study of Federalism, Temple University (Philadelphia, 1972).

Fira, Aleksandar. "Autonomous Provinces," *Yugoslav Survey* 6 (July-September 1965), pp. 3185–92.

Friedman, Francine. "Yugoslav Foreign Policy's Ambivalence Towards *Detente*," *International Perspectives* (January-February 1979), pp. 19–24.

Friedrich, Carl J. "New Tendencies in Federal Theory and Practice: General Report," Paper delivered at the Sixth World Congress of the International Political Science Association, Geneva, September 21-25, 1964.

——.Trends of *Federalism in Theory and Practice*. New York: Praeger, 1968.

Gurr, Ted Robert. *Why Men Rebel*. Princeton, N.J.: Princeton University Press, 1970.

Hondius, Frits W. *The Yugoslav Community of Nations*. The Hague: Mouton, 1968.

Horvat, Branko. *An Essay on Yugoslav Society.* White Plains, N.Y.: International Arts and Sciences Press, 1969.

Jambrek, Peter. *Development and Social Change in Yugoslavia: Crises and Perspectives of Building a Nation.* Lexington, Mass.: Lexington Books, 1975.

Jelicic, Milivoje. "The Economic Functions of the Republics Within the Federation," *Socialist Thought and Practice* 14 (January 1974), pp. 34–52.

King, Robert R. *Minorities under Communism: Nationalities as a Source of Tension among Balkan Communist States.* Cambridge, Mass.: Harvard University Press, 1973.

Lang, Nicholas R. "The Dialectics of Decentralization: Economic Reform and Regional Inequality in Yugoslavia," *World Politics* 27 (April 1975), pp. 309–35.

Lederer, Ivo J. "Nationalism and the Yugoslavs," in Peter F. Sugar and Ivo J. Lederer, eds. *Nationalism in Eastern Europe.* Seattle: University of Washington Press, 1969, pp. 396–438.

Lendvai, Paul. *Eagles in Cobwebs: Nationalism and Communism in the Balkans.* London: Macdonald, 1969.

Lenin, Vladimir Ilich. *Collected Works.* 45 vols. Moscow: Foreign Languages Publishing House, 1961.

Macesich, George. *Yugoslavia: The Theory and Practice of Development Planning.* Charlottesville: University Press of Virginia, 1964.

Marriott, J.A.R. *The Eastern Question: An Historical Study in European Diplomacy.* Oxford: Clarendon Press, 1958.

Milenkovitch, Deborah D. *Plan and Market in Yugoslav Economic Thought.* New Haven: Yale University Press, 1971.

Miljevic, Dorde, Stefanovic, Nikola, and Marinkovic, Dusan. "The Latest Changes (1971) in the Constitution of the Socialist Federal Republic of Yugoslavia," *Yugoslav Survey* 12 (November 1971), pp. 1–36.

Remington, Robin Alison. "Yugoslavia and European Security," *Orbis* 17 (Spring 1973), pp. 197–226.

Riker, William H. *Federalism: Origin, Operation, Significance.* Boston: Little, Brown, 1964.

Rubinstein, Alvin Z. *Yugoslavia and the the Nonaligned World.* Princeton, N.J.: Princeton University Press, 1970.

Rusinow, Dennison I. "The Other Albanians: Some Notes on the Yugoslav Kosmet Today," *American Universities Field Staff* (Southeast Europe Series) 12 (November 1965).

———.*The Yugoslav Experiment 1948–1974.* Berkeley: University of California Press, 1977.

Shaw, Stanford. *History of the Ottoman Empire and Modern Turkey.* 2 vols. Cambridge: Cambridge University Press, 1976.

Shoup, Paul. *Communism and the Yugoslav National Question.* New York: Columbia University Press, 1968.

———. "The National Question in Yugoslavia," *Problems of Communism* 21 (January-February 1972), pp. 18–29.

———."Yugoslavia's National Minorities under Communism," *Slavic Review* 22 (March 1963), pp. 64–81.

Singleton, F.B. "Albania and Her Neighbours: The End of Isolation," *World Today* 31 (September 1975), pp. 383–90.

——. *Twentieth-Century Yugoslavia*. New York: Columbia University Press, 1976.

Temerinac, Radovan, and Ferovic, Abedin. "Legislative Powers of the Socialist Autonomous Provinces," *Yugoslav Survey* 15 (February 1974), pp. 37–52.

Temperley, Harold W.V. *History of Serbia*. New York: Fertig, 1969.

Teune, Henry. "The Future of Federalism: Federalism and Political Integration," in Valerie Earle, ed. *Federalism: Infinite Variety in Theory and Practice*. Itasca, Ill.: Peacock, 1968, pp. 213–33.

Wolff, Robert Lee. *The Balkans in Our Time*. Cambridge, Mass.: Harvard University Press, 1956.

Italian Accommodation of Cultural Differences

Fabio Lorenzoni

Ethnic and Cultural Differences in the Italian Population with Reference to Linguistic Minorities

In Italy the problem of ethnic and cultural differences among various segments of the population and among various geographical areas within the country is one of linguistic minorities settled in limited parts of the national territory. They are concentrated both near borders or as linguistic enclaves in which ancient cultural traditions have continued throughout the centuries. Imported with the original immigrant settlements, the language of the country of origin has been handed down to the present day.

The phenomenon has little numerical significance; all the populations habitually using a language other than Italian amount to little more than half a million people out of a total of approximately 55 million Italians.[1] The habitual use of a language other than Italian is also the only sign, or at least by far the most important one, that distinguishes these communities. It is basically for this reason that foreign languages are singled out as a criterion by the legal system.[2]

In fact, the protection of linguistic minorities is the object of a system of regulations, varying according to the individual case. This system is based on a fundamental principle of the Constitution with regard to rights of freedom—Art. 6. Under this principle particular minorities are given a wide range of types of protection, defferentiated according to their total number, the historical-political qualification of their origin, and the extent of the socio-cultural expressions through which they demonstrate their special distinguishing features.[3]

Thus, there are parts of the country in which the minority population is more numerous than the Italian-speaking population of that same area; there are minorities whose protection is based on international obligations made by Italy following the Second World War; and, finally, there are minorities which represent no more than the remains of remote cultures originating from migrant settlements from other countries. Due to special local events, these groups have maintained a particular attachment to their original languages and traditions, delaying over the centuries

89

the process of assimilation into the predominant cultural and national environment which normally takes place after a few generations.

The types of protection given to various minority groups demonstrate the different realities and historical origins of each minority. Taken as a whole, these types of protection represent an evolution in ways of putting into effect the principles of freedom as guaranteed by the Italian legal system according to the Art. 3 of the Constitution. In its two sub-sections, Art. 3 very clearly states the two sides of the problem: on one hand, there is the traditional clause which guarantees that "all citizens have equal social rank and are equal before the law without regard to sex, race, *language*, religion, political opinions, personal and social conditions"; on the other hand, there is the progressive clause which solicits change and social evolution aimed at reaching objectives of fundamental equality. In this regard, the second sub-section of Art. 3 of the Constitution requires "the Republic to have the duty of removing all social and economic obstacles which, by limiting *de facto* the freedom and equality of citizens, prevent the full development of the human person and the effective participation of all workers in the political, economic and social organization of the country."

Commenting on this apparent contradiction, Pizzorusso ("Tutela delle minoranze linguistiche e competenza legislativa regionale" in the *Rivista trimestrale di diritto pubblico* 1974, p. 1097) states that "with reference to this, it becomes necessary to go back to the well known difference between "voluntary" minorities and "unwilling" or "necessary" minorities. To this last category belong the social groups which, as victims of discrimination or persecution, long to see these phenomena end in order that they may integrate into the society in which they live. Those, on the other hand, belonging to voluntary minorities are social groups which not only wish to see an end put to the discrimination to which they may be victims, but also, and frequently above all, wish to see shown off to their advantage those factors which make them different from the majority. As a consequence, whereas the unwilling minorities aspire to seeing the principle of formal equality, principally understood as prohibiting discrimination, put into effect, the voluntary minorities aspire to attain a special legal system which, in a certain sense, is a privileged one. This could also be considered putting the principle of equality into effect, but only if it is understood in that particular sense generally known as "essential equality."

As linguistic minorities usually belong to the category of voluntary minorities, it is considered that this is the kind of protection referred to in Art. 6 of the Constitution. Certainly, this is what is referred to in Art. 3 of the code of laws of the Friuli-Venezia Giulia Region and in Art. 2 of the code of laws of the Trentino-Alto Adige Region, which distinctly calls for "equality of rights among citizens, no matter which linguistic group they belong to" (applying the principle of formal equality) and the safeguarding of their "respective ethnic and cultural differences" (applying the principle of essential equality).

These principles are closely connected to those which guarantee forms of association[4] and those which protect the national historical wealth, favoring the development of culture which is not endangered but, on the contrary, is enriched by making the most of minority and local distinguishing features which are safeguarded by Art. 6 of the Constitution.

Indeed, in the case of some minorities settled at the country's borders, protection goes beyond mere linguistic and general cultural safeguards. This is true of the German minorities in the province of Bolzano and of the Slavs of Friuli. In these cases, however, there are international agreements which serve as a basis for the different systems which govern these communities; these agreements were included in the internal constitutional structure—with much delay—after the end of the Second World War.

For this reason the treatment of the minorities in question reflects a special situation; the use of a language different from Italian is the expression of the link between the minority and the border nation and thus is much stronger than that of other linguistic minorities within the country.

However, now that the problems of an international character have been thoroughly settled—although until just a few years ago they had much influence on the matter, involving several particular linguistic minorities—it is possible to describe the measures taken to protect these minorities. Even though such measures vary, depending on specific situations, everything centers around providing a safeguard for the rich cultural wealth frequently embodied in these minorities with their special local traditions. However, the measures do not take into account matters of a nationality or, vice versa, matters that do not concern national unity, but, instead, enrich its pluralistic structure.

It is specifically in this way that the role of the Italian regional system can fully carry out its function as a participant and assist in putting the constitutional principles of fundamental equality into practice, bringing about the country's cultural growth by showing off the expressive capacities of cultural plurality, of which the linguistic minorities are a part, to their best advantage.

Protection of Minorities as the Application of the Principles of Pluralism and Equality

In contrast to what occurred during the Fascist era when the State's objective was the forced assimilation of every expression of cultural difference, the Republic's legal system now pursues a positive policy toward linguist minorities, using more and better means to protect and favor them. This legislative evolution, set in motion by the approval of the Constitution on December 27, 1947, and by its coming into effect on January 1, 1948, brought about the progressive recovery of the values inherent in protecting minorities. The reason for this is the change in an ideological assumption. Today we no longer hold the conviction that the principle of nationality must be carried out in preference to anything else. Instead, present-day public opinion is in favor of adapting the different aspirations of individuals and social groups, and this goal is realized mainly by putting the principles of pluralism and equality into practice.

In fact, the principle of pluralism consists of placing increased value on the forms of association by which man's personality is realized. He is no longer considered as an isolated individual but, rather, is viewed within a social context. This context is respected even in the case of communities or associations which are smaller than the State's community, or in the case of communities which cross the State's border in one way or another.

As for the principle of equality, it implies above all—as is obvious—the prohibition of discrimination. This results in the illegitimacy of any oppressive measure against particular categories of individuals, and thus, against members of ethnic-linguistic minorities as well. This "negative protection" (in the sense that it prevents discrimination), although by and large sufficient to protect the "unwilling" minorities by allowing them to assimilate with the majority, is not enough to protect voluntary minorities. They aspire to having their distinguishing characteristics shown off to best advantage by "positive protection," which can only be the result of special regulations creating an exception, thus bringing about a system privileging them in a certain sense."[5]

In this framework it is possible to see how the role of the regional system, and the system of local authority in general, can contribute much to promote distinguishing cultural characteristics in limited areas of the territory. Before taking a look at how positive protection of linguistic minorities is regulated in individual regions, let us note that it is brought about both directly, through measures safeguarding the use of the language, and indirectly, through guarantees of proportionality among the members of different ethnic-linguistic groups. The direct way includes measures which ensure school teaching in the same language that is spoken and written by the minority, or, at least, the teaching in public schools of the minority language and culture in addition to other subjects. After the school age, linguistic protection requires that, generally, in all relations with public offices the citizen can communicate with authorities using his own language, and, vice versa, that the authority addresses him using the minority language. In the Valle d'Aosta and Trentino-Alto Adige regions, this is demonstrated first of all by, publishing the Official Gazettes in two languages (Italian and French in Valle d'Aosta, and German and Italian in Trentino-Alto Adige). In the province of Bolzano all public employees are required to know German as well as Italian.

There are also measures providing for forms of incentive and special protection of the use of minority languages in the fields of mass media, the daily press and periodicals, motion pictures, radio and television, not only for local and private stations, but for the national networks broadcasting in protected areas as well.

The other category of means for safeguarding minority cultures (that is, those with an indirect influence on the use of language) includes regulations which aim at maintaining a fixed proportion among populations belonging to different ethnic groups. In Italy there are no measures which directly limit people's freedom of movement in this sense. On the contrary, with reference to the Slovene minorities in the region bordering Yugoslavia, protection includes guaranteeing the possibility to emigrate or immigrate with easy terms for the loss or gain of citizenship and for the transfer of title-deeds to property.

Generally the citizen has the free choice of making or not making a declaration stating that he belongs to a minority group

Moreover, as has already been said, since official policy favors the protection of minorities and the enrichment of distinguishing cultural characteristics, there are measures designed to grant easy terms and social and economic benefits in favor of minorities, as well as guarantees of proportionality for employment in govern-ment posts for members of different ethnic groups.

Finally, in the political organization of representative public authorities, favorable conditions are guaranteed to exponents of minority groups. In the first place, this takes the form of public financing of political parties. Notwithstanding general regulations, this is granted even to political parties which have participated in national elections, but which, being an expression of minority ethnic groups, are found only in limited areas of the country. The condition necessary for this exception to the norm is that the parties represent minorities protected by the special code of laws concerning autonomy approved by every region through constitu-tional law.

The composition of the local, regional, provincial and munici-pal elected assemblies, as well as those in mountainous commun-ities, provides for the specific situation of minorities so that a system of ethnic proportionality is guaranteed, creating an excep-tion to the true numerical proportion of voters.

The German and Latin Linguistic Minorities Protected in the Trentino-Alto Adige Region

The most extensive protection given to ethnic and linguistic minorities in all of Italy is granted to the German population of the province of Bolzano, which represents 62.4% of the inhabitants of the entire province.

The solution to the Alto Adige question was finalized by the De

Gasperi-Gruber agreement of 1946. However, until the end of the 1960s, the matter was the source of different kinds of tension which led the two parties concerned, Italy and Austria, to appeal to the United Nations. Eventually Italy requested that the controversy be brought before the International Court of Justice in the Hague. In short, a change in the government of territorial autonomy of Alto Adige (also called South Tyrol, which corresponds to the province of Bolzano) was desired by the Austrians in order to separate it entirely from the Trentino. However, in 1969 a set of 137 points intended to bring about a more favorable treatment of the German-speaking minority led to the end of the controversy and a thorough reframing of the special code of laws for autonomy of the Trentino-Alto Adige region. The new code of laws was issued with the constitutional law of November 10, 1971, N.1. It was then inserted into a unified text of laws concerning the special code for the Trentino-Alto Adige region. This was followed by a series of regulations for implementing the individual powers assigned to the jurisdiction of the region and the province.

The main difference between the Trentino-Alto Adige region and all the other regions in Italy is that the two individual provinces which make up the region, Bolzano and Trentino, are granted wide legislative powers, which normally are granted only to the regions. All the other provinces are at a territorial level of government which has no legislative powers at all.

Among the legislative and administrative powers of these special provinces, many seem to be specifically designed to favor the minority's particular interests. For example, the powers enable cultural autonomy to be put into practice; they deal with economic activities carried out mainly by members of the minority; and they are concerned with the organizational activities necessary for local collectivities. (Pizzorusso, Minoranze, p. 553). Moreover, with the reform of 1971, the region as a whole was granted the power to make laws regarding the protection of linguistic minorities. This ended the period which, beginning with the promulgation of the Constitution in 1948, had excluded this power from those granted to the regions.

On more than one occasion the Constitutional Court had delivered a judgement on the matter, deciding that measures for the protection of linguistic minorities were connected with the State's international relations. It is probable that the members of the Constituent Assembly had not intended to give these measures this significance; however, without doubt, in the historical context in which the Alto Adige question remained subject to dispute, it was difficult not to take them into consideration. Therefore, today the system of regulations regarding German minorities in the province of Bolzano is part of the range of measures favoring cultural pluralism instead of matters of national plurality existing within the State.

In addition, another minority which uses the Ladin language

lives in the Trentino-Alto Adige region. This minority benefits by specific protection in the province of Bolzano. A constitutional law concerning the Ladin population in the province of Trento was voted on by the Chamber of Deputies on June 9, 1977, and is in the process of being approved. This law will guarantee that the Ladins are represented in the Trento provincial council, that the language is taught in school, and, in short, that the Ladin minority is treated on an equal basis with the others protected in the region.

Without going into detail over individual measures for minority protection of which there are many—I refer the reader to the texts mentioned in the bibliography for a more thorough analysis of the subject—it is enough to say here that it is assured by guaranteeing the minorities that their language and culture would be taught in public schools. In addition, relations with public offices may be held in the language of the minority, and regulations ensure ethnic proportionality both in government employment and in elective posts.

The Trentino-Alto Adige law of July 23, 1973, N.9, for example, put into effect the guarantee that the Ladin linguistic group would be represented in the regional and provincial councils of Bolzano, as was provided for by Art. 62 of the region's code of laws for autonomy. Art. 8 of D.P.R. (decree of the President of the Republic) November 1, 1973 N. 691 establishes that the provincial board of RAI (the Italian radio and television broadcasting company) be composed of the President of the Board and three members, one each of the Italian, German and Ladin languages. According to to Art. 9 of this D.P.R., the staff of RAI in Bolzano in charge of programs in German and Ladin must belong to the German and Ladin language groups respectively.

With the law of March 11, 1972, N.118, steps were taken in favor of the economic development of the population of Alto Adige. These steps encourage protection of German linguistic minorities in very different sectors—German motion picture screenings, incentives for production, registry activities and changes in judicial districts. Moreover, ethnic proportionality is guaranteed in legal offices. On the basis of a 1971 census, in the province of Bolzano 63% of all posts are reserved for the German group, 33% for the Italians, and 4% for the Ladins. The regulation (D.P.R. July 26, 1976, N. 752) dealing with all public employment in general provides for the distribution of posts among the respective linguistic groups.

Belonging to a linguistic group is left up to the free choice of the parties concerned. This choice must have some kind of stability, but it is revocable. It is modified or changed every time a general census is taken of the population. Regulation D.P.R. July 26, 1976, N. 752, concerning ethnic proportionality in public bodies clearly confirms the distinguishing characteristics of the minorities —which are considered voluntary minorities—to be protected in this region. It is the State's concern that through public bodies the minority's cultural characteristics are cultivated as a specific demonstration of pluralism which is complied with in the entire legal system.

The Linguistic Minorities in the Friuli-Venezia Giulia Region

Another linguistic minority in Italy has had problems of an international nature, not resolved until many years after the end of the Second World War. It is the Slavic-speaking group settled at the border with Yugoslavia.

In fact, the international importance of the Slovene minority is shown by the outcome of the "memorandum d'entente," signed in London on October 5, 1954, by the governments of Italy, Great Britain, the United States and Yugoslavia, containing detailed regulations for the protection of minorities in both sides of the Trieste territory. As is known, the governmental system of the free territory of Trieste could not be put into practice, because, in order to function, the appointment of the High Commissioner for Trieste was necessary, and this never occurred. On the other hand, the Constitution provided the foundation for Art. 116 of the fundamental Charter, on the basis of which the Friuli-Venezia Giulia region has a special code of laws for autonomy. This was put into effect with the Constitutional Law of January 31, 1963, N.1, which approved the code of laws. However, the provisional system of government dictated by the Tenth Transitory Regulation of the Constitution had already provided for leaving the measures for the protection of linguistic minorities intact, in accordance with Art. 6.

As far as the Slovene minority is concerned, three different forms of protection are recognized for the three nuclei which reside respectively in the provinces of Udine, Gorizia and Trieste. In the province of Udine linguistic discrimination is prohibited, based on the principle of formal equality. In the province of Gorizia, the State's legislation on the subject of teaching applies (the law of July 19, 1961, N. 1012, which was modified and integrated with the law of December 22, 1973, N. 932). Accordingly, the right of the members of the minority to have nursery, elementary, secondary and vocational schools where teaching carried out in Slavic is recognized. In the ex-territory of Trieste, besides this legislation, international protection based on the special code of laws included with the "memorandum d'entente" also applies.

With the Osimo Treaty signed on November 10, 1975, by Italy and Yugoslavia, relations between the two countries were settled definitely, including a series of commitments for the protection of minorities. Italy implemented the treaty by approving it with its own law of March 14, 1977, N. 73. In Art. 8 of the Osimo Treaty, both parties commit themselves to guarantee, within their respective systems, "the maintenance of the level of protection given members of the two respective ethnic groups provided for in the special code of laws no longer applicable." This put an end to international protection, now replaced by measures guaranteeing and favoring the linguistic characteristics of the Slavic communities living in the Friuli-Venezia Giulia region.

The region, on the other hand, had already taken over these objectives with more than one law. Among these, the following should be noted: the regional law of July 2, 1969, N. 11, which included among the duties of the regional administration that of encouraging activities and initiatives regarding the cultural wealth of linguistic minorities; the law of October 9, 1970, N.36, which, besides repeating this provision and developing it, establishes that one of the experts called upon to be part of the regional socio-economic committee must be an expert in socio-economic problems of the Slovene linguistic minority (Art. 1 and 2); the regional law of Friuli-Venezia Giulia of July 21, 1971, N. 27, which in the same way controls the composition of the regional committee for cataloging and making inventories of the cultural and environmental wealth of Friuli-Venezia Giulia (Art. 10, subsection 1, letter e, and Art. 11, letter g); the law of March 14, 1973, N. 20, which provides for refunding by the regions of expenses incurred by local boards for the needs of bilingualism.

Thus the situation in Friuli-Venezia Giulia is very different from the one in Trentino-Alto Adige. Here even before international relations were thoroughly defined, the region adopted measures of protection in favor of the linguistic minorities, already expecting that the measures would favor cultural pluralism, instead of simply directing the relations between representatives of different nationalities. In the Trentino-Alto Adige, on the other hand, this other kind of protection did not come about until after the reform of the code of laws of 1971, when the provisions of the set of 137 points, agreed upon on an international level, were put into effect. This was possible because the tenth transitional regulation of the Constitution had already provided for minority protection in the region, even apart from the definition of the special code of laws for autonomy. It was also possible because the number of members of the Slavic linguistic group represented only 4% of the residents in the region, whereas the German group represented over 62% of the population in the province of Bolzano.

Linguistic Minorities in Valle d'Aosta, Calabria, and the Other Newly-Established Regions

The autonomous region of Valle d'Aosta is the only region in Italy which is composed of one single province. Its territory corresponds to an area settled by a French-speaking minority.

No problems of an international nature exist in this region, and minority protection dates back to before the Second World War. A special code of laws for autonomy, approved by the constitutional law of February 26, 1948, N. 4, states that "in the Valle d'Aosta the French language is recognized as equal to Italian" (Art. 38). Documents under the seal of a public officer may be written in one or the other of the two languages. Preference in the employment of government officials is given to natives of the region, and, at any rate, knowledge of the French language is a prerequisite. Both teaching in the minority language and teaching of the protected language and culture are guaranteed in every type of school at every level.

The region also benefits from a financial system based on several tax exemptions which permits its population to enjoy a better standard of life. Even through these indirect measures, the constitutional principle of Art. 6 can be considered put into practice, and the development of cultural and linguistic character-istics of the minority settled in the region is favored.

In the newly-established regions instituted in 1970 on a nation-wide basis, several codes of laws, deliberated on by the regions' respective councils and approved by law of Parliament, have expressly provided for the protection of local minorities as one of the regions' duties. Among these regions, Calabria has the most detailed regulations on the subject. It recognizes its duty to favor "with respect for their traditions, the value of the historical, cultural and artistic wealth of the populations of Albanian and Greek origin" as well as "the teaching of the two languages in places where they are spoken" (Art. 56, letter r of the code of laws). Other regions use a more general expression in their code of laws, for example: "the region favors placing value on the original wealth of language, culture and customs found in local communi-ties" (Art. 5 of Basilicata's code of laws); "favoring the protection of the linguistic and historical wealth and the popular traditions of the ethnic communities existing in its territory, in agreement with the municipalities concerned (Art. 4, Molise's code of laws); "defends the original wealth of language, culture and customs of local communities and places value on them" (art. 7 of Piemonte's code of laws); "agrees with placing value on the cultural and linguistic wealth of individual communities" (Art. 2, Veneto's code of laws).

In the Veneto region, the regional law of August 1, 1974, N. 40 is already in effect; it protects Ladin-Dolomite minorities of Alto Cordevole and Ampezzano in the province of Belluno, the Ladin-Friulian minorities of the Portogruaro district in the province of Venice and the German minorities in the towns of Sappada, Roana, Rotzo and Giazza.

Bibliographical Note

On the problem of linguistic minorities, a general treatment may be found in: Tullio De Mauro, *Storia linguistica d'Italia unita, Bari 1963;* Id., *La lingua italiana e i dialetti,* Firenze 1969; Sergio Salvi, *Le Lingue tagliate, storia delle minoranze linguistiche in Italia,* Milano 1975; Bernardini, *Le mille culture,* Roma 1976; on the legal side of the problem: Alessandro Pizzorusso, *Le minoranze nel diritto pubblico interno,* Milano 1967; Id., *Il pluralismo linguistico in Italia fra Stato nazionale e autonomie regionali,* Pisa 1975; Id., *Commento all'art. 6 Cost.,* in Commentario della Costituzione edited by G. Branca, Bologna 1975; Id., *Minoranze etnico-linguistiche,* in Enciclopedia del diritto *ad vocem,* Milano 1976; Gianfranco Mor, *Minoranze linguistiche,* in: Guida per le autonomie locali 1978, Roma 1978; Manlio Udina, *Sull'attuazione dell'art. 6 della Costituzione per la tutela delle minoranze linguistiche,* in: Giurisprudenza costituzionale 1974, p. 3602. As regards the two minorities protected on the basis of international agreements, see: Manlio Udina, *Scritti sulla questione di Trieste,* Milano 1969; Mario Toscano, *Storia diplomatica della questione dell'Alto-Adige,* Bari 1967; Sergio Bartole, *Profili della condizione giuridica della minoranza slovena nell'ordinamento italiano,* in: Studi in onore di Manlio Udina, Milano 1975. For more general information on the regions' powers with reference to the protection of minorities, see: Alessandro Pizzorusso, *La garanzia di rappresentanza del gruppo linguistico ladino nel consiglio regionale e nel consiglio provinciale di Bolzano,* in: Le Regioni 1973, p. 1118; Id., *Tutela delle minoranze linguistiche e competenza legislativa regionale,* in: Rivista Trimestrale di Diritto Pubblico, 1974, p. 1093; Id., *Verso il riconoscimento della soggettivita delle comunitá etnico-linguistiche?,* in Studi in onore di C. Furno, Milano 1973; Raffaele Ingicco, *Minoranze linguistiche: due iniziative regionali rinviate dal Governo,* in: Le Regioni, 1977. p. 971.

Matching Peoples, Territories and States
Post-Ottoman Irredentism in the Balkans and in the Middle East
Myron Weiner

Irredentism—the demand by one state for the territory of another either because it contains a *people* whom it considers to be its own, or *land* over which it claims historical rights—is a common feature of state formation and its aftermath. Irredentism in the contemporary Third World has been an issue between India and Pakistan; Indonesia, Malaysia and the Philippines; Morocco and Mauritania; Afghanistan and Pakistan; Iran and Iraq; Ethiopia and Somalia; Ethiopia and French Somaliland; Rwanda and Burundi; Togo and Ghana; and the Ivory Coast and Ghana. It emerged when the European powers withdrew from Africa and Asia, leaving behind states whose boundaries often cut across tribes and linguistic groups, and whose boundaries rarely matched any historic kingdoms.

But irredentism is not simply a phenomena of post-European colonialism. It has its roots in the process of state formation in Europe—the word *irredenta* is of course Italian—and its most consistent expression was in the European states that emerged following the break-up of the Ottoman empire in Southeast Europe. The Ottoman empire was in fact a multi-continental empire: it spanned both the Dardanelles and the Suez across three continents. Its breakup, and the subsequent emergence of independent states, thus had repercussions far beyond the boundaries of Europe, repercussions that are still felt in the contemporary process of state-formation in the Middle East.

The Ottoman empire was one of the largest and certainly among the most enduring of the great multi-ethnic states in world history. At the peak of its power it dominated the Arab-speaking world of North Africa and the Middle East and the polyglot, multi-religious Balkans. It contained Slavs, Turks, Greeks, Armenians, Arabs and Kurds and numerous other linguistic communities, and Muslims, Roman Catholics, Greek and Russian Orthodox, and Jews, all in their varied sects and denominations. It was a world of extraordinary religious, linguistic and cultural diversity with a variety of institutional arrangements that permitted autonomy to a greater or lesser degree within what would be described today as an authoritarian political framework. It was the disintegration of this empire in the nineteenth and early twentieth centuries that stimulated the drive for independent statehood on the part of its many ethnic communities, and at the same time generated the ambitions and anxieties of the major European powers.

One phase of the empire's disintegration took place in Southeast Europe, beginning in the early part of the nineteenth century and culminating by the end of World War I in the emergence of five successor states—Rumania, Yugoslavia, Greece and Albania.

Another phase occurred in Western Asia at the close of the First World War, and by the 1950s it also culminated in the emergence of five independent successor states—Israel, Lebanon, Syria, Jordan and Iraq. In both regions the successor states, and the borders assigned to them, were created by powers external to the region. In both regions state boundaries neither matched the distribution of ethnic groups in any precise fashion, nor matched the territory that each of the new states demanded on the basis of what they asserted as their historic national rights. One of the most important similarities in the two regions in this process of state formation was thus the emergence of irredentism—the demand by many of these states that their boundaries be revised so that they could incorporate the ethnic minority and/or territory of one of their neighbors.

Though there are many variants of irredentism, and as we shall see there are important differences between irredentism in the Balkans and in the Middle East, this paper suggests that irredentism constitutes a category of behavior or class of relationships with many common features and, most importantly, some common determinants and consequences. Irredentism as it now exists, as well as in the forms it may take in the future, in the Middle East is in many ways similar to the irredentism that existed earlier in the Balkans.

Since there are dangers both in the misuse of historical analogies and in the neglect of historical experiences, it may be useful to dwell briefly on both the limits and uses of history for a consideration of contemporary policies. Permit me for this purpose to invoke a medical analogy.

Medical researchers isolate a pathology. In some instances the cause of the disease may be discovered in the laboratory. In other instances, epidemiologists may reason inductively about the cause of the disease by observing and comparing the frequency of its occurrence in different population groups, places, times and circumstances. Often the epidemiologists will speak of "risk factors" rather than "cause."

But whatever the "cause," the disease itself is studied: its characteristic symptoms, its course of development, and its probable outcome. The researcher constructs a model of the disease, but the model is only an approximation of reality. The model conceptualizes and generalizes certain features of the disease and the dynamics of its development, but it is not capable nor intended to accurately describe and predict every case. Medical clinicians then use this model for diagnostic purposes to predict the probable course of the disease's development and to prescribe treatment. In his diagnosis and prescription a competent doctor is aware that each individual case has its own pecularities so that neither prediction nor prescription should be mechanically made. Cancers do go into remission. Patients can die of measles. Antibiotics do fail. Aspirins can kill. The model guides the clinician, but he is not driven by it.

The danger in reasoning by historical analogy is that we may simply choose a particular historical event to suit our current preferences. "No more Munichs, no more Vietnams" are slogans, not the basis for an informed use of history. To use history, we must have a construct, a framework within which we place individual events or cases because they belong to a class of events. The analyst must demonstrate that he has defined such a class, and then developed a model in which events occur in sequences and one event tends to lead to another. The model remains an approximation of historical reality. It does not incorporate and explain every significant feature and variation of the events it attempts to describe and explain. Both in the natural universe and in human affairs, concrete cases are invariably unique, while all scientific conceptualizations are abstractions that never fully exhaust or reflect concrete reality.

Elsewhere I have tried to develop such a model for the study of irredentism[1] and later in this paper I shall restate the main outlines of the model. The primary objective of this paper is to demonstrate that irredentism in this region can be understood not as a unique event, but as part of a class of events that other countries that came out of the Ottoman empire also experienced. I shall try to show how irredentism first worked in the Balkans and that, variations not withstanding, there were many uniform patterns of development. I shall then suggest how some of these patterns now appear to be replicated in the Arab-Israeli conflict, and that by understanding them we may be in a better position to predict and therefore influence their outcome.

We shall begin, then with a set of historical statements concerning how and why irredentism developed in the Balkans.

The Rise of Balkan Irredentism

1. The decline of the Ottoman empire in the beginning of the nineteenth century was accompanied by the intervention of the then Great Powers, especially France, Britain and Russia, in the process of forming new states in the Balkans. The creation of these states—Greece in 1829, Serbia, Montenegro and Rumania in

1878, Albania in 1912, and the union of the Serbs with other southern Slavs to form the state of Yugoslavia in 1918—was largely determined not by the relationship between the Ottoman authorities and the successor states, but by the Great Powers at international congresses to which the successor states were often not parties. It was the intervention of Great Britain, Russia and France in 1829 that led to the creation of Greece as an independent state following the Greek revolution against the Turks in 1821. In the 1870s Russia proposed the formation of a Greater Bulgaria—but the French and British overruled the proposal and created a smaller Bulgarian state, and Albania was created by the major powers in 1912. One international conference after another—Trianon, San Stefano, Berlin and Paris—set the international boundaries. It would not be an overstatement to say that every question of state formation and boundaries in the Balkans involved one or more of the Great Powers.[2]

2. The primary concern of each of the European powers was to prevent any other European power from having too decisive a voice in the Balkans. France and Britain were concerned that Russia not dominate the region, that Italian influence on the states bordering the Adriatic be limited, and then later that German power not be extended. But apart from the exigencies of great power relationships, each of the European powers was influenced by the dominant *zeitgeist* of the time which conceived of each people or nationality having a state of its own.

It was a notion that underlay the movements for the political unification of the Italian-speaking and German-speaking peoples. And it was a sentiment that shaped the demands by the various peoples living under the multi-ethnic Hapsburg and Ottoman empires for independent statehood. The demand for breaking up these empires—as distinct from their democratization—soon emerged as the central political force among each of the peoples in southeastern Europe.

It was a sentiment that was widely supported in the West. The Hellenophile British supported the Greek demand for independence against the Ottomans. The French supported their fellow Latin Rumanians, and the British (and the Russians) supported the Bulgarian independence movement. Woodrow Wilson's belief in "self-determination," with its notion of ethnicity as the central criteria for state formation, was very much in the spirit of nineteenth century European nationalism. Thus, the process of state formation in central and eastern Europe was widely based on the assumption that each people had the *right* to create its own state.

3. What constituted a "people" was, of course, one of the most difficult questions. Were the two major tribes, the Gheg and Tosk, a common people—Albanians? Are Moldavians and Walachs a common people, Rumanians? Are Macedonians a separate people or, as some Greeks asserted, merely Slavic speaking

Greeks? Should Serbs, Croatians, Montenegrins, and Slovenes be brought together as southern Slavs? What constitutes a people? Their religion? Language? Shared historical memories? What if these do not match?

For the better part of a century a great battle ensued for the secular souls or identities of the people of southeastern Europe, a struggle involving the churches, princes, boyars, tribal chiefs, landlords, the urban middle class, intelligentsia, new political leaders and emigres. The relationship between smaller and larger identities remained fluid for, even as nationalist movements emerged emphasizing the importance of language, there remained strong sentiments for a larger pan-Slavic movement.

4. Equally problematic was the question of how one related an imprecise definition of a people with the very precise notion of a state, a territory, and clearly demarcated borders. The villages of one community often faded off into another. Border peoples sometimes spoke syncretistic languages, mixing the structure of one language with a large vocabulary from another. Some people linguistically belonged to one community, but by religion to another. Sometimes the urban centers contained one people, but the rural areas in which the towns were located contained another. And, of course, the towns themselves were often mixed as various peoples came together in search of education and modern employment. Each Balkan state had "national" minorities who belonged to other states, and minorities who had no state at all. Bulgaria, for example, had Turks, Rumanians and Greeks, not to mention Jews, gypsies and Armenians or non-national minorities; and the Yugoslavs had Germans, Hungarians, Albanians, Rumanians and Bulgarians plus Macedonians.

5. Compounding the uncertainties of whether a particular local community belonged with one people or another, and the tensions that arose among peoples who shared the same space, was the additional conflict that arose over historical claims. As each people asserted its own ethnicity and insisted that a people could become a nation only when it possessed a state of its own, ethnic groups turned to their past greatness to define where their borders should be. Invariably, each ethnic group discovered that the moment of its historic greatness coincided with the point when the state encompassed the largest territories under its control. Each ethnic group, therefore, demanded that contemporary boundaries be based upon historical boundaries, generally of great antiquity, irrespective in some instances of the existing distribution of ethnic groups. Needless to say, the claims of the Albanians, Macedonians, Bulgarians, Greeks and others were incompatible with one another.

6. Thus, the Balkans that emerged out of the Ottoman empire consisted of states whose boundaries were largely shaped by outside powers, where every state contained a majority and one or more minorities that it shared with a neighbor, and with

governing elites who believed that the state boundaries should include all those who shared their nationality, or along boundaries that coincided with a period of historic greatness. The result was that there was not a single state in southeastern Europe that either did not make irredentist claims upon a neighbor or was not the object of irredentist claims, and often both. Thus Hungary wanted the Vojvodina region of Yugoslavia and the Transylvania region of Rumania with their Magyar populations; the Italians demanded Italian speaking areas of Yugoslavia (and of Austria); the Greeks wanted the Greek populated areas of southern Albania and Turkey; Albania claimed the Kosovo region of Yugoslavia; and Bulgaria, Yugoslavia and Greece quarreled over the future of Macedonia, an area straddled by all three.

7. Irredentism became the single most important determinant of how states behaved and how they developed in the Balkans. How they interacted with other states in the region, how they related to the Great Powers, how they treated their minorities, and what received priorities in their internal development, were all largely shaped by whether they made claims upon their neighbors, or were the objects of their neighbors' claims. This will become clearer as we turn now to a brief review of the internal politics and foreign policies of three of the Balkan states, Greece and Bulgaria, both irredentist states, and Yugoslavia, the object of revisionism. At the conclusion of these cases, we shall codify some of the general patterns of behavior. Then we shall consider how relevant these general patterns are for examining irredentist conflicts in the contemporary Middle East.

Greece and the Megali Dream

It is appropriate that our first example of an irredentist power should be Greece, for Greece can properly be described as the first "new" nation, that is the first country under the rule of an ethnically alien colonial people to break free to become in independent nation in modern times. It is now fashionable to speak of the United States as the "first new nation," but in the contemporary sense in which we speak of new nations, the United States is not one. The U.S. belongs to a different class of states, along with Australia, Canada, New Zealand, and most of Latin America, countries established and populated by European powers whose governing elites and masses of people shared similar values, language and ethnicity with the imperial power. As Louis Hartz has pointed out, these countries were fragments of European cultures and have had quite a different set of development problems and characteristics from the contemporary newly-independent states.

Colonial rule of the Greeks by the Turks began in 1453 with the conquest of Constantinople, the former capital of the Byzantine Empire, and came to an end with the Greek war for Constantinople in 1821. Ottoman rule was not completely unwelcome at first, since it freed the Greeks from the Venetians and other western Catholic crusaders who had played such a decisive role in destroying the Byzantine Empire. Moreover, the Ottomans permit-ted freedom of trade to the Greeks and allowed Greek merchants and seamen to expand throughout the Aegean Sea, permitted education in the Greek language, and gave official recognition to the Greek Orthodox Church. The result was that the schoolmas-ters, priests, intellectuals, and merchants of Greece were among the first people under Ottoman rule to develop a nationalist revolutionary movement.

But to understand the revolution launched by the Greeks against the Turks in 1821 and the subsequent expansionist sentiments of the new Greek state, we must appreciate one very significant feature of Greek social structure under the Ottomans. The Turks welcomed the Greeks into the Ottoman civil service so that by the seventeenth century there was an important class of Greek officials, called the Phanariots (after the quarter of Constan-tinople in which the Patriarchate of the Greek Orthodox church is located). The Phanariots, even though they did not become Muslims or adopt the Turkish language, achieved positions of great authority—as Dragoman of the fleet in charge of administra-tion and tax collection in the islands of the Aegean, as rulers of Moldavia and Walachia (later Rumania), and as Dragoman of the Porte (private secretary to the Sultan's Grand Vizier)—four of the highest offices in the Empire.

In short, the Greeks had considerable social social mobility within the Ottoman system and it was these opportunities, rather than any severe repression, which account for the rise of the nationalist movement earlier in Greece than elsewhere in the Balkans. They also account for one other feature of the Greek revolution. As Toynbee has pointed out, the Greek revolutionaries were inspired by two incompatible ambitions: to gain control over the Turkish empire and place it under Greek management—that is to say, re-establish the Byzantine Empire with its capital at Constantinople; or, alternatively, to secede from the Ottoman Empire to create an independent Greek state. The earliest revolts by the Phanariots in Moldavia understandably received no support from the Rumanians who had no interest in furthering imperial Greek interests; the revolt did, however, win widespread support in the Peloponnese, with enthusiastic support from Greek merchants and their families abroad. It soon became clear that the merchants, the priests and the intellectuals did not share the interests of the Phanariots and other leading Greek families with positions in the buraucracy in preserving the Ottoman Empire intact, but felt instead that if the Greeks were to become a nation, the Ottoman Empire must be broken up.

It should be stressed that the Greeks of the nineteenth century had a conception of their national identity different from the conception of Greek identity held by Western Europeans. British Hellenophiles, for example, supported the Greek War of Independence as if the classical Greek heritage were their own, as, indeed, it was felt to be. But for most Greeks, the greatest event in their own history was the introduction of Christianity and the rise of the Orthodox Church. Though in the eighteenth and nineteenth century it became fashionable in the west to despise Byzantine culture (the term Byzantine is still a pejorative with overtones of intrigue and decadent opulence), most Greeks took more pride in the great empire which governed the eastern portions of the Christian world for some eleven centuries than in the small, pagan republics of ancient Greece. Like many people, the Greeks defined their period of historic "greatness" as the period of greatest territorial control, not the periods of highest cultural achievements.

The details of the Greek War of Independence need not concern us, but three aspects of the war and the immediate aftermath are relevant for our analysis. The first, a very familiar problem in new states, is that from the very beginning, indeed in the midst of the struggle against the Turks, there was a conflict between the new central government and local authority. The first president, Capodistrias (who was assassinated a few years after he took power), engaged in a continuous struggle with local landowners and independent rulers known as primates. A number of scholars have argued that Capodistrias and his successors were ultimately so successful, both in destroying the system of local auto-nomy (because it was essentially hostile to the central government) and in replacing it with a national hierarchically centralized bureaucratic structure centered in Athens, that the development of administrative initiative at the local level was subsequently prevented.[3]

A second consequence of the struggle was that the new state included within its boundaries only a small percentage of the Greeks living around the Aegean Sea. Thessaly and the Aegean islands, including Crete, were not part of the territory of the new Greek state. From the very beginning, therefore, the leaders of the new state felt that their territory was incomplete. It has been suggested by historians that Prince Leopold of Saxe-Coburg, who had first agreed to be king of Greece, subsequently changed his mind when he became convinced that the new state would be so geographically limited that it would not be viable. This sense of territorial incompleteness had a decisive effect on the kind of priorities and policies chosen by Greek leaders for the next hundred years.

Thirdly, the new government established itself as a monarchy, not a republic, thereby setting a precedent followed by every subsequent successor state emerging out of the disintegrating Ottoman Empire. Why Greece—then Bulgaria, Rumania, Albania and Yugoslavia—all chose to become monarchies in the nineteenth century is a fascinating issue in institutional development worthy of more detailed examination than we can provide here. In the Greek case it had something to do with the desires of the British, who had played such an important role in helping the Greeks achieve independence that they had a decisive influence on the kind of political system the Greeks established. The British wanted to prevent the Russians or any other major power from having influence in Greece and thought that a monarch from one of the smaller states (they tried Saxe-Coburg and when that failed found Prince Otto of Bavaria) would reduce the chances of Great Power penetration. Moreover, the Greeks themselves were politically so divided, and so fearful that one faction or another might dominate the system, that they welcomed bringing in an outside ruler—at least at first. And finally, the concept of monarchy played an important part in what we would today call the political development theory which prevailed among many educated Europeans of the nineteenth century. This concept emphasized the legitimizing function of the monarch, and in the minds of conservative elements both in Greece and in Britain the monarch was also seen as a possible barrier to revolution. Sovereignty, in this conception, rested in the hands of the monarch (and in practice the elites with access to him) rather than with the "people." In short, the monarchy could assure order, restrain popular elements,and protect the power of the upper classes.

Every account of Greek political history for the hundred years after the War of Independence has stressed the obsession by all Greek governments with what the Greeks called the "Megali Idea," the great idea which brought together the irredentist urge to unite all Greeks with a desire to revive the Byzantine Empire. The disagreements among politicians centered on the issue of *how* to achieve this goal, not whether it was worth struggling for, and virtually every crisis in Greek politics during this period was related to this expansionist goal. This obsession with expansion or, as the Greeks saw it, with making the nation whole, was one which other peoples in the Balkans also felt intently and which they shared with other self-conscious peoples divided by international boundaries. George Bernard Shaw captured this sentiment well when he sought to explain why Irish nationalism seemed so hysterical, fierce and uncontrollable. "Nobody in Ireland of any intelligence, likes nationalism any more than a man with a broken leg likes having it set. A healthy nation is as unconscious of its nationality as a healthy man of his bones. But if you break a nation's nationality it will think of nothing else but getting it set again."[4]

The strength of the "Megali Idea" was described by one Greek scholar who wrote that "to understand this nationalist behavior one must always bear in mind that the Greek feels emotionally much closer to Byzantium than to ancient Athens. The classical world is admired, venerated and studied—but it is dead. The Byzantine Empire, on the other hand, is very much alive in every

Greek heart and has conditioned all reactions since 1453. The Turkish occupation was always considered temporary and from the first years of childhood every boy and girl was taught that eventually all the Greeks will be united again and form one nation with its capital in Constantinople, or, as the Greeks usually say, with its capital in "Polis." For there are many "cities" in the world, Andrianoupolis, Philippoupolis and Alexandroupolis, but there is only one "Polis," and this is "Constantinoupolis." And even today, when one says that he is leaving for the "city" or that his father was born in the "city," or that a great fire destroyed many shops in the "city," everyone understands that he is referring to Istanbul...This zealous desire of incorporation all the irredentist Hellenes in one Greek nation (was) transubstantiated into the policy of the "Megali Idea."[5]

It would take many detailed pages to recount the various steps which successive Greek governments took to satisfy Greek irredentist claims. For our purposes it is more important to look at the effects this policy had upon the internal political development of Greece and its international alliances.

Though it is empirically impossible to demonstrate that if a given policy had not been pursued, something would have happened that did not happen, a reasonable case can nonetheless be made that the focus on expansion reduced the pressures and probabilities of internal social and economic reforms. One piece of limited evidence for this argument is provided by the Balkan historian William Miller, who described the conflict between two Greek leaders in the 1840s, Mavrokordatos and Kolettes. Mavrokordatos adopted a view, supported by the English, that before pursuing a policy of uniting Crete, Epirus, Macedonia and the rest with the small Greek kingdom, the Greek government should create a competent internal administration, engage in prudent finance, and establish a model of good, orderly government so that when Turkey did fall apart, Greece would be the only heir. Kolettes, his political opponent who, incidentally, came from Epirus, argued that territorial expansion should be be the first object of the new government. His argument appealed, wrote Miller "to imperialist sentiment which animates all Balkan nationalities and is fostered by their long and mutually conflicting historical traditions, and their strong feeling of exclusive nationality."[6] It was Kolettes who took power and whose policies were pursued.

There was an unsuccessful war between Greece and Turkey in the 1850s, an unsuccessful insurrection in Crete with Greek support from 1876 to 1886, an unsuccessful four-week war in 1897 when Greek troops landed in Crete, and another unsuccessful uprising in Crete in 1909. The 1909 uprising was a major event in the development of the Greek political system for it was accompanied by the rise of the "Military League" of younger officers who attacked the professional politicians for their surrender to Turkey on the Crete issue. In a coup in Athens in 1909, members of the officer corps overthrew the Greek government and took steps to strengthen the position of the profes-sional military staff by insist- ing upon the exclusion of royal princes from commands in the army and the appointment of professional military personnel as ministers of war and marine. Though we lack detailed studies of the social composition of the Greek military, there is some evi- dence that, as in other developing countries, the military was becoming an instrument for social mobility for the non-landed middle classes who resented the domination of the Greek political system by the crown and by upper class landed elements.

The League proceeded to force the King to invite the Cretan politician M. Venizelos to become prime minister. Venizelos, who was thoroughly committed to the incorporation of his Crete home- land into Greece, devised a new, tough-minded strategy for defeat- ing the Turks. Greece, under his leadership, joined the Balkan League with Serbia and Bulgaria in a successful attack against Turkey in 1911. The Balkan League defeated Turkey, and as a result, Greece enlarged her territory from 25,000 to 42,000 square miles and her population from 2.7 million in 1912 to 4.8 million in 1914. Venizelos' greatest triumph was to incorporate his native Crete into Greece in 1913.

Throughout the nineteenth century and well into the twen- tieth, almost no Greek politicians paid attention to questions of internal reform and development. Since the achievement of their goal of expansion was dependent upon the kind of external allian- ces Greece built, politicians and citizens alike became more con- versant with international politics than with internal social and economic issues. One example of this can be culled from a report based upon the work of a Rockefeller Foundation team in Crete after the Second World War.[7] The author of that report observed that once Crete was joined with Greece, it became part of the highly centralized Greek bureaucratic structure which would not tolerate any independent local authority. The Governor-General of Crete, the mayors of each city, the presidents of villages, and even school teachers, were all appointed, paid and removed by minis- tries in Athens. Crete had no legislative body. Businessmen who wanted to import goods had to travel to Athens for permission. Even the roads on Crete had to be built by Athens. The people of Crete, wrote Allbaugh, had a concern for politics, but that meant world events and what was taking place in Athens, not matters involving local initiative.

The international alliance strategy of the Greeks was also shaped by her irredentist claims. In the nineteenth century, the issue was comparatively clear cut; any country that was anti-Turk was an ally of Greece. By the end of the nineteenth century the issue became cloudier. When Greece first became independent no one considered the possibility of a revived Bulgarian state or an enlarged Serbia, each seeking to restore its own medieval empire.

But by the latter part of the nineteenth century, both the Serbs and Bulgarians were laying claim to Macedonia, a region which the Greeks considered theirs by historic right. The Serbs pointed out that their great medieval ruler, Tsar Stephen Dushan, had his capital in Skopje, and the Bulgarians argued that their Tsar Samuel had his residence on the Macedonian lake at Ochrid and that Ochrid was the center of a number of important Bulgarian religious sites. Greece had joined with both Bulgaria and Serbia against the Turks in the First Balkan War, but almost immediately thereafter Bulgaria unsuccessfully attacked Serbia and Greece.

The rivalry between Greece and Bulgaria took form from the 1878 Treaty of San Stefano which followed a Bulgarian uprising against the Turks and the Russo-Turkish War of 1877. The Treaty provided for the establishment of a "Greater Bulgaria" which gave Macedonia to Bulgaria and left Salonica in Turkish hands, thereby ignoring the claims of Greece. It was essentially a Slavic settlement pressed by the Russians. The Treaty was superseded the following year by the Treaty of Berlin which recognized the complete independence of Serbia, Montenegro, and Rumania from Turkish rule, and reduced "Greater Bulgaria" to a small self-governing principality with tributary status under the Sultan. Thrace, Macedonia, Epirus and Albania, all claimed by the Greeks, remained under Turkish rule. The borders provided by the aborted Treaty of San Stefano, however, remained the dream of the Bulgarians and became a source of continued conflict between Bulgaria and Greece.

In short, throughout the first half of the nineteenth century, Greek claims for provinces almost exclusively Greek, such as Thessaly and the Aegean islands, brought her into conflict with Turkey, while in the latter parts of the nineteenth and the beginning of the twentieth centuries her aspiration for areas of mixed populations, such as Epirus, Macedonia and Thrace, brought her into conflict with the Balkan states of Bulgaria, Yugoslavia and, later, Albania.

When the First World War began, the Greek government was divided. Venizelos wanted to support the allies and the Serbs against the invading Germans and Bulgarians. King Constantine (crowned, incidentally, like his predecessors, not as King of Greece, but as King of the Hellenes, emphasizing the Greek aspiration for incorporating all Hellenes into Greece) supported by the military, backed the Germans. Though ideological and sentimental attachments affected the strategies of the two groups—Venizelos viewed himself as a Liberal and as pro-British, and Constantine had a German wife—each group was in effect banking on the military success of one side or another. The outcome of the war did indeed determine the internal political outcome for Greece. In 1917-18, with the successes of the allies, Venizelos overthrew the Greek government, forced the abdication of King Constantine, and brought his son Alexander to the throne.

After the coup of 1911 and the two Balkan wars which followed, the military became a well-established, independent political force within Greece, allying itself with one party, then another, sometimes supporting the crown, sometimes opposing it. The military itself was never a unified force and the shifting alliances of the military often reflected the shifting struggles within the military.

The events of the 1920s more than any other period in Greek history illustrate the overwhelming effect which the national expansion issue had upon the political struggles within Greece, struggles not only over who should govern but about the very institutional structure of the country—on such questions as whether Greece should be a monarchy or a republic, or whether the country should be governed by military or civilian institutions.

In 1920 Venizelos and the Liberals were defeated in a national election. Thereafter, following the sudden death of Alexander, the monarchists pressed for and won a plebiscite recalling his father, King Constantine. In 1921, the Greek army launched an attack upon the Turks in Asia Minor in an effort to conquer Constantinople, with the dream that Constantine would be crowned emperor in the holy Orthodox church of Santa Sophia. One writer described the attack as a "typical Balkan fit of nationalist megalomania," an "attempt to invade Turkey and restore the Byzantine Empire, the last remnant of which had disappeared in 1453, half a millennium earlier."[8]

The attack resulted in a major defeat of the Greek army by the Turks, and, had not the western European powers restrained the Turks, Greece itself might have been badly crushed. As it was, the long-term consequences for Greece were considerable. The Turks drove out large colonies of Greeks from all along the coast of Anatolia. It is estimated that more than a million Greeks migrated from Turkey and Bulgaria into Greece, thereby bringing to an end possible Greek claims on the basis of the presence of ethnic brethren in neighboring states. A number of defeated military officers, bitter at the outcome of the war, formed a revolutionary committee, forced the abdication of Constantine, appointed King George II (the oldest son of Constantine) to the throne, and called for the return of Venizelos. Several ministers of the former government were arrested, tried and, in spite of strong opposition from the British, executed. Bitterness against the crown, which had been associated with the military disaster, was widespread, but it was especially great among the million refugees concentrated in Macedonia, central Greece and Thrace. With the support of most of the refugees, a plebiscite held in 1924 proclaimed the establishment of a republic, and shortly thereafter the members of the royal family were deprived of their Greek nationality. The issues of the war, the defeat, the execution of members of the government, the dismissal of the King and the establishment of a republic, divided Greeks for the next two decades and even beyond.

Of the many effects of the war and, more broadly, of Greece's expansionist efforts, three were of great significance in the decades which followed. The first was the consequence of adding over a million refugees to Greece. As a result of this influx, the political balance in Greece was drastically altered. Before the arrival of the refugees, the Populist Party (the pro-royalists) enjoyed slightly more support than the liberals. Thereafter, the Greeks from Turkey, an estimated 300,000 male voters, swung the balance behind the Liberal Party of Venizelos and against the monarchy. The bitterness of the refugees toward the monarch was a significant factor in the outcome of the 1924 plebiscite when 70% of the voters cast their ballot for a republic as against 30% for the monarchy. The Peloponnese and much of old Greece was for the monarchy, while Macedonia, with its large refugee population, and the refugee quarters of Athens and Piraeus voted decisively against the monarchy. Since the refugees constituted 20% of the population, their vote may very well have been decisive. A generation later the refugees and their children were again to play an important role in Greek political development. The Greek Communist Party (the KKE), though formed in 1918, only became a force in Greek politics after the Asia Minor debacle. Much of the KKE's support in the civil war which tore Greece after World War II came from the refugee settlements in Macedonia, and throughout the 1960s and 1970s this region has continued to support left-of-center political movements.[9]

A second consequence of the defeat was the impetus it gave to the military in Greek politics. As noted earlier, the military coup of 1909 was the first in a series of direct interventions on the part of the military into Greek politics. The military, or at least one section of it under General Dousmanis, supported the pro-German policy of King Constantine during the First World War and supported his recall to the throne after the defeat of Venizelos and the Liberals in the elections of 1920. And we have already noted the role of the military, first in the expansion into Turkey and then in the formation of the revolutionary committee to force the abdication of Constantine. The republic which was proclaimed in 1924 was overthrown the following year by a military coup led by General Pangalos who then imposed a dictatorship. A year later another military coup took place, this one led by General Kandylis who, as premier, permitted new elections and paved the way for the formation of a civilian government under Venizelos. In 1933, Venizelos and his party were defeated by the pro-royalist Populist Party, and this time, much to the chagrin of his supporters abroad who associated Venizelos with democratic traditions, he threw his support behind an attempted coup by General Plastiras. But the coup failed and Venizelos went into disgrace and exile. A plebiscite was again held in November 1935 and, with the support of pro-monarchist elements in the army, there was an overwhelming vote for the restoration of the King. In 1936 following a political deadlock between the Liberals and Populists, General Metaxas, with the support of the King, took power and established himself as a dictator, a position he held till his death in 1941, just a few months after the Italian attack. In the postwar era the military played an important role in suppressing the insurrection led by the Communist Party, and in April 1967 the military overthrew a left-of-center government and established a military dictatorship.

There can be little doubt that during the inter-war period, the Greek army was very much affected by the rout of its forces in the Greco-Turkish War in which the Greeks were driven from Turkey and the ancient Greek settlement of Smyrna was destroyed. This overwhelming defeat instilled in the officer corps a desire for revenge and honor and since there was little chance for military action abroad, the military turned to politics within the country.

The third effect of the war was its impact on the Megali dream. How powerful a force that dream was is dramatically illustrated by the fact that May 29, 1921, when King Constantine personally landed in Smyrna in Anatolia to undertake personal command of the Greek army, was the anniversary of the fall of Constantinople and the death of the last Byzantine Emperor, Constantine XI, in 1453. But the dream proved to be a total disaster. From all over Anatolia, Greeks fled to Smyrna seeking protection from the attacking Turkish army. Smyrna itself was destroyed and the ports of Greece were jammed with refugees. "It was the tragic end of an adventure," wrote Pentzopoulos, "which obliterated in blood and fire a civilization that had flourished and progressed in Ionia since the time of Homer. It was the complete uprooting of Hellenism in Asia and the burial of the magnificent dream of the "Megali Idea."[10] Though thereafter the Greek government continued to make revisionist claims on Albania (for northern Epirus in which substantial numbers of Greeks continued to reside) and sought *enosis* (union) with Cyprus, the dream of a larger Greek empire came to an end with the transfer of populations.

Why had the Greek government launched an attack against Turkey? The precipitating event had been the London Conference of February 1921 which the Greek government saw as an effort to undermine the earlier, more favorable, Treaty of Sevres. Nonetheless, it is unclear as to why the Greeks attacked when they did and whether they had any realistic hope of achieving their dual aim of conquering Greek-populated areas of Turkey and conquering Constantinople with all its overtones of Byzantine glory. The evidence on these points is unclear, though a few writers claim that the Greeks had reason to believe that they would win British support in the attack. There is also some reason to believe that the Greek army overestimated its own strength and underestimated how much the Turkish army had been rebuilt by Ataturk since the 1913 debacle. But even taking these factors into account, one consideration of some theoretical importance should be noted and that is the importance given to chance in the calculation of the Greek military, the monarchy and governing Greek politicians. Since one did not have any exact measure of ones own strength in relation to the enemy's, and one could not be sure how the Great Powers might act, then, so many Greeks reasoned, one might just as well take a chance! One English writer, Forster, observed that "the 'Great Idea' has always induced the Greek patriot to throw prudence to the wind on the slightest provocation, and there was no statesman strong enough to oppose the irresistible impulse of popular excitement."[11] To Greek leaders, the rewards of victory appeared to be so great that it seemed worth the risk, and no one seemed to have any awareness of what the full consequences of defeat might be—an understandable failing since none of the previous defeats had produced consequences of any overwhelming importance. How common such high-risk policies are on the part of revisionist powers, how much chance becomes part of the calculation of governing elites, is a theme we shall have occasion to explore again as we look at the behavior of another revisionist state.

Bulgaria: Turning Plowshares into Swords

With the establishment of a Bulgaria independent of Ottoman rule, in 1878, there emerged still another Balkan revisionist state. In pursuit of its irredentist objectives, Bulgaria fought against Turkey in 1911 and against its Balkan neighbors, Greece and Serbia, two years later—losing in the process 58,000 lives and 105,000 wounded (in a total adult male population of an estimated 713,000). In World War I, again in pursuit of its irredentist claims, Bulgaria supported the Germans in a war that cost it a hundred thousand lives and an estimated 300,000 wounded. And, as in the case of Greece, its internal politics and modernization was largely shaped by its revisionist objectives.

In some respects Bulgaria had a promising beginning. It was the site of two major historical kingdoms in the ninth and twelfth centuries, whose power extended over a considerable portion of the Balkan peninsula. These historical kingdoms provided the basis for contem-porary unifying myths—and also for its revisionist claims. The Turks subsequently occupied Bulgaria and took control over much of ihe land, but permitted Bulgarian culture and language to persist. When independence came, Turkish landowners were expelled, with the result that Bulgaria was left with one of the most equitable systems of land distribution found anywhere in Europe. In the early nineteenth century it is estimated that two-thirds of the land holdings were smaller than five hectares and there were few large landowners. Moreover, when a measure of independence was achieved in 1878 it adopted a relatively liberal constitution which provided for universal suffrage—along with an imported German King. At the end of the century, the country experienced a considerable amount of economic growth, a rise in literacy, and an increase in urbanization. According to Gerschenkron, the country had begun the process of industrialization and modernization.

For the Bulgarian government, however, the most pressing issue was her claim upon Yugoslavia and Greece over Macedonia. Macedonia was a disputed region of the Balkans, bordered on the west by mountains of the Albanian frontier and on the east by the River Mesta, separating Macedonia from Thrace. In the south, it extended to the Gulf of Salonika and in the north the frontier was at Crna Gora. The area had not been an independent state since the fourth century B.C. and it had successively been under Byzantine and the Turkish rule. Since some of the main trading routes in the Balkan peninsula pass through Macedonia, it was an area in which a wide variety of different ethnic groups had come to live making it virtually impossible to draw any boundaries separating one ethnic group from another. A substantial number of Greeks had settled, as elsewhere, in the towns and were engaged in trade. There was a substantial Muslim community, not necessarily ethnically Turkish, in positions of authority, nomadic Vlachs, an Albanian element, and—largest of all—a mass of peasant cultivators described variously as Macedonians, modified Bulgarians, or Slavophones, the first being the definition preferred by the Yugoslavs, the second by the Bulgarians, and the third by the Greeks.

The claims made by the Yugoslavs, the Bulgarians and the Greeks, each of whom claimed exclusive right to the disputed territory, were variously based upon historical claims or upon ethnicity. Historically, each ethnic group in the Balkans had enjoyed some period of political supremacy over substantial portions of the peninsula. Earliest, perhaps, were the Albanians, successors to the Illyrians; then the Greeks, both in their classical epoch and in the Byzantine era; then the Macedonians, whose power under Alexander extended across the Near East to the Indus River in south Asia; then the Wallachians (ancestors of the Rumanians), a cross between the Roman invaders and the official inhabitants who became Latin in speech, the only people in the Balkans to do so; then the Slavs as represented by the Serbs, who established a great medieval state; then the Bulgarians, thought to be Tartar in origin, who gradually merged with the Slavs and developed a Slavonic language akin to that of the Serbs; then finally the Turks who extended their power over the entire peninsula after the fifteenth century.

As the Serbs, the Greeks, and the Bulgarians each freed themselves from Turkish rule, their leaders laid claim to the disputed Macedonian region. It should be remembered that the newly-independent states of Serbia, Greece and Bulgaria, established in the nineteenth century, contained only portions of the ethnic groups which were a majority in the new states. Substantial portions of the peninsula remained under Turkish rule well into the twentieth century. In 1911, Serbia, Greece and Bulgaria joined together in a combined attack against Turkey in what is generally referred to as the First Balkan War. The result was a surprise victory for the three small states. It was almost inevitable that the three states would quarrel over the spoils, especially over Macedonia, and in 1913 Bulgaria attacked both Greece and Serbia in order to establish her control over the disputed regions.

The first dispute over Macedonia among the three states took place in the 1870s and centered around an ecclesiastical matter. The Orthodox Church in the Balkans has historically played quite a different role in the development of nationalities and nation-states than did the Roman Catholic Church. Theologically, the Orthodox Church did not subscribe to the universal conception of the Roman Catholic Church. The Roman Catholic Church, both in its theology and in its institutional structure, cut across ethnic and state boundaries. It had considerable difficulty adapting itself to the rise of nation-states in western Europe and, in the case of Italy, was positively hostile to the formation of an Italian state. In contrast, the Orthodox Church recognized a considerable degree of autonomy in its ecclesiastical structure. The Turks gave official sanction to the establishment of the Patriarch in Constantinople, but throughout the Balkan provinces the churches were relatively autonomous. One important consequence was that the churches in Wallachia, Moldavia, Serbia, and the principalities which ultimately made up Bulgaria, each became centers for the preservation of local languages and cultures. Some of the churches were desecrated by Turkish soldiers. The Orthodox attack against conversion to Islam was as much in defense of nationality as it was in defense of religion. The analogy to the position of the Buddhist hierarchy in Sri Lanka and Burma, the Arya Samaj movement in India and the mosques in Iran is quite apparent, for there too, religious institutions played an important role in defining and defending nationality.

Though the Patriarch of the Greek Orthodox Church in Constantinople was considered by the Porte to be the head of the Christian community, in reality the Orthodox churches were administered by what has been aptly defined as an oligarchy of patriarchs. Indeed, the Turks permitted the Christians to create autocephalous ecclesiastical administrations. The link between the local churches and the ecclesiastical administration was relatively weak. This autonomy, one might even say isolation, was strengthened by the fact that the Orthodox Church was strong in the rural regions and had little strength in the cities, wherein resided the Turks, Jews, and minorities generally. For example, Salonika, the chief city of Macedonia, was a Jewish-majority city before World War I.[12] Confined as they often were to rural communities with little contact with the cities, other areas of the Ottoman Empire, or the Patriarch in Constantinople, local churches became centers for the preservation of indigenous cultures and languages, often intensely narrow-minded in their outlook.

From the very beginning of their national movement, the Bulgarians laid claim to Macedonia. The Russians, because of their proximity to the Bulgarians and their religious kinship, supported the Bulgarians in their claims against the Turks and, ultimately, against other national claims in the Balkans. In 1870, the Turks gave in to the Russian-supported Bulgarian agitation for the formation of a separate Bulgarian Orthodox Church or Exarchate, with authority extending into parts of the Turkish province of Macedonia. The ecumenical Patriarch in Constantinople excommunicated the Exarch and all his flock, having declared the new autocephalous Bulgarian church to be schismatic.

The Russians, as patrons of the Bulgarians, pressed for the inclusion of all of Macedonia, except Salonika and the Chalkidic peninsula, under Bulgarian rule in the Treaty of San Stefano (1878). For generations thereafter, San Stefano became the rallying cry of Bulgarian nationalists—since this Treaty, and only this Treaty, provided for the creation of a Bulgarian state which matched the territorial limits, more or less, of the medieval Bulgarian states. Why the Russians wanted a "Greater Bulgaria" is an issue which need not detain us, although briefly one can say that the Russians presumably felt that a Bulgarian state, Slavic in language and cultural heritage, Orthodox in religion, geographically adjacent to Russia, still under Turkish domination (unlike the Serbs, who had on their own fought and won their independence) was likely to be the most pliable state in the Balkans.

"Greater Bulgaria" was never created. The western powers, fearful of an enlarged Bulgaria under Russia influence, intervened at the Treaty of Berlin, and Macedonia remained under Turkish rule. From this point on, through the Second World War, the goal of virtually every Bulgarian government (with one significant exception) was to gain control over Macedonia. What were the consequences of this policy, both on the internal political development of Bulgaria and upon its external relations?

First of all, in its external relations Bulgaria sided with whatever power was most likely to help her achieve her objective. In the latter part of the nineteenth century, the Conservatives were generally pro-Russian and sought Russian support for Bulgarian expansion, while the Liberals were suspicious of the Russian government and of Russian influence. The differences between these two groups were as much the result of their differences on internal political reforms within Bulgaria as they were over their respective judgment on international matters. The Conservatives were in favor of extending executive authority and were sympathetic to the extension of monarchical powers, while the Liberals were in favor of expanding the powers of the legislative assembly. The Conservatives and the Prince had the sympathy of Russian officials since Russian interest in the 1880s was in expanding and influencing the Bulgarian military with the intention of preparing the army to win a "Greater Bulgaria."[13] The upper clergy generally supported the monarchy, while the parish priests and school teachers sided with the Liberals. In 1881 Prince Brattenberg, with the support of the Conservatives and the Russians, organized a coup d'etat to extend his own authority and weaken that of the assembly. According to Black, the ideas of nationalism and equalitarianism were so dominant in Bulgaria in the 1880s that, in the absence of external considerations, the Liberals would have easily won popular support. But Russian intervention played a significant part in the internal political conflict and its outcome.

Bulgarian relations with Russia were always complex and ambivalent, for there were differences both within the Bulgarian and the Russian elites on fundamental issues of internal development and external goals. But the central elements in the relationship were that Russia had been the liberator (in 1877) of the Bulgarians from the Turks, the Russians and the Bulgarians were both Slavs (elements which made the Russians popular with the Bulgarian peasantry) and, Russia backed the goal of a Greater Bulgaria. Yet in spite of these ties, when it seemed expedient the Bulgarian government turned against the Russians.

The period from 1911 to 1918 was one in which the Bulgarian government sought to achieve its objective through combined military-diplomatic strategy. In 1911, Bulgaria joined with two of her rivals, Greece and Serbia, to attack Turkey and to free Macedonia, along with other areas, from Turkish occupation. In 1913, after this first triumph, Bulgaria turned against Serbia and Greece to fight for the spoils, a war which Bulgaria lost with a considerable sacrifice of life. In World War I, Bulgaria sided with the Central Powers against Russia, this time with the expectation that a German-Austrian victory would lead to their acquisition of Macedonia. Though the redemption of Macedonia and southern Dobruja was popular, the war itself was not, particularly since neither the troops nor the peasants were eager to fight against Russia.[14] In the Second World War, Bulgaria sided with the Germans, again in the expectation that her territorial claims would thereby be satisfied.

Bulgarian governments from 1913 onward had an uncanny instinct for engaging in losing wars and allying the country with the losing side. Perhaps the most significant internal political effect of this alliance strategy was that it served to strengthen the most conservative, right-wing elements within Bulgarian society. The events of the years 1919 to 1923 demonstrate this point rather dramatically.

The anti-Russian, pro-German policy pursued by the Bulgarian government during the First World War was opposed by a political party known as the Peasant Union, led by Alexander Stamboliski (1879–1923). Stamboliski was himself a rare figure in Bulgarian politics, a man of peasant background, who won the devotion of

Bulgaria's peasant masses and the hatred of its town dwellers. Stamboliski believed that since some 80% of Bulgarians were peasants, the country should be governed not only by a peasant party, but by a peasant dictatorship. After he became prime minister in 1919, the result of an election in which the Peasant Union emerged with the largest number of seats in the Sobranie or Bulgarian parliament, Stamboliski took steps to crush all opposition parties.

It is not easy to briefly capture the strong antagonism which existed between town and country, urban dweller and peasant, in Bulgaria in the 1920s. Partly the hostility had to do with the historic role of the town under Turkish rule as exploiters of the countryside. Partly it had to do with the contempt felt and shown by the educated urban middle class toward the backward, crude, primitive peasant. Partly it had to do with the fact that Bulgaria was a country of small landholders, with almost no large landowners or aristocracy who might have linked the countryside to the city. Partly it had to do with the suffering experienced by the countryside as a result of three successive wars which killed off, without gain to anyone, such a large number of young peasants through combat, hunger and disease. Partly, and this was explicit in Stamboliski's outlook, it represented a revulsion for the Great Powers with whom the urban intelligensia were always allied; Stamboliski wanted Bulgaria and Eastern Europe generally to stand against the industrial capitalist West and the Bolshevik East. He sought an entente of non-aligned peasant states of Eastern Europe that would not only be ideologically apart from the Soviet Union and the Western powers, but would be an independent political force—in the language of contemporary politics, a "third" force.

Stamboliski and his Peasant Union government thus sought to bring to an end the policy of revisionism and expansion. In so doing, Stamboliski succeeded in antagonizing every significant political force in the country outside of the peasantry—the army, the monarchy, the urban middle classes, the intelligentsia, the urban working class, the Macedonians. Stamboliski exercised all the power at his command to beat down this powerful array of forces. The new government passed laws restricting the press, prohibiting lawyers from practising their trade while serving as mayors, deputies, etc., closed the university at Sofia for six months and reduced its budget, jailed opposition leaders, used the Orange Guards to break up protest rallies, passed land limitation laws, and revised the credit system for cultivators. In international affairs, Stamboliski worked toward a rapprochement with Yugoslavia in an effort to end the dispute over Macedonia.

But in the early morning hours of June 9, 1923, the army occupied the police, government and communications buildings in Sofia and seized provincial town centers. Stamboliski was captured by a group of Macedonians, reportedly tortured, his hands cut off—"the hands that had signed the Nish Convention" with Yugoslavia, and was officially "shot while attempting to escape."[15] The successor government appointed by the King, suppressed the Peasant Union and the Orange Guards, shortly thereafter crushed an abortive Communist coup, and increased the political power of the Macedonians.

The position of the Macedonians within Bulgaria warrants some attention for the Macedonians played a role in Bulgarian politics far more important than their numbers would suggest.[16]

The Paris Peace Conference divided Macedonia into three: Greece received the largest portion of 34,600 square kilometers, then Yugoslavia with 26,776 square kilometers, and Bulgaria with only 6798 square kilometers. The portion of Macedonia within Bulgaria was known as the Petrich Department and had a population of 220,000 in 1926. Another 100,000 Macedonians lived within Bulgaria, of whom 70,000 were refugees from Greek Macedonia and another 32,000 were from Yugoslavia. Rothschild reports that in 1919 the number of Macedonians holding key political and professional positions within Bulgaria was: eight cabinet ministers, 14 diplomats, 54 Sobranie deputies, 11 metropolitans of the Orthodox church, 12 professors, 90 writers and journalists, 100 judges and lawyers, 71 higher civil servants, 262 active army officers, and 453 reserve army officers.[17]

But what is most striking is how institutionalized the power of the Macedonians had become in the Bulgarian political system, to a large extent as a result of the commitment which virtually all political groups in the system had made toward the incorporation of Macedonia into Bulgaria. This might be a useful point to reflect on the great influence which minorities can exercise when the political system in which they live is committed to rectifying the injustice done to them; the Palestinian refugees in the Arab states come quickly to mind.

A group of Macedonians formed the Internal Macedonian Revolutionary Organization—IMRO. IMRO was, of course, particularly strong in Petrich and Kustendil districts of Bulgaria—that is, the portions of Macedonia within Bulgaria. Stamboliski was aware of the danger of IMRO to his objectives and sought to break their power by arresting IMRO leaders. In turn, IMRO recognized that Stamboliski's success would spell the end of their power and of their objective of uniting Macedonia. IMRO leaders played a significant role in the coup which overthrew Stamboliski, and IMRO leaders reportedly executed the peasant prime minister.

In the 1920s IMRO became such a powerful force that it prevented the central Bulgarian government from extending its authority into Petrich Department. According to Elizabeth Barker, IMRO was a Mafia-like organization, collecting taxes within the Petrich Department (on the three million kilos of tobacco grown), forcing the inhabitants of the department and Macedonian migrants elsewhere in Bulgaria to buy immunity from blackmail and terrorism through "voluntary" patriotic subscription or "taxes" and trafficking in illegal drugs. IMRO had support from emigrants who had fled into Bulgaria during the Balkan Wars, mainly peasants who, according to Barker, hated being uprooted from their original homes and who were not easily assimilated into Bulgaria. "The upheaval in their lives had often left them thriftless and discontented and turbulent and they were not particularly popular with the ordinary Bulgarian. So they provided a reservoir of manpower on which IMRO could draw for its terrorist cadres and its unofficial militia; and, since they had lost their roots, they could easily be browbeaten into obedience to IMRO."[18] IMRO engaged in terrorist acts and assassinations both in Yugoslavia and in Bulgaria and, again according to Barker, deliberately tried to keep Macedonia in such a state of unrest that news of it would constantly appear in the world press so that the Great Powers would feel forced to redraw the Balkan frontiers. The movement mixed political idealism and self-seeking opportunism. It was bitterly divided, not only along political lines, but between rival groups seeking to gain profit. Its last leader Ivan Mihailof, writes Barker, "was, in fact, a killer and a gangster on a large scale, not a revolutionary."[19] The willingness of IMRO leaders to commit assassinations, their economic independence, and the bitter internal divisions within Bulgarian political life which permitted them to throw their weight readily behind one group or another, all combined to make them one of the most powerful elements in the Bulgarian political system in spite of their relatively small numbers.

Since its formation at the turn of the century, IMRO had been divided into two streams, one favoring the creation of an independent Macedonian state, and the other advocating annexation with Bulgaria. So long as the entire region was under Turkish rule, the group advocating independence was active in setting up a shadow administration of its own and organizing uprisings against the Turks. According to Rothschild, the Bulgarian Communist Party gave its support to those elements of IMRO in the 1920s which favored the creation of a separate Macedonian state, since, from their point of view, the demand tended to fragment three "bourgeois" states and disrupt the hateful Versailles settlement.[20]

After the assassination of Stamboliski the power of IMRO continued to grow. They not only extended their authority in Petrich Department, but engaged in assassinations and terrorism within Bulgaria and exercised great influence at the highest levels of government. In 1934 an army coup dismissed parliament, dissolved all political parties, censored the press, and dissolved IMRO. But while IMRO had come to an end, the claim on Macedonia continued. The persistence of this claim was a significant element—perhaps the most important element—in the Bulgarian decision to join with Austria, Hungary and Germany in the Second World War, against Yugoslavia, Rumania, Czechoslovakia and the Western Allies. To the very end, Bulgaria's revisionist goals dominated her foreign policy, even when it meant becoming a supporter of German efforts to militarily occupy all of the Balkans.

One final aspect of the revisionist goal deserves our attention, and that is its effects upon Bulgaria's economic development policy. Alexander Gerschenkron in his brilliant analysis of pre-World War I economic development policies in Bulgaria considered why Bulgaria had only a modest rate of industrial development from 1909 to 1937 and why so little structural change occurred; he concluded that a concern for foreign and military policy obstructed serious preoccupation with industrial development, so that the Bulgarian government let many opportunities pass unused. Thus, Gerschenkron reports that the premier, once a great advocate of economic development, turned his attention to preparing for a military attack upon the Turks, expressing the sentiment that he felt, in his own words, "responsible to History for the conclusion of the Balkan Alliance."[21]

Yugoslavia: Falling Apart

Yugoslavia during the inter-war period was not a revisionist power, but was the object of revisionist claims by all its neighbors, Greece, Albania, Bulgaria, Austria and Italy. It had to integrate diverse ethnic groups into a single state, a problem so immense that under the very best—i.e., the most isolated—circumstances, these tensions might not have been resolved; as it was, Yugoslavia's problems of integration were inextricably bound up in the international order of which it was a part.

Yugoslavia, established as a newly-independent nation in December 1918, was a union of the independent kingdoms of Serbia and Montenegro with the newly-freed territories of the Austro-Hungarian state. From its very beginning, Yugoslavia was probably the most diversified European country west of the Soviet Union. In its diversity it was much more like many of the newly-independent areas of Asia and Africa than any other European state. First of all, there were major structural differences. The new state contained several different legal and administrative systems. There was Serbia, a monarchy, with a well developed administrative structure and political parties, independent through most of the nineteenth century; Montenegro, also an independent kingdom, a loose collection of tribes which had gradually become a bureaucratically administrative state; Croatia and Slovenia, both quasi-autonomous provinces of the Hungarian half of the Hapsburg monarchy; the province of Vojvodina which had been an integral part of Hungary; Slovenia and Dalmatia, both of which had been parts of the Austrian half of the Hapsburg state; and Bosnia and Herzegovina, formerly under Ottoman rule which had fallen under an Austro-Hungarian condominium and had

been administered by their Joint Ministry of Finance. Each area
had some historic individuality. Each region was well defined and
commanded some local allegiance, some identification from a
majority of the local population. And each had an operating legal
and administrative apparatus, and, in several instances, especially Croatia and Serbia, they had their own functioning political
parties prior to the creation of the new state.

Within the country were also differences of language, religion,
and culture. Croatia and Slovenia were predominantly Catholic;
Serbia and Montenegro were Orthodox; and Bosnia and Herzegovina were largely Muslim. In 1931, 48% of the country was Orthodox,
37.5% was Roman Catholic, and 11% was Muslim. As for language,
most of the country spoke Serbo-Croatian, two variants of a
common tongue, but Serbian was written in Cyrillic script as are
most other Slavic languages while Croatian is written in Roman
script. Moreover, two major groups do not speak Serbo-Croatian:
the Macedonians, with a language close to Bulgarian, written in
Cyrillic; and the Slovenes, speaking a Slavic language, under
strong German, Hungarian and Italian influence, written in the
Roman alphabet. These cultural differences appeared to be so
great that one Frenchman wrote:

> More and more obvious appear the illusion and chimera of
> those who hope to unite all the Slavs of the south: Croatia,
> Bosnia, Serbia, Montenegro and Bulgaria. This is perhaps a
> beautiful dream, but it is only the dream of literary artists and
> poets, As for the Croats and Serbs, religion and civilization,
> spirit and historical tradition turn the former toward the
> Occident and the latter toward the Orient. To wish to unite
> them is to wish to unite two contrary things, to reconcile
> Rome and Byzantium.[22]

To these religious and linguistic differences we should also
add differences in levels of development. The areas which lived
under Austrian rule, particularly Croatia and Slovenia were more
developed—had more industry, transportation, communication
and education—than the areas which had lived under Turkish
rule, such as Macedonia, Serbia and Bosnia-Herzegovina. The
Serbs and Montenegrins, with their traditions of historic independence, looked down upon the Croatians and were particularly
proud of their traditions and their martial values of honor, heroism,
masculinity, the strong sense of pride and self-confidence. The
people of Slovenia and Croatia, in turn, were part of the Central
European tradition and viewed the Serbs as part of an inferior,
backward, almost barbaric Balkan tradition.

Finally, we should also note that there were large minorities;
some three-quarters of a million Albanians, a half million
Hungarians, a quarter million Turks, and a quarter million other
Slavic peoples from Bulgaria, Czechoslovakia and the Ukraine.

From the very beginning, the new state was torn between two conflicting approaches to the issue of national integration. One group, the Serbs, advocated a centralized structure: the other, the Croatians, were in favor of a more federalized system with considerable autonomy for each "nationality." The Croatians viewed the Serbian approach as simply an extension of Serbian power: central authority, felt the Croatians, meant Serbian author-ity since the monarch was Serb, the army was Serb, much of the bureaucracy was Serb. And since the Serbs were the largest single group their political parties and elites would dominate the government. Serb leaders, on the other hand, saw the proposal for federalism as a way of disrupting the Yugoslav state, and the Croatians as essentially disloyal to the idea of a united southern Slav state of Yugoslavia. One writer, summing up two decades of conflict between these two groups concluded that:

> From the outset the conflict that raged between the Croats who argued for federalism and the triumphant Serbs who insisted on centralism warped the growth of democracy in Yugoslavia. Because the Croats would not willingly accept defeat and the Serbs would not willingly compromise in victory, the processes of constitutional government broke down. Because the major politicians and parties lacked common political traditions and could come to no agreement on the fundamentals of government, the leaders of the new state were left to run the country by force and intrigue.[23]

The Yugoslav situation in the inter-war years had some of the attributes of contemporary Nigeria, with its conflict between the Hausa and Fulani in the north and Ibo in the south; the one Muslim, with strong traditions of religious and tribal authority, the other, smaller in number, more enterprising and modern in its orientation. The one difference is in the interests of outside powers. Nigeria had a civil war on its own without great power intervention or, for that matter, any substantial intervention by its neighbors. In contrast, internal Yugoslav tensions were nurtured by outside powers who saw the struggle between the Serbs and Croatians as an opportunity to undermine the Yugoslav state and bring about its disintegration. Both the Bulgarians, with their eye on the Yugoslav portions of Macedonia, and the Italians, not only hungry for the Italian populated areas in the north, but interested in extending their influence all along the Adriatic as part of Mussolini's quest for a "second Rome," had an interest in breaking the Yugoslav state apart.

In all fairness, however, it should be stressed that the major struggles between the Croatians and the Serbs involved little foreign intervention. Certainly the most dramatic event of the 1920s was strictly a Serb-Croatian matter: the assassination of Radi, the leader of the Croat Peasant Party on the floor of parliament (the Skupstina), by the Serbs. Almost immediately thereafter the King set aside the constitution, dissolved political parties, transferred power from the Skupstina to himself, and in effect established a royal dictatorship. Though of great interest to her revisionist neighbors, none of these developments occurred as a result of external intervention.

The assassination of the King in 1934 in Marseilles by a Macedonian, in a plot planned by Croatian extremists had more direct international implications, not only because of the Bulgarian sponsorship of Macedonian claims for independence (or for merger with Bulgaria) but because of reported Italian and Hungarian support for the Croatian separatists.

Within a few years it became clear that the revisionist and expansionist claims of her neighbors, Bulgaria, Italy, Hungary and, ultimately, Germany, were to become decisive factors in the wartime disintegration of the country.

When we speak of Yugoslavia "disintegrating" we need to be analytically more precise. Central to the question of Serb-Croatian relations was the issue of the legitimacy of central institutions of authority. The Serbs demanded loyalty to the existing political system, to the monarchy, the army, the centralized administrative structure. The Serbs viewed these institutions as legitimate, worthy of allegiance irrespective of how well they functioned at any particular time. The Croatian separatists, on the other hand, viewed these institutions neither as legitimate nor as supportive of the maintenance of an independent Croatian identity. The issues of identity and legitimacy were thus inextricably linked, both for the Serbs and the Croatians.

We have no attitudinal surveys conducted in Yugoslavia during the inter-war period which would give us any "hard," i.e., statistically measureable data on the type and distribution of a sense of national identity or on the extent to which the populace felt loyal to the political institutions and procedures under which the country was governed. But far more relevant is the way in which people behaved when the system was under attack from outside. On the eve of the Second World War, the government of Yugoslavia was confronted with one of the most difficult tasks of diplomacy ever encountered by the political elite of a country. The revisionist powers of Central and Eastern Europe—Germany, Italy, Hungary and Bulgaria—were on the offensive and the Yugoslav government had to choose a strategy most likely to reduce the possibility of an armed attack from Italy or Germany. The Yugoslav government feared that an alliance with the Germans might result in a German occupation, while a pro-Allied or neutral stance would alienate the Croatians whose separatist leaders would receive German and Italian encouragement for the establishment of a Croatian state. By 1941 almost no alternative seemed workable, as German troops moved into Bulgaria, Italians moved into Albania and Greece, and the British had moved troops into Greece, unless, as one scholar of this period (Hoptner) has suggested, the Great Powers themselves were prepared, as they obviously were not, to respect Yugoslavia's neutrality as they did Switzerland's and Sweden's. The Yugoslav government, in its effort to avoid civil war with the Croatians while keeping the Germans out, signed a treaty with the Germans which allied the two nations but forbad the entrance of German troops into Yugoslavia.

The difficult choice facing the Yugoslav government, leading to its momentous decision to sign a pact with its greatest enemy, is described by Hoptner in this incident:

> Prince Paul and Princess Olga were under no illusions about the United States position when they dined privately with (U.S. Minister) Lane on March 20th (1941). They were told by their host that although they admitted the democracies would eventually win the war, they, unlike President Roosevelt, would not look to the future. The Prince's advisers, he said, were men who looked only to the present and to their material interests. Then he touched on a nerve. Signing the pact, he reminded the Prince Regent, meant striking a blow against an ally, Greece, Princess Olga's homeland. Why not, then refuse to sign?

> The Prince Regent seemed self-possessed. He agreed that the pact would be no guarantee against a future German attack; past events had proved that German guarantees were useless and that the pact would only tie Yugoslavia's hands for future diplomatic or military action. But if he refused the German guarantees, and war came, he was certain that the Croats and Slovenes would not fight. He had been urged to sign the pact by the Croats and Slovenes, the other two, and the opposition Yugoslav Nationalist Party. If, after giving Yugoslavia specific guarantees, the Germans attacked, only then, in Prince Paul's opinion, would the country unite against the aggressor.

> Lane argued that public opinion was opposed to the signing of the pact. He thought of the fierce anti-German and anti-fascist talk so often heard in the streets, restaurants, and coffee houses of Belgrade; many Serbs showed open disdain for the "blond ones."

> Prince Paul again disagreed. What was true in Belgrade was not necessarily true in Zagreb. There was not only public opinion; there was, indeed, a nation deeply and tragically disunited. He had only a few more months of service as a trustee for King Peter. During those months he was going to do everything he could to avoid taking the step that would lead inevitably to bloodshed.[24]

A week later on March 27th, the military, viewing the pact as a pro-German move and a bowing to Croatian sentiments, launched a successful coup against the government. According to Hoptner, the Serbs, especially the generals, the intelligentsia and leftists, the opposition, the army, the air force, and the Orthodox church felt the signing of the pact was a betrayal of old allies and that it would encourage Croat separatism and Italian territorial claims. A few hours after the coup the streets of Belgrade filled with cheering crowds.

The new government, suddenly fearful of a German attack, reversed itself by announcing that it would honor Yugoslavia's commitment to the Tripartite Pact but the Serb-sponsored coup brought to an end the efforts of the regent to bring about a Serb-Croatian rapprochement.[25]

How little feeling of legitimacy and loyalty there was within the political system, especially among the Croatians, is dramatically demonstrated by the behavior of Yugoslav troops after the German invasion of April 1941. Within twelve days, 254,000 Yugoslav soldiers surrendered to the Germans. Entire Croatian units surrendered or simply went home. "One Croat group, in the midst of an officer's party when overrun by a German regiment, stopped the festivities long enough to surrender and then went back to their fun as if nothing untoward had happened."[26]

The German invaders established an "independent" Croatian state and, on paper at least, carved Yugoslavia up, giving portions to its Bulgarian, Hungarian and Albanian allies. A powerful resistance movement arose, among the most powerful movements in occupied Europe, but it had to fight against the right-wing Ustashi movement in Croatia as well as against the Germans, and it was divided into the Tito-led Partisans and the Serbian, strongly anti-Croatian, Chetniks, who soon turned against each other.

The Yugoslav government had sought to use diplomacy as a means of preserving both her independence and her unity; by April 1941 she had lost both.

Two features of the Yugoslav case warrant further reflection because they illustrate more general theoretical perspectives of the problems of national integration of a state subjected to revisionist claims.

First of all, the Yugoslav experience suggests the limitations of a communications theory of national integration. This theory stresses the unifying effects of the spread of railroads, post and telegraph communications, the press, commerce, education and internal travel, in short, of the whole process of modernization. On each of these variables, Yugoslavia ranked higher in 1941 when the war began than in 1919 when the state was created. Trade, commerce and communication between Croatia and Serbia even during the worst periods of the 1920s and 1930s was higher than at the end of the First World War when these politically separate regions were initially brought together. This is not to say that the

growth of communications and commerce may not be a necessary condition, only that it is far from sufficient. When there are
discrete ethnic groups as in Yugoslavia, the growth of communication and transportation may, and often does, increase the sense of
identity within each group as much as these developments effect
the pattern of relationship among ethnic groups. What is more
decisive in creating national loyalty toward the political system is
the kind of political arrangements the ethnic groups make with
one another. The "treaties," "coalitions" and constitutional arrangements ethnic groups make may appear to the outsider to be
tampering with the surface of things rather than with the
essentials, for these coalitions, treaties and the like seem so
tentative and do not involve the fundamental changes in attitudes
which we assume are essential if a sense of national identity and
legitimacy are to be achieved. Yet these political arrangements
are the conditions necessary for attitudinal change. Structural
arrangements need not follow, they may precede attitudinal
changes.

There is a kind of reductionist position in the melting-pot
communications theory which tends to see political change
simply as a consequence of more "fundamental" changes in
social relationships, economic development and the growth in
communications. It is well to remind ourselves that the pattern of
interaction may very well be in the other direction, that political
changes may bring about changes in social relations, economic
development and patterns of communication.

From time to time various efforts were made to bring about a
rapprochement between the Serbs and the Croatians. Some
historians have suggested that by the late 1930s, especially in the
Croatian-Serb "pact" of 1939, such a rapprochement was becoming possible. We know that in other political systems, such as in
Belgium, Canada and India, structural arrangemnts and pacts of
various sorts have been critical in whatever degree of integration
is sustained. In fragile political systems torn by ethnic conflicts,
arrangements of one sort or another have often proven critical in
avoiding civil conflict and even civil war.

The Yugoslav political system might not have held together
even if there have been no revisionist claims upon it, but the
claims and expansion of her neighbors proved to be decisive in
her disintegration. The Yugoslav system was in many ways
analogous to a bar stool with three or four legs linked to the seat,
but without cross bars holding the legs together.[27] The chair could
stand, but if any substantial weight was put upon it, the legs would
draw apart and the chair would collapse. In this instance, the
pressure of the Italians and the Germans "broke" the system. Even
earlier in the 1920s and 1930s, the Macedonians, the Croatians,
and the Slovenes all had reason to think that the system might not
last, that the intervention of one or more outside powers would
destroy the system and change its boundaries. So long as this

feeling of tentativeness persisted, the incentives for withholding loyalty were greater than the pressures for integration.

In exploring the factors at work in the development of national integration and political legitimacy it is important that we pay particular attention to political variables, and resist the tendency to rely upon economic, social or psychological explanations for political facts. If we use psychological variables to explain psychological behaviors, and social facts to explain social facts, so ought we first turn to one set of political facts to explain another.

The second significant feature of the Yugoslav case is the inverse of the first. We have suggested that international events had a critical effect on Yugoslavia's internal political development; Yugoslavia's external behavior was also decisively influenced by it. As the Bulgarian-Hungarian-Italian-German noose tightened, it became apparent to most Yugoslav leaders that they lacked a sufficiently powerful or united army, or a sufficiently loyal population, to depend upon the country's internal strength to cope with the external threats. That Yugoslavia had the potential, at least in determination if not resources and manpower, to ward off the German army is demonstrated by the ability Yugoslavia demonstrated in the late 1940s, less than a decade later, to deter Soviet military intervention. But by 1948, Yugoslavia was far more unified politically—her army, in spite of wartime losses, far more capable of coping with a potential enemy. In 1940-41, the Yugoslav elite had to use diplomacy as a substitute for internal strength and the tool of diplomacy alone proved to be unsatisfactory. As an adjunct to military power and a loyal population, diplomacy might have rescued the Yugoslavs from a German attack, but by April, 1941, especially after the coup (which, ironically, cheered the West because of its anti-German character), the Germans knew that their army could invade and occupy Yugoslavia relatively easily.

Yugoslavia's allies, France and Britain, had no vital interest in preserving Yugoslavia's territorial integrity; ultimately, Yugoslav leaders realized that neither their alliances nor the League of Nations could or would protect them from attack. By the late thirties, it became apparent to all the countries of Central and Eastern Europe challenged by revisionist and expansionist powers, particularly the Czechs, the Yugoslavs and the Romanians, that the Western powers could not be relied upon. In time both their internal political development and their international behavior became dominated by their need for security. The uncertain relationship betwen peoples, territories and states in a European world which assumed that nation and state should be coterminous was the central determinant of Balkan developments. As John Campbell expressed it so clearly:

> ...There emerged in the nineteenth and twentieth centuries the classic model of what the world has come to know as Balkanization—a group of small, unstable and weak states,

each based on the idea of nationality, in an area in which nation and state did not and could not coincide; all with conflicting territorial claims and with ethnic minorities that had to be assimilated or repressed, driven into unstable and changing alignments among themselves, seeking support from outside powers in order to protect their national existence or to satisfy national ambitions, and in turn being used by those powers for the latters' own strategic advantage.[28]

The Dynamics of Irredentism

What generalizations can one draw from these diverse historical cases? Can we say that there are uniform patterns of international behavior or of internal political development on the part of irredentist states or of the states against whom irredentist claims are made? It would appear that in spite of the many individual variations there are characteristic patterns of political develop-ment within both irredentist and anti-irredentist states, that states engaged in irredentist disputes form a syndrome—that is, they are generally found together, are causally interrelated, and they owe their origin to common factors. Since the model has been developed in more detail elsewhere, here I shall only suggest some of the main features.[29]

1. The first characteristic is that irredentist states tend to form alliances to threaten the state containing the ethnic minority. Their natural allies are both neighboring states of their enemy, and great powers that are anti-status quo with respect to the international or regional balance of power. In turn, the anti-irredentist state with the ethnic minority will seek defensive alliances to preserve its borders; its natural allies are neighbors of its irredentist enemy and other powers that wish to preserve the international or regional status quo. Neighboring states and more powerful outside powers find it difficult not to be drawn into the dispute, and often have much to gain by supporting one side or another.
2. The persistent concern of the irredentist state for the status of the ethnic minority in the neighboring state creates hopes within the ethnic minority that it may be incorporated into the revisionist state. Typically, a substantial portion of the ethnic minority becomes hostile to efforts to nationalize it into the anit-irredentist state in which it lives. The growth of irredentism tends, therefore, to undermine efforts by the government to integrate its ethnic minority.

Some members of the ethnic minority may strive to improve their status (often demanding greater autonomy or some kind of federal arrangement) within the country in which they are a minority and press for improving relations between the two countries, viewing themselves as a "bridge." Often there will develop an acute conflict within the ethnic minority as to the character of their own identity, their affinity, or lack of affinity with other ethnic communities, and the risks and benefits of supporting the regime in which they live or supporting union with their irredentist neighbor.

How to treat the population under dispute typically becomes an acute issue within the governing elite. While one group may advocate a federalist policy aimed at increasing the autonomy and decreasing the fears of the minority, another group may press for a centralist policy and an increased reliance upon coercion against dissident elements, arguing that those who are unwilling to accept the authority of the state should leave. The more threatening the revisionist power, the more likely the centralist group will win.[30]

3.   To the extent that the irredentist power is obsessed with the question of boundary rectification this issue rather than matters of internal development will receive the highest priority. How to bring about a change in the international or military situation so as to redeem their kinsmen and correct territorial injustice are goals on which citizens and the governing elite may unite. In foreign policy, the government searches for allies and arms and in domestic affairs it gives priority to military development. Those politicians and intellectuals who dare to advocate shifting priorities to internal development and the resolution of tensions with their neighbor may find themselves accused of disloyalty and may even be faced with personal danger.[31] Though the government may pursue economic development efforts as a means of increasing its military power, since its primary concern is with military preparedness it is likely to pass up economic opportunities, or to put aside proposals for internal reforms that do not facilitate the achievement of its military objectives.

The political culture of both the citizenry and the elite are molded by the desire to redeem the "repressed" minorities and to reunite with one's kinsmen. Militancy, self-sacrifice, the readiness to die for one's country become highly valued and there is hostility to all those within and outside who do not support the "just" demand. There may be hostility to internal dissent because it weakens national unity, and affection for the military on which, ultimately, hopes for redemption rest. The rhetoric of public discourse becomes highly charged with emotion so that rational discussion of alternative courses of action becomes impossible.

Just as the ordering of priorities and the political culture is shaped by irredentist demands, so is the internal distribution of power likely to develop in such a ways as to favor those advocating order and unity at home and militancy abroad. There is a strong tendency for the military to assume political power in irredentist political systems, for voluntary institutions and the mass media to become subservient to central authority, and for the central government to resist genuinely free elections and a representative process that might change the existing power structure. Opponents of the regime may be arrested and charged with espionage and collaboration with the enemy; existing elites, whether "radical" or "conservative," may use the irredentist issue to prevent competitive politics and changes in the existing power structure. Some form of military rule is common among irredentist states.

The irredentist state may take chances without careful calculations as to the probability of a successful outcome for it has an interest in keeping the issue alive and in provoking external intervention. It may provoke military skirmishes on the border; commando units of "volunteers" may be encouraged to make forays across the line. The irredentist state may launch an abortive military attack, even when it knows it cannot win, in order to trigger the involvement of one or more of its neighbors or one of the great powers. Because it tends to overestimate the capacity of its own military (usually by exaggerating the high morale and moral fervor in the army), underestimate the capacity on its enemy (by assuming that there will be an uprising of the dissident minorities within) and, because it will grasp at any suggestion that its allies and one of the great powers will give it support (or be forced to give it support rather than allow its defeat), the irredentist state may take risks that others view as irrational and even self-destructive.

4. Among all three actors in the dispute—the irredentist state, the anti-irredentist state and the disputed ethnic group there is likely to be a concern, almost an obsession with the past as each actor seeks to define or justify its identity. The exact location and extent of historic kingdoms, the special merits attributed to historical heroes, and the historic distinctive qualities of the people—their language, literature, folk songs, traditional social institutions and practices and their deeply revered values are all explored and publicized by the country's historians, poets, priests, politicians, schoolteachers and journalists. There is often a tendency for poets to be hawks and the military to be dovish, for the literary elites are inclined to want to take military risks whereas sections of the military, aware of their own limitations, may prefer to be cautious.

5. Political leaders advocating a position contrary to the majority view are likely to be considered disloyal. A kind of Gresham's law of leadership is at work with the most militant groups assuming a growing voice in the country's political life. Political leaders in the irredentist state advocating a military solution are likely to drive out those who want to end the dispute by accepting the status quo; in the status quo power, those who advocate a firm stand are likely to drive out those who wish to surrender the disputed territory and those who want to be "tough" on the minorities may drive out those who want to be more accommodating; and within the contested ethnic group, those who advocate a policy aimed at reuniting the divided community are likely to drive out those

willing to accept the status quo or seek some autonomy within the existing borders.

Post-Ottoman Irredentism in the Middle East

Now let us consider how some of these features of irredentism associated with state formation in the Balkans may be relevant to an analysis of the contemporary Israeli-Arab conflict

In one significant respect the outcome of state formation in the Middle East was the same as in the Balkans: what states were created and with what boundaries was a matter largely determined by the European powers. France created the modern boundaries of Syria and redrew the borders of Lebanon; Jordan was carved out of the Ottoman province of Damascus, to which was added the lands west of the Jordan. And the territories incorporated into Iraq were drawn from several Ottoman provinces. Finally, Israel as a state, and the territories initially assigned to it, was created by the United Nations resolution of November 1947. As in the Balkans, differences arose within the successor states in the Middle East as to whether there should be several "national" states or a single Arab nation, whether some of the existing states should be still further divided into smaller units, and whether boundaries created by the Europeans were legitimate or not. There was, of course, one significant difference between developments in the Middle East and in the Balkans: one of the successor states was viewed as illegitimate by every other state in the region.

The borders which Israel obtained by January 1949 and which continued until the Six Day War in 1967, bore little relation to those sought by the Zionist movement. The proposal submitted by the Zionist Organization to the Paris Peace Conference in 1919 which considered, among other things, the fate of the territories under Ottoman rule, called for the creation of a state whose boundaries included all of the territories that had been included in the Hasmonean kingdom (165–63 B.C.E.) as well as some areas (the western Galilee and Negev) that had been part of the Jewish kingdom of Solomon (11th Century B.C.E.).[32] These boundaries were based upon a conception of Eretz Yisrael, that is a territory that more or less approximated the biblical land of Israel. It included, in addition to the territories that are now part of the state of Israel, all of the West Bank plus portions of the East Bank of the Jordan which, according to biblical accounts, were occupied by the tribes of Reuben, Gad and a branch of Manasseh. For Zionists, Israel represented not simply a state for Jews, but a *return* by Jews to a land which belonged to them and from which they had been expelled by the Romans and subsequent invaders. Thus, the demand was not for land presently settled by Jews, but for land in which historically they had lived, from which they had been excluded, and to which they now wished to return. For some religious Jews, the return to the biblical lands was part of the redemptive process. As Kevin Avruch observed, they criticized the secularists for distinguishing between the "religious" and "political-national" concepts of Judaism and argued that the territorial integrity of Eretz Yisrael was central to this process of redemption, for there was an intrinsic holiness to the land itself.[33] From the perspective of many Zionists, Jews had a right to all of historic Palestine, that is, those lands that were given to Moses and Joshua and which were part of the first or second Commonwealth as described in the Old Testament. From this point of view Jewish rights were no less in Hebron and Nablus than in Tel Aviv or Jerusalem since rights were defined as independent of the existing settlement of Jews.

It is impossible to speak of a Zionist point of view when the movement, like contemporary Israeli politics, reflected so many ideological perspectives.[34] There were those who spoke of Eretz Yisrael as simply the territory within which Jews had the right to create settlements, those who conceived of a bi-national state within these boundaries, as well as those who defined Eretz Yisrael as the boundaries of a proposed Jewish state. And there were those who would put aside the ideological question of what constituted Jewish territorial rights for a consideration of the practical political question of what boundaries could be obtained.

As a practical matter, the question of including portions of the eastern bank of the Jordan in a Jewish state was precluded by the British decision to partition Palestine, create the state of Transjordan, and close the area (after 1921) to further Jewish settlement. Thereafter, various proposals were made by the British and by the Jewish Agency for partitioning the remainder of Palestine between a proposed Jewish and a proposed Arab state. These discussions between the British and Jews came to an end with the United Nations Partition Plan of November 1947 which gave the proposed Jewish state approximately 54% of the land, made Jerusalem an international zone, and gave the remaining territory to a proposed Arab state. The Arab rejection of the UN plan and the subsequent Arab attack led the Israelis to fight not only for the territory assigned to them by the UN, but for Jerusalem and for areas assigned to the proposed (but now rejected) Arab state. When the cease fire was declared in early 1949, Israel controlled an additional 25% or so of the area west of the Jordan that had not been included in Israel by the UN Plan. This included, in addition to West Jerusalem, all of the western Galilee (including the towns of Nazareth, Acre and Nahariya), some areas along the Mediterranean (including Jaffa and Ashdod), an area known as the "Little Triangle" to the south of Nazareth, and some areas to the west of Jerusalem (including Lod and Ramla) and to the south (including Beersheba).

Until 1967 Israel viewed the 1949 cease fire line as the de facto boundaries of the state of Israel. In a situation in which her neighbors did not recognize the right of the state of Israel to exist, there was no discussion between Israelis and Arabs as to what ought to be the final borders of the state. Though a distinction continued to be made by many Israelis between *Eretz Yisrael* (the Land of Israel) as opposed to *Medinat Yisrael* (the State of Israel, within its existing borders), the government of Israel made no claim upon its Jordanian neighbor other than to press for recognition of the state of Israel within, more or less, existing borders. In short, irredentism played no part in the internal politics or the external behavior of Israel between 1949 and 1969; but it is important to note that no change took place in the Zionist conception of Israel's territorial rights to Eretz Yisrael, The ideological question was simply, as the phrase goes, put on the back burner.

The extension of Israeli control over the West Bank as a result of the 1967 war brought back the ideological question. Many Zionists argued that all of the West Bank, not only East Jerusalem, should be annexed by Israel since these areas are part of Eretz Yisrael. Others rejected this position, not on ideological but on practical political grounds. Though Israel had a legitimate claim to the territories, they reasoned, its incorporation into Israel would mean the addition of a million Arabs to the country. These, alongside the existing half-million Israeli Arabs, would constitute an enormous political threat to continued control of the country by the Jewish population, a threat further compounded by a sharp disparity in the population growth rates of the two communities. As a practical matter, they argued, the right to annex the West Bank should not be exercised. Instead the territory should be retained for bargaining with the Arab states until they recognized the state of Israel; meanwhile its control by Israel would enhance Israeli security.

Israeli discussions of the future of the West Bank are thus clouded by two sharply conflicting conceptions. There are those who are content with a state largely within the 1949 borders (or the 1967 borders, that is, 1949 plus east Jerusalem) whose thinking on the question of the West Bank is based entirely on security considerations, as opposed to those who see the West Bank in ideological, that is Zionist terms, as part of a Greater Israel. This latter position is taken by various groups within Likud, including Herut, the largest party, the Greater Israel movement, Shlomzion and La'am and by the National Religious Party and it is supported by sections of the Labor Party. The most articulate spokesman for a Greater Israel is the Gush Emunim (the "Bloc of the Faithful") who make irredentist claims not only on the West Bank, but on all the "administered territories," including Sinai, the Gaza Strip and the Golan Heights and who, in pursuit of their objective, created Jewish settlements in territories outside the 1949 boundaries.

The quarrel between those who want to return the West Bank under certain conditions, or retain some areas for security purposes (e.g., the Allon plan) but return the rest, and those who argue for the annexation of the West Bank is not merely a difference between doves and hawks. More fundamentally, it is a dispute over the very conception of a Jewish state, between those who want a Jewish state in a portion of Eretz Yisrael in return for security and those who believe that the Zionist dream will not be complete until the Third Commonwealth is established within all of the Land of Israel.[35]

The government has sided with the irredentist view. Most recently, it was expounded by Prime Minister Begin who said that "The Green line no longer exists—it has vanished forever. . . . We want to coexist with the Arabs in Eretz Yisrael. . . Jews and Arabs will coexist in Judea and Samaria as they do in Jerusalem, Ramle, Jaffa and Haifa."[36]

The debate therefore among Israelis over autonomy is not simply over the question of what kind of autonomy should exist on the West Bank, but whether autonomy should be viewed as a step toward the return of the West Bank to Arab control (either to a new Palestinian state or to Jordan), or whether it is a step toward the annexation of the West Bank. The Prime Minister and members of Likud believe that it is the latter. The Arab rejectionists agree. The United States and Egyptian governments believe that it should be the former, as do many Israelis including a substantial part of the Labor Party.

The question of the settlement of Jews on the West Bank (especially in Arab populated areas, as opposed to the "security zone" proposed in the Allon plan) is heavily invested with the ideological question of whether the Zionist dream of an Eretz Yisrael remains to be fulfilled. Its supporters believe that the West Bank should be part of Israeli sovereignty, that Jews should *retain* their *right* to settle, that the land itself should be under Israeli control (including the disposition of its waters, and control over settlement, immigration and, of course, security). By expanding the Jewish population on the West Bank, and by giving Arabs on the West Bank some rights of self-rule outside the framework of Israeli citizenship it then becomes feasible, so members of the government believe, to consider annexation. The incorporation of *Eretz Yisrael* into *Medinat Yisrael*, the expansion of the Jewish population to more of the biblical lands which many hope can be accelerated by additional migration of Jews from the diaspora (in fulfilment of the messianic vision of *kibbutz galuyot*, the "ingathering of the exiles") is an expression of the Zionist goal. The Gush Emunim thus represents the vanguard of the Zionist dream no less than the *halutzim* or pioneers did in the era of the *Yishuv* (the pre-state Jewish community), and irredentism is the central ideological expression of that vision.

Israeli irredentism is, of course, a peculiar kind of irredentism for it is a demand for territory over which the state already exercises control. The reluctance of the government to annex the

West Bank results only partly from the complex international situation it is in; it has been reluctant largely because of its concern over the impact of annexation on the demographic composition of the country and its implications for continued Jewish rule within the framework of a democratic political system. For many members of the government, therefore, the autonomy experiment is intended to explore avenues for annexation which would provide Arabs on the West Bank and Gaza with some measure of self-rule, but which would exclude them from the Israeli political system. The formula, "self-rule for peoples, but not for territories," is intended to serve this purpose. It also permits the government to continue its policy of creating Jewish settlements on the West Bank and keeping these settlements free from the control of any Palestinian-run autonomy councils. Many Israelis see the formula, and the settlements, as a strategy to prevent both the emergence of a Palestinian state or, alternatively, what would in effect be a bi-national state for Israel.[37] At the end of this experimental period, the prime minister has declared, Israel would then annex the West Bank. While such a formula of annexation plus autonomy for peoples might resolve the dilemma for Israel, it is likely to be seen by outsiders as a retrograde measure reminiscent of South Africa's policy of. giving blacks a "homeland" of limited self-rule and denying those who live within the homeland, as well as those blacks who live and work within white dominated areas, rights to participate in the South Africa political system. It is not difficult to envisage the reaction to such a policy not only in the Arab world, but among friends of Israel in the west as well. There is likely to be strong feeling that Israel's moral standing as a state for Jews has been undermined by the imposition of Jewish domination over an Arab population, justified not on the painful grounds of security considerations, but on the religious-ideological grounds of annexing territories to which Israel claims historic rights. Whether advocates of annexation are prepared to pay the price of declining international support for Israel, with all its implications for financial assistance, immigration and security, is at the heart of the controversy within Israel over autonomy and the question of Israel's long-term objectives for the West Bank.

Palestinian Irredentism

The Palestinian National Covenant of July 1968, which still represents the official ideological position of the Palestinians, takes an explicit irredentist position. "Palestine is the homeland of the Arab Palestinian people; it is an indivisible part of the Arab homeland, and the Palestinian people are an integral part of the Arab nation" (Article 1). "Palestine, with the boundaries it had during the British mandate, is an indivisible territorial unit"[38] (Article 2). "The Palestinian Arab people possess the legal right to their homeland and have the right to determine their destiny after achieving the liberation of their country in accordance with their wishes and entirely of their own accord and will" (Article 3). Other Articles explain that only Jews who lived in Palestine prior to the "Zionist invasion" (beginning in the nineteenth century) can remain (Article 6), that the partition of Palestine in 1947 and the establishment of the state of Israel are illegal (Article 19), and that Jews do not "constitute a single nation with an identity of their own" (Article 20).

In his November 1974 speech to the United Nations, Yasser Arafat largely reconfirmed the Palestinian position as stated in the Covenant. In his speech he called for the establishment of "an independent national State on all liberated Palestinian territory." The "Political Programme for the Present Stage of the Palestinian Liberation Organization" drawn up by the Palestinian National Council several months earlier, made clear that a state created on "liberated territories" would not be the final boundaries of a Palestinian state and that it would not live side by side peacefully with a state of Israel whose boundaries it recognized. "The Liberation Organization will struggle against any proposal for a Palestinian entity the price of which is recognition, peace, secure frontiers, renunciation of national rights and the deprival of our people of their right to return and their right to self-determination on the soil of their homeland." The Council also reaffirmed its opposition to Resolution 242.

Some observers of the internal politics of the Palestinian movement have argued that the PLO is prepared to accept a Palestinian state living side by side with Israel (but not recognizing a "Zionist entity") without planning its armed overthrow, and they will cite as evidence of this view statements by various moderate Palestinians. Those who argue this position suggest that even if a Palestinian state persisted in its unwillingness to recognize the state of Israel, and even if it held the position that *through peaceful means* there could eventually emerge in the area a single "democratic state" in which Muslims, Jews and Christians would live together, this dream would soon give way to the realities of international politics, and the two states would then live side by side, if not in friendship, then at least not in a state of armed tension.

However, in the absence of assured recognition by a Palestinian state of Israeli boundaries, it is not difficult to envisage a Palestinian state making irredentist demands for border revisions. The Palestinians would clearly insist, as they do now, that the 1967 borders be re-established, with East Jerusalem incorporated into the Palestinian state as its capital. Even should East Jerusalem be returned, or some formula found that permitted shared rule of a united city, the Palestinian state might call for a return to the proposed (but never established) 1947 United Nations Plan under which two states would have been created West of the Jordan. Israel would then be asked to "return" to the Palestinians

Nazareth, Acre, Jaffa, Lod, Ramla, the Little Triangle, Beersheba, and the western Galilee. The Palestinians could argue that a large part of the Palestinian population that fled from Israel in the 1947-48 war came from the areas that would have been included in the Arab state in accordance with the UN partition plan. At a minimum, the Palestinian state might call for the return of those areas that continue to have large Arab populations, namely, the Western Galilee, (including Nazareth), and the Little Triangle.

Thus, on the grounds of reuniting Palestinian peoples on both sides of the border, providing for the resettlement of many of the Palestinian refugees who have left the region, and on legal grounds, a case could be made by a Palestinian state for incorporating all or portions of the territories Israel captured in the 1948 War that had not been awarded to Israel by the UN Partition Plan of 1947.

If an irredentist Palestinian state behaved as have other irredentist states, one would expect such a state to seek support for its irredentist demands from its Arab neighbors and from states outside the region, including one or more of the great powers. But the most important ally of the Palestinian state would be the Israeli Arabs or, as they now call themselves, the Palestinians, who live within the 1967 borders. Faced with the "offer" to join with their brethren in Palestine without having to physically move, many would soon join in the demand for redrawing the international borders.[39] Those few who wanted to integrate within Israel would find themselves isolated; the radical elements would grow and their strategy would probably be to provoke Israeli authorities in an effort to demonstrate their "repressive" character, and thereby attract support for their cause outside. The attitude of the Israeli government toward the Arab minorities would be influenced by the extent to which sections of the minority expressed support for the irredentist movement and thereby explicitly abjured loyalty to the regime. Members of the government and the opposition who argued for policies intending to integrate Israeli Arabs within the country's economy and educational system would find themselves pushed aside by those who advocated a "hard line" toward the Arabs based upon security considerations. As tensions grew between Arabs and Jews within Israel, and between Arabs and the Israeli state, the Palestinian state would seek to win international support for its irredentist claims by widely publicizing real, exaggerated and invented reports of mistreatment by Israelis and Israeli authorities of the Arab minority.

How aggressive an irredentist Palestinian state might be in attempting to smuggle arms to terrorists within Israel, provoke clashes at the border and launch raids would only partially be influenced by the kinds of support it received from other states, or if a Palestinian irredentist state behaved like other irredentist states, it would be in its interest to constantly provoke tensions and crises that would keep the issue on the international agenda. As a state it would be inclined to take high risks, even though such behavior might disrupt its internal development.

What conclusions can be drawn from this analysis? The first is that while many would view the creation of a Palestinian state which recognizes Israel along agreed-upon borders as a major step toward peace in the Middle East, it would be a step backward if a Palestinian state were created that did not recognize Israel and did not have mutually agreed-upon permanent borders. The only possibility of avoiding irredentism on the part of such a state is if representatives of the Palestinians who were accorded legitimacy both by the Palestinian population and by the Arab governments agreed to negotiate directly with the Israeli government. At present, and for the foreseeable future, only the PLO has such a status. It has not yet indicated its willingness to negotiate, nor has it been invited by Israelis to do so.[40]

Should such a Palestinian body refuse to respond to an expressed willingness on the part of the Israeli government to negotiate over the the question of creating a Palestinian state, it would seem unwise as well as unlikely for any Israeli government to accede to demands for the creation of a Palestinian state even were it under substantial external pressures. An externally imposed state would invariably be irredentist.

At the same time, Israel's case for retaining control over the West Bank in the event the Palestinians are unprepared to recognize the state of Israel with agreed upon borders is weakened by Israel's present position that there are no conditions under which it would return the West Bank to Arab sovereignty, and that annexation of the territory (allowing some autonomy to the local Arabs) is the ultimate and preferred objective. Israel's long-term security, which rests so substantially upon its relationship with the United States, and now with Egypt, can be jeopardized by any categorical position on the Israeli side that its objectives are irredentist and that it therefore permanently denies the people of the West Bank and Gaza any opportunity to live in an independent Palestinian state even under terms that are congruent with Israeli security.

Israel will have to choose between its goals of colonization and irredentism and agreement with its Arab neighbors. In turn, the Palestinians will have to choose between their goals of a limited Palestinian entity or an irredentist Palestinian state that seeks to absorb large portions if not all of Israel. A half century ago the successor states of the Ottomans in the Balkans had to make similar choices: to make expansionist claims based upon, as they saw it, history, morality and justice, or in the interests of peace with their neighbors to opt for some modified version of existing international borders. They opted for the former and brought death and destruction upon themselves and others. Can the successor states in the Middle East make wiser choices?

Notes

1. "The Macedonian Syndrome; An Historical Model of International Relations and Political Development," *World Politics*, Vol. XXIII, July 1971, pp. 665-683

2. For a description of the interrelationship between the European alliance system and the development of the Balkan states in the nineteenth century, see W.L. Langer, *European Alliances and Alignments, 1871-1890*. New York, 1931. For a summary of irredentist claims in the Balkans see Robert L. Wolff, *The Balkans in Our Times*. Cambridge, Mass.: Harvard University Press, 1956, pp. 143-156.

3. See, for example, William P. Kaldis, *John Capodistrias and the Modern Greek State*. Madison: The State Historical Society of Wisconsin for the Department of History at the University of Wisconsin, 1963.

4. Quoted by Brian Inglis, *The Story of Ireland*, London: Faber and Faber, p. 212.

5. Dimitri Pentzopoulos, *The Balkan Exchange of Minorities and its Impact Upon Greece*. Paris: Mouton, 1962, pp. 25-26.

6. William Miller, *A History of the Greek People (1821-1921)*, New York: Dutton and Co., p. 39.

7. Leland G. Allbaugh, *Crete: A Case Study of an Underdeveloped Area*. Princeton: Princeton University Press, 1953.

8. R.V. Burke, *The Dynamics of Communism in Eastern Europe*. Princeton: Princeton University Press, 1960, p. 64.

9. *Ibid*.

10. Pentzopoulos, *op. cit.*, p. 48.

11. E.S. Forster, *A Short History of Modern Greece, 1821-1956*. 3rd edition, London: Methuen, 1958, p. 32.

12. 12. Joseph Rothschild, *The Communist Party of Bulgaria: Origins and Development, 1883-1936*. New York: Columbia University Press, 1959 p. 214. Rothschild reports that in 1897 the population of Salonika was estimated at 120,000 of whom 75,000 were Sephardic Jews, 14,000 Greeks, 11,000 Slavs, and the remaining 20,000 were Turks, Vlakhs, Albanians and Gypsies. In 1913, the city population was 153,000 consisting of 61,000 Jews, 46,000 Moslems, 40,000 Greeks and only 6000 Slavs.

13. For a detailed account of the early years of the Bulgarian state and the complex maneuverings of Prince Brattenberg, the Great Powers and Bulgarian political leaders, especially in the period from 1878 to 1885, see C.E. Black, *The Establishment of Constitutional Government in Bulgaria*. Princeton: Princeton University Press, 1943.

14. For an account of internal political developments after the Brattenberg coup, see J. Rothschild, *op. cit.*

15. In this discussion of Bulgarian revisionist policies I shall only consider the Macedonian issue since it was the central focus of Balkan disputes and the most significant element in Bulgaria's internal political life. But Bulgaria was also engaged in a dispute with Rumania over southern Dobruja lost during the Balkan wars of 1912-13. The Bulgarians argued that 2% of the population of Dobruja were Rumanians, 38% Turks and 48% were Bulgarians. The Rumanians sought to resolve this claim by establishing a Rumanian majority in the province. In 1924 a law was

passed expropriating land from non-Rumanians. As a result, 40,000 Bulgarians migrated to Bulgaria and another 20,000 Turks returned to their homeland. The policy of forceable movement of population pursued by the Rumanians was part of a general policy of most Balkan countries striving for ethnic homogeneity and for the population settlement of disputed territories based upon historic claims. In a similar fashion, the Turks sought to "solve" their Greek problem, and the Greeks their Macedonian problem.

17.   Rothschild, *op. cit*., p. 174.

18.   Elizabeth Barker, *Macedonia: Its Place in Balkan Power Politics.* London: Royal Institute of International Affairs, 1950, p. 37

19.   Ibid., p. 39. In the 1920s, wrote Barker, IMRO "became more a financial racket, selling its services to the highest bidder—the Bulgarian government, the Italians, possibly for a brief period Soviet Russia," Barker, *ibid.,* p. 39. According to Burke, the government which replaced Stamboliski virtually handed over Petrich Department to IMRO—allowing IMRO to collect tobacco taxes and appoint the Petrich delegation to the Sobranie, and in return, IMRO provided new governments with a corps of assassins. See Burke, *op. cit.* For a history of IMRO, see J. Swire, *Bulgarian Conspiracy,* London: R. Hale, 1939.

20.   Rothschild, *op. cit.*, p. 177.

21.   Alexander Gerschenkron, *Economic Backwardness in Historical Perspective*, Cambridge: Harvard University Press, 1962, p. 230.

22.   Quoted by C.A. Beard and G. Radin, *The Balkan Pivot: Yugoslavia.* New York: Macmillan, 1929, p. 29.

23.   Jacob B. Hoptner, *Yugoslavia in Crisis, 1934–41.* New York: Columbia University Press, 1962, p. 293.

24.   *Ibid.*, p. 235–236.

25.   *Ibid.*, p. 287. Hoptner says that the key people in the coup were Serbian officers and that they chose not to take into their confidence any ranking officers who had ever been attached to the army of the Hapsburg monarchy and very few from Croatia and Slovania. He also noted that while the Croats criticized the coup as a strictly Serb matter, many welcomed it on the grounds that it would hasten Germany's attack on Yugoslavia which they viewed as a necessary step toward the achievement of an independent state of Croatia.

26.   *Ibid.*, p. 288.

27.   A significant missing linkage was the absence of political parties that transcended ethnic boundaries. The People's Radical Party and the Democratic Party were almost exclusively Serbian. The Croatians had their own Peasant Party, the Slovenians had the People's Party, and there was the Yugoslavia Moslem Organization in Bosnia-Herzegovinia. The struggle among parties, therefore, invariably intensified regional conflict. The Communist party subsequently emerged as the only significant political party to cut across ethnic lines. It has been estimated that the Communist army in the spring of 1944 was composed of 44% Serbs, 30% Croats, 10% Slovenes, 4% Montenegrins and others. See J. Frankel, "Communism and the National Question in Yugoslavia." *Journal of Central European Affaris*, Vol. 15, April 1955, pp. 54. For an analysis of the multi-ethnic character of the Communist party after the war, see Paul Shoup, "Yugoslavia's National Minorities Under Communism," *Slavic Review*, Vol. 22. 1963; and "Membership of the Socialist Alliance of the Working Peoples of Yugoslavia," *Yugoslav Review*, Vol. 5, April-June 1964. Tito himself, it is worthy of note, had a Croat father and Slovene mother.

28.   John C. Campbell, "The Balkans: Heritage and Continuity," in Charles and Barbara Yelavich, *The Balkans in Transition: Essays on the Development of Balkan Life and Politics since the Eighteenth Century.* Berkeley: University of California Press, 1963, p. 397.

29.   Weiner, "The Macedonian Syndrome," *op. cit.*

30.   In Yugoslavia the Serbian centralists won. It is interesting to note that post-war Yugoslavia found it easier to pursue a decentralist policy when irredentist demands subsided.

31.   Though there were many proposals for a federation of Balkan states which would thereby bring an end to irredentist claims, political support for such a solution was lacking. See L.S. Stavrianos, *Balkan Federation: A History of the Movement Toward Balkan Unity in Modern Times.* Northampton, Mass, 1944. Unilateral solutions, especially those calling upon a government to renounce its irredentist claims, were regarded as disloyal.

32.   For a description of these and other boundaries proposed for the state of Israel, see Martin Gilbert, *The Arab-Israeli Conflict: Its History in Maps.* Weidenfeld and Nicholson, London, 1976

33.   Kevin A. Avruch, "Gush Emunim: Politics, Religion and Ideology in Israel," *Middle East Review*, Vol. xi, no. 2, Winter, 1978-79, pp. 26-31.

34.   For various pre-independence views, see Ben Halpern, *The Idea of the Jewish State*, Cambridge: Harvard University Press, 1961, and Walter Laquer, *A History of Zionism.* New York: Schocken, 1972.

35.   For a particularly useful summary of post-1973 Israeli attitudes on the West Bank, the Palestinians and related issues, see Larry Fabian and Ze'ev Schiff, ed. *Israelis Speak.* New York: Carnegie Endowment for International Peace, 1977. The views of various political parties are described in Efraim Torgovnik, "Accepting Camp David: The Role of Party Factions in Israeli Policy Making, *Middle East Review*, Vol. xi. no. 2, winter 1978-79, pp. 5-10.

36.   "Begin: There is No Green Line," *Jerusalem Post*, April 30, 1979. The government's official views have been set forth in its proposals for autonomy. It calls for an extension of Israeli sovereignty over the territories at the end of the five year transitional self-rule period. See the *Jerusalem Post*, May 18, 1979, for details. For an Israeli view on autonomy predicated upon security considerations alone, see Yigal Allon, "Anatomy of Autonomy," *Jerusalem Post*, May 31, 1979, and "An Israeli Dialogue on Peace," *Middle East Review*, Vol. xi, no. 1, Fall 1978, pp. 42-50.

37.   It should be pointed out, however, that the presence of Jewish settlements does not necessarily preclude the establishment of a Palestinian state nor the return of the West Bank to Jordanian rule. Apart from the option of removing the settlements, there is no reason why the status of the settlements and of its Jewish population living in an area of Arab sovereignty could not be negotiated. The West Bank need not be *Judenrein*, free of Jews, anymore than Israel itself need be without Arabs.

38.   The PLO Covenant, Yasser Arafat's speech to the United Nations, and other Palestinian documents are conveniently reproduced in Fabian and Schiff, *op. cit.*

39.   According to a Ford Foundation-financed survey conducted among Israel's Arabs by the Institute for Research and Development of Arab Education (Haifa), 59% favored returning to the borders proposed under the 1947 UN partition proposal. Fifty percent of Israel's Arab population rejected Israel's right to exist. *Jerusalem Post*, June 10, 1979.

40.   It should be noted, however, that under the Camp David

agreement, Israel is committed to negotiate with the Palestinian representatives of the autonomous councils concerning the future status of the occupied territories four years after autonomy is put into effect.

Irredentism, Power Politics and Multi-Ethnic Polities
A Discussion

Daniel J. Elazar, Robert Pranger, Shmuel Sandler,
Emanuel Gutmann, Myron Weiner, Eliezer Yapou,
Don Peretz, Francine Friedman

Daniel Elazar: Governmental institutions that are well run from a technical point of view are not the solution to political problems, though they may be useful in other respects. Today national and municipal institutions in our world are so closely intertwined that they cannot be separated in the quest for self-determination and self-government, on one hand, and efficient, democratic government on the other. I think that as we get further into our discussion we will see how the municipal institutions in the territories are of considerable importance in building the kind of infrastructure upon which whatever is developed in the next few months or years will be very significant.

The question, however, that Francine leads us to is almost the reverse of this observation. There is a certain level of political satisfaction that has been provided to minorities in Serbia which permits better government to have a real influence on political ties. That leads me to the question: what is the threshold of political satisfaction which makes it possible for better economic conditions, better services, and the like to tip matters in the direction of political stability.

Just as it is foolish to assume that "good government" will satisfy national aspirations, it seems to me that it is not enough to suggest that political issues and interests will overrule all other considerations in all cases. At some point there is a threshold of minimum political satisfaction that allows these other factors to come into play in a serious way. As Francine Friedman's paper shows, a group does not have to get everything that it demands politically in order for it to reach and cross a kind of substantive and maybe symbolic threshold, and then to allow these other

147

factors to come into play. Obviously something like this happened in the Balkans. All the irredentist claims which made the Balkans the tinderbox of Europe for two generations still have not been settled. The conflict is there, but obviously some sort of threshold has been crossed.

Robert Pranger: I wonder whether the situation in the Balkans hasn't changed because the great power strategies vis-a-vis the Balkans have changed, not the irredentism itself. I am still struck by the interest that the great powers have in the Middle East and in a settlement in that region. Whatever has happened in the Balkans, in terms of great power interests or changes in the position of Germany or of other powers in Eastern and Central Europe, has really not happened in the Middle East. I think this interaction between irredentist claims and great power strategy is very significant. In that sense, I think matters will continue in the Middle East regardless of what happens elsewhere. But I was struck by the point that Myron made about this interaction, that, in essence, Britain drew lines on a map, just as the French and the British divided up the Middle East once by secret treaties. I am also frankly curious as to whether, if some very deep division in this part of the world threatened peace between the United States and the Soviet Union, it would not be settled that way again. I think this is an issue that ought to be kept in mind, this interaction between great powers and irredentism.

Shmuel Sandler: For years I thought, as did many Israelis, that our conflict is unique, and if only it would become a problem of irredentism, then it would be a normal situation. Irredentism was better than illegitimacy. But you just pointed out that even in such a situation, things are not stable, and there are other problems.

Now, because you just cannot uproot irredentism with political solutions, I would like to ask whether a federal solution isn't the only way to avoid this problem which is going to exist after a peace treaty. Because, as I understand it, in the places where federalism has succeeded, the problem of irredentism seems to have been solved. It is only the nation-state model that aggravates the problem of irredentism.

Emanuel Gutmann: I wish I knew the answer to the question of the threshold of politics. I don't. There are so many answers, and they differ from place to place. In one sense, nothing succeeds like success; that is to say, you see that it works somehow, and you do a little more of it. For example, the big dividing issue in Belgium in the nineteenth century was really one of liberalism vs. the church. In the first half of the twentieth century, the big issue was the class issue. This issue has now been displaced. One can actually see the way politics has changed in Belgium, as the central issues change.

Myron Weiner: How do you end irredentism? One might ask the question, how is it we do not have irredentist movements in the Balkans any more? This was the tinderbox of the world. It was a major element, some people would consider it the most decisive element, in the outbreak of the First World War and, of course, it was important in the Second as well. Why did irredentist move-ment more or less come to an end in this part of the world?

There are several possible explanations. Some of the irredent-ist claims were reduced by shifts of population. Some were reduced by redrawing borders in Eastern Europe. I would submit, however, that the most important reason is, as Robert Pranger suggested, that the international balance of power changed. Once the Soviets became the dominant power throughout the Balkans, no Balkan state would make claims on any other Balkan state, thereby contending with Soviet power. There was no way that any of them could get any outside country to support their claims. Certainly the United States and countries of Western Europe were not at that point going to challenge the Soviets' power, and they had no reason to do so.

The only possible claim that could exist was if the East Euro-pean countries persisted in making their claims upon Yugoslavia. It was quite clear that if they were to do so, it would be understood as a Soviet confrontation with Yugoslavia. The Soviets, for a var-iety of fairly obvious reasons, have thus far been unwilling to make those kinds of claims upon Yugoslavia. One cannot rule it out in the future; indeed that is one reason why people are so anxious about what Yugoslavia will look like later. Clearly the option of opening up irredentist claims, not simply by the Balkan states but by the Soviet Union or by the Balkan states on behalf of the Soviet Union is an option for Soviet power in the future, and that is why that issue cannot be viewed as permanently closed.

So what I am suggesting is that, although in the past the great powers set the boundaries in the Balkans, they were also willing to join one political state or another in trying to redraw those boun-daries. Each of the states in the area had reason to believe that by creating an alliance with an outside country they could change the boundaries. The Greeks thought they could get British support. The Bulgarians thought they could get Russian or, later, German support. And even within Yugoslavia, each of the groups within the country thought it could appeal to a different international power to defend its particular claim. After the Second World War, that option closed.

Robert Pranger: The question was raised as to whether irredent-ism is somehow linked to great power interests. As an example, the Quebec Party is now sounding out various great powers about their position on the referendum which is going to occur. They are sounding out the French. They are sounding out the United States government and quite closely following opinion in the U.S. Under these circumstances, I wonder whether in any irredentist situation it is better to have the great powers in conflict or to somehow be able to factor that conflict out, as far as irredentist demands are concerned. This can be done either by creating one power hegemony in an area or by some kind of cooperation which seems much rarer between the great powers. In the case of Greece and Turkey, in contrast to that of Bulgaria and Yugoslavia, the United States controlled Greece and Turkey; that is to say, through the NATO alliance and their military establishments, the U.S. in essence controls the course of events, although they have been near the brink of war on several occasions.

I am curious, because some of the patterns of behavior in the Middle East seem to encourage great power conflict here in various ways. The Arab countries draw a patron to one side and then the other, and everyone wonders why irredentism runs wild in the vicinity. Why not encourage different big power behavior?

Shmuel Sandler: The United States is a good federal state, and still it objected to the right of secession in the middle of the nineteenth century. As for the Soviet Union, although the right of secession is written into the constitution, that still does not mean a lot.

What I mean by federalism is basically increasing the pie and sharing it, instead of dividing the existing one and thus creating irredentism. A federal solution does not have to be fashioned after the American federal model or the Swiss federal model or any other such model, as Daniel Elazar said, it can take other forms. It can be a permanent league of nations; it can be a common market; and so on. When we talk about federalism, we do not always mean the American or any other model.

Daniel Elazar: Just one semantic point; the term "federal state" is often used by practitioners of international relations to describe federal systems. It is not used by people inside any federal system that I know of. Unlike people governed by other kinds of systems, who use the term "state" to describe the system which embraces them, people living under federal systems do not use that term except, perhaps, to describe the constituent units. I think this suggests a broadening, rather than a limiting of the term.

Myron Weiner: Again, on the question of termination, it seems to me that irredentism can be terminated because one state has dominant control over the area and in fact refuses to allow the irredentist issue to come to the surface. Another way is for several powers to agree on control. As has been said, the Soviet Union dominates the Balkans. The United States has a very substantial voice in Greece and Turkey, although it does not quite dominate in the same way. Clearly, Greece and Turkey cannot challenge any of the states under Soviet control without American support. They can challenge each other, which in fact they do. Of course, one version of that irredentism is the Cyprus dispute. We could have stopped that only if we had the kind of power over those states that the Soviet Union has over the Balkans. The Soviet Union can go further than we can for a very simple reason. The Soviet army is based all over the Balkans and can prevent Bulgaria from going to war against Yugoslavia. That, it seems to me, is a very big difference.

On the question of federalism as a way of dealing with internal ethnic differences, one big difference between post-war and pre-war Yugoslavia is that prior to the war there were three national institutions—the army, the monarchy, and the bureacracy—which were national in scope but not in ethnic composition. They were all Serbian. With the establishment of the Communist regime, not only was a national institution created, a political party which cut across ethnic lines, but the Serbian monarchy was eliminated, the army's leadership base broadened, and the bureacracy decentralized. It was not simply that the Communists created a federal system, but that the national institutions also came to represent the different groups within the political system and provided, therefore, a framework within which autonomy could develop.

Eliezer Yapou: Does autonomy, to be full autonomy, require that the right of secession be included? I think that that is extremely important. As far as I know, the Yugoslav regime today theoretically exists on the recognition of the right of secession of each of the republics. It is, however, assumed that there is an undertaking on the part of each not to use this right.

Irredentism is, in one way or another, a fight for the right of secession. In the conflict that we have here in the Middle East, we, the Israelis, keep repeating that we shall not allow under any circumstances a Palestinian state to arise. In fact, if we grant them autonomy, it again raises the question of the right of secession. All right, we grant them autonomy, but up to a point; they will not have the right to secession.

Don Peretz: I wonder if we could return to the question of the right of secession. It was mentioned that the Yugoslav federation of six republics was based on the 1936 USSR constitution which, as I recall, did include the right of secession. To what extent was that right instrumental in obtaining the ratification of the constitution by the republics, and to what extent is it instrumental in providing satisfaction in meeting their national problem? On a theoretical level, I think an important question in the whole discussion of federalism is, to what extent is federalism likely to be an acceptable solution for any problem of conflicting ethnic groups without the right of secession? Ultimately, is not federalism really tantamount to independence and sovereignty, if it does include the right of secession?

Emanuel Gutmann: Let me say a word about the right of secession. There is a formal side to it, that is to say, whether a country has this right mentioned in its constitution or not. If it is purely for tactical reasons, to make the partners more agreeable and confortable, then I would say by all means put it in. But basically speaking, I do not think it makes any difference whether you put it in or not. The fact that the right of secession is not in your constitution will not keep people from claiming tomorrow that they are seceding. Whether they succeed is a question of power.

Francine Friedman: On the question of secession, I think what is significant, adding to what Prof. Gutmann has said, is that the Yugoslavs, both going into World War II and coming out of it, were socialists, very dyed-in-the wool socialists. I think that the theory was very important to them. Despite the fact that the practice was obviously not important, the theory was. And I think that for that reason whether or not the right of secession was included in the constitution was significant to them. What is also significant is that in the 1946 constitution of Yugoslavia, the right of secession was specifically provided, not only in the basic principles, but also as a separate article. In the 1974 constitution, it is mentioned only in the basic principles. I think possibly the Yugoslavs are starting to backpedal a little bit. They are possibly starting to regret that they followed the Soviet constitution so closely, because for the first time there is a possibility that somebody will take them up on it. The Kosovo-Albanians, particularly, are notably unhappy in Yugoslavia.

In 1971, the major area of secessionist feeling was that of the Croatians. They were saying that they were not getting enough of a return for their foreign currency, and they were not represented equally in the officer corps, which was mostly Serbian. They also tried to separate the Croatian language from Serbian and said that Croatian should be used as an official language within Croatia. For these reasons, they began to talk in secessionist terms. Lately, I understand, some of the cooler heads have begun to prevail and to say that possibly Croatia would not be such a viable state in the area that it is. Some people disagree because there are smaller states with fewer economic advantages. Nevertheless, the Croats have started to re-think what the advantages are to a Yugoslav union. So possible secession, they feel, is not to their economic advantage.

Arrangements For Self-Rule and Autonomy in Various Countries
The Situation in 1979

Daniel J. Elazar

In its search for a solution to the problem of the territories occupied by Israel as a result of the Six-Day War—one that will provide an acceptable level of self-determination for their Arab residents—the present Israeli government has proposed a system of autonomy for the inhabitants of those territories. Designed to provide some context of shared rule at least for an interim period, this plan has been presented by the Israelis *de novo*, virtually without reference to similar arrangements presently extant elsewhere. As a result the plan has been treated by the world at large as if it were a device designed to prevent the exercise of self-determination by the local inhabitants. Israel itself has helped foster that impression, perhaps unwittingly, by rejecting or ignoring accepted terminology in presenting its plan and failing to link its plan with the many existing manifestations of what it has proposed.

While our age is generally—and properly—considered to be the greatest age of state-building yet known in human history, not every state or polity to emerge in the twentieth century or in the five centuries since the emergence of the modern state has opted for conventional sovereignty. Nor has every people or nation seeking political self-determination taken that turn. Simultaneously with the emergence of the idea of the "sovereign state" has come the idea that political sovereignty is property vested in the people who delegate powers to political institutions and who, in their sovereign capacities, can delegate such powers to different institutions for different purposes. Thus the statist revolution has been paralleled by another kind of revolution, one which seeks to adapt

153

the institutions of governance to different human realities whether internally or on an interstate basis.

Thus, in addition to the over 150 examples of "sovereign" states recognized as such under international law, we have identified 91 examples of self-rule, home rule, or autonomy within or involving 52 different sovereign states. If each separate self-governing comprehensive political entity were to be counted, the number would be in the hundreds and if local home rule arrangements were added, in the thousands. The examples reflect the same purposes that have led to the creation of "sovereign" states, namely the achievement of self-determination by collectivities (nations, peoples, even tribes) under conditions that require at least a formal commitment to democratic republicanism. Since over 90 percent of all "sovereign" states encompass significant ethnic diversity not to mention historical and traditional territori-ally-based differences and interstate regional ties, they represent necessary responses to a real human condition. Israel's attempt to forge such a response for its area should be seen in that context.

What follows is the latest summary of the continuing survey of existing forms of self-rule and autonomy across the world, as of July 1980, which up dates the earlier inventories prepared by the Jerusalem Institute for Federal Studies in 1977 and 1978. A number of the cases referred to in the following pages deserve further study for their relevance to the Israeli/Palestinian context.

Africa
Comoros Islands
The Federal and Islamic Republic of the Comoros is a federation of three islands under a federal constitution approved by a referendum in 1978.
Egypt
The Egyptian-Sudanese border is so drawn that there are enclaves on either side attached for certain purposes of governance to the other country.
Ghana
Ghana's 1979 constitution divides the country into nine regions, guarantees their territorial integrity and some internal self-government through a mixture of traditional (houses of chiefs) and modern institutions, and provides a role for them in the national government.
Nigeria
1. Nigeria is a full-fledged federal system. Originally a three-unit federation, it has been reorganized three times and is now divided into 19 states to accommodate the major ethnic groups.
2. Because of the 100 plus tribal groups in Nigeria, many remain minorities and certain states have no single ethnic majority. To accommodate this, Nigeria has created sub-state units with municipal powers like counties, which, while officially organized on a strictly territorial basis, actually are designed to provide many

smaller tribes with a unit of government to call their own.

Southwest Africa (Namibia)

While the final form of its regime has not been set, the Turnhalle constitution provides for a kind of non-territorial federation of ethnic and tribal groups. The constitutionally-established division of powers is between a general government in which each group is represented more or less proportionately and is protected as a group by appropriate constitutional guarantees and what are, in effect, constituent governments for each of the constituent groups.

South Africa

1. A fairly complex arrangement involving a white-controlled Republic of South Africa, originally a union of four provinces, two originally Afrikaner-dominated and two originally English-dominated. Their powers are less than those of federated states but more than municipal although they have been diminished in recent years.

2. The Republic territory was further divided into nine black homelands, three of which have been given full independence but are still bound by customs union and a multitude of bilateral agreements with South Africa and are dependent upon it in other ways as well. Two others formally are defined as associated states with full internal self-rule

3. In addition, the three black countries of Botswana, Lesotho and Swaziland are linked to South Africa through a customs union although otherwise fully independent.

4. South Africa also attempts to encourage autonomous institutions among Coloureds and Asians on a non-territorial basis. These are resisted by the Coloureds who want integration with the whites and partially accepted by the Asians, who wish to preserve their own identity.

Sudan

1. To settle its civil war between north and south, Sudan granted the southerners regional autonomy, whose implementation has been real but limited because of a lack of resources to pay for it. In 1980, the Sudanese government announced that the rest of the country would be regionalized as well. This followed on the transfer of most domestic functions from the national government to the provinces.

2. In addition, Sudan has a number of autonomous enclaves along the border with Egypt (see above)

Tanzania

A union of Tanganyika and Zanzibar preserves substantial home rule for each essentially on a federal basis. Zanzibar's constitution provides for a popularly elected government within the union.

Asia

Afghanistan

While Afghanistan's formal constitution conforms to centralized French-style models to make it seem Western, the Afghanis have reported that they have a well-rooted two-tiered system whereby the formal Western-style institutions of government serve the country as a whole, while local affairs are in the hands of the tribes, with the provinces functioning as mediating institutions through which the general government can deal with tribal leaders on a day-to-day basis. In 1978, the seizure of power in Kabul by a pro-Communist group brought with it efforts to impose central government control over the tribes, which are bastions of Islamic fundamentalism. This, in turn, led to tribal revolts which gained considerable ground in the first half of 1979, and to the recent Soviet intervention.

Brunei

Linked to the United Kingdom as an associated state since 1963 when it withdrew from the Malaysian Federation, it has reluctantly acquiesced to Britain's insistence that it become independent in 1983.

Bhutan

Bhutan is linked to India as an associated state.

Burma

Officially a union, it has various autonomous "states" or tribal regions, of which little is known except that in certain cases very real state autonomy is maintained by tribal military forces which keep the central authorities out of their areas.

China

China is a unitary state which has had to utilize federal principles and arrangements to accommodate two kinds of ethnic groupings despite its Communist reluctance to do so. They include:

1. autonomous regions such as Tibet, Sinkiang and Mongolia which serve the non-Han populations that rim the country to the northwest and south;

2. tribal federations serving the non-Han tribal groups to the northeast.

While in both cases the autonomy is of the Communist style with all its limitations (Maoist principles are not too different from Leninist ones), even this limited autonomy is worthy of note.

India

1. A federation of 17 states and nine Union Territories which appears quite stable, especially now that the states have been reorganized on an ethnolinguistic basis wherever serious demands of that nature have been raised, and in one case on a religious basis, to give the Sikhs a state of their own. While seemingly centralized with regard to certain aspects of policy-making, the federal system is particularly attuned to providing cultural home rule and autonomy for ethnic, linguistic and religious and other interests within its framework. This is very important in the Indian setting.

2. India is of particular interest because states representing particular ethno-linguistic groupings often provide services to people of the same grouping outside of the state boundaries, either as

individual states or, where there are several states representing the same grouping, through joint programs or institutions. Thus school systems for different ethno-linguistic groups exist in major cities sponsored by the different states or groups of states.

3. In addition, India has devised arrangements to accomodate special situations which demonstrate the flexibility of federal principles. For example, with the division of Punjab into two states, the capital city of Chandigar became a Union Territory so that it could serve as the capital of both. The government buildings were literally divided in half to do so.

4. Several Union Territories are actually frameworks for local federations of relatively primitive tribes.

Iran

Once considered by outsiders to be a classic example of a homogeneous nation-state, since the fall of the Shah in 1978, Iran has been revealed as a state with strong ethnic minorities now actively demanding regional autonomy. The Islamic republican constitution provides for elected regional councils to serve those minorities but not autonomy.

Israel

1. A compound of ethno-religious communities, each state-recognized and aided, with powers in the fields of religion, culture, language, and matters of personal status.

2. Consociational arrangements linking the various "camps" and parties into which the Jewish majority is divided, at least in theory.

3. Municipal home rule for Arab cities and villages in the administered territories.

Japan

As result of the American occupation and the constitution written for Japan by the United States, the Japanese prefectures have been strengthened and given elected legislatures and governors of their own in a manner somewhat similar to the Italian regions. Most domestic functions in Japan are actually handled by the prefectures or local governments, often as agents of the central government.

Lebanon

Until the civil war, a consociational state with rule shared by the several confessional communities, each of which maintained a kind of internal self-government in many fields. Now the country is divided into three regions: a Syrian-dominated region under nominal control of the Lebanese government, a Christian-controlled enclave in the north, and a Christian-controlled region under the protection of Israel along Lebanon's southern border. The country's future is unclear except that unless it is fully incorporated by Syria, some kind of federal or consociational arrangement probably will be reestablished out of necessity.

Federation of Malaysia

A federation with two sets of relationships between the constituent states and the federal government.

1.   The nine states of the Malay peninsula, the original federation of Malaya, stand in a classic federal relationship with the general government.

2.   The two states on the island of Borneo which subsequently joined the federation enjoy greater powers and hence greater autonomy.

Nepal

Originally a group of petty principalities, it was united in the late eighteenth and nineteenth centuries but retained much of the basis for the old system because of the separation of populations among the valleys within the Himalaya mountains. As a result, it has a three-tier system of indirectly elected councils that, in theory, at least, is designed to encourage local autonomy.

Pakistan

A four state federal system even after the secession of East Pakistan, rather unstable, with continuing problems between the general government and the provinces plus, in some cases, among tribes within the provinces, but surviving as a system nonetheless.

Singapore

This personally-governed city-state fosters a kind of communal cultural autonomy in an urban setting.

Sri Lanka

The 1978 constitution defined it as a unitary state with a decentralized administration, two national languages, Sinhala and Tamil, and an electoral system based on proportional representation and multi-member constituencies to accommodate the island's Tamil minority.

United Arab Emirates

The one functioning federal system in the Arab world, and the only one to have taken hold. It consists of seven sheikdoms and represents a particularly interesting kind of power-sharing since few functions are actually undertaken by the general government. Instead, what passes for a general government parcels out common tasks to different emirates, which then take responsibility for their implementation throughout the federation. This could be a useful model to explore, especially considering that it is an Arab one.

Australia and Oceania

Australia

A classic federation. On the countrywide plane, it has no features of special interest other than the fact that it is quite successful. More interesting is the borough system of metropolitan organization that possibly could be useful in designing a solution for Jerusalem.

Cook Islands–New Zealand

An associated state relationship, with New Zealand the associate power and the Cook Islands the associate state.

Republic of the Philippines

Although designed as a centralized state, the islands have varying degrees of *de facto* home rule and there is also an off again–on again *de jure* autonomous status for the Moro Provinces in southern Mindanao.

New Hebrides

Formerly A British-French condominium, since August 1980 a decentralized state; each island has considerable autonomy.

Papua/New Guinea

A federated system. Some of the offshore island groups attached to the new state enjoy constitutionally guaranteed autonomy.

Fiji

A consociational arrangement prevails between the native Fijians and the descendants of Indian contract laborers who are now a majority of the local population.

Solomon Islands

A new state established as a decentralized republic with each island having almost complete self-rule in all domestic matters.

Europe

Andorra

This polity in the Pyrenees mountains is formally under the joint rule of the President of France, as successor to the French King, and the Bishop of Urgel in Spain. In fact, rule is exercised locally through local institutions, including an assembly of all male citizens and a small elected council, with the two nominal rulers maintaining limited oversight and, in effect, a mutual check on one another to preserve Andorran independence.

Austria

1.   Austria is a federation of nine *Lander*, all of which are equal in their powers vis-a-vis a strong general government.

2.   The Burgenland includes special arrangements for its linguistic minority.

Belgium

After prolonged constitutional crisis, Belgium has reconstituted itself as a quasi-federal state consisting of three primary regions based upon linguistic differences of the country's two cultural communities, the Flemings and the Walloons. The actual structure is more complicated than that, since it has been built upon an earlier structure in which the provinces and communes of Belgium retained very great powers of self-government and the central government actually functioned as little more than a collective holding company. In addition, a German-speaking minority is also accommodated through a further territorial division of powers. The resolution of the Belgian conflict is of particular interest because it represents one of the first apparently successful efforts to come to grips with the new ethnic nationalism of the post-World War II period. Belgium is also a consociational polity.

Cyprus

The 1960 constitution provided for a consociational distribution of power among the Greek majority and the Turkish minority with the cultural rights of each group provided for and certain offices within the general government guaranteed to each. This constitution was the result of an explicit rejection of territorial division. It failed to satisfy either party, each for its own reasons. The Turkish invasion brought about a *de facto* partition of the island designed to force a federal solution. Strictly speaking, the parties to the Cyprus conflict have not yet concluded on a particular form of regime but it seems clear that they will perforce adopt some form of federal solution, probably a two-unit federation following the Turkish plan because of the power of the Turkish army, although the Greeks have suggested a multi-unit federation. *De facto*, a two-unit federation exists without an effective general government.

Czechoslovakia

A two-unit federation of Czech and Slovak republics, carefully bound together through a single, highly-centralized Communist party. Essentially, federalism is designed to provide a certain amount of home rule, particularly for the Slovaks.

Denmark

1.   While Denmark is formally a unitary state, the position of the local government units is established in the constitution in such a way as to give them the primary and almost exclusive responsibility for the delivery of services with the national government serving almost exclusively as a policy-making and standard-setting body. This tendency has been strengthened in recent years as a result of constitutional and administrative reforms.

2.   The Faroe Islands and Greenland stand in a federacy relationship with Denmark, the latter since the passage of a 1979 referendum.

Note: The Nordic Union, which embraces Denmark, Finland, Iceland, Norway, and Sweden, resembles the Benelux arrangement in its general character but has certain unique features of its own which make it worth examining with regard to sharing of functions on an intergovernmental regional basis.

Finland

1.   Like Denmark, the Finnish state is structured so as to give local governments a strong constitutional position and primary responsibility for most governmental activities within the state framework2.   The Aaland Islands in the Gulf of Bothnia between Finland and Sweden, while formally a Finnish county, actually have a status equivalent to that of an associated state, guaranteed by Russia and Sweden. As Swedish-speaking territory of strategic importance, the Swedes have a major interest in the inhabitants and the Russians have a major interest in keeping the islands out of Swedish hands. Consequently, the territory has been given this particular status within Finland, which conquered the islands sev-

eral centuries ago. Of particular interest are the provisions as to who can. obtain citizenship in the islands, land purchase restrictions, and the structure of the governing institutions.

France

France itself provides no examples of internal self-rule or autonomy even though it has very real ethnic groups within its boundaries who are now demanding same. Whatever regional and local government structures it has, have very limited formal powers, plus whatever they are able to gain through participation in the highly centralized French political system. The French overseas possessions, on the other hand, for the most part have self-rule through locally elected assemblies with the governors appointed by the ruling power. France is a partner in two condominiums: Andorra and the New Hebrides.

Federal Republic of Germany

1. A classic federation with substantial powers granted to the *lander* (states) and based upon a relatively sharply maintained constitutional division of powers in which shared powers are also constitutionally defined in very precise terms. Particularly interesting because the states range from relatively large entities, in terms of both territory and population, to city-states such a as Hamburg. The federal government is so structured that the states as states have a major voice in federal decisions as well as in their own internal matters.

2. West Berlin is attached to the Federal Republic in the manner of an associated state because of the requirements of the four occupying powers. The form of this association is of significance because of the reason why it has come about, namely the role of international forces in shaping the internal constitution of the two entities on what is a permanently temporary basis. On one level, Berlin is treated like any other *Land* in the federation, but it must reenact all federal legislation through its own legislative body because of its legal status as an associated state.

Italy

After World War II, under pressure from the Allied powers, the Italians wrote a regional structure into their constitution. They borrowed the Spanish approach to regional self-government as a basis for satisfying those regionally-based national aspirations which had been suppressed in the process of the unification of Italy in the previous century. While all of Italy is divided into regions, the regions themselves are of two orders.

1. Five regions, either islands like Sicily and Sardinia or territories on the country's northern periphery with special ethnic, historical, or geographic circumstances, are constitutionally autonomous in the sense that they are virtually the equivalent of states in a federal system. The two island regions are designed to preserve regional ways of life while the three territorially contiguous regions were established to accommodate ethnolinguistic minorites. In the latter cases, the government in Rome has been ambivalent

and has encouraged their "Italianization" as a matter of national policy.

2. The other 15 regions have more limited powers of regional governance, something more than municipal powers but less than the status of federated states, reflecting the presumably less sharply pronounced differences between Tuscany, Lombardy, Piedmont, and the like. Since each of these regions has a relatively strong sense of identity, their reality extends beyond their formal governmental powers.

Of particular interest is the fact that the Communist Party of Italy has captured control of a number of regional governments through which it has attempted to demonstrate its ability to govern responsibly and well to the Italian public thus leading to their involvement in the Italian political system in what has, to date, proved to be a positive (if, perhaps, dangerous) way.

3. Special arrangements for cultural autonomy have been introduced for minority linguistic groups.

4. In 1978, at the initiative of Venice (Veneto Region), an interstate regional grouping for economic development involving three regions in Italy, four Austrian *bundeslaender*, two Yugoslav republics, and one West German *Land* was established.

Liechtenstein

This principality is one of the original small units in the Holy Roman Empire that could have become a canton of Switzerland but which did not want to give up its princely institutions in order to do so, a requirement in that democratic republic (and one that points to the fact that forms of regime must be the same in close federal relationships). Instead, Liechtenstein became an associated state linked to Switzerland for certain purposes but retaining greater autonomy for others. This arrangement has permitted both to retain their particular orientations and forms of regime.

The Netherlands

1. The Netherlands constitution opens with a declaration that the polity is a unitary decentralized monarchy. This provision is the result of a constitutional compromise reached in the period after the Napoleonic conquest between defenders of the rights of the eleven provinces which had previously constituted the Netherlands Confederation and the revolutionaires who sought a strong central government. The provinces and municipalities retain strong self-rule powers by virtue of the constitutional system and the informal elements linked with it, powers that have been somewhat reduced or reoriented in the twentieth century, primarily as a result of the conflict between Socialists, Calvinists, and Catholics which has led to a consociational political system within the formal framework. Today the consociational arrangements seem to be declining while the territorial units remain strong within a highly integrated framework.

2. The former Netherlands colony of Curacao is linked with it in a federacy or associated state relationship, much like that of the

United States and Puerto Rico. Suriname was also linked to the Netherlands in that way, but recently opted for independence.
Note: The links among the Benelux countries are worth examining as reflecting other relevant possibilities for shared arrangements. The links are something more than a cultural league or common market, but something less than a federated polity.

Norway

Spitzbergen is fully incorporated into Norway but the U.S.S.R. has extra-territorial mining rights on the islands guaranteed by the treaty establishing their status, which it exploits extensively.

Poland

Poland has formally decentralized internal planning and administration to regional governments.

Portugal

The Azores and Madeira Islands have been given substantial powers of self-rule along the lines of Northern Ireland in the United Kingdom, in response to their demands for even greater autonomy. The final details of that arrangement have yet to be worked out under the present Portuguese democratic regime.

Rumania

In theory, the cultural and linguistic rights of the Hungarian minority are constitutionally protected and maintained through a communal council. In fact, standard pressures toward homogenization common in Communist countries prevail.

Spain

Regional demands for autonomy have a long history in modern Spain, and in fact date back to the pre-modern period when Spain was a united monarchy rather than a unitary state. The Spanish constitution of 1931 is considered the classic model of the regionalist approach to self-rule which provides regional autonomy on a constitutionally devolved rather than a federal basis. Under it, autonomous regional governments functioned until suppressed by the Franco regime. Post-Franco Spain has revived regional autonomy for Catalonia and the Basque provinces. Its new constitution includes provisions for establishing autonomous regions throughout the country, as mutually agreed upon by local inhabitants and the Madrid government, more or less on the model of the 1931 republican constituion. The Spanish approach has been to grant each region its own statue of autonomy tailored to its particular situation or based upon a particular set of compromises negotiated between Madrid and the regional leadership. Andalusia is close to acquiring autonomy. By the end of 1978, pre-autonomous status had been granted to ten regions and regional councils established in each.

Switzerland

The classic federal system, it is significant in a number of ways:
1. the small total size and population of the country and the number of small cantons into which it is divided (in effect 26, with the 26th, the Jura, carved out of the Canton of Berne in 1978),

ranging in size from a few tens of thousands to several hundred thousand population;

2.   the way in which a federal structure has been used to accommodate a variety of linguistic and religious differences so as to mitigate the effects of serious cleavages;

3.   the way in which the Swiss Confederation grew during centuries of prolonged warfare, through an expanding series of bilateral and multilateral pacts, compacts, or covenants entered into over a period of more than 500 years, formed or modified as conditions warranted;

4.   the device of demi-cantons as a means of handling new demands for self-rule within the federation most recently applied in the case of the Jura. (Switzerland seems to be accommodating the Jura conflict much more easily than a unitary state like France, for example, is able to accommodate the Bretons, or even a state like Spain is able to deal with the Basques, precisely because of its commitment to principles of power-sharing on a territorial basis.)

5.   the links Switzerland has with its neighbors, particularly in the Basel and Geneva regions, to provide shared facilities on a local regional basis across each other's borders; and

6.   the relationship between Switzerland and Liechtenstein (see above).

Note: While Switzerland is often rejected as a proper example because of its reputation as a peaceful neutral, it should be recalled that the Swiss fought with their neighbors for some 600 years or more on a continuing basis in order to achieve their present framework, and the framework emerged out of the struggle itself.

U.S.S.R.

This is the classic Communist federation, the original expression of Leninist doctrine in which federalism is deemed a transitional phenomenon designed to provide for cultural autonomy until the new Communist man energes. In fact, federal arrangements have become deeply entrenched as reflected in the recent abortive effort to weaken them through constitutional change. The Soviet system is more complex than most federations since its primary purpose is to accommodate ethnic differences in a large, highly diverse country.

1.   The principal units of the federation are the 15 union republics, each of which is theoretically sovereign, even to the point of having the right of secession, although in fact all are dominated by the highly centralized Communist Party. Of the 15, the Russian Soviet Federated Socialist Republic embraces over three-fourths of the total area of the U.S.S.R.

2.   Four of the union republics are further divided into 20 autonomous Soviet socialist republics and eight autonomous regions.

3.   In addition, the Russian Soviet Federal Socialist Republic has ten national districts. Each of these categories represents a particular arrangement designed to provide certain kinds of home

rule for different nationalities within the overall Communist system. Needless to say, the Communist Party holds the whole system tightly together.

The United Kingdom

As its official name suggests, the U.K. is a union, in its case a compound of various forms of local autonomy within a nominally centralized parliamentary system, as follows:

1. Scotland is a separate country, united with England and Wales by the Act of Union of 1707, through which it retains its own legal system, established church, fixed number of representatives in the British parliament, and home rule in a substantial number of areas, including the structuring of the local governments within its boundaries, education, and various social and technical functions. There exists a Scottish Office in London and Edinburgh, in which are concentrated most administrative functions exercised separately by Scotland. A Secretary of State for Scotland sits in the British Cabinet. Because of the separate legal system, Scotland has its own comprehensive system for the administration of justice, including courts and police.

2. Wales is a separate country that was absorbed into the United Kingdom, on far less favorable terms, in the fifteenth century. Consequently, it has less in the way of reserved powers and the degree of home rule available to it has fluctuated. It is presently increasing. The Welsh Office is responsible for the administration of many programs for Wales and special powers are given to Wales in the cultural field, the major area through which Welsh nationalism is expressed. However, Wales does not possess a separate legal system or established church.

3. Northern Ireland was created as a separate political entity as a result of the partition of Ireland in the early 1920s. At that time, it was given substantial home rule, including a legislative body of its own and reduced representation in the British parliament in return for the broad grant of powers to its own legislature. For all intents and purposes, it had the powers of an American state until the disturbances of the past decade led the British parliament to revoke that devolution of powers and abolish the structure that accompanied it, a power which the British parliament had reserved to itself and which made the arrangement in Northern Ireland a matter of home rule rather than federalism. However, it is an accepted principle of the British constitution that Ulster is entitled to self-government or autonomy, even if the form of that autonomy and the institutions which embody it are determined by act of the British parliament. The parliament itself has consistently emphasized local efforts within Ulster to develop suitable institutions, retaining a veto over the final character of those institutions. Efforts continue to rebuild Ulster's political structure.

4. The Isle of Man is essentially a self-governing state irrevocably associated with the United Kingdom. The British parliament has limited legislative authority over it and the Manx assembly func-

tions in almost sovereign capacity to control the internal affairs of the island, even to the point of issuing its own stamps. The relationship is best described as federacy or associated statehood.

5.   The Channel Islands—Jersey and Guernsey—have a status dating back to the feudal period which makes them, for all intents and purposes, associated states as well. While the British parliament nominally possesses greater powers of intervention, in fact a constitutional crisis would be provoked were it to exercise them.

6.   The major Scottish offshore island archipelagos, the Shetlands and the Orkneys, have substantial home rule within Scotland which is constitutionalized through a combination of traditional usages and formal legislative enactments.

7.   The remaining British colonial possessions, most of which are small entities if not islands, have mostly ceased to be colonies in the traditional sense and now possess substantial powers of self-government or home rule with elected legislative bodies sharing power with governors appointed by the Crown, frequently from among the local residents.

8.   Proposals are also being aired for the division of England itself into regions with their own institutions of administration and governance and possessing home rule powers. Among other things, this has encouraged the resurgence of Cornish demands for self-rule, since Cornwall also has a certain traditional status as a country within the British Isles.

Note: In March 1979 Scottish and Welsh voters rejected acts of devolution submitted to them by the British Parliament which would have established legislative assemblies for Scotland and Wales with limited powers.

Yugoslavia

1.   The People's Federal Republic of Yugoslavia consists of six national republics linked together in what has become increasingly more of a confederation than a federation. The federal government is structured so as to make decision-making a joint inter-republican matter. Thus the formal locus of power is increasingly with the republics,and even the structure of the League of Communists (the formal name of the Yugoslav Communist Party) reflects this.

2.   In addition, there are two autonomous regions within Serbia with special powers of their own which have evolved in recent years to become almost identical to those of the republics.

3.   The republics are further divided into communes with substantial municipal powers that are protected in the federal constitution on the theory that the federal compound in Yugoslavia involves local, republic, and federal arenas equally.

North America

Canada

1.   A federation of ten provinces and two territories in which the federal government formally possesses all powers not specifically

granted the provinces by the Canadian constitution (the British North American Act). In reality, the provinces have become very powerful.

2.   Since the 1960s there has been an informally recognized special relationship with Quebec that increases its autonomy *de facto*. Canada is officially multi-cultural but Quebec is the only autonomous unit dominated by a minority culture. It refers to itself as l'Etat de Quebec and its legislative body as the National Assembly. The attempt to accommodate Quebec has increased the autonomy of the other provinces as well.

3.   The territories embrace vast, sparsely populated areas of Canada's north and consequently have home rule powers but under federal control.

United Mexican States

1.   Formally a federation like the U.S.A. In fact, its 29 states exercise limited autonomy on what is, in effect, a home rule basis under the aegis of a strong federal government.

2.   Mexico City, the capital, is located in a federal district.

3.   Mexico has two territories which have more limited home rule powers because they are underdeveloped.

United States of America

1.   The classic modern federation, consisting of 50 states formally possessing all powers not delegated to the federal government, actually exercising substantial powers albeit within the framework of a strong federal government.

2.   Washington, the capital city, is located in a federal district.

3.   The U.S. maintains separate federacy (associated state) arrangements with Puerto Rico and the Northern Mariana Islands, whereby the two associated states are internally autonomous while linked to the United States as their associate power. A third federacy arrangement is presently in the process of being implemented with the Federated States of Micronesia, a local federation of Pacific islands that have been under American control. Each such arrangement has its own character and constitutional framework.

4.   There are home rule arrangements for such possessions as American Samoa whereby local residents elect their own governor and legislature and possess substantial powers of internal self-government.

5.   Over 40 states provide for constitutional home rule for counties and/or municipalities, whereby local voters within those jurisdictions may elect to adopt their own charters and thereby acquire powers of home rule protected by the state constitution.

South America

Argentina

A federation in which most power is lodged in the federal capital. The states are essentially vehicles for home rule and for local oligarchies to maintain a power base.

Brazil
1.   A federation in which the powers of the 22 states depend upon the character of the national regime at any given moment. The States remain strong politically in any case.
2.   Brasilia, the capital, is located in a federal district.
3.   Brazil has 5 territories.

Colombia
A decentralized unitary state with strong provisions for provincial home rule, including elected provincial councils with significant powers. Decentralization is maintained to the degree that it is by virtue of the strong demands for autonomy that exist in some of the major provinces.

East Caribbean Regional Arrangements
The failure of the West Indies Federation did not lead to the demise of federal arrangements in the eastern Caribbean. Instead a variety of regional arrangements have been initiated as the islands became independent. Five such arrangements stand out:
1.   Caribbean Community and Common Market (CARICOM).
2.   East Caribbean Currency Authority—issues common currency for seven island states.
3.   East Caribbean Supreme Court—the appellate court for the above states.
4.   Organization of East Caribbean States (OECS)—a coordinating council of ministers.
5.   East Caribbean Common Market (ECCM)—associated with CARICOM.
By 1979, virtually all of the former British island colonies had moved through associated statehood to full independence within this network of institutions.

Venezuela
A federation of 20 states and 2 territories formally similar to the U.S.A. Its states have real home rule powers but no more than that because development resources remain concentrated in the hands of the federal government. Various federal agencies are established on statewide basis to manage state and local development.

Note: All Latin American countries emphasize municipal autonomy and generally have strong provisions in their constitutions to that end, but these are primarily norms to be achieved rather than maps of existing reality except insofar as underdeveloped national governments do not assert their authority over municipal oligarchies. Because Latin American municipalities are not separated on an urban-rural basis but combine urban and rural settlement in relatively large municipal units many of the municipios are the size of Judea and Samaria together or are even larger.

Part Three
Realities

Israeli Administration and Self-Rule in the Territories
The Israeli Perspective
Maj. Gen. Rephael Vardi

The policy regarding the territories was formulated and developed immediately after the Six Day War, and based primarily on four principles. The first was formally entitled, "Restoration and Normalization of Civilian Life," later retitled, "Normalization and Development." The second principle was called "Maintenance of Security and Public Order." Principle three was given no formal title, but it concerns self-government for the territories. As early as 15 November 1967, the Israeli government had decided to allow and encourage the population to manage its own affairs as far as possible. I shall concentrate mainly on this decision and how it was implemented by the Israeli Military Administration in Judea and Samaria.

The principle of self-government soon evolved two maxims. The first was non-intervention in the daily life of the population, and the second was non-presence of Israelis as long as security is not impaired. These maxims followed logically from the main policy regarding the civilian population: that as far as possible Israel should encourage the population to manage its own affairs.

The Military Government or, more specifically, Military Commander is invested with the powers of chief legislator as well as of chief executive of the government. He also holds judiciary powers, as he is responsible for the administration of justice, including the authority to appoint and dismiss justices. According to Proclamation No. 2, concerning law and administration, promulgated by the Commander of the I.D.F. in the West Bank on June 7, 1967, all the powers of the former sovereign were to be taken over by the Military Commander, including the powers of the King of Jordan, the legislative powers of the parliament (to the extent that parliament participates in legislation in Jordan), and the powers of the Council of Ministers of the government. In this proclamation, the Military Commander declared that the law in force on the day of his assumption of these powers shall remain in force unless amended by him and subject to any changes that may arise from the institution of I.D.F. rule in the area.

To what extent was there devolution of power and authority to

171

the local population through the classic division of the three powers— legislation, judiciary and administration?

Legislation: The chief legislator is the Military Commander.
Legislation is almost entirely divided into two areas, the first of
which is the legislation of security matters concerning the armed
forces, its installations and members, and public security in the
territories. In this security legislation the inhabitants (Jews and
Arabs alike) have not participated, and their advice has not been
sought. The sole authority remains the Military Commander, who
enacts laws according to necessity for security purposes.

On the other hand, the policy with respect to legislation on
civilian matters, involving amendments or changes in existing Jordanian laws, has been to adhere as far as possible to the principles of international law and not to tamper with the prevailing
Jordanian law. The only exceptions would be if there arose an
absolute necessity for action to maintain public order, to promote
the welfare of the population, to effect an efficient and good
government, or to meet new developments for which the Jordanian laws had not provided, in order to oblige the population itself to
effect changes for its own sake. For instance, when in 1971 there
arose a dispute among three towns, Bethlehem, Beit Jalla, and Beit
Sahur, which endangered the regular water supply to the inhabitants, the Military Commander responded to the demands of the
mayors of these towns and established by decree a common
water authority for them within the framework of Jordanian law.
The Commander took this step after consultations and discussions with the mayors and their legal advisers, who could hardly
agree among themselves about the provisions governing the
water authority.

Initiative to amend Jordanian laws sometimes comes from Military Government departments. There were instances in which
the law had been found lacking, and amendment or change was
necessary in order to meet economic developments, an improved
standard of living, adjustment to open borders, and the free movement of persons and goods between Israel and the West Bank (for
example, the standardization of road safety regulations). In all
such cases, amendments of the existing laws have been promulgated with great caution and care in adherence to international
law. Otherwise, the existing policy is not to touch Jordanian law.

In all these instances, although the Military Commander was
not obliged to act, and no formally constituted body exists, we
usually took advice from those among the population concerned
about the amendments, such as the mayors, etc. The decision
was, however, in the hands of the Military Commander. All this
applies to major legislation.

In addition, the law empowers the mayors of the municipalities to enact by-laws, and the Military Administration encourages
them to act accordingly. The fact is that they were not always
willing or ready, for a variety of reasons, to initiate and enact by-

laws, even when these were vital to the municipality. In order to facilitate the enactment of by-laws by the mayors, the Military Commander enacted certain by-laws which each and every municipality may, if it wishes, adopt as its own. For instance, responding to a request by some of the municipalities, the Military Commander enacted a law enabling the municipality to establish a municipal magistrate or court which would deal with offenses against municipal by-laws committed within the limits of the town. The proceeds of the hearings—fines, etc.—would create additional income for the municipality. In conclusion to this point on legislation, since, there has seldom been legislation on civilian affairs, the participation of the population in the proceedings has been limited.

The Judiciary: Only one of the former powers of the King of Jordan has remained under the authority of the Military Commander—the appointment of judges. The local courts have retained their competence to adjudicate all civilian cases and criminal offenses. The status and competence of the local courts has not been changed except for one major amendment which increased their authority and independence. Since the Jordanian system of government is a centralized one, the highest court was located in Amman. Appeal and other cases from the West Bank courts were referred to the Court of Cassation for final judgment. Therefore the Military Commander empowered the Court of Appeal, first sitting in Jerusalem and later, after Jerusalem was unified, in Ramallah, to exercise the powers of the Court of Cassation as well as the authority of the High Court of Justice.

Once the judges were appointed, there was no intervention whatsoever in the judicial process. The offices of Attorney General and district attorney remained in local hands. Prosecution is at their full discretion, as is execution of the decisions of the court.

Two more points deserve emphasis: 1) the appointment of judges is done after consulting the President of the Court of Appeal; 2) there has not been not a single dismissal of a judge in the West Bank.

The Civil Administration: We inherited the Jordanian system of administration, which, was centralized. Branches of the various departments of the ministries in Amman operated in the West Bank, down to the district and sub-district levels. Their authority was limited, and they acted according to directives and instructions from the center in Amman.

Another structure of the Jordanian centralized administration was the office of District Governor (in Arabic, the *Muhafez*), which was responsible for security and public order, and had a certain power of supervision over civilian affairs, including the government departments operating in the district and the municipal corporations. Subordinate to the Muhafez were the *Mutazarif*, who was in charge of the sub-district with similar authority and the *Kaimekam*, the sub-district officer. Their major task was to observe and report on the loyalties of the local government officials, mayors and other leaders, to the regime in Amman. This structure of government has been abolished. Some of their responsibilities were invested in the District Military Commander.

The system of government established by the Military Government consisted of Israeli civilian officials representing the Israeli governmental departments. These officials operate within the framework of the Headquarters of the Military Government. To each of them has been delegated the authority of the appropriate former minister of the Jordanian government according to Jordanian law. For example, the officer in charge of agriculture under the Military Government has the powers and authority of the Minister of Agriculture in Jordan according to the prevailing Jordanian law. Only a few Israelis work under these officials, and the rest of the departments consist of former Jordanian officials or new local officials employed by the Israeli military government.

The administration consists of two layers: 1) the Central Headquarters in which Israeli civilian Military Government officers in charge of the departments operate; 2) the districts. The West Bank is divided into seven districts. The various governmental departments in the districts are managed by local Arab officials and staff. The Israeli officer mainly controls the budget and limits his involvement to policy, general directives, and supervision of the orderly and efficient operation of the department. He is not involved in the day-to-day work of the local governmental departments. Virtually all the local departments in the districts now have much more authority and power than they had when they were discharging the same functions under the Jordanian government.

In his daily life, the West Bank citizen meets only local Arab officials whenever he requires government services such as health, welfare, and education, or when he pays for these services through income and property tax collectors. Even if the Israeli officers are willing to intervene more thoroughly in the work of the departments, they are virtually unable to do so, because they are very few in number. At present about 350 Israeli officials operate in the West Bank of Jordan in civilian government, in contrast to about 11,000 Arab officials. For example, the department of education consists of about 20 Israeli officials, including clerks, accountants, and so forth, with only four Israeli supervisors. The number of Arab teachers is about 7,000. One does not need much imagination to envisage the scope of supervision when the number of supervisors does not exceed three or four.

For all practical purposes, on the district level, the civilian government is managed by the local Arab officials.

Local Government

Although it was not part of their official functions, the mayors became the primary representatives of the population to the milary government on matters far beyond strictly municipal affairs. They bring to the attention of the military government in the district or to the commander of the area all kinds of problms, requests, and compl ints of the citizens of their municipalities and villages.

Immediately in June 1967, we restored and reactivated all municipal corporations existing at that time. Then, in response to demand from the population—and in accordance with Jordanian law—we established two new municipalities, Yata and Kabatya.

The municipalities continue to function according to Jordanian law and their competence was extended. Under the Municipalities Law, the municipal corporations are invested with vast authority. In fact, only part of these were exercised under the Jordanian regime. For instance, the law empowers the municipalities to construct hospitals and clinics and operate them. Their competence extends to education and culture as well. In fact, those matters were managed by the Jordanian government.

Under the Israeli Military Government, municipalities have extended their powers and authority in three ways: 1) informally, they extended their influence and representation in a variety of affairs to villages beyond the boundaries of the town; 2) the boundaries of most of the municipalities have been extended due to the demands of the mayors—both the town planning area and the town boundaries (the reasons for this were rapid economic and public services development, construction of thousands of new houses, roads, etc. under the Israeli Military Government during this period); 3) we gave them more powers whenever they asked for them. Usually we were willing to invest them with more authority than they were ready to take, but we avoided coercion. The reason for their reluctance was quite obvious. Generally, more authority meant competence to collect more municipal taxes. It was of course more popular to demand grants from the Military Government and from abroad than to tax the citizens, especially under the Military Government.

Most of the towns have their own electricity and water supply systems which were extended by the Military Government. Some of the towns supplied water and electricity to the surrounding villages, and some were connected to the Israeli electricity system, but only when they requested it. Israeli generated electricity was sold to them in bulk, and the municipalities distributed to the town and surrounding villages, as they did formerly. Since Israeli electricity was much cheaper than that of local power stations, the municipalities continued to sell at the former rates and increased their income considerably.

I wish to stress another point, perhaps the most important one, about local government. There are many interpretations of the development of self-rule. At the end of the nineteenth century and early in the twentieth century, self-rule was still considered to be the amount of participation by the population in the government of its own country, i.e., the extent of democratization of government and local institutions. In the light of this interpretation, we, perhaps, for the first time in the history of the region, effected elections by the population to local government organs under so-called occupation. The first elections were held in 1972, strictly according to the Jordanian law. Then later on, in 1976, the population eligible to vote elected their own councillors.

The elections were organized and held by local election committees without any interference by Israeli officials. According to the Jordanian law, the government has the privilege of appointing two un-elected councillors to the elected municipal council, as well as to appoint the mayor. We did not take advantage of these provisions, and in no case was a councillor appointed to the elected councils of the municipalities. We introduced the practice of the mayor being elected by his fellow councillors, both in the 1972 elections and again in 1976.

Security is one of the basic problems in the area and dominates matters of policy. Even when security was involved, however, we preferred not to intervene in the election results. In 1972, for example, one of the councillors elected to the newly formed municipality of Yata had just recently been released from jail after serving a long sentence for participating in terrorist activities. In spite of that, he was not denied his candidacy to the council and then, having been elected, his membership. Moreover, his fellow councillors elected him as mayor. We then faced the question of whether to permit a man convicted of terrorism to become mayor and represent the population. We decided not to intervene, and the man became the mayor of the town of Yata.

The 1972 elections were held strictly according to Jordanian law. We were severely criticized in Israel as well as abroad for not amending the law in order to extend the franchise to women and allow them to participate in the elections. In 1976 we amended the law on two points: one, granting the franchise to women, and the other, relaxing some property tax regulations which limited the number of eligible voters. Through these two amendments, the number of voters rose from about 32,000 in 1972 to roughly 88,000 voters in 1976, over one-third of whom were women. If self-rule is considered to be the participation of the local population in establishing their own local government organs, these elections permitted the utmost expression of self-rule.

We also reactivated the village councils, and today almost 90 village councils are operating. In 1975 elections were held to the village councils as well, applying the same rules as those used for the municipal elections. In addition, elections were held to the chambers of commerce whenever requested by the members, again according to Jordanian law.

Culture, Religion, Education

Autonomy is often defined in terms of culture. It is measured by the degree to which a certain population can live in its own cultural environment, manage its own education in its own language, and control its religious affairs. In this sphere, self-rule or self-management of the population has achieved its greatest independence.

Education: Education is free of charge. The Military Government employs the teachers, pays their salaries, constructs new schools, furnishes them and distributes free books. The Jordanian curriculum is used, and the sole language of instruction is Arabic. Hebrew is not taught in government and private schools, not even as a second language. The books are the Jordanian texts. In 1967, immediately after the Six Day War, the Israeli Ministry of Education, struck by the anti-Israeli and anti-Semitic contents of some of the textbooks used in the West Bank and Gaza, decided to introduce the Israeli Arab program of studies. The immediate reaction of the local leaders, teachers, and students was the declaration of a strike. They did not open the schools on the scheduled date. The Military Government realized that there was a genuine apprehension among the Arabs that the Israelis were trying to intervene in their own education and culture and impose Israeli views on them. The government then decided that it would only review the books and the Jordanian program of study, and unless it found something which was anti-Israeli or anti-Semitic, it would continue to allow them to teach according to the Jordanian texts and curriculumm. We reviewed hundreds of books and only partially censored 58 of them.

A committee of local educators called "The Committee for High School Examinations" was established. Formally, the Committee is responsible for the preparation of the exams, but it virtually directs education in the West Bank, introducing changes in the programs according to changes effected in Jordan. Here we see how complicated the self-rule issue is. Their problem is not only with Israel, because they still receive directives from Jordan in almost all matters effecting changes in curriculae and exams, in adherence to developments in Jordanian educational programs. Due to the absence of universities in the West Bank until 1972, the graduates had to continue their studies in Amman or in universities in other Arab countries. The Jordanian government issued Jordanian graduation certificates to the high school students that were examined in the West Bank, and only then were they admitted to the Arab universities.

During the entire period, therefore, education has been managed by the local educators, while the Military Government provided the budget and all the necessary equipment.

Religious Affairs: From the very beginning, the Military Government was anxious not to interfere in any religious affairs. It absolutely safeguarded religious freedom, free access to the holy places, and so forth. The justices of the religious courts, the Shariah courts, according to Jordanian law, are appointed by the King. The

Military Commander did not demand to appoint them. They were appointed by the self-nominated Chief Justice in Jerusalem (the Kadi Kudat) who at most notified the Military Government, on his own initiative, about the new appointments. He did not ask for approval, but just forwarded the notifications.

This non-interference applies to all religious matters and to the relationship between the military government and the Moslem religious establishment. In fact, the religious establishment, including the courts, the self-appointed Supreme Moslem Council, and the management of the Ukaf estates, enjoy under Israeli government far more independence in the management of their religious as well as temporal affairs than under the Jordanian government.

Several attempts were made, mainly on Israeli initiative, to extend administrative self-government. The first was as early as 1968. We conducted negotiations and talks with the local leaders, with the aim of establishing an all-West Bank administration or executive of local leaders. This has not materialized. Later on, in 1969, talks were resumed, among them a program for restoring the function of the *Muhafez* and appointing local leaders as heads of the *Muhafeza* with full authority, according to the law, including internal public security matters and local police. This has not materialized. Throughout the period these negotiations have been resumed, but without result due to threats from the Jordanian Government and the PLO.

Another attempt was made by handing over more authority to local Arab officials, creation of all-West Bank functions, and appointment of Arab directors general to government departments which in due time would take over from the Israeli officials. This endeavor has not been successful so far. Although some authority was delegated and a few all-West Bank functions created, most of the Arab officials were unwilling to take part in this program. There were cases in which good administration required an overall local manager-director; in the health services, for instance. In a few cases in which a local official has been appointed, such a person was usually called to Jordan and instructed not to accept or to resign if already appointed. All these efforts, which were mainly initiated by us to devolve more authority on local officials, by and large failed. In the management of civilian affairs we were ready to give full powers, including a certain control of the budget. (It should be remembered that the budget comes mainly from the government of Israel and not from local taxes.) Unfortunately, for reasons of Arab external and internal pressure, the population, leaders, mayors and government officials were unwilling to take more responsibility than that established in practice throughout the period.

Conclusion

In the realms of the judiciary, education, cultural and religious affairs, and local government, the population enjoys a great amount of self-government, both legally and in practice. In administration, it enjoys a certain degree of self-government, and to a much lesser degree in legislation. Regarding the future, a firm basis has been established for a local self-governing body, whenever it may be decided upon, to create an administration in the widest sense of the word.

It should be noted that the Israeli military authorities, were, during these twelve years, always ready to grant the population more independence and freedom in managing their affairs than the population was ready to accept. I have mentioned many endeavors that have not materialized, not because Israel was unwilling to devolve authority, but always because some external body, sometimes the Jordanians, sometimes the PLO, instructed local leaders to refuse.

Such was the case in the municipal elections of 1972. Jordan, the PLO, and other Arab countries demanded that the population should boycott the elections. The mass media, propaganda, threats, bribes, physical violence, were all harnessed to sabotage the elections. Usually, in civilian affairs we do not impose our will upon the population. But in the case of the elections of 1972, we had to use some measures of counter-pressure in Nablus only. In spite of that overwhelming opposition, the elections were held and carried out freely and smoothly in Samaria as well as in Judea. Hardly a month later, the Jordanian government recognized the elections and recognized the elected mayors under occupation. In 1976 no such problem arose. The Jordanian government and the PLO pushed forward their supporters to participate in the elections and present their candidacy.

Here we reach the crux of the problem. Throughout the twelve years, the population and the leaders were not free to formulate their independent opinion about their own present and future, because of external pressures by Jordan, the PLO, and others. It is interesting to point out that in this triangle of Jordan, the PLO, and Israel, the latter although present in the territory, is the least influential. The voice that is being heard and obeyed is that either of Jordan or of the PLO.

Note

The above presentation is not given in an official capacity. The preference throughout is for the term "administered" rather than "occupied" regarding the territories, as this is the accepted Israeli terminology.

Israeli Occupation and Self-Rule in the Territories
The Inhabitants' Perspective
Professor Emile A. Nakhleh

Some of my statements may bring discomfort to many readers. For this, I apologize. However, to be committed to peace, to be seriously involved in the peace process, and to be optimistic about the results, one must face the issues head on, unpleasant as they may be.

My discussion will consist of several parts:

- An overview of my research
- Basic assumptions
- Occupation as a system
- The inhabitants' reaction to the "self-rule" proposal
- Concluding remarks

My research, which is based on extensive interviews conducted in the West Bank and Gaza, focused on three topics: 1) the political and institutional infrastructures in the West Bank and Gaza; 2) the roles which these institutions would play in building a national entity once a political settlement is reached, and; 3) the specific issues and problems to be encountered in the initial post-settlement period.[1]

An Overview

For purposes of this study interviews were conducted with mayors, town managers, city councilmen, lawyers, professors, writers and representatives of charitable groups. The municipal interviews focused on the largest towns in the West Bank and the Gaza Strip: Gaza, Ramallah, al-Bireh, Nablus, Jenin and Hebron (al-Khalil). Data on the charitable groups were obtained primarily from Dr. Amin al-Khatib (Jerusalem), the head of the Federation of Charitable Societies. Related data were also obtained from the Office of Research and Documentation at Birzeit University, near Ramallah. Concerning economic and agricultural development, the available written data were supplemented by interviews with Arie Bregman at the Bank of Israel in Jerusalem and with Professor Hisham 'Awartani at the Khadduri Agricultural Institute in Tulkarm and more recently at al-Najah University in Nablus. Related issues were also discussed with professors at Birzeit University and in Ramallah, Hebron, Jerusalem and Gaza.

Interviews with municipal officials sought information relevant to the following ten questions:

- What is the existing municipal structure and how does it function?
- What are the operative laws and what is the source of municipal authority?
- Since municipalities are theoretically subject to Jordanian law and are in practice subject to military occupation, what is the functional relation between Jordanian law and military occupation in terms of municipal operations?
- What services do the municipalities offer?
- What are the major problems facing the municipalities? Are there problems common to the different municipalities?
- What are the major sources of municipal revenues and what are some of the serious budgetary problems they face?
- On the assumption that the municipalities would be called upon to play an expanded role in a transitional regime, what changes would have to be made?
- How soon and under what conditions would they be able to assume their new role?
- What type of economic development and economic projects would they undertake under the new regime?
- What are the major economic, social, demographic,and legal issues that should be included in the negotiating process?

With the charitable organizations, interviews were directed toward the following five questions:

- What are the major societies and what functions do they perform?
- What are the outstanding problems they face in their health, educational and welfare services?
- What functions would they perform under a new (transitional and posttransitional) regime?
- How would these services be integrated into the new regime once a national authority is established?
- What are the major economic and social issues that should be included in the negotiating process?

Those interviewed indicated with genuine enthusiasm that once a workable political process is put into effect, the basic economic, social, and legal problems can be solved. It is also possible, they indicated, for interstate linkages to be established once occupation comes to an end and they can participate freely in the process of transition.

Most likely to create friction during or after the negotiations, however, is the issue of land. Specifically, who owns what lands in the occupied areas? It is believed that Israel's Jewish National Fund has acquired through purchase and other means hundreds of thousands of acres in the West Bank since 1967. This is obviously in addition to the so-called state lands which Israeli authorities have confiscated for settlements, military posts, and other purposes. The expansion of metropolitan Jerusalem beyond the so-called green line in the areas of Shu'fat, Beit Hanina, Bethlehem, and Beit Jala is another example of the complex land question.

Basic Assumptions

In the course of these interviews it became apparent that before any changes can be made in the status quo, and before leaders of political and social organizations would be willing to cooperate in any new arrangement, the following conditions must be met:

1. Economic, social, and legal issues cannot be meaningfully discussed or ultimately resolved apart from the political question.

2. No political arrangement or settlement can be expected to endure without the cooperation of Palestinian community leaders in the West Bank and Gaza. While these leaders admit that the Palestinians are not an active partner in the negotiation process and that a settlement might be imposed upon them, they maintain that by apathy and non-cooperation they could render any imposed settlement ineffective.

3. Cooperation in solving non-political issues would be forthcoming only after a political arrangement acceptable to the Palestinians was underway. Furthermore, such cooperation would not materialize without the approval and encouragement of Palestinian leadership outside the West Bank and Gaza. The Palestine Liberation Organization (PLO), not necessarily any one leader, is perceived to be the only credible representative of Palestinians.

4. Perhaps the most adamantly and widely held position of the Palestinian leadership in the West Bank and Gaza, regardless of ideological affinity, is that to be acceptable the transitional regime must be preceded by: 1) termination of the Israeli military occupation as a system, as a symbol, and as a physical presence, and; 2) clear recognition of the Palestinians' ultimate right to self-determination. The rejection of Mr. Begin's self-rule plan of December 1977 by Palestinian leaders was caused primarily by Begin's refusal to accept the centrality of these two prerequisites. Palestinian leadership viewed Begin's plan as relying on continued Israeli military presence in the occupied areas in order ot perpetuate Israeli rule and to retard aspirations for self-determination.

5. Palestinian institutions in the West Bank and Gaza would have to play a significant role in any political arrangement,

whether in a two-state scenario (Israel and Palestine/Jordan) or a three-state scenario (Israel, Palestine and Jordan).

6.   Once the pressing economic, social, and legal issues have been identified, the cooperation of Palestinians outside the occupied areas must be obtained for these issues to be solved and for any regional linkages to work. This cooperation is particularly relevant in such areas as population relocation, economic development, investment, trade, banking and housing.

7.   On a more positive note, while most of those interviewed strongly supported the establishment of a sovereign Palestinian state or a national authority in the West Bank and Gaza following the with-drawal of Israel, they also admitted, with cautious approval, that such a state or national authority would not come into being immediately, but that some sort of a transitional regime would be instituted. They further admitted that during this transition Palestinian sovereignty would most likely be shared and legitimacy would continue to be debated. The other expression of moderation that emerged clearly during the interviews was the Palestinian acceptance of the reality of the state of Israel.

8.   The centrality of the Palestinian issue in the Arab-Israeli conflict is no longer in doubt. Accordingly, Palestinian leaders assert that any bilateral peace accord between Israel and any Arab state that does not take the Palestinian element into active consideration would be doomed to failure. Peace by proxy, as one Palestinian stated, will not work.

9.   The military occupation has permeated all segments of the inhabitants' daily life. And while it is more obtrusive in the political sector, it is much more insidious in the economic life of the territories. The numerous examples cited by Palestinian farmers, citrus growers, laborers, merchants and businessmen point to an economic colonialism governed by a concerted Israeli policy designed to benefit the economy of the occupier to the detriment of the occupied. This perception of economic life in the West Bank and Gaza is widely held throughout the region.

10.   Finally, the issue of Israeli settlements in the West Bank and Gaza is viewed by Palestinians as closely allied with Israel's perception of the land. Many Palestinians believe that Prime Minister Menahem Begin's attitude toward "Eretz Israel" or the "Land of Israel" is a deterrent to any prospective settlement. These Palestinians believe that Israeli settlements are a symbol of the system of occupation; they were created by it and have been maintained by military might.

Basic Issues

When negotiations eventually begin, a wide range of vital issues will need to be discussed that do not directly involve broad political or military questions. These issues, which will directly affect the building of a Palestinian society, are primarliy economic, social and legal. Though not explicitly political, these issues might act as an incentive for a settlement and sustain it, or they might create frictions before, during, or immediately after the negotiations.

For the purposes of this work, the nonpolitical issues involve seven broad categories:

1. Relocation of refugees and non-refugees
   a. Within the region (West Bank and Gaza)
   i. From camps into established towns and cities
   ii. From camps into new towns
   iii. From towns of current residence into towns of origin
   b. Across the region's boundaries
   i. Jewish settlers moving out of the region
   ii. Displaced Palestinians moving into the region
   c. Long-term and short-term relocation of Palestinian profes-sionals, skilled workers, and prospective bureaucrats
   d. Population distribution both at time of settlement and in the future
2. Housing
   a. New residential settlements for immediate occupancy
   b. New developments within existing towns and cities
   c. Remodeling of old and condemned sections within existing towns and cities
   d. Construction timetables (availability of labor, materials, plans and permits)
3. Municipal services—water, sewage, sanitation, public security and order, electricity and telephone
4. Regional services—health, education, welfare, transportation, and communications
5. Municipal and regional planning—rural and urban planning, land use, zoning laws and subdivision regulations, and development
6. Basic economic issues—agriculture; tourism; trade arrange-ments; industry; banking, monetary and financial policies; and manpower planning.
7. Legal issues
   a. Fundamental laws for the postoccupation state—constitu-tional, civil and criminal laws
   b. Legal relations among Palestinians, Israelis, and Jordanians; citizenship laws, travel documents, and accomodation of stateless persons
   c. Property laws
   d. Regional and international governments and treaties, eco-nomic and political
   e. Legal status of Jerusalem
   f. Legal arrangements beyond the transition stage
   g. Legal implementation of various UN resolutions applicable to the conflict.

Military Occupation in the West Bank and Gaza

The ubiquity and pervasiveness of military occupation are evident to all strata of the population in the West Bank and Gaza. Military control has been exercised on practically every level of the inhabitants' daily life—transportation, agriculture, municipal government, employment, education, commerce, banking, development and, of course, political activity. Occupation as a system has been involved in the expropriation of lands, the establishment of settlements and public services and, of course, the control of water and electricity. It seems to me that many Israelis are not really aware of, or perhaps are not interested in being fully informed about, the nature, function and policies of occupation in the West Bank and Gaza.

Municipal government in the West Bank derives its authority from Article 41a of the Jordanian Municipal Law of 1955 as amended until 1967. Although this law has been updated since 1967 on the East Bank, the changes have not been applied to the West Bank municipalities. When asked, several attributed this fact to their refusal to deal with the Israeli military occupation on legal matters. They stated that such dealings might have been misperceived as granting a form of legitimacy to the occupation. As a result, West Bank municipal government has been run, on the one hand, by military occupation policies serving the interests of Israel and, on the other, by an outdated Jordanian law serving, at least theoretically, a Jordanian *ancien regime* that no longer exists.

A wide gap exists between the theoretical or legal authority of West Bank local governments and the way they actually function. Article 41a of the Jordanian Municipal Law gives municipal government authority to act in 40 different areas. In practice, however, every action must have the prior approval of the military government, otherwise it would be nullified by the authorities. Before 1967 municipal government came under the authority of a district commissioner (*mutasarrif*), who in turn reported to the minister of interior in Amman, who acted in the name of the Jordanian monarch. Except in extremely serious cases, most municipal functions and actions were routinely conducted with the approval of the commissioner.

After 1967 one of the first orders issued by the military government was that Israel's minister of defense would assume the authority of the Jordanian monarch over the West Bank, and the authority of the district commissioner was to be vested in the Israeli military governor. The role of the Jordanian minister of interior was taken over by a civilian liaison officer from Israel's Ministry of Interior who was assigned to the West Bank's military headquarters near Ramallah. Israeli civilian officers from other ministries were also assigned to the military headquarters to handle issues pertaining to their own ministries.

Once this flow of authority under occupation was established, the military government proceeded to issue orders requiring prior approval on every activity of municipal government. These orders in effect nullified the Jordanian municipal law in its entirely and placed day-to-day civilian municipal functions under the direct control of the military government, thereby subjecting those functions to the political influence and authority of the occupation. The military government accordingly became the executive as well as the legislative branch of local government.

The military government added a bureaucratic layer above the municipal government, called the Supreme Planning Council, whose members are appointed by the military governor. The primary purpose of this Council has been to implement the Israel government's settlement policy in the occupied areas. Nowhere is the power of this Council more apparent than in planning, zoning and general land use policies, particularly in relation to land annexation and to the proposed expansion of the corporate limits of Arab towns. In almost every instance, the Supreme Planning Council ruled against West Bank towns and cities and in favor of the Israeli settlement policy. Furthermore, the Council has the power, by military decree, to overrule or nullify any municipal decision regarding planning and zoning and to forbid housing development in any area, within or outside the corporate limits of any town, even though that area had alreay been zoned residential. Such an order is usually issued in the name of the military government.

The mayors interviewed unanimously agreed that rule by military fiat compounds the vicissitudes of municipal government. And the manner in which military orders are conveyed makes it extremely difficult for local officials to contest or question them. Orders often come from headquarters in the form of phone calls and are rarely confirmed in writing. When they are communicated in writing, they are rarely signed by an individual but bear the name *al-hukm al'-Askari*, "The Military Rule." Hence municipal officials often find it extremely difficult to contact the right person in the military hierarchy. Although orders are written in both Arabic and Hebrew, municipal officials—none of whom speak Hebrew but all of whom speak Arabic— have been informed that the Hebrew version of the order is the official one and the Arabic is an official translation. Written orders are rarely officially stamped, yet they carry the force of law.

According to the mayors interviewed, the areas which are subjected to and severely hampered by military government control within the municipal administration include the budget, taxes, planning and zoning, industrial development, loans, education, collection of grants from the Arab world and capital improvement. In addition, West Bank mayors are forbidden by the military government to meet with each other even socially, and West Bank towns and cities are prohibited from establishing any cooperative regional programs. This is particularly harmful in the area of economic development, for which regional cooperation is essential.

The problems cited by municipal officials may be attributed to three major conditions: first, the Israeli occupation and the political, psychological, economic, social and strategic constraints placed on the Arab population in this context; second, the outdated municipal laws and ordinances governing municipal functions; third, the vague sources of legal authority under which municipal government has operated since 1967 in both the West Bank and Gaza. During this period, local government has been based on a mysterious combination of Jordanian law, mandate law, military orders and the personal temperament of local or regional military governors. Local government operations, fiscal and otherwise, have often been subject to political interpretations of local and regional powers. Accordingly municipal budgets are frequently at the mercy of the conflicting interpretations of outside governments, primarily Israel, Jordan and the Palestine Liberation Organization (PLO), and secondarily, Egypt, Syria, Saudi Arabia and Arab Gulf states.

Most of these constraints are expected to disappear or to diminish once a new political arrangement is implemented, and the prospects of municipal government playing an important and perhaps central role in a post-occupation transitional arrangement are encouraging. Whether the transitional order is based on one Palestinian sovereignty or a mixture of sovereignties directly or indirectly involving Jordan and Israel, the legal authority and the police powers of local political jurisdictions will have to be redefined and definitely expanded. This optimistic prognosis is in no way linked to any particular form of post-occupation regime. It does assume, however, that no real improvement, at least in the context of this discussion, can be expected under occupation and that improvement is possible once the system of occupation is replaced by a new regime. Again, this discussion assumes that improvement carries with it the cooperation of the local indigenous population and local leaders.

Reaction of West Bank and Gaza Inhabitants to the Israel-Egypt Peace Agreement

West Bank and Gaza inhabitants have strongly rejected the Sadat initiative, the Camp David accords, and the peace treaty between Israel and Egypt. They have viewed "self-rule" as a continuation of Israeli rule in the territories by another name. Palestinian collective public rejection of the Egypt-Israeli peace process in the West Bank was stated in at least seven major declarations:

1.   Declaration opposing the "self-rule" guidelines, mid-August 1978.

2.   Declaration by the Administrative Board of the Arab Graduates Union, September 21, 1978.

3. Declaration from the Union of Professionals, Jerusalem, September 24, 1978.

4. Undated declaration from the occupied territories, which was circulated clandestinely during the last week of September 1978. It contained more than 121 signatures (some were illegible), half of which by members of town and village councils.

5. Declaration by the Arab Graduates Union, September 28, 1978. The signatories included leading clerics, former Jordanian officials, members of the Jerusalem Chamber of Commerce, and representatives of professional societies.

6. Declaration by the conference of the popular organizations in the occupied lands, held in Beit Hanina (outside Jerusalem) on October 1, 1978. The convening of the conference was announced in the Arabic press on October 1 and its resolution received prominent coverage in the papers the following day. *Al-Fajr*, for example, printed a large photograph of the gathering, a summary of the resolution, and a complete list of the 96 signatories.

7. Declaration submitted to the Ramallah Municipality by the students of the UNRWA Men Teachers' Training Center in Ramallah on October 3, in support of the resolution of the October 1 meeting in Jerusalem.

The above declarations focused on the following five points:

- The Palestinian Arabs are one people.
- The PLO is their sole legitimate representative.
- The self-rule plan legitimizes the occupation and prevents self-determination.
- A just and lasting peace can come only through the Palestinians exercise of their right to self-determination and national independence, after complete Israeli withdrawal.
- Palestinian sovereignty must be returned to East Jerusalem, which is an inseparable part of the West Bank.

On the basis of interviews conducted for this research, it can be stated with certainty that two fundamental conditions must be met before the cooperation of West Bank and Gaza leaders can be obtained: termination of the Israeli occupation and a recognition of self-determination, leading to an eventual Palestinian sovereignty over the West Bank and Gaza.

A majority of Palestinian elites interviewed in the West Bank and Gaza exhibited a genuine attitude of political moderation and a sincere commitment to peace. This moderation was reflected in at least three specific attitudes:

1. They are inclined to negotiate with Israel on the future of the occupied areas.

2. Many of them recognize at least tacitly, the possibility that some sort of transitional regime, in which sovereignty will be vaguely shared with others, will replace the occupation. They disagree, however, on the length of transition.

3. They also realize that, at least for the foreseeable future, Palestinian independence and sovereignty, when established, would be subject to constraints imposed by neighboring states, particularly Jordan and Israel. While they find it difficult to accept this eventuality, many of them have resigned themselves to it.

This moderation is generally congruent with the public position taken by West Bank and Gaza elites. The sporadic incongruence seems for the most part to have been generated by the exclusion of the two fundamental demands fequently voiced by Palestinian leaders: the end of occupation, and a statement of principles regarding ultimate sovereignty.

While the purpose of this study is not to chronicle the myriad of peace proposals offered over the years regarding the future of the occupied territories, it might be useful to take a brief look at the position taken by Palestinian elites on specific proposals. Most of those questioned agree on the following:

1. They support Security Council Resolution 242. While some elements of the Palestine Liberation Organization have tacitly accepted this resolution, the PLO has officially rejected it as written because it treats the Palestinians as refugees only.

2. They reject Israel's self-rule plan announced by Prime Minister Menachem Begin to the Israeli Knesset on December 28, 1977. They maintain that the twenty-six-point plan is designed to perpetuate Israeli military control of the area by other means.

3. While some Palestinian leaders desire to involve the Soviet Union actively in the peace process, along the lines of the Soviet-American statement of principles of October 1, 1977, most of them accept the position that the United States is the only outside power capable of bringing about a settlement. These same people have serious doubts, however, whether the United States would bring about such a settlement. Many Palestinians, while readily pointing out the pervasive pro-Israeli sentiment in American policy, state with satisfaction that a discernible shift in American public opinion concerning the Middle East has begun to crystallize.

4. Palestinian leaders in the West Bank and Gaza and even the PLO leadership itself have on numerous occasions expressed serious interest in opening dialogue with the United States regarding the Middle East conflict. While numerous covert contacts are reputed to have been made between certain U.S. government officials and PLO representatives, publicly and officially the United States has persistently refused, with an uncharacteristic stubbornness, to initiate such a dialogue.

5. West Bank and Gaza leaders believe that the PLO is the only recognized representative of the Palestinian people. However, the strength of their clinging to the PLO seems to be in direct proportion to the extent of U.S. and Israeli refusal to deal with it. The negative reaction of the elites to the September 1978 Camp David "Framework for Peace in the Middle East" is a case in point. While West Bank leaders did not reject the framework outright,

they decried what they perceived to be a total denial of the PLO's leadership.

Aside from the above factors, the study has demonstrated that viable social and administrative infrastructures do exist in the West Bank and Gaza and can function as a nucleus of a post-settlement regime. Given the proper circumstances, these institutions, which have operated out of necessity under occupation, could function out of expertise in the post-occupation stage.

Note

1. For a more detailed presentation of this research, see Emile A. Nakleh, *The West Bank and Gaza: Toward the Making of a Palestinian State* (Washington, D.C.: American Enterprise Institute, 1979).

Autonomy in Judea, Samaria and Gaza
Legal Aspects of its Implementation
Moshe Drori

As a result of the Camp David agreements and the Israeli-Egyptian peace treaty, the coming years will see a long and intricate negotiation process over autonomy in Judea, Samaria and Gaza. Legally, Israel is bound to negotiate with Egypt and other Arab representatives "and to start negotiations within a month after the exchange of the instruments of ratification of the Peace Treaty." Furthermore, "Egypt and Israel set for themselves the goal of completing the negotiations within one year."[1]

It is not our intention to forecast the outcome of the negotiations. Our purpose in this article is to describe the legal framework for the negotiations, to try to point out several key issues to be discussed, and to suggest legal solutions for them. These are not the sole issues to be negotiated, but due to the short space available, only these few will be dealt with. Some of them apply to any variation of autonomy, whereas the ones discussed later are specific to the autonomy suggested in our region (especially Israeli settlement in the administered areas). Therefore their treatment will be more extensive.

Sources and Legal Documents

Four documents establish the framework for discussing the legal system that will exist after autonomy is implemented. First and foremost is the detailed agreement concerning autonomy, neither drafted as yet nor signed, which should result from the year-long negotiations. Since this agreement is unavailable as yet, we will consider all its alternative versions in accordance with documents to be described. Second, and most recently signed, is the letter written by Israel and Egypt on March 26, 1979, the day of the peace treaty in Washington, DC; this in effect reiterated most points included in the third and so far the central document—the Camp David Agreement.[2] The fourth is not a bilateral document; rather, it reflects Israel's position, as expressed in the Israeli Prime Minister's peace proposal of December 1977, and approved by the Knesset (Israel's Parliament).[3]

The binding document, serving as a basis for our discussion, is the Camp David Agreement. It should be stressed, however, that the Agreement is relatively brief on details of the autonomy plan and actually leaves most issues for further discussion (apparently those which remained unresolved at Camp David).[4]

On the other hand, Israel's peace plan is more detailed and touches upon the main issues with regard to autonomy, though it too lacks some detail. This plan, though obviously not binding upon the other party, may be said to constitute an Israeli public and moral undertaking not to deviate from the plan and not to restrict rights granted through it. The opposite may be contended too: the plan has not been accepted by Egypt, and thus Israel may deviate from it in future proposals made in the negotiations. However, it would clearly be both morally and politically difficult for Israel in future negotiations to disassociate itself from its peace plan, especially if the U.S. claims that this is exactly Israel's proposal of December, 1977.[5]

The Parties in the Negotiations

At this stage Israel, Egypt and the United States intend to establish autonomy following an agreement between Israel and some Arab party. (We will later discuss a possible unilateral establishment of autonomy by Israel.) Who will decide on the parties to the negotiations preceding the autonomy agreement? Who will the actual parties be, and will they change in various stages of the negotiations? Do they have to participate in the negotiations, and will any decisions reached bind them?

It should be stressed at the outset that the parties which have agreed to negotiate are Israel and Egypt,[6] with the participation of the United States.[7] Israel and Egypt have also decided at Camp David that the autonomy agreement will be trilateral—among Egypt, Israel, and Jordan—and that "the delegations of Egypt and Jordan may include Palestinians from the West Bank and Gaza or other Palestinians as mutually agreed."[8]

It should be noted here that the term "Palestinians" is far from unequivocal, as it may at first seem. Israel regards the term as meaning only "Palestinian Arabs," i.e., only Arab inhabitants of "Palestine" (the Land of Israel—"Eretz Israel"), and not representatives of the P.L.O. or others from outside "Palestine." This Israeli position was expressed in a letter from the President of the U.S. to Israel's Premier—thus Israel may at least view it as part of the agreement, without which she would not have signed.[9] Those Palestinian representatives joining the Jordanian or Egyptian delegations require prior unanimous acceptance, so that, in effect, Israel may veto P.L.O. participation. Neither Jordan nor any Palestinian Arabs are party to either the Camp David Agreements or the letter. They therefore are not legally bound to join the negotiations, and even less so the agreement.

Legally we are faced in this situation with a document similar to a contract "in favor of/against a third party" in private law. Such a contract cannot bind the third party—at most it can confer certain rights upon it. However, does Jordan's refusal to participate in the negotiations absolve Egypt and Israel from their undertakings in that article? It seems that, since both countries knew Jordan was not bound by the framework agreement, the article should be interpreted as a form of invitation to join in the discussions. If Jordan refuses to do so, they must negotiate until they reach agreement to establish autonomy.[10] In such case, President Sadat has declared to President Carter in his letter of the date that the Camp David Agreements were signed that Egypt will assume the "Arab Role," following consultations with Jordan and representatives of the Palestinian people.[11]

So far we have examined only the parties to the autonomy negotiations, but the Camp David Agreements also refer to additional negotiations—to determine the "final status of the West Bank and Gaza"—which will commence no later than three years after autonomy has been established. The negotiators will include, aside from representatives of Israel, Egypt and Jordan, "the elected representatives of the inhabitants of the West Bank and Gaza."[12]

Several remarks should be made at this point: first these representatives have a *right* to participate, as opposed to the first negotiations, in which it was stated that Jordan and Egypt *may* include Palestinian representatives. Second, these representatives are elected and not appointed[13]; thus Israel cannot veto participation of P.L.O. members, if in fact these are the elected representatives of the inhabitants. It remains unclear whether these are the same representatives elected to the administrative council, or special ones for this purpose alone (and, if so, how are they to be chosen?). Third, these representatives do not necessarily have to be Palestinians, but only representatives of the inhabitants. If so, Israelis who reside in Judea, Samaria and the Gaza District may elect and may be elected representatives for these negotiations to determine the final status of the areas in which they reside.[14]

To what extent will the agreement reached bind the inhabitants themselves? Regarding the first negotiations in 1979–80 to achieve the autonomy agreement, it has already been noted that participation of representatives of the inhabitants in this case is merely an option for Jordan and Egypt. Politically, at least, it may be contended that the agreement does not bind the inhabitants, as the representatives appointed by Jordan and Egypt with Israel's consent do not represent them. Legally, the inhabitants' consent is not mandatory, neither in advance nor *post factuna*, and autonomy may be imposed. Autonomy would clearly require—politically, publicly, practically, but not legally—the consent and cooperation of the population.

The situation differs for the negotiations concerning the final status of the West Bank and Gaza. In this case the elected representatives of the inhabitants are their delegates, and as such any agreements bind the inhabitants. This obligation, however, is only legal and cannot prevent the rise of another leadership (e.g., through revolution), which may not view itself bound by the previous obligations of the elected representatives.

The Basic Legal Norm-"The Source of Authority"

The autonomy we are considering differs from an autonomy in which a country grants some of its powers—at its sole discretion—to one of its regions. The object of autonomy in our case is presently under Israeli military rule, and Israel has undertaken to hold negotiations which, when completed, will lead to the establishment of that autonomy. After the parties successfully complete the negotiations—within the expected one-year period—a treaty will be signed, which should define the framework for the autonomy's powers, methods for electing its institutions, its operation, its links with Israel, Jordan and others, etc. As far as bilateral relations between the signatories (at least Israel and Egypt, and Jordan, too—if it joins) are concerned, the agreement is binding. It forms the basic legal norm, or the source of authority, for autonomy, in the sense that a party which unilaterally takes action contradicting this agreement will be considered to be in breach of the agreement.

Still, this is not sufficient; the agreement must also be given validity under the local legal system which will prevail in Judea, Samaria, and Gaza. Considerable disagreement concerning this issue exists between Israel and Egypt, as neither the Camp David Agreements nor the letter make any provisions in this regard. Egypt views the agreement as constituting the basic norm in the local legal system as well and as forming the supreme constitutional document within it (the regular legislative powers will be considered later). On the other hand, Israel views the military government of the areas, which has been operating since 1967, as the "source of authority" and obeying its orders as the basic norm. The wording of the Camp David Agreements and the letter tends towards the Egyptian interpretation[15]:

> ... the Israeli *military government* and its *civilian administration*[16] will be withdrawn as soon as a self-governing authority has been freely elected by the inhabitants of these areas to *replace* the existing military government.

This wording, explicitly stating that the self-governing authority replaces the military government which will be withdrawn, means the end of the military government. It therefore cannot continue to be the source of authority for the autonomy's operation. An additional opinion may be that the military government will enact the Autonomy Law as its final action and will then be abolished. However, within the five autonomy years there will be no military government at all.

Other Israeli experts view the matter differently. At the Camp David negotiations, a proposal had been made to include an explicit provision that the military government would be abolished. Israel objected and this wording was not accepted. Instead, the word "withdrawn" was used, and hence the interpretation was made that the military government will withdraw to some point outside the administered areas (such as Tel Aviv) from where legally it will continue to act as the source of authority.[17]

A third possibility, as yet not publicly raised, is that the basic norm would be fixed by an act of the Knesset (Israel's parliament) which would establish the powers of the various autonomy authorities. Under Israeli law, the Knesset's legislation is also valid in territories under military occupation, as was decided in the very first criminal appeal brought before the Supreme Court as soon as the state was declared.[18] Such legislation would therefore not alter the existing status of the autonomy, which at present is still under the military government. However, such an act would be suspected as tending towards annexation, and the Arabs would view it as even more distasteful than continuing the military government. The latter has existed for the past twelve years and is legally recognized under international law and the law of occupation. Knesset legislation, however, alters the situation and openly establishes the area or population under the autonomy plan as a *de facto*—if not *de jure*—part of Israel.

In concluding this section about the source of authority, I should point out that the press has raised the possibility that if the parties fail to reach an agreement about autonomy, Israel will establish it unilaterally, either in Gaza alone, or in both Gaza and Judea and Samaria. In such case, an Israeli act would obviously be the source of authority (either an Order of the Area Commander or a Knesset act, as per above).

The Autonomy's Legal System

What would be the nature of the legal system in Judea, Samaria and Gaza? If the agreement is viewed as the source of authority, an obvious question arises: what was the validity of the law in force prior to the agreement? If an Order of the Area Commander is viewed as the source of authority, we have an additional layer in the area's legal system, and thus the law previously in force continues as it is.

The Camp David Agreements do not deal with the question of the continued application of the legal system. Article 19 of the Israeli peace plan provides that a committee of representatives of Israel, Jordan and the Administrative Council will rule unanimously which legislation will continue in force and which will be abolished.[19] However, until such rulings are made by the joint committee, a legislative vacuum will exist in all areas of life (civil, criminal, economic, etc.). In doing, its work the committee must consider all existing law, not only that legislated since 1967, but also earlier layers of the system (Jordanian, Mandatory and Ottoman law).[20] Due to this substantive obstacle the following approach should be used: the founding document of the autonomy must expressly provide for legal continuity, in an arrangement similar to Article 11 of Israel's Law and Administration Ordinance of 1948,[21] the "unification" of the West and East Banks and Jordan's annexation of the West Bank in 1950,[22] and Article 2 of the Law and Administration Proclamation promulgated upon the establishment of the Israeli army's rule in the area in 1967.[23] Only on the basis of such legal continuity can a committee be required to decide on methods for coordinating the law and the existing state of affairs by amending or abolishing legislation. This committee will also have to determine, (if the document itself does not so provide), who will possess the various powers under the existing legislation, including "translation" of powers of the King of Jordan, his government, ministers and high officials into "parallel" offices in the autonomy.

Branches of Government in the Autonomy

The branches of government in the military government had a dual structure—officers of the military government on the one hand, and inhabitants of the areas on the other.[24] Will this structure fundamentally change upon establishment of autonomy, or will there only be a shift in the borderlines between the extent of powers of the Israeli authorities *vis-a-vis* the local authorities?

On one hand, the autonomous region is obviously not a state and hence its powers will not be unlimited. On the other hand, there are changes which will occur in the local powers of the administered areas, and the term "full autonomy"[25] in the Camp David Agreement must be given meaning.

It should be emphasized that the Israeli plan, though entitled "Self Rule," has dealt all along with one body, the Administrative Council, with the understanding that this is merely an administrative organ, with no control over other branches of government. On the other hand, in the Camp David Agreements the term used is "self-governing authority,"[26] which is wider and includes other branches. At one point the Camp David Agreements employ the term "self-governing authority (administrative council)."[27] The brackets narrow down the wider term and imply that the only expression of the "self-governing" concept is the administrative council; hence, the authority cannot act outside the administrative sphere, However, this term appears only once, and in the first and important instance, the term "self-governing authority" appears without reference to the administrative council, referring to the authority as existing "in order to provide full autonomy to the inhabitants." Since further interpretation is still possible, it may be contended that the sole reference to the "administrative council" indicates that in all other cases in which the term "self-governing authority" appears, it means "administrative council."

In any case, we will now examine the branches of government as they appear in the autonomy plan under the various documents and interpretations.

The Legislature

Which body will constitute the legislative branch during the life span of the autonomy?

At the outset we must emphasize that it is almost inconceivable not to have a legislature and to freeze the legal situation in a given area for five years. To use the words of the President of the Supreme Court on the legislative powers of the military government, "Society's needs change with time and the law must provide solutions for them. . . Life does not remain stagnant, and no government, whether in occupation or otherwise, properly fulfills its obligation towards the population if it freezes legislation and does not adapt it to the changing needs.[28] These words apply more emphatically to the five autonomy years. Any understanding person would see that the situation may not remain unchanged; taxes would stay the same, criminal law could not be made stricter or lighter, social or other benefits could not be added. In any legal structure of the autonomy period a body should be established which will have the power to make laws and amend and abolish existing legislation. There may be reasons to restrict that body's legislative powers to specific matters, or to expressly exclude from its authority security, external affairs and clearly political matters (such as legislation regarding a national flag and anthem and, obviously, a declaration of independence). In any case, however, the "legislative authority" of the autonomy plan must be clearly designated.

This key issue, at least for jurists—some regard the body authorized to enact "Supreme Legislation" as the sovereign in the state structure—is not mentioned in the Camp David agreements, which avoided detail. The agreements left this definition of powers of the self-governing authority (clearly including its legislative power and its nature, whether "supreme" or "subsidiary") to the agreement to be signed by Israel, Egypt, Jordan and the Palestinians.[29] The Israeli peace plan partially provides for this problem. The article detailing the departments of the Administrative Council says, "the Administrative Council will. . . promulgate regulations relating to the operation of these Departments."[30] It remains unclear from this wording whether the article means regulations in the strict sense (that is, only subsidiary legislation), or regulations as a general heading for legislation.[31] The source of authority empowered to promulgate these regulations also remains unclear. Is it this very article? If so, then the *extent* of this power is in question. Can the chief of the health department promulgate any regulation on health? Or is it the existing legislation? Then the question is whether the department chief is vested with the authority of the "parallel" minister—with the powers of the minister of health transferred to the health department chief, as in the above example. What then happens to the powers Jordanian law gave to the body "above" the minister—the King, and the Council of Ministers—or "below" him—the director-general, the district director, etc? The difficulties we have raised are further tangled if we closely consider Art. 19 of the peace plan. Whereas Art. 10 clearly establishes the Administrative Council's power to promul-gate regulations, Art. 19 provides that this issue is to be decided by the joint committee of Israel, Jordan, and the Administrative Council.

The legislating entity remains unclear as well. Is the above styled Administrative Council authorized to promulgate regula-tions with regard to all departments—and then a simple majority, and not a special one, appears sufficient—or does each depart-ment chief have the power to make subsidiary legislation in his own department, just as a minister in Israel promulgates regula-tions in his own ministry.

If the Administrative Council or each department chief has the power to promulgate regulations, who approves them? Is this an exclusive power of the Council similar to that of a minister in Israel, or is there a need for the approval of another body, such as a municipality in Israel, whose regulations require approval by the Minister of the Interior? If the second alternative applies, which body? Is it an Israeli body—an Israeli minister, e.g., the Minister of the Interior? This would indicate that Israel views Judea, Samaria, and Gaza as an internal region in this minister's jurisdiction. Or the Knesset, one of its committees, or perhaps the military govern-ment—if it still remains? Another question applies to local munici-pality by-laws, today approved by the Israeli Interior Staff Officer, through his exercise of the powers of the Jordanian Interior Minis-ter and Government.[32] In the autonomy, will this approval power pass on to the Administrative Council? If so, to which department, since it does not have an Interior Department?

What of judicial review and the legislation. If an Administrative Council regulation contradicts an existing law or is *ultra vires* the legislative power in the founding document, which body will declare it void? Will any court be authorized to do so, even within any action (indirect attack), or will this be within the jurisdiction of a special, local court (since the Court of Appeal has the powers of the High Court of Justice—a court of Cassation—under Jordanian law),[33] or an Israeli court?[34] Should a mixed, special legal forum be established to form a constitutional court to decide these sensitive issues?[35]

This discussion of the nature of legislative powers under the autonomy period may seem to be legal quibbling; however, the issue is not limited to legalities. Law only serves as a tool to bestow powers, and thus an accurate definition of the extent of power will actually decide the nature of the administrative authority.[36] Such a definition will avoid future confrontations, and each side will clearly know its place and extent of powers.

The Judiciary

The local courts which had operated in the area up to 1967 have continued their work under the occupation. They have ascending levels of power, the highest of which is the Ramallah Court of Appeal. These courts handle all civil and criminal matters, excluding security offenses, which are tried before military courts. Lately municipal courts have been instituted as well.[37] In addition there are religious courts of the various denominations for matters of marriage, divorce and family law.

There is little doubt that any conceivable autonomy plan, even the most limited, would allow the local judiciary to remain as it is. Moreover, it is quite probable that all powers now in the hands of military government officers, especially the appointment of judges, will be executed by the autonomy authorities and, naturally, by the department for the administration of justice and supervision of local police forces (the 11th department under the Israeli peace plan[38]).

The situation differs with regard to the military courts. These have been established by the military government and draw their powers from it; the military government is responsible for appointing judges, confirming judgments, etc.[39] If the military government remains the source of authority, even if it moves outside the administered areas, the military courts will face an identical fate. Moreover, it may be said that even if the military government is wholly abolished, military courts may still be essential for security needs. It has been established that there will be a "redeployment of the remaining Israeli forces into specified security locations."[40] If so, a military judicial arm obviously should continue to exist in the autonomy plan. If the army, fully armed, is permitted to remain for security reasons, its judicial system should operate as well.[41]

Israel's High Court of Justice now has the power of judicial review over military government actions in the civilian, security, legislative and administrative areas.[42] If the military government remains the source of authority, the High Court of Justice will retain this power. Moreover, this court will retain its judicial review over actions of that part of the army which will remain within the security zones. If these actions were committed in Israel, they would be subject to such review. In civil actions against the army, such as those resulting from road accidents caused by military vehicles, no change is expected in Israel's policy of opening its courts to inhabitants of the areas for actions against Israeli authorities.[43] The local autonomy authorities will not be subject to judicial review of the High Court of Justice, since they do not form an authority acting under Israeli law.

The Executive

The Camp David Agreements intentionally left the executive issue open, providing that "the parties will negotiate an agreement which will define the powers and responsibilities of the self-governing authority to be exercised in the West Bank and Gaza."[44]

Under the Israeli Prime Minister's plan, the Administrative Council is the executive body, and all "administrative affairs relating to the Arab residents of the areas of Judea, Samaria and the Gaza district will be under the direction and within the competence of the administrative council."[45] According to this plan, the executive arm will consist of an Administrative Council, which will include the following offices: Education, Religious Affairs, Finance, Transportation, Construction and Housing, Industry, Commerce and Tourism, Agriculture, Health, Labor and Social Welfare, Rehabilitation of Refugees, Administration of Justice and the Supervision of Local Police Forces.[46]

As this list demonstrates, the Council will possess the means to execute all governmental capacities except for foreign affairs and defense. Although an office of the interior is missing from the list, this was probably due to an oversight. Presumably the Administrative Council will also fulfill the interior ministry functions especially in supervising municipalities. Generally speaking, the executive capacity would seem to be concentrated almost entirely in the hands of the local residents through the Administrative Council, although the local authorities (municipalities and rural councils) and the Chambers of Commerce will continue to function. However, it must be emphasized that some of the executive capacities, namely, security and public order will be subject to a unique arrangement to be described later.

State Comptroller

In a modern state, the Comptroller is generally regarded as a fourth branch of government in addition to the Legislative, Judicial and Executive branches. All documents dealing with the autonomy period disregard this issue altogether. Under proper administrative rules, a special body of the autonomy comptroller which would be independent and would submit its reports to the chairman of the Administrative Council should be established. The comptroller's jurisdiction would extend not only to the Administrative Council and its departments, but to other local bodies as well, especially the municipalities. This would in no way infringe upon the continued activity of Israel's State Comptroller, who will go on reviewing military government actions (if it stays on), or actions of military units in the area as he has since 1967.

Security

Art. 11 of the Israeli peace plan provides explicitly that security and public order in Judea, Samaria, and Gaza will be the responsiblility of the Israeli authorities. This principle has been diluted in the Camp David Agreements. First, Israeli armed forces are to withdraw and redeploy in specified security locations.[47] The security of the borders will be assured, among other means, by joint patrols and control posts of Israeli and Jordanian forces.[48] The central new point of the agreements is the establishment of a strong local police force which may include Jordanian citizens and which will maintain a continuous link in internal security matters with the Israeli, Jordanian and Egyptian representatives appointed for this purpose.[49]

Security problems are numerous and varied and should not be detailed here; we will settle for a general description of the main points.

Against an external threat such as war by Jordan or the entire Eastern Front, it appears the Camp David Agreements will not impose limits on Israeli defense. In other words, if war breaks out between Israel and its eastern enemies, the Israeli army would be able to enter Judea and Samaria, both in order to reach the front with Jordan or Syria and to defend the area against invaders. In such cases there will be no limits on the number of Israeli soldiers and their location. If in a war a state of emergency may be declared within Israel, including curfew, etc., it is obvious that it may also be declared in the autonomous area or upon its population as well.

An act against Israeli soldiers in Judea, Samaria, or Gaza would permit immediate reaction. Under the "Hot Pursuit" doctrine the perpetrators may be pursued even beyond the security locations into the local cities and villages. The same may apply to Israeli citizens and even tourists. Israel has a security interest in guarding its citizens' personal safety (under International Law a state must protect its citizens) and even that of tourists visiting an area for which it is responsible. The difficulty is in criminal, and even security offenses, in their early stages (organization for sabotage arms gathering, etc.), or when directed against local "collaborators" or not specifically against Israelis; e.g., setting up roadblocks, etc. Apparently the local police are authorized to deal with these matters, but from Israel's side it seems clear that exclusive handling of them by local police will gradually and necessarily injure vital Israeli interests, until free movement of Israelis within Judea and Samaria is curtailed, to the detriment of Israeli settlements in the area (which will be discussed below).

It thus appears that Israeli interests require a clear definition of powers given to the Israeli authorities in security and public order matters.The security activities required are of a wide range—intelligence reports, presence of the security service in areas inhabited by local residents, apprehension of suspects, arrests and searches, curfews, and court trials and sentences, including imprisonment. If the military government remains in force, its powers on these fields continue to exist and no legal changes are necessary.[50] If it is abolished, special legislation will be needed to provide Israeli authorities with powers of arrest and search, investigation and prosecution.

It will also be necessary to maintain a system of military courts to try these offenders. It seems reasonable that, if an Israeli soldier is permitted to shoot to kill so as to protect security, then a jurist wearing an officer's uniform should be able to try security offenders in a fair trial. However, public sensitivity also has its influence, and the Arab side may not be convinced that establishment of such judicial bodies is advantageous. It thus appears preferable to authorize Israeli courts (either regular criminal courts or the Lod Military Court, under the 1945 Emergency Regulations) to try these offenses. This method also solves the problem of establishing the confirming authority or the body authorized to reduce and mitigate sentences if the Area Commander, who fulfills this function now, will have disappeared.

It may be noted that the "strong police force" is local, and no express provision is made that it be composed exclusively of Arab residents of the areas. One may contend that it should include residents of the Israeli settlements in Judea, Samaria and Gaza, since they are also local residents

Israeli Settlement

Various kinds of Israeli settlements exist in Judea, Samaria and the Gaza District—towns, kibbutzim and cooperative agricultural settlements (moshav). Several general problems already exist with regard to Israeli settlement in Judea and Samaria stemming from the fact that the settlers live in a region where a system of law other than that of Israel applies. These problems have existed for the past twelve years with only a few having been resolved.

The core of the issue is as follows: except for a few laws of a personal nature Israeli law is territorial, and as such it applies solely within Israel proper. The law in Judea and Samaria is also territorial and applies generally only within this area. Israeli settlers in the area feel linked to Israel, and thus to Israeli law and administration, but the law which applies to them is essentially the territorial law of the area, i.e., the legal system of Judea and Samaria. As a result of the clash between the (preferred) personal law and the (actual) territorial law, several problems both legal and practical, arise in various spheres.[51]

The settlement issue was frequently raised during the lengthy negotiations between Israel and Egypt, but the Camp David accords and the letter fail to mention it. Israel views settlement in the territories as a legal act consistent with its rights and claims for sovereignty in Judea, Samaria and the Gaza District; the peace plan itself declares explicitly that "residents of Israel will be entitled to acquire land and settle in the areas."[52] The estimate of the situation at this stage is that Israeli settlements will remain intact even after the establishment of the autonomy. This situation raises numerous and varied problems in legal, economic, and other fields, the essence of which will be presented here with proposed legal solutions.

Land for Settlement

Jewish-owned land: some land in the territory had been acquired prior to 1948 by Jews and had been registered in their names in the Land Registry. This was the case regarding part of the land of Gush Etzion in Judea and Kfar Darom in the Gaza Strip. During the era of Jordanian rule in Judea and Samaria, the Jordanian government enacted a Custodian of Jewish Property Law and orders were issued on the basis of that law transferring Jewish-owned land and property to the Jordanian Custodian. The status of Jewish-owned land still registered as such in the Land Registry would not change with autonomy, since the Jordanian Custodian of Jewish Property did not employ his powers and the land remains with its owners. Since 1967, Jewish-owned land registered under Jordanian law in the Land Registry in the name of the Custodian of Enemy Property has been transferred to the Israeli Custodian of Government Property, an Israeli army staff officer. While those lands are formally government-owned, it is fair to contend they are actually Jewish-owned and should remain so.[53]

Government land: an accepted principle of international law and the laws of war expressed in Proclamation No. 2 and a special order promulgated in the territories is that government property, including land, passes into the occupying country's possession.[54] According to an order promulgated in Judea and Samaria, a Custodian of Government Propoerty was appointed in the area.[55] This Custodian, actually the representative of the Israel Lands Administration in the area, is authorized to sign contracts and manage the property. A substantial part of the land used for Jewish settlement is government land; at times the Jordanian Crown's (or the British High Commissioner's) title is expressly registered as such in the Land Registry, and at times government ownership is determined by the established legal system which holds, for example, that no-man's land or land which cannot be cultivated belongs to the government.

It must be stressed that under international law the Custodian's authority is based upon the assumption that he holds the property in trust until the end of the occupation and the conclusion of peace treaties, whereupon it will be returned to its former owners i.e., the occupied country. As the autonomy agreement is not a final one, the Custodian's obligation as trustee still stands until such time as it is determined who has sovereignty in the area and who holds title to government land. Moreover, the Jordanian government, which had previously ruled Judea and Samaria, declared that under the Rabat Conference decisions it does not claim sovereignty over the area, thereby weakening the Custodian's trust obligation. However, the Custodian remains bound by that trust until the conclusive determination of sovereignty at the end of the five autonomy years. Practical difficulties may impede the application of this reasoning if the military government is completely abolished; if it merely withdraws, but remains in authority, the Custodian of Government Property will retain his powers anyway. It therefore appears that, at least in private law, one solution would be to make long-term contracts even at present, so as to "freeze" the current situation and to avoid any possible Arab claim for rights in the property. Then, if the autonomy authorities viewed themselves as responsible for government property, they would have to deal with the long-term leases and rights already in existence.

Abandoned property: The unattended property of any person who has abandoned the area is considered to be abandoned property and is transferred to the Custodian, that same representative of the Israel Lands Administration.[56] He holds it in trust for the owner, and if the latter returns to the area, the Custodian must restore the property to him, including any income derived from it.[57] Settlements have been established on this land as well, especially where on one piece of land, there are both some government plots and some belonging to absentees. The problem here would be more difficult in the autonomy era, for even now the law recognizes the right of the original owner to his actual property.

Moreover, under Article A(3) of the Camp David accord, a special committee would be established to handle the return of these absentees to Judea and Samaria. Though this committee's decisions would have to be unanimous (i.e., Israel would retain a veto), it would most likely try to have as many Arabs as possible return to the area. One of the obvious criteria justifying the repatriation that would be suggested by the Arab members would be land ownership. This is a very reasonable criterion; land ownership reflects strong links with the area, and the return of a land owner would not cause an economic problem nor "disruption and disorder," as this article states. Although the U.S. has no delegate on this committee, it appears doubtful that Israel could persuade the U.S. and public opinion of the justification for preventing a resident of the area who had lived there up to 1967 from returning to his lands, which the military government held as trustee for him.

It is thus suggested that an order be promulgated, or that it be agreed with the Arab party and then be promulgated by order, that if such an absentee owner returns and his land is occupied, he would be entitled to monetary compensation and not to his actual property. Though this constitutes "post factum" expropriation, it appears the proper way to prevent evacuation of settlements or part of them and their replacement with Arab residents. This may be seen as parallel with the Israeli decision in 1967 not to expel Arabs who lived in Jewish-owned houses in Hebron. In order to avoid confrontation between the nations the interest of the status-quo should be posed against specific private titles.

Private land: under international law the military government may not as a general rule infringe upon private property,[58] but if security needs so require, it may be used, expropriated, or destroyed.[59] Israel's official policy has been that new settlements are established to fill military and security need. Thus Israel's opinion is that private land may be seized for military purposes in order to establish settlements on it. Seizure does not mean confiscation. Title to the land remains with the original owner but he loses use of it. Orders of seizure have been issued by the area commanders in Judea, Samaria and Gaza under which private land has been seized. Under such orders the military government has acquired the right of use of the land.[60] The orders provided for annual rent to be paid the owners and/or lawful tenants, even though international law does not require their compensation. In fact, certain owners accept the annual rent, while others refuse on principle to accept any monetary compensation. With the establishment of autonomy this issue will be more difficult to resolve than all other kinds discussed above. First, the inhabitants may demand, in civil action, that the settlements be vacated (a similar problem may arise regarding abandoned property as well). Second, the claim

of security needs will be weaker when the military government is totally abolished, or even if it merely withdraws.

A somewhat radical solution may be suggested, one which could provide a suitable means of avoiding future litigation and would allow the continued status-quo with regard to the existing settlements. It is proposed that land for settlement be expropriated for public needs under the Jordanian Land (Expropriation for Public Needs) Law, No. 2 of 1953. The Israeli authorities have so far avoided using this law for Jews and it was only used to fulfil the needs of Arab residents, such as expropriation for a road within an Arab town. However, in 1973 the Supreme Court recognized that Kiryat Arba residents are residents of the area, so that the military government must provide them with electricity, just as for other residents.[61] Thus, land may be expropriated for Israeli settlers. If this method is adopted, it may be applied to all kinds of land described above, especially that of absentees. Land would be expropriated for a public body, preferably the Israeli municipal body, as detailed below.

Planning and Construction

The Jordanian Planning of Towns, Villages and Buildings Law, No. 79 of 1966, applies in Judea and Samaria. Order No. 418[62] provides that the powers of the various planning and construction committees be divided as follows: the powers of the District and Supreme Committees are vested in the Supreme Planning Committee, composed of Israeli Military Government staff officers and headed by the Staff Officer of the Interior. Municipalities form the local committees within town limits and village planning committees outside of the towns. The latter include Arab members only: the Planning Department engineer, who also serves as chairman, the District Physician, the District Public Works Department engineer, and the Arab village committee representative.

Order No. 418, as amended in Order 604, provides that the Area Commander may appoint special planning committees (instead of village planning committees), which would have the powers of local and even district committees. This Order may be employed to provide for planning and construction of Israeli settlements.

It is proposed that the Israeli municipal body recently established be given planning and construction powers similar to those of local or district committees, including supervision over illegal or deviant construction, whereas the Supreme Planning Committee will retain its powers. If autonomy is territorial and its authorities are vested with planning and construction powers, the area should then be divided regarding these matters into two regions: an Arab region served by a Supreme Planning Committee composed of Arabs and Israeli settlement regions (the Jordan Valley, Gush Etzion, Kiryat Arba, and routes linking Israeli settlements to I.D.F. camps) under the authority of a Supreme Planning Committee comprised of Israelis. Coordination procedures for borderline areas between the two regions will have to be established, just as the planning authorities in Judea and Samaria now coordinate actions with their Israeli counterparts in adjacent regions (Jerusalem with Bethlehem and Ramalla, Kfar Saba with Kalkilia, etc.).

Infrastructure

Water: substantial Jordanian legislation exists with regard to water, including powers of expropriation, licensing, supervision, etc. Nevertheless, as Dr. Y. Boneh and Mr. Uri Beida state, "in contrast with the Israeli Water Law, state ownership over water sources has not been established in Judea and Samaria."[63]

The importance of the water issue cannot be overemphasized. Not only must ownership and supervision of existing water be determined, including safety of pipelines, but definite rules must be established regarding use of water and drilling for water outside Israeli settlement areas. From a geologic aspect, the granting of absolute freedom to Arab residents of the territories to drill for water as they wish would interfere with the level of water freshness and may produce water shortages, not only for Israeli settlements in Judea and Samaria, but also for those within Israel proper. With respect to this sensitive issue, the preferable solution seems to be the establishment of a common authority, comprised of delegates from Israel and the Administrative Council, which would unanimously decide the following issues: division of the present water supply, its price, new drilling rights, water projects, etc. This authority must have extensive powers, including expropriation of water found in private land, so as to divide it among residents of Judea and Samaria, Arabs and Jews.

Roads: freedom of movement on the roads is a primary condition for the welfare of Israeli settlement, and it must be viewed as part of Israel's security needs. One question which comes to mind concerns the authority to expropriate land in order to pave new roads or improve existing ones. Will that right remain with the Israeli authorities (the military government, which may remain in the area, or some other official representative of Israel), or will it be transferred to the autonomy authorities? The suggestion that a common body be created, as in the case of water, may apply here as well.

Electricity: at the first stage in the forming of a new settlement electricity is supplied by generators, and only later is it linked with an electric power network. In the Jordan Valley, settlements are linked to the power system of the Israel Electricity Company, which has built a line from Mehola southward through the valley. The rights of the Israeli company must not be interfered with after autonomy is established. The autonomy authorities would not be empowered to enact a law transferring the concession to sell electricity to another company.

In the Judea region the Jerusalem District Electricity Company Ltd. has a concession, and Israel respects it within its limits. (An attempt to extend it towards Hebron failed by a decision of the High Court of Justice.[64]) At any rate, in order to avoid the need to link with the Jerusalem company, the Gush Etzion settlements were declared military grounds. Thus the Military Government did not have to comply with the concession and linked the settlements to the Israeli Electricity Company when the line was extended to Kiryat Arba. On the other hand, Maaleh Edomim, east of Jerusalem, is linked to the East Jerusalem company. The High Court of Justice has ruled that providing electricity to Kiryat Arba and to Israeli settlements is within the Military Government's authority, as part of its duty to care for the inhabitants.[65]

Arrangements must be made for supplying electricity to the settlements by the Israeli company. Israel is able to exert substantial pressure upon the East Jerusalem company (which in effect receives all of its power from the Israeli company). On the other hand, the safety of the Israeli line must be ensured, since in some places it passes through densely populated Arab regions, such as the Jerusalem-Gush Etzion-Kiryat Arba line.(This line will probably be safe anyway, since it also supplies electricity to Arab Hebron). From the legal aspect, it should be demanded in the negotiations that the Israeli company be given the right to supply power to geographic areas where Israeli settlements or municipal bodies exist, whether within the concesion area of the East Jerusalem company or outside it.

Telecommunications: telephone lines, telex, cables, etc., in Judea and Samaria serve the Israeli settlements, the I.D.F., and local residents as well. These must also be under the supervision of Israel and the Administrative Council, both regarding their security and their development and maintenance.

The common denominator in the issues of water, electricity, roads and telecommunications is their being part of the area's infrastructure, and threfore their control should be a combined Israeli and local one. It is hence proposed to establish a common coordination body for all infrastructure issues, similar to the one for water, expressing the interests of both sides and producing optimal efficiency in operating the infrastructure for the welfare of all residents, Arabs and Israelis.

Settlement Security

Guarding settlements: arrangements for guarding the settlements have been made in a special order of the Military Commander[66] similar to Israel's Guarding in Settlements Law.[67] It is suggested that this order be left in force even after autonomy is established. If the military government is abolished, the guarding arrangements must be made through Israeli legislation, thus providing settlements with the ability to ensure efficient guarding and offering suitable compensation to any person hurt in all these activities.

Police: as we have seen, the Camp David Accords mention a strong local police force comprised of local residents. The wording enables Israeli settlers, as area residents, to participate in this police force as well. Moreover, under the agreements Israel retains the authority to maintain security, and it may view the police in the settlements as a means to maintain this security. It is still too early to know how the negotiations about the local police force will develop and what would be its size and organization. In any case, an Israeli demand to have a police force in the Israeli settlements linked with the proposed municipal body is legitimate and conforms with the Camp David Accords. Structurally this force may be viewed as part of the Israel Police or the local autonomy police, but in any case there is a need for a police force which would be authorized to arrest persons, both security offenders and criminal offenders, of all kinds

Developing Settlements

The above analysis deals mainly with methods of maintaining the status quo when autonomy is established. However, if Israel intends to develop and extend settlement and not just "freeze" it, more extensive powers are required than those suggested.

Concerning land, for example, it is insufficient to find a suitable legal solution just for the present situation; legal means must be provided permitting future seizure or expropriation of land for new settlement areas or extending the present ones. The proposed peace plan, which mentions the right to settle and purchase land,[68] is too general. Legal means must be provided to oblige land registries within the autonomy government to register land purchases by Israelis. At any rate, regarding land areas on which settlements already exist, the borders of the area to be expropriated should be determined according to maximal planned sizes of settlements, and of the proposed Israeli municipal bodies, and of the amount of required water.

Proposed Solutions

In addition to the solutions suggested above regarding specific issues—and many others exist—the critical issue which arises is autonomy's applicability to Israeli settlers. Two methods are proposed so as to prevent the applicability of the present territorial law i.e., Jordanian law in Judea and Samaria, to Israeli settlers and to bring them under the protection of Israeli law.

a.   *Municipal bodies*: the Israeli agricultural settlements in Judea and Samaria have been recently organized into regional councils dealing with purely municipal issues.[69] It is suggested that these bodies have more extensive powers than those of municipal bodies in Israel, so that they could serve as a means for transferring Israeli administration and government to the Israeli settlers. They would be provided with land to be leased, water to be distributed, and powers to supervise roads, electricity, guarding of the settlements, police, education, health and welfare. A court may also be established under this framework which would not be merely a municipal court. The areas under the jurisdiction of the Israeli municipal bodies will not be subject to laws and regulations of the Arab Administrative Council, and the local police would not be authorized to enter their territory. The roads leading to these municipal areas from Israel should also be under the jurisdiction of those bodies and not that of the Administrative Council.

b.   *Applying Israeli law to settlers*: to strengthen the link between the settlers and Israel, Israeli law and jurisdiction apparently may be applied to Israeli settlement areas. However, in the present political constellation this would be difficult. Thus a Knesset law is suggested, to provide as follows:

Israeli law, jurisdiction, and administration shall apply to citizens of the State of Israel or to persons registered at the Population Registry in Israel as permanently residing within the area of Judea and Samaria, and they shall be deemed to be residents of Israel with respect to any law.

This is not an annexation of territories to Israel, as was done with East Jerusalem under Article 11b of the Law and Administration Ordinance, 5708-1948 (as amended in 1967), but a personal application of Israeli law to settlers in Judea and Samaria.

For external purposes, both in negotiations with Arabs and in discussions with the United States, it may be argued that establishing the municipal body and the personal application of Israeli law to settlers are legal means that Israel employs to protect its citizens within the autonomy period, just as any country protects its citizens, both within and outside its territory.

Thus autonomy in Judea and Samaria would in effect apply to part of the area where Arab residents are concentrated, whereas the Israelis would have an autonomy within autonomy, wherein Israeli law would apply.

Reciprocal Relations between Israel and the Autonomous Areas

We should note at the outset that the areas of Judea, Samaria and Gaza are geographically in the heart of Israel and that, during the last twelve years, the previous border between these areas and Israel was only imaginary.[70] In practice there was freedom of movement of people and goods between them. Reciprocal relations are quite extensive: tens of thousands of local residents work in Israel; residents of the areas are influenced by the spirit and democratic institutions of Israel; the economies of Israel and these areas form one unit, etc.[71] The Israeli peace plan provides for continued open borders, or, more accurately, for the absence of borders: "Residents of Israel and residents of Judea, Samaria, and Gaza district will be assured freedom of movement and freedom of economic activity in Israel, Judea, Samaria, and the Gaza district."[72]

The Camp David agreements disregard this issue. Israel, however, is probably going to insist on it, since this constitutes one of the major factors in viewing Judea, Samaria and Gaza as part of Eretz-Israel (Land of Israel), which the Israeli government holds is never to be divided again. Thus freedom of movement without visas or permits is an important element of the Israeli government's outlook. Against an Egyptian contention that the autonomy government may form its own independent policy of entry and exit permits, one may reply that this is a power of a sovereign state, which the autonomous areas are not.

This freedom of movement is significant in creating the proper atmosphere of continued economic and social cooperation between Judea, Samaria and Gaza on the one hand, and Israel on the other, which constitute, at least *de facto*, one economic unit. The lack of borders has numerous effects on the freedom of movement between Israel and the autonomous areas. Thus, to use an innocent example, unlimited power in the hands of the chief of the Department of Helath may permit him to declare the area of Judea and Samaria closed due to a fear—whether real or imaginary—of disease. In so doing freedom of movement will be curtailed. This may have extremely adverse effects on Israel's economy, which employs tens of thousands of workers from the administered areas.

Freedom of movement also necessitates detailed arrrangements concerning reciprocal recognition of vehicle and driving permits, determining communication routes passing through the autonomy, etc. These reciprocal relations are a bit more intricate in the economic field. Our estimate is that a solution may be reached here too, provided the autonomy and Israel continue as one economic unit, especially externally. Thus the border with the East Bank, i.e., the Jordan bridges, will be open to the movement of goods according to the rules prevailing in Israel, not only because of security reasons (and hence the legitimacy of Israel's demand for continued security checks at the bridges), but also because of economic ones. If the Administrative Council could form a customs policy contradicting Israel's, it could flood the market in Judea and Samaria, and hence in Israel (as no border exists), with cheap goods that would harm Israel's economy. Therefore the power to promulgate even customs regulations would not be left entirely with the autonomy authorities, but with Israel. Israel would at least be able to veto one-sided changes by the Administrative Council. This also applies to other indirect taxes—Purchase Tax and Value Added Tax. This last tax is easily understood; its logic applies in one economic system, where, in each production stage, the deductible tax may be set-off. Two separate economic systems, one of which has the tax and the other does not, or has different amounts of tax, would produce unfair competition, smuggling and tax evasion.

The situation differs for direct taxes, which the autonomy authorities may be expected to collect themselves at their own rates. However, an additional problem which in itself may require a separate article appears: methods for determining the autonomy budget and its sources of income. If Israel finances part of the budget, the autonomous authority's burden will be eased and Israel will have some means of supervision over the Administrative Council. If the Arab party demands budgetary independence, many difficulties will arise. Capital import through contributions would cause one such difficulty. It may damage the whole monetary market throughout Israel and the autonomous areas. Another apparently reasonable demand would be that taxes deducted at source from local residents working in Israel be transferred to the autonomous authority, which supplies them with most of their services. Hence, a coordination system between Israel and the autonomous areas must be formed, and this has already been hinted at in the peace plan.[73] However, it appears this system must be stronger and rooted in more operative levels of departments vis-a-vis government offices, and not only in one representative of the Administrative Council who will serve as a contact with Israel.

The Citizenship Option

We conclude this discussion of autonomy with an Israeli proposal which has not, as yet, had an Arab reaction, nor been mentioned in the Camp David Accords. This is the option offered to inhabitants of the areas to choose between Jordanian and Israeli citizenship.[74]

It should be noted that this step offers political expression to local residents, many of whom had no citizenship at all. Up to 1948 residents of Palestine had citizenship given them by the British Mandate under the Palestinian Citizenship Order, 1925.[75] With the Mandate's end on May 15, 1948, Palestinian citizenship disappeared. Those Arab residents of Palestine who did not remain in the newly-formed State of Israel and merely acquire Israeli citizenship had no citizenship whatsoever. The overwhelming majority of the residents of the Gaza Strip have remained without citizenship. Even during the years of Egyptian military government prior to 1967, they received no Egyptian citizenship and did not take part in elections for Egypt's parliament.

In Judea and Samaria, the Jordanian Citizenship Act, No. 6. for 1954, prevailed; it gave Jordanian citizenship to anyone who had held Mandatory citizenship up to May 15, 1948. Under this act, Jordanian citizenship was bestowed upon permanent residents of Judea and Samaria but, with few exceptions, those who had fled to the area from Israel during the 1948 war and were considered refugees did not receive Jordanian citizenship and so remained without citizenship. Thus for most of the Gaza residents and part of those in Judea and Samaria who hold no citizenship the Israeli pleace plan has an outlet for their political aspirations.

Even if most residents who consider themselves Palestinians refuse Israeli citizenship, this very option, which depends on individual choice, constitutes a change of status for the inhabitants. Upon obtaining Israeli or Jordanian citizenship, the local resident will be entitled to take part in elections for Israel's or Jordan's parliament, respectively, *in addition* to his right to participate in elections for his autonomous institutions.

Warnings have been voiced, especially in Israel, regarding the possibility that many Arabs would opt for Israeli citizenship which could cause a radical change in the Israeli political balance of power. If all the residents of Judea, Samaria and Gaza were to obtain Israeli citizenship, they plus the Israeli Arabs in the Galilee and the "little Triangle" would constitute about one-third of all residents of western Palestine and could form an Arab party that would win about one-third of the seats in the Knesset.

However, the citizenship issue is part of future prospects, and it seems to be last on the priority list as far as negotiations are concerned; hopefully it will be resolved following the successful conclusion of the autonomy discussions.

Conclusion

Implementing the autonomy plan in Judea, Samaria and Gaza entails many problems. The autonomy's origin would be military rule, unlike a "normal" autonomy bestowed by a country upon one of its own regions. Interests which seem vital to Israel, not only those directly linked to security, but also including Israeli settlement and its continued development, lack of *de facto* borders, and the continued economic state of affairs—all these create a unique situation. Historic examples cannot be immediately applied, except with appropriate modifications. This essay has pointed out several basic problems which we feel will be the centre of discussion and which, once resolved, will determine the final autonomy document.

Many have remarked that autonomy raises a political rather than a legal problem. It is not our aim here to disprove this view and to show it to be a solely legal issue. On the contrary, the legal aim is to clarify problems and to define the borderlines of the powers of various authorities in this delicate state. When politicians avoid decisions, or reach only general ones, leaving the formulation of documents to jurists, it seems that the jurists raise all of the problems, thus producing the impression that the autonomy plan is a legal issue. The reason is clear: politicians evade concrete decisions, settling for a formula acceptable to all or for an empty slogan. Then at the stage of legal formulation, which requires sharp and clear terminology, the political problems swept under the carpet emerge again. Discussion of issues by jurists in fact serves the politicians. Problems are clearly presented, everyone knows his specific authority, and the unequivocal and binding solutions found may enable the parties to operate the autonomy plan.

Notes

1.　These quotations are from a letter by the President of Egypt and the Prime Minister of Israel to the President of the United States on March 26, 1979, which began, "This letter confirms that Israel and Egypt have agreed as follows. . ." It will be referred to hereafter as "the letter."

2.　"A Framework for Peace in the Middle East Agreed at Camp David, September 17, 1978." The text of the agreements, with commentary and notes, is included in: R. Lapidoth, "The Camp David Agreements: Some legal Aspects, "*The Jerusalem Quarterly*, No. 10 (Winter 1979), pp. 14–37. The accord will be referred to hereinafter as C.D.A., followed by the article number.

3.　See: Minutes of the 9th Knesset, Second Session, Meeting No. 61, of December 28, 1977, p. 925 (in Hebrew). The plan was approved by a majority of 64 to 8, with 40 abstentions. The Prime Minister of Israel said that various statesmen in the world reacted positively to the plan, how-ever, the President of Egypt did not accept the plan. A brief discussion of the legal aspects of the plan are included in M. Drori, "The Legal System in Judea and Samaria: The Previous Decade and a Glance at the Future," *Israel Yearbook on Human Rights* (1978) p. 144, p. 171.ff.

4.　Dr. Eliahu Ben Elissar, Director General of the Prime Minister's office, in a discussion on Israeli television, On May. 14, 1979, has indeed voiced the opinion that this trait of leaving certain points open to different interpretations was one of the virtues of the Camp David accords.

5.　According to the letter: "The United States Government will partici-pate fully in all stages of negotiations." One may enter into more intricate elaboration and ask, for example, is there legal "estoppel" here? Does this doctrine play any role in international negotiations? If so, under what con-ditions, and do these exist in the present circumstances? However, these questions are beyond our present discussion.

6.　See C.D.A., Article A.

7.　See the last part of the letter and note no. 5 *supra*. The wording of the letter fails to make it clear whether the United States must legally partic-ipate in the negotiations or has the option of so doing. Hence it may be viewed as a proposal which the U.S. may accept or reject. However, the status of the United States in the negotiations will obviously be of great importance.

8.　C.D.A., Article A1(B), and the letter.

9.　Letter written the day the C.D.A. were signed. It is interesting to note that the explanatory note (note 3 *supra*) of the letter written by the Prime Minister of Israel and the President of Egypt on March 26, 1979—which also reiterated the provisions of C.D.A., Article A1(B)—did not mention the Palestinians, but only that the term "West Bank" is understood by Israel to mean Judea and Samaria. It should be noted that this explana-tory note is not binding upon Egypt, as it was not written to Egypt and was omitted from its copy of the letter and agreement.

10.　This may also be shown by the fact that in both the C.D.A. and the letter the wording is,"Jordan will be *invited* to join the negotiation." Since Jordan is invited, it may accept or reject the invitation.

11.　Letter No. 8, Appendix 2.

12.　C.D.A., Article A1(c).

13.　Cf. Daniel Potshuvitzki, "Regarding the Camp David Agreements and the Linkage to Establishing the Autonomy," *Ha'uma* (The Nation), 56 (December, 1978), p. 9–13, at p. 11 (in Hebrew).

14.　On the other hand, the term "inhabitants" appears in the C.D.A. as connoting the residents entitled to self-rule and to participation in determining their own future; it may therefore be said that this envisages Arab residents only, and the term "inhabitants" has been used so as to avoid the problem of citizenship of Arabs in Judea, Samaria and Gaza.

15.   C.D.A., Article A1(a).

16.   An Israeli concession has been made here. The first article of the 1977 Israeli Peace Plan proposed that only "the administration of the military government. . . will be abolished," assuming that this type of government—especially its military character—will be maintained in the area, as part of maintaining security (Article 11 of the Israeli plan).

17.   See Professor Ruth Lapidoth's brief comments, *supra*, no. 2, p. 26. The Egyptian argument, meant to prevent the continued activity of the military government, is a double-edged sword. If the agreement is the source of authority, it cannot bestow more than each of its components possesses. Egypt has no sovereignty claim over Judea and Samaria, and if only a bilateral Israeli-Egyptian accord is reached, it may be seen as admitting Israel's sovereignty over the area, or, at any rate, that Israel may bestow autonomy there. The situation would differ if the military government were to bestow autonomy, as no doubt is the case, since it carries out *de facto* the powers of government in the occupied area under international law.

18.   Criminal Appeal 1/48, *Sylvester* vs *The Attorney General*, Psakim Elionim (Supreme Court Decisions), Volume 1, p. 513, 15 pp. 533-534.

19.   This committee must also decide the extent of the Administrative Council's authority to promulgate regulations. See below.

20.   Concerning the layers of the legal system in Judea and Samaria, see: Drori, *supra*, n. 3, at pp. 144-145, 146-147.

21.   See in detail: A. Rubinstein, *The Constitutional Law of the State of Israel* (Second Edition, Shocken, 1974), pp. 33-54 (Hebrew). A similar provision will be required regarding individual acts according to the principle in Article 19 of the Law and Administrative Ordinance: loc. cit., pp. 55-56.

22.   See: S. Shitrit, "Civil Rights in Jordanian Law," *Mishpatim*, Vol. 1 (5728-1968), p. 113, at p. 114 (Hebrew); M. Shamgar, "The Observance of International Law in the Administered Territories," *Israel Yearbook on Human Rights*, 1 (1971), p. 262, at p. 265.

23.   See in detail: M. Drori, *The Legislation in the Area of Judea and Samaria* (Hebrew University, Jerusalem, 1975) (Hebrew), pp. 38-39, 213.

24.   See: Drori, *supra*, n. 3, Ch. 4-7, at pp. 147-161.

25.   C.D.A., Article A1(A).

26.   C.D.A., Article A1(A) (twice); Article A1(B) (twice); A2; A3. This term also appears twice in the letter.

27.   C.D.A., Article A1(C). This term also appears once in the letter.

28.   High Court of Justice Decision No. 377/71, *Aljamaya Almassihiyah Lilarachi Almakadssah (Christian Holy Places Assoociation)* vs. *Minister of Defence*, Piskei Din (Supreme Court Judgments), Vol.26(1), 574, at p. 582. For a detailed discussion of this decision, see: Drori, n. 23, p. 79 ff.

29.   C.D.A., Article A1(B).

30.   Article 10 of the Peace Plan.

31.   Compare: Drori, *Supra*, n. 3, Ch. 12.2, at p. 171 ff.

32.   See generally: M. Drori, "The Relationship between Central Government and Local Government in Judea and Samaria from a Legal Viewpoint," *Ir Ve'ezor* (Town and Region), Volume 2, No. 3 (5735-1975), pp. 57-69.

33.   Drori, *ibid.* (*Supra*, n. 23), p. 188.

34.   Regarding jurisdiction of Israeli courts on matters concerning the administered areas see: Drori, *ibid,*. p. 74 ff.

35.   Questions of composition of the court arise—who will preside, will a majority of the judges be Israeli, local, or will the court comprise of foreign members as well?

36. Compare with regard to municipalities the article mentioned in n. 31.

37. Regarding the court system in Judea and Samaria see in detail the article in n. 3, Ch. 6, p. 150 ff.

38 Article 10(K) of the Israeli plan. The Camp David accord does not deal with these details, but one may assume its drafters also envisaged government departments, one of which would, no doubt, be responsible for courts.

39. Regarding Military Courts see in detail: Drori, *supra*, n. 3, Ch. 6. 3, at pp. 153–154; n. 23, p. 160ff.

40. C.D.A., Article A1(B).

41. Even though this is not expressly mentioned in the C.D.A., it may be included in "arrangements for assuring internal and external security and public order," to be achieved in an agreement as provided for in that article of the C.D.A.

42. Drori, n. 3, Ch. 6.6, at pp. 156–159; Drori, n. 23, pp. 74–90.

43. See, example, Shamgar, n. 23, p. 273, 277.

44. C.D.A., Article A1(B), and compare with the letter as well.

45. Article 9 of the Israeli peace plan.

46. Article 10 of the Israeli plan.

47. C.D.A., Article A1(B).

48. C.D.A., Article A1(B), last part.

49. C.D.A., Article A1(B) and A2. The term "strong local police force" appears in both places. Some may interpret the role of this police force as maintaining both public order and internal and external security—thus fulfilling the functions of police and army simultaneously: D. Potshuvitzki, *op. cit*, n. 14, at pp. 11–12. However, this is not our opinion, as it appears quite clear that the role of the local police is limited to police functions only.

50. Regarding all criminal law and military government powers in this area, see Drori, *op. cit.* (n. 23,), pp. 176–185.

51. These issues were extensively discussed by me in a series, "The Autonomy and Israeli settlements in the West Bank," *Ha'Aretz*, October 20, 22, 24, 1978.

52. The initial part of Article 20 of the Peace Plan.

53. However, this is a double-edged argument. If Israel does not recognise the validity of Jordanian legislation regarding Jewish absentees' property, the other side may similarly claim that the Israeli Absentee Property Law of 1950 is invalid. Thus the road is open for claims and counterclaims regarding Arab and Jewish refugees.

54. See also: G. von Glahn, *The Occupation of Enemy Territory: A Commentary on the Law and Practice of Belligerent Occupation* (Minneapolis, University of Minnesota Press, 1957), p. 176 ff.

55. Order Concerning Government Property (West Bank Area) (No. 59), 5727-1967, Proclamations, Orders and Appointments (of the Military Government), No. 5, p. 162; Drori, n. 24, p. 193.

56. Order Concerning Abandoned Property (Private Property) (West Bank Area) (No. 58), 5727-1967, Proclamations, Orders and Appointments, No. 5, p. 158.

57. The aforementioned Order, and Drori, *op. cit.*, n. 23, p. 192.

58. See for example, Regulation 46 of the Hague Regulations, 1907.

59. See, for example, Regulation 23(g) of the Hague Regulations, 1907; Article 592–593 of the British Manual.

60. This was also recognized by the Supreme Court when sitting as a High Court of Justice in the Raffah Approach case; High Court of Justice Decisions No. 302/72, 306/72, *Suleiman Hilu and Others, Sabah El Salaimah and Others v. the Government of Israel and Others*, Piskei-Din, Volume 27(2), 169, and see Drori, *op. cit.*, n. 23, p. 88–89.

61. High Court of Justice Decision No. 256/72, *The Jerusalem District*

Electricity Company Ltd. v. The Minister of Defense and Others, Piskei-Din, Volume 27(1), 124, Drori, *op. cit.*, p. 84–85.

62.   Order Concerning Planning of Towns, Villages and Buildings Law (Judea and Samaria) (No. 418), 5731–1971, *Proclamations and Orders,* No. 27, p. 1000.

63.   See: Y. Boneh and A. Beida, "Sources of Water and their Use in Judea and Samaria," in A. Shmueli, D. Grossman, R. Zeevi (editors), *Judea and Samaria-Chapters in Settlement Geography* (Canaan, Jerusalem, 1976), p. 34, at p. 40.

64.   See sources in n. 61.

65.   See n. 64.

66.   Order Concerning Guarding in Settlements (Judea and Samaria) (No. 432), 5731–1971, *Proclamations and Orders,* No. 28, p. 1056.

67.   Local Municipalities (Guarding) Law, 5721–1961, *Sefer HaHukim* (Book of Statutes), No, 346, p. 169.

68.   See Article 20 of the Peace Plan.

69.   See Order Concerning Administration of Regional Councils (Judea and Samaria) (No. 783), 5739–1979, and also Order Concerning Administration of Maaleh Edomin (Judea and Samaria) (No. 788), 5739–1979. An Order concerning the management of Kiryat Arba as an administration was promulgated a few years ago. See: Order Concerning Administration of Kiryat Arba (Judea and Samaria) (No. 561), 5735–1974, *Proclamations and Orders,* No. 34, p. l384.

70.   The areas were considered as closed, and exit and entry were allowed only by permits, but following the general permits, the "Green Line" has almost totally disappeared. See also: Drori, n. 23, pp. 144–145.

71.   Cf. Drori, n. 24, p. 96; Drori, n. 3, Ch. 11, pp. 168–170. This has been viewed as a "common market that has been created between Israel and the territories." A. Bergman, "Economic Development in the Administered Areas," in D.J. Elazar (ed.), *Self Rule/Shared Rule: Federal Solutions to the Middle East* (Turtledove, Ramat Gan, 1979). p. 46.

72.   Article 22, of the Peace Plan.

73.   Article 23. of the Peace Plan.

74.   Articles 14–18 of the Peace Plan.

75.   Drayton, *Laws of Palestine* (London, 1934), vol III, p. 2640.

Partition Versus Sharing in the Arab-Israeli Conflict

Shmuel Sandler

Israeli public opinion and the foreign policy making elites have been divided since the 1967 war on the issue of the territories acquired during the war. While an absolute majority agreed that a return to the pre-1967 lines, even in exchange for a genuine peace, was unacceptable, the question of how much Israel should give back was not resolved. If this problem remained somewhat academic so long as there was no sign of a real peace, the November 1977 initiative of President Sadat and the ultimate signing of a peace treaty with Egypt rendered the question more acute. Moreover, Israel's agreement to return all of the Sinai peninsula to Egypt narrowed the problem to the Golan Heights, the West Bank, and the Gaza Strip. With Egypt committed to the latter two areas and Syria showing no signs of compromise, the political debate came to focus on the future of Judea, Samaria, and the Gaza Strip.

In general, it can be agreed that from Israel's point of view a radical solution along the lines of total withdrawal or absolute annexation of these territories is impossible and even undesirable. The first option has to be rejected because of the strategic threats that such a move would constitute for Israel. Full integration of all the territories is impossible because of international and demographic considerations. The practical conclusion is therefore that a political solution would have to be based on some kind of a compromise between the two options.

If we accept this conclusion, there are two alternatives for a compromise: territorial partition or power-sharing. The general task of this essay is to examine these alternatives from two perspectives: historical and strategic.

It is interesting to note that this dilemma is not new to the contending parties in Palestine. Since the early 1920s, the Zionists

221

have been faced with these two options. As we shall demonstrate in the first part of this essay, this dilemma has accompanied the Arab-Israeli conflict throughout its history. While partition prevailed in the early stages of the conflict and was responsible for the emergence of two states—Jordan and Israel—in geographic Palestine, this did not resolve the national conflict in the Middle East.

The second part of the essay examines the strategic dilemma which Israel has faced since the Six-Day War. Following this war, western Palestine—Eretz Israel in Hebrew—was reunited, but the dispute between Jews and Arabs was not resolved. If the 1967 war proved the fragility of the 1949 armistice lines, the ensuing violence and particularly the 1973 war revealed that neither could the new lines promote stability. The various plans that have emerged since June 1967 were designed to resolve this dilemma. These plans can be distinguished, *inter alia*, by their attitude towards repartition versus powersharing.[1]

Partition Versus Sharing:
The Historical-Political Dimension

Future historians will probably describe the Arab-Israeli conflict as the Hundred Years' War of the Middle East. The conflict is already approximately eighty years old and, although it is difficult to point to the exact year in which the conflict was generated, we do know around what time the foundations for the dispute were laid.

The origins of the struggle between the Arabs and Jews over Palestine go back to the end of the nineteenth century. At that time, two powerful national movements were born—Zionism and Arab nationalism. Despite the fact that they were founded in different parts of the world, since both focused their attention on the same region, they were destined to cross each other. Although one movement, Zionism, directed its demands to only a small portion of the region—Palestine—while the other had larger regional ambitions, they were ultimately to confront one another. And despite the fact that both movements had ancient historical and religious origins, their modern manifestations were primarily influenced by European nationalism.[2]

In retrospect, the emerging nations of the Middle East had a choice between a nation-state and a federal model. Had they chosen the latter model, the region would probably have saved itself many wars, struggles, and instability. But, with the assistance of their European mentors, they chose the first route and thus were heir to the destiny of Europe.

The actual conflict between Arabs and Jews emerged when the Zionist movement started to implement its design for establishing a Jewish state in Palestine. The recurrent argument that the Jews misled the Arabs and other nations as to their ultimate political goal is unfounded. One had only to read *Der Judenstaat*, written by Theodore Herzl, the founder of political Zionism, and published in 1896, to see that what he had in mind was a state.[3] But so long as the Jews in Palestine did not present a potential threat and Arab nationalism was limited to small elites, there was no significant national dispute between Jews and Arabs. It was only on the eve of World War I, and particularly following the Balfour Declaration issued on November 2, 1917,[4] that an active struggle against Zionism was put into motion. The recognition of Zionism by a global power, accompanied by certain disappointments with regard to the promises given by Britain to the Arabs during the war, increased hostility towards both Britain and the Jewish national movement.

Nevertheless, the Arab attitude towards the Jews was not homogeneous. On the one hand, the Palestinian Arabs, who were divided on various issues, were united in their objection to Zionism and particularly to the Balfour Declaration. In their struggle against the Jews, both the Moslems and the Christians of Palestine were united, a unity represented by the foundation of the Moslem-Christian Association. Their general position was that there was no room for a Zionist political entity. Thus, they were opposed not merely to a Jewish state in Palestine but even to a national home for the Jews.

On the other hand, there were more moderate forces among the Arabs, represented by the Hashemite monarchs. Hussein Ibn Ali, sheriff of Mecca and later king of Hejaz, who was Britain's Middle East partner against the Ottomans, in a meeting with D. G. Hogarth—the head of the Arab Bureau in General Allenby's headquarters—welcomed Jews to come and settle in Arab lands. His son, Emir Feisal, who was later nominated king of Syria, met with Dr. Chaim Weizmann, the leader of the Zionist movement, and also called for the immigration of Jews into Palestine in larger numbers.[5] In a memorandum dating from the first day of the peace conferences in January 1919, Emir Feisal made a friendly statement on Zionism and supported, in essence, the idea of a protectorate in Palestine in which Jews and Arabs would live peacefully.[6] To be sure, these proclamations did not support a Jewish state. Yet, such attitudes were a far cry from the positions held by the Arabs of Palestine demanding the abolition of the Balfour Declaration and a halt to Jewish immigration.

In the period immediately following World War I, both the Hashemites and the Palestine elites supported—though for different reasons—a similar solution for Palestine. The essence of their plan lay in the creation of a greater united Syria which would include Syria, Lebanon, and Palestine on both sides of the Jordan River. Feisal's support for such a solution was obviously motivated by the fact that the British government intended to designate him as king of Syria. The Palestinian position, in contrast, was primarily motivated by the objection to Zionism. They hoped that, by the annexation of Palestine to Syria, they would prevent the establishment of a Jewish state.[7]

The creation of a greater Syria, however, was contrary to the wishes of Britain because, according to the Sykes-Picot Agreement, the area was to be divided between France and Britain, with Syria going to the former and Palestine to the latter. This was also one of the reasons why the British did not welcome the Feisal-Weizmann Agreement.[8] The division of the area between the two great powers led to the expulsion of Feisal from Syria by the French in 1920, at which time the independence of that country was abolished. This put an end to the plan of creating a greater Syria under the auspices of the great powers, and the Palestinian Arabs now had to create a new identity for themselves to counterbalance the Zionist claims.

The First Partition of Palestine

The collapse of the greater Syrian kingdom left the British with the problem of eastern Palestine. The territories east of the Jordan had been under Feisal's rule but, with the latter expelled from Syria, there was nobody to rule them. Historically, these territories were part of Palestine, and indeed they were included under the British Palestine mandate set up by the San Remo conference. The lack of a central government, accompanied by the presence of Syrian nationalists in these areas, led to tribal raids on Syria, prompting the French government to warn the British to put an end to these actions.[9] Under these circumstances, the arrival of Emir Abdullah, Feisal's eldest brother, at Ma'an solved the British dilemma.

Emir Abdullah, who came to eastern Palestine under the pretense of liberating Syria and restoring his brother's throne, lived up to the pragmatic expectations of Winston Churchill, then Colonial Secretary. (As a result of the San Remo conference, Palestine had been transferred from the Foreign Office to the Colonial Office.) At the conference on Palestine which met in Cairo in March 1921, it was decided that Feisal should be compensated for his losses in Syria and be nominated king of Iraq. But since Iraq had been promised earlier to Abdullah, there was now a need to compensate Feisal's older brother.[10] Moreover, it was necessary to promote a central government for Transjordan (as eastern Palestine came to be known) and, since Britain did not desire to invest in the maintenance of a regular army in the area, Abdullah's rule there was an ideal solution.[11] In a meeting between Churchill and Abdullah held in Jerusalem, the latter agreed to the British conditions—namely the acknowledgement of the British mandate in his territory and the abandonmnet of any war plans against France.[12]

The Zionist reaction to the partition of Palestine was mixed. It is true that there had been no Jewish settlement in Transjordan; however, the Balfour Declaration and the British mandate included both sides of the Jordan. Hence, the partition of Palestine and the establishment of an Arab government in eastern Palestine could have been considered as the first British violation of the

Balfour Declaration. Moreover, the establishment of the Abdullah Emirate closed the door to a compromise in which the Palestinians would have received the other side of the Jordan. The Zionist feeling of betrayal was further aroused when on September 16, 1922 the British government issued a memorandum declaring that Jews were forbidden to buy land in Transjordan.[13] This action amounted not only to the violation of the mandate but to religious discrimination as well. In any case, the first partition of Palestine, or Eretz Israel—the land of Israel—as it was called by the Jews, crystallized the struggle between Palestinian Arabs and Jews over the western part of Palestine, in the future to be known as Palestine, whereas the eastern part became a national Arab entity named Transjordan.

Although the reaction of the Palestinian Arabs to the partition was a positive one, since the ruler of that region was an Arab, this partition also had a negative impact on them. Whereas previously they had had a clear cause for expressing their nationalism, with the collapse of the greater Syria idea and the detachment of eastern Palestine, they were left with no positive cause. Their nationalism was now expressed even more strongly in their hatred of the Zionists and the British administration. It was at this time and under these circumstances that the leadership of the Palestinian Arabs shifted to Haj Amin el-Husseini, the Mufti of Jerusalem. This man, who was interested primarily in religion, translated the frustrations of the Arabs into a religious cause. Under his leadership, the national feelings were interwoven with anti-Jewish, not merely anti-Zionist, feelings. This new trend expressed itself in the greatest outbreak of hostilities since the arrival of the first Zionists in Palestine. In August 1929, rumor advanced by the Supreme Moslem Council spread throughout Palestine to the effect that the Jews planned to take over the holy sites in Jerusalem. The hostilities which this provoked began in Jerusalem and spread to other cities such as Hebron and Safad, where more than one hundred Jews were murdered and hundreds wounded.[14]

At the same time, the new attitudes also prompted anti-British feelings, and the Mufti preached the view that the foreign rulers were allies of the Jews and therefore to be regarded as an enemy. Consequently, in October 1933, the first Arab rising against the British took place — an event which was followed by the great Arab rising in the years 1936–39.[15]

Besides the violence brought about by these attitudes, the practical result was that the Palestinian Arabs continued to resist any compromise with the Zionists. In contrast, throughout that period, Abdullah continued his contacts with the Zionists, trying to convince them to invest in Transjordan. In a meeting held on January 24, 1924 between the Emir and a Jewish delegation headed by Colonel F. Kish—the head of the Executive Committee of the Jewish Agency—Abdullah said:

Palestine is one unit. The division between Palestine and Transjordan is artificial and wasteful. We, the Arabs and the Jews, can come to terms and live together in peace in the whole country, but you will have difficulty in reaching an understanding with Palestinian Arabs. You must make an alliance with us. . . Please come to Transjordan. . . Together we will work for the benefit of the country.[16]

The negotiations were resumed in 1933 and, on several occasions, Abdullah and tribal leaders from Transjordan met with Zionist leaders to discuss Jewish settlement in these areas. Ultimately, these discussions failed to produce practical results because of threats from the Palestinian Arabs and the objection of the British government to Jewish immigration into Transjordan.[17]

The First Partition Plan of Western Palestine

If the Zionists, in the period preceding the Balfour Declaration, did not fully realize the problems they would encounter in establishing a Jewish state in Palestine, in the 1920s these realities started to penetrate their cognitive values. The Arab revolts and the British responses to them began to convince many of the Jews that a purely Jewish solution was not practical. In the Zionist camp, the main factions can be divided into two. On the one hand, there was the moderate group headed by such people as Dr. Chaim Weizmann, Dr. Chaim Arlozoroff, and David Ben-Gurion; and, on the other, "maximalist Zionism" (*Grosszionismus*), within which the Revisionists under the leadership of Vladimir Jabotinsky were the most prominant group. The Revisionists demanded an immediate declaration that the final goal of the Zionists was the establishment of a Jewish state within the historical boundaries of Palestine, including Transjordan.[18]

Within the moderate camp, there was no clear operational solution to the problem of the Arab population in Palestine. In general terms, however, it would be accurate to state that the parity principle was dominant until 1937. Although most of the groups saw their final goal as achieving a Jewish majority, many of them perceived that enterprise as a joint state for Jews and Arabs as equal nations. In operational terms, this could be accomplished only through one of two ways—a binational state or cantonization.

The binational idea was supported primarily by two movements—*Brit Shalom* (Peace Union) and *Hashomer Hatzair* (The Young Guard). The first group was composed primarily of intellectuals at the center of the political spectrum, whereas the second was a leftist Zionist faction. Despite their differences on social issues, both movements supported the creation of an Arab-Jewish state. There were also supporters of the idea of binationalism among *Hapoel Hatzair* (The Young Worker) and *Achdut Haavoda* (United Labor)—two socialist movements—but none of these parties came out with binational programs.[19] Ben-Gurion, who saw the territorial issue as crucial, supported a federal solution based on cantonization.[20]

Thus, the Zionist position between 1917–1937 can be defined as moderate. Except for the Revisionists, they all accepted the fact that historic Palestine was divided and tried to reach an accommodation with the Arab population in the country. Since the Arab population was a majority—and, clearly, even if the Jews should become a majority, there would still be a large Arab population—a federal solution to reconcile the national aspirations of both peoples was seen as unavoidable. This situation began to change only after 1937

The foundations for the partition of western Palestine were laid in 1937, when a British Royal Commission arrived in Palestine to investigate the disturbances caused by the Arab revolt of 1936. In 1936 the Palestinian Arabs called a general strike in order to obtain a ban on Jewish immigration, the prohibition of land transfers from Arab to Jewish hands, and the establishment of an Arab national government in place of the British mandate. The strike was followed by a boycott of the Jews, which gradually developed from sporadic acts of violence into open warfare against the Jews and the British administration. Although the rebellion failed, as the Arabs suffered more from the disturbances than did the Yishuv (as the Jewish community in Palestine was known), the government in London nominated a committee headed by Lord Peel to investigate the crisis and to recommend a solution to the Palestine problem.[21]

The proposals that were put before the commission followed along the ideological lines of the various camps. The Arab Higher Committee, representing the Palestinians, demanded that Palestine be established as an Arab state. The Revisionists urged the establishment of a Jewish state on both sides of the Jordan. The Jewish Agency submitted a parity proposal according to which a legislative council would be established in which Jews and Arabs would be granted equal representation. Were this proposal to be accepted, the Zionists were prepared to commit themselves to maintaining this parity, "whatever the future ratio between Arab and Jewish populations might become."[22]

The Royal Commission rejected all these proposals on practical, moral and political grounds, and instead, recommended the partition of Palestine into sovereign Arab and Jewish states and a British mandatory zone. The general outline of the partition was that the Jewish state would comprise the north and the coastal plain, while the remainder would go to the Arab state, which would be united with Transjordan. The British mandate would embrace the holy places (Jerusalem and Bethlehem) and a corridor linking them to the Mediterranean.[23]

The reaction to the partition plan among the Zionists was mixed. They were divided into two camps, for and against partition, independent of social and economic ideologies. The anti-partition camp was composed of the leftist *Hashomer Hatzair*, the religious *Mizrahi* movement, the conservative wing of the General Zionists (a free-trade and anti-socialist party), and the nationalists of the Jewish State party. The pro-partition camp included parties from the moderate left and the center, headed by Dr. Chaim Weiz-mann and David Ben-Gurion. In the debate over partition, those in favor emerged victorious, and the Zionist Congress accepted the principle of partition, though with reservations as to the borders suggested by the Royal Commission.[24] In contrast, the Arabs rejected the partition plan. Not only was the plan rejected by the Palestinians, but all the Arab rulers, except Abdullah, came out against it.[25]

In the long run, the events of 1937 laid the basis for the even-tual partition of Palestine in 1947. Although the British government later withdrew its support for the establishment of two separate states, the plan reemerged after World War II. But what was more significant was the fact that, on both sides—both Zionist and Arab—the idea of partition was adopted by certain leaders who would pursue it in the future. Ben-Gurion and Abdullah were ready to accept the partition for different reasons. The Zionists real-ized that a federal solution with the Arabs was inconceivable. Their primary goal of increasing the Jewish population in Palestine to a majority was unattainable so long as the Arabs objected to it and the British government was influenced by these objections. Thus they preferred a compact Jewish state in which they would become a majority to a state encompassing the whole of Palestine in which they would remain a minority. Abdullah, on the other hand, who had ambitions of establishing a "Greater Syria" under his leadership, understood that the partition could eventually serve his purposes. Transjordan, in order to become a viable inde-pendent state, could not remain in its present form. The establish-ment of a Palestinian state would have meant a total separation between his country and the West Bank. In contrast, partition could result in the annexation of certain parts of the western side of the Jordan River. Thus, the Hashemite king, who had previously advocated cooperation with the Jews in order to improve the eco-nomic situation of his country, now became the only partner in the Arab camp—even if only a tacit partner—with whom the moder-ate Zionists could negotiate. The forces of partition were thus born in 1937.

The Second Partition of Palestine

The events of the years between 1939 and 1945 demonstrated to the Zionists the urgent need for an independent Jewish state. The British White Paper of 1939, which put heavy restrictions on future Jewish immigration to Palestine, was published as a result of Arab pressure on Britain, which was now entering a struggle against

Germany and needed all the support it could get in any part of the world, including the Middle East. It proved to the Zionists that, despite their commitment to a Jewish National Home, the British were ready to abandon their promises in the face of considerations of realpolitik. The new restrictions were particularly fatal at a time when millions of Jews were being slaughtered in Europe. The inability of the Jews in Palestine to assist their brethren in Europe demonstrated more than ever that the Jewish problem could be solved only through the establishment of an independent Jewish state.

It was against this background that in 1942 the Zionists came out openly with a request for the establishment of a Jewish state in Palestine. The Biltmore program (as the resolution came to be known), which was adopted in New York, was then submitted to the Yishuv, but here it met with formidable opposition. While Ben-Gurion succeeded in obtaining the support of the parties of the right and center, he encountered stiff resistance in his own party, and among the binationalists. The leftist opposition in *Mapai* (Ben-Gurion's socialist party), known as Section B, objected to the establishment of a Jewish state before the Jews attained a majority in Palestine, on the grounds that this could only lead to a partition of the country. The leftist parties of *Hashomer Hatzair* and the Zionist Workers objected to the establishment of a Jewish state through partition, for they saw the final solution in the establishment of an Arab-Jewish state in all of Palestine. The binational idea was also supported by such non-political organs as the League for Jewish-Arab Rapprochment founded in 1939 and the *Ihud* (Union) Association founded in 1942, whose leader, Judah L. Magnes, had been one of the founders of *Brit Shalom* in the mid-1920s. Magnes won over to his position Henrietta Szold, the founder of Hadassah (the American women's Zionist organization)—a fact which could have led to that organization's withholding its support for the Biltmore program. However, despite this opposition, the statists, as they now became known, defeated the binationalists at both forums— the political institutions in Jerusalem and Zionist organizations in New York— and the Biltmore program was adopted.[26] The victory of the statists also represented, in essence, the victory of the pro-partition camp, since it was clear that the establishment of a democratic Jewish state would require the partition of Palestine.

In the following years, however, in negotiations with the British government, the Zionists opposed the partition of Palestine. In September 1943, Churchill informed Weizmann of a decision by the British cabinet committee on Palestine to grant the Jews full sovereignty in a divided Palestine. But the Zionists, in a memorandum submitted to the British government, requested the establishment of a Jewish state in an area specifically defined as Palestine west of the Jordan. In November, Weizmann was told by the British Prime Minister that he favored the inclusion of the Negev in the Jewish portion of Palestine.[27] But in 1946 the Jewish Agency Exec-

utive in reaction to the Morrison-Grady Plan which recommended
the conversion of the mandate into a trusteeship and the division
of the country into Jewish and Arab provinces,[28] suggested the
partition of Palestine along the lines of the Peel Commission proposal plus the Negev, while the rest would go to the Arabs.

Finally, in 1947 the problem of Palestine came under the jurisdiction of the United Nations, which appointed an international
investigating board—the United Nations Special Committee on
Palestine, or UNSCOP—which recommended the termination of
the British mandate. But on the final scheme the committee was
divided between a majority recommending partition with economic union and a minority recommending the establishment of
a federal government comprising Arab and Jewish states with Jerusalem as the capital.[29] The Palestinians and the Arab states
rejected both partition and federation, while the Zionists dismissed
the federal proposal but accepted the partition plan. On November
29, 1947 the General Assembly endorsed the partition proposal by
a vote of 33 to 13, thus giving it the necessary two-thirds majority.

Although on the surface the positions of both sides seemed
clear, internally the situation was quite different. King Abdullah,
despite pledges to support the Arab cause, was striving for a partition of Palestine in which he would annex the new Arab state. In
two meetings between Abdullah, Golda Meir and Moshe Sharett in
November 1947 and April 1948, it was agreed that the monarch
would control the Arab portion of Palestine if he did not interfere
with efforts to establish a Jewish state. But Abdullah could not
keep his promises and, under Arab pressure, had to join in the war
effort against the new Jewish state which was established on May
14, 1948. Nevertheless, he continued to try and reach an agreement with the Israeli leaders. In a series of secret meetings which
took place in the second half of 1948 and early 1949, the two sides
negotiated and finally reached an agreement granting Transjordan those areas which later came to be known as the West
Bank.[30] Another part of geo-historical Palestine—the Gaza Strip
—went to Egypt.

In the Jewish camp, too, the attitude vis-a-vis partition was not
unanimous; objection arose on both sides of the political spectrum. The Revisionists were willing to delay the establishment of
the state in order to prevent partition. On the other side of the
spectrum, *Hashomer Hatzair* objected to the resolution in accordance with its binationalist view of Arab-Jewish relations. The
leaders of the leftist *Ahdut Haavoda*, who also objected to the
partition of Palestine, supported the establishment of an international mandate which would encourage Jewish immigration to
Palestine until the Jews should constitute a majority, at which time
a Jewish state would be established.[31]

Despite differences of opinion, a Jewish nation-state was
established in a portion of western Palestine, and the entire area
was divided between Transjordan, subsequently known as Jor-

dan, and Israel. This reality came into being because of several reasons. First, strong international forces supported a division of the area along national lines. Second, the Arab inhabitants of the area were not open to any compromise with regard to powersharing and sovereignty, nor to any other federal solution. The only moderate force within the Arab world, King Abdullah, had an intrinsic interest in the partition of Palestine, as he had come to power through an earlier partition and hoped to gain from the new one. Third, the integrationist forces within the Jewish camp were either very weak, i.e., *Brit Shalom* or dogmatic, i.e., the Revisionists or *Hashomer Hatzair*. The moderate forces in the Jewish camp, while supporting parity in the early stages of the discussions, gave up the idea in face of Arab extremism and the urgency of absorbing millions of Jews who were now waiting to immigrate to Palestine. It was only natural that the moderate and pro-partition forces in both camps should cooperate and thus bring about the second partition of Palestine.

From Partition to Partial Reunion

In spite of early expectations that the armistice lines of 1949 would eventually become the recognized borders between Israel and its Arab neighbors, the 1949 agreements were not followed by a formal peace treaty. In the years that followed, the hostile attitude of the Arabs towards the Jewish state continued to intensify, becoming increasingly dogmatic. Arab hostility was translated into terrorist actions which were launched and supported by various Arab governments. These terrorist actions ultimately led to the Sinai Campaign in 1956 in which Israel militarily defeated the Egyptians, and subsequently enjoyed a period of relative tranquility, until hostilities were renewed in the mid-1960s.

Nevertheless, in the period between 1948 and 1967, tacit cooperation between Israel and the Hashemite Kingdom was maintained. The prospects for a separate peace between Israel and Jordan suffered a setback when Abdullah was assassinated on July 20, 1951 by a 21 year old Palestinian. Ben-Gurion, Israel's first Prime Minister, tried, however, to preserve the tacit understanding between the two countries. Israel responded to terrorist actions from Jordan wth a restricted policy of retaliation. Despite the hostilities originating in Jordan, Ben-Gurion confined the 1956 war to the Egyptian front. Israel and Jordan cooperated tacitly against the internationalization of Jerusalem and in the utilization of the Jordan-Yarmuk river system.[32] But most important was Israel's declaration with regard to the preservation of the status quo on the West Bank. Israel warned that control of the Jordan "bulge" by a state or a united command other than Amman would constitute an automatic *casus belli*. Finally, by permitting British troops to fly over Israeli territory in 1958 and land in Jordan, Israel actively assisted in preserving the independence of Jordan and its pro-Western regime as well as countering Nasser's attempt to rule a united Arab world.

This tacit alliance between two elites which maintained the status quo—and thus the partition of Palestine—came to an end in the latter half of the 1960s. The renewal of terrorist actions against Israel by a new Palestinian group, al-Fatah—actions planned and controlled by a new leftist junta in Damascus—brought about the breakdown of stability in the Middle East. The Syrian actions and Israeli warning triggered the Egyptian dictator, Abdul Nassser, with Moscow's support, to concentrate an Egyptian army in the Sinai—a fact which ultimately caused the Israelis to react militarily. King Hussein's inability to stay out of the Six-Day War, despite promises and pleas from the Israeli leadership to this effect, brought about Israel's conquest of the West Bank. In addition to the Sinai peninsula and the Golan Heights, the Gaza Strip, too, was taken over by Israel, and the various parts of western Palestine were now united under one central authority. Nineteen years after their separation, the West Bank, or Judea and Samaria as they were called in Hebrew, and the Gaza Strip were reunited in the hands of Israel.

But the repercussions of the 1967 war extended beyond territorial integration; it had far-reaching political and social implications in both the Jewish and the Arab camps. First of all, it weakened the common interest between Israel and Jordan, which had maintained the partition of Palestine. Secondly, it strengthened the Palestinians—who had consistently been against the partition of Palestine and objected to any Jewish entity in the area. The Arab defeat in the war strengthened the Palestinian contention that the only way to destrroy the Zionist entity was through a prolonged guerilla war, thus elevating the status of the terrorist organizations in the Arab world. Thirdly, and perhaps most importantly in the long run, the identity of the Palestinian Arabs underwent modification. In the period prior to 1967, the Palestinian Arabs were primarily divided among three countries. Following the 1967 war, Arabs who had previously been living in three separate countries—Israel, Jordan and Egypt—were now reunited. The merging of the Arabs from the Gaza Strip, the West Bank, and Israel into one entity was bound to create new realities and identities. The contacts between the Arabs from Israel and the territories generated the Palestinization of the Israeli Arabs, and strengthened the separationist feeling among the other Palestinians.

The acquisition of the new territories also had a profound impact on Israeli political attitudes and structure. It aroused nationalist feelings among the general populace and the elites with respect to these areas. Ideas and aspirations which had previously been limited to the Revisionists (and even there had already begun to fade) now crossed traditional party lines, and even within the Labor Party there were those who objected to a new partition. Figures like Moshe Dayan and Shimon Peres, students of David Ben-Gurion, now spoke of new arrangements to replace the previous partition. The National Religious Party (N.R.P.), a pragmatic party which had always supported Labor's foreign policy and a very important factor in Israel's coalition governments, now adopted a platform that objected to withdrawal from ancient Jewish land. Moreover, the 1967 war brought about the creation of a national unity government which lasted until 1970 and in which *Herut* (the successor of the Revisionist movement) participated for the first time in Israel's history, thus acquiring legitimacy as a ruling party. In the years that followed, Menahem Begin increased his power by absorbing various smaller parties, thus creating an alternative to the ruling Labor Party. In short, in both camps the moderate forces that had supported and maintained partition became weaker while the integrationists increased their power.

To be sure, in the first ten years following the Six-Day War, this trend was as yet indefinite. The Labor government aspired to reach an agreement with Jordan which would satisfy its strategic needs in the West Bank, but would also return most of the land to its eastern neighbor. This policy of territorial compromise basically implied the repartition of western Palestine. The Allon Plan, which was never formally adopted by the Labor governments, in effect guided the Israeli settlement policy in the new territories.[33] Moreover, Israel and Jordan cooperated during two crises. In September 1970, when King Hussein cracked down on the Palestinians and expelled their organizations, Israel deterred Syrian intervention on behalf of the Palestinians. Likewise, during the 1973 war, Jordan limited its participation on the Arab side. Nevertheless, these interactions were not followed by a comprehensive territorial compromise, and, as a matter of fact, the direct beneficiaries were the anti-partition forces in both camps. Following the Yom Kippur War, the Palestinian organizations were recognized in the Arab world as the sole representatives of the Arabs living in the West Bank and the Gaza Strip. On the world scene, they were accorded observer status in the United Nations and representation in various European capitals. In Israel, the Rabin government, which came to power in the wake of the 1973 war, was torn between hawks and doves, and was ultimately defeated in May 1977 by the *Likud* party headed by Menahem Begin. After decades of Labor leadership, Israel was now ruled by a coalition in which integrationists from various parties provided the dominant tone.

Thus, from a federalist perspective, the dilemmas which confronted the Jews and the Arabs in geographic Palestine (Eretz Israel) in 1978 were to a certain extent similar to those of the 1930s. There are two ways in which the national aspirations of Jews and Arabs in the area can be reconciled. One is to share sovereignty and power, the second is to divide the territory. The first solution implies a federalist-oriented solution, the second a solution based on the nation-state model.

The Strategic-Political Dimension

The acquisition of territories by Israel during the 1967 war infused two new principles into Israel's foreign policy. The first element was that for the first time in her history, Israel had acquired a bargaining card which she could exchange for Arab recognition of the Jewish state. While until 1967 the Zionist state did not possess any tangible assets with which it could encourage its neighbors to bring the state of war between the two peoples to an end, the Arab defeat in the Six-Day War changed this situation. At the same time, it was accepted that the astonishing victory in 1967 provided the besieged state with more comfortable borders, or strategic depth, which Israel had been lacking throughout its nineteen years of independence. While the 1949 armistice lines were preceived by most of Israel's national security analysts as an invitation to war, many believed that Israel would in the future enjoy more secure borders.

However, there was to a certain extent an inherent contradiction between returning territories for the sake of achieving legitimacy, and keeping them for strategic reasons. In order to resolve this dilemma, the Israeli policy makers developed the formula of territorial compromise whereby Israel would relinquish certain territories in exchange for genuine peace, but would retain other areas for strategic reasons. In other words, in a final settlement, Israel would attain both legitimacy and security, two elements that are required for stability.

As long as all the Arab states rejected any recognition of the Jewish state and the situation remained static, the Israeli position was sound and stable. Subsequently, however, two new realities emerged. First, it was demonstrated that Israel's improved defense lines did not deter military action on the part of the Arab states. If the 1967 war demonstrated the vulnerability of Israel's borders, the war of attrition and particularly the Yom Kippur War made it clear that neither could the new ceasefire lines deter its neighbors from initiating a military offensive. Second, it became apparent that several Arab states were ready to make peace with Israel in exchange for the return of territories. President Sadat's public statements, followed by his historic visit to Jerusalem and finally the actual signing of a peace treaty, indicated that peace could be achieved. In recent encounters between Israeli ministers and King Hussein, the Jordanian monarch also displayed a readiness to sign a peace treaty with Israel in exchange for a total Israeli withdrawal from the West Bank and East Jerusalem.[34]

These developments have sharpened the question of territories versus peace, peace versus secure boundaries, secure versus accepted borders. The moderate Arab position, even after the signing of a peace treaty between Israel and Egypt, is that Israel's legiimacy would be established providing that it withdrew to the pre-1967 borders. On the other hand, Israel maintains that a complete withdrawal would endanger its existence in the long run, if not immediately. How can these two positions be reconciled? This question serves as the basis for the following analysis.

Territories and War Motivation
An Analytical Framework

Although the core of the Arab-Israeli conflict has focused, since its inception, on the question of Israel's legitimacy, the territorial question was also of primary importance. As in other international conflicts, territory has always been a major issue in the dispute between Arabs and Jews. In the era of the territorial state, national existence and territory are linked. If a nation or a certain group is not ready to accept the legitimacy of another, then it is in effect denying that nation the right to a certain territory. Accordingly, the dispute between Arabs and Jews could be described as a confrontation over the question of who should control a certain territory within the geographic boundaries of Palestine. Since the Jews did not possess any other territory, the question of legitimacy or national existence and that of territory were in this case congruent.

In the following pages we shall present a framework that describes the relationship between Israel's control of territory and Arab war motivation. We shall assume that the dependent variable, Arab war motivation (axis M) is a function of the independent variable, territorial aggrandizement, described here by axis T. The curve describing the relationship between the two variables is curve I. Our basic assumption is that Arab war motivation is in direct proportion to Israel's territorial aggrandizement; as Israel increases its territory, Arab war motivation also increases. We do not argue that any increase or decrease on axis T would be followed by a corresponding increment on axis M. However, we assume that the general direction of curve I would conform to that

Figure 1

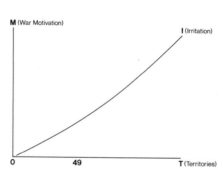

shown in Figure 1—moving upward from left to right. The acquisition of Arab lands by Israel enrages the Arabs and thus increases their urge to go to war.

It is not our intention to provide an exact description of the relationship between the two variables, but to describe the general direction. We can assume that the Arab states in the aggregate would be totally satisfied only if Israel's territory were to be reduced to zero; only a reduction of the state to zero territory would reduce the war motivation to zero. Another indication of the validity of the irritation curve is the time interval between wars. It took nineteen years from the initial attempt to prevent by force the establishment of the Jewish state in 1948 until the Arabs moved on several fronts towards the second major confrontation. It took only six years after Israel had increased its territory in 1967 for her defeated neighbors to launch a direct military assault against her. It is true that, in the interval between 1948–1967, various attempts were made to make life difficult for the besieged state. Nevertheless, all these actions can be classified as either non-military or sub-limited warfare. In the period between 1967–1973, the intensity of Arab economic, political and sub-limited warfare did not decline and may even have increased in comparison to the pre-1967 period. Moreover, in the second inter-war interval, Gamal Abdul Nasser initiated a war of attrition in which both sides suffered severe casualties. In response to the argument that the Sinai Campaign of 1956 postponed an Arab attack by demonstrating Israel's military superiority and destroying the Egyptian army, it may be argued that, in the Six-Day War, Israel presented a much more convincing superiority, yet the Arabs did not wait eleven years to retaliate.

However, the war motivation-territory relationship is also influenced by another factor—the temptation factor. This curve moves in a direction opposite to that of the irritation curve. It implies that the increments in Israel's territory resulting from the 1967 war which provided her with natural borders in the south and west and geo-strategic superiority in the north as well as with strategic depth mitigated the Arab temptation to launch a strike against the Jewish state. Israel's withdrawals from these lines, therefore, tend to increase the war motivation of the Arabs as a result of the increased temptation. While marginal withdrawals would only increase the temptation slightly, deep retreats, especially beyond certain strategic points, would increase the temptation significantly. A return to the 1967 borders, for instance, would increase the temptation drastically. This phenomenon, which may be common to the security interests of other countries, is particularly important given Israel's geo-strategic position. (See Figure 2)

Since its inception, Israel has suffered from a clear geo-strategic inferiority vis-a-vis its neighbors. Although its boundaries were improved during the War of Independence in comparison to the partition plan, the 1949 armistice lines were far from constituting secure borders. This fact was especially significant in light of other tangi-

Figure 2

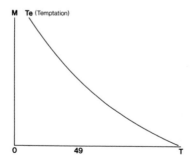

ble Arab advantages in the balance of power equation. While Israel succeeded in counterbalancing the Arab states' tangible superiority (e.g., population, munitions, etc.) primarily through intangible means, the geographic factor remained problematic. The ability of the Arab countries to concentrate armies in the Sinai near Israel's border or on the West Bank where the entire width of the coastal plain at one point is not more than about ten miles, to mention only two of several strategic options, provided them with a clear strategic advantage.[35] In order to counter such a move, Israel would have had to mobilize its entire reserve force—an action which would have crippled its economy. Moreover, the northernmost points in the Gaza Strip and the western points in the West Bank directly threatened the main centers of Israel's population, including the heavily populated Tel Aviv metropolitan area and Jerusalem. In short, as Yigal Allon, late foreign minister of Israel, put it:

> The most cursory glance at the map is sufficient to ascertain how little the armistice lines of 1949 . . . could be considered defensible borders. And even the most superficial fingering of the pages of history should be enough to demonstrate how attractive these lines have been to the Arab states as an encouragement to try their strength again against us.[36]

In retrospect, the development of the 1967 crisis demonstrates how Israel's geo-strategic vulnerability played a major role in triggering the Six-Day War. The Syrian geographic advantage which enabled them to shell Israeli settlements was a major factor in the Soviets' fear that an Israeli retaliation was imminent. The Egyptian concentration of troops on the border with Israel, the closing of the Straits of Tiran and the agreement between Nasser and Hussein permitting Egyptian forces to move into the West Bank posed a strategic threat to Israel, thus forcing her to take preemptive action.[37]

The geo-strategic realities together with historical experience thus provide us with sufficient evidence that the temptation curve moves in a direction opposite to that of Israeli expansion. Withdrawal from territories would thus provide the Arabs with increasing incentives to attack Israel because of its vulnerability. Consequently, whatever gains Israel would achieve by reducing Arab war motivation through withdrawal would be set off by the impact of the temptation factor. In short, the relationship between territories and war motivation in the Arab-Israeli context, from a strategic point of view, can be seen as influenced by two factors which move in different directions: irritation and temptation. Whereas the first factor implies that Israeli territorial expansion increases Arab war motivation while withdrawal reduces it, the second has a reverse effect. The Yom Kippur War demonstrated the strength of the irritation factor, whereas the war of 1967 confirmed the temptation factor.

Under such circumstances, it might be valid to argue that there is not much room for a compromise. If the choice with which Israel is faced is that between even the most moderate Arab position —total withdrawal to the pre-1967 borders—and maintaining the status quo, the latter alternative is the better one.

A more profound examination of the analytical framework presented in the preceding pages, however, leads to other possible conclusions. The underlying principle of this framework is the distinction between various degrees of war motivation. While the pessimistic view is that the Arab war motivation is constant—no matter what Israel's size, the Arabs would be equally motivated to attack her—we have argued that this motivation is influenced by both temptation and irritation. Thus, if irritation could be reduced without temptation being increased, the result would be a net decline in war motivation. In our terms, this would mean withdrawal on the teritorial axis to the point where the temptation curve crosses the irritation curve and starts to independently influence the war motivation axis (see Figure 3). Beyond that point, any further withdrawal would not decrease the war motivation but rather increase it.

Figure 3

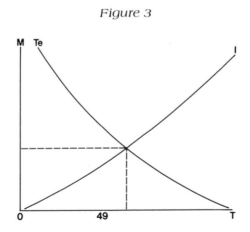

Repartition of Western Palestine
The Allon Plan vs. the American Plans

Since the termination of the Six-Day War, a multitude of peace plans have appeared, designed to bring stability to the Middle East. The components common to most of the serious plans concentrated on three elements: Israeli withdrawal from territories acquired during the Six-Day War, the Palestinian problem, and secure borders for Israel. While the first two elements are designed primarily to resolve the irritation factor for the Arabs, the third element—secure borders—is aimed at resolving the temptation problem for Israel. The main problem is obviously that of reconciling the first two elements with the third, or, according to the logic of our framework, to find an equilibrium between irritation and temptation in territorial terms.

In fact, there does exist an operational plan which, at least from the point of view of certain sectors in the Israeli body politic, was tailored more or less in accordance with the rationale of the equilibrium framework presented above—the Allon Plan, which, from the summer of 1967 until the fall of the Labor government in 1977, dictated Israel's settlement policy.

The overall objective of the Allon Plan, named after its sponsor Yigal Allon and first published by its author in *Foreign Affairs*, is to "provide Israel with the minimal defensible borders that are indispensable, without impairing to any meaningful extent, the basic interests of the other sides, including those of the Palestinian community."[38] In exchange for peace, he was ready to give up the large majority of the areas which Israel had acquired in the 1967 war, but not beyond the point which would "provide Israel with that vital element so lacking in the pre-1967 war lines."[39] From our point of view, it could be argued that what Allon suggests is to retreat as far as possible on the territorial axis in order to satisfy basic Arab desires (the irritation factor) without impairing what he considers minimal security requirements. Further withdrawal, in Allon's view, would bring about an increment in Arab motivation to attack Israel (the temptation factor). He admits that "if the sole consideration were the purely strategic military one, then possibly the most convenient security borders would have been those Israel maintained following the Six-Day War, or perhaps those which it maintains today."[40] But since such borders would not be acceptable to the Arabs, the best available solution is to exchange territories for legitimacy, though not at the expense of returning to borders where "the Arab states may be tempted to hit Israel with a first strike, preventing the latter from hitting back effectively. With such lines as those existing prior to the 1967 war, this would be a concrete and intolerable threat."[41]

The Allon plan is influenced by two additional considerations, which, while not mentioned explicitly in our framework, are

implicitly included in it: the demographic factor and the establishment of a Palestinian state. By returning the heavily populated
areas in Judea, Samaria and the Gaza Strip to Jordan, Allon hoped
both to avoid the problem of a demographic threat to the Jewish
state and to prevent the establishment of a Palestinian state
between Israel and Jordan.

The establishment of a Palestinian state between Israel and
Jordan is related to both the irritation and the temptation factors.
From the Arab point of view, the foundation of such a state would
restore at least part of the injustice done to their brethren by the
establishment of the Jewish state in Palestine. From the Israeli
point of view, such a state would mean the installation on its
border of a political entity having strong feelings towards the rest
of geographic Palestine. While in the case of the Arab states the
return of territories might at least reduce the irritation factor, this
does not apply to the Palestinians. Thus, whatever Israel might
gain from satisfying certain aspirations of the Arab states, it would
lose by the creation of such a revisionist factor. Moreover, such a
state might open its doors to other neighboring Arab forces—e.g.,
Syria, Iraq, or even the Soviet Union—and thus impair the balance
of power. In short, by satisfying the irritation factor in the short run,
Israel would create a new equation of irritation and temptation
with strong war motivation on the Arab side like that which
existed at the pre-1967 borders.

Returning now to the Allon Plan, it would be accurate to state
that the Allon Plan is influenced by the logic of both irritation and
temptation, with the problem of the Palestinian state interwoven
on both curves and the demographic threat in the background.
The territorial compromise put forward by Allon can be perceived
as the point of equilibrium between two opposing linear curves.
The return of most of the territories to Arab sovereignty would
reduce Arab irritation and enable them to resolve the problem of
Palestinian self-determination in a Jordanian framework. At the
same time, Israel would maintain control over certain essential
territories, thus keeping the temptation factor to the minimal point
available under such circumstances.

The principal shortcoming of this plan, which was sound from
a strategic point of view, was that the Arabs found it unacceptable.
It is by now an established fact that the outline of this plan was
presented on several occasions to the king of Jordan and rejected
by him. From Hussein's point of view, the only way he could legitimize peace with Israel was by achieving the return of all of the
West Bank as well as East Jerusalem. In exchange for merely the
return of the populated areas of the West Bank and the Gaza Strip,
a population with a strong Palestinian identity, he was not ready to
risk his relations with neighboring Arab countries, particularly
Syria and Saudi Arabia.

Another significant aspect of the Allon Plan was that it viewed
the final solution in terms of a repartition of western Palestine

between the Jewish state and its eastern neighbor. Despite the fact that it saw the Jordan River as Israel's security border, it nevertheless recommended a territorial division based on the nation-state paradigm. In short, this plan should be viewed as a continuation of the option which had prevailed since the Peel Commission's recommendations of 1937.

The American view of the final solution for the territories, whether the Rogers plan under the Nixon administration or the Brookings plan whose main elements were adopted by the Carter administration, is also based on the partition principle.[42] The American position is closer to that of the Arabs, demanding in essence an Israeli withdrawal from almost all of the territories in exchange for a genuine peace between Israel and its Arab neighbors. But the American approach and Sadat's approach as well can also be understood in terms of the equilibrium framework presented here. It is true that their main concern is with reducing the irritation curve and thus minimizing Arab war motivation. With regard to the temptation curve, their main argument is that the combination of a genuine peace, the solution of the Palestinian problem, and Israel's military strength would be sufficient to curb temptation. In other words, they want to substitute Israel's demands for secure boundaries with non-territorial elements. In addition, Sadat is willing to compensate Israel for its loss of territorial advantages with security guarantees extended by the great powers.[43] In terms of our framework, what they suggest is to move the temptation curve leftwards, thus finding another point of equilibrium which would coincide more or less with the pre-1967 boundaries (see Figure 4).

Figure 4

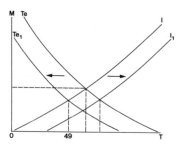

Integration and Powersharing
The Dayan and the Begin Plans

In the period following the Six-Day War, there evolved alongside the Allon Plan another approach to the problem of the territories, a plan which had a certain impact on the integration of the West Bank and the Gaza Strip into Israel. While Yigal Allon's plan dictated the Labor governments' settlement policies between 1967 and 1977, the other plan put forward by Moshe Dayan, Israel's

Defense Minister between 1967 and 1974 and as such responsible for governing the territories, influenced the administrative, economic and internal security aspects of the territories. Since Dayan
has never explicitly outlined his plan as Allon had done, we shall
utilize here a fair summary of the guidelines of his approach, also
known as "functional compromise." Professor Gidon Gottlieb has
pieced together from various sources five principles which serve
as the guidelines for this approach:

- Under the prevailing conditions in the Arab world, Israel must
  retain full military control, if need be, throughout Judea and
  Samaria. Israel cannot allow any other army to establish a
  presence there and must retain the capability to combat terrorist actions in the territories.
- Any peace agreement must provide for the right of Jewish
  settlement everywhere in Judea and Samaria.
- There must be a special and unique relationship between
  Israel and the West Bank. (There can be no closed borders
  anywhere west of the Jordan.)
- Israel must refrain from the inclusion of a large Arab minority
  in the State of Israel.
- When a final settlement is reached, all Israeli citizens, Jews
  and Arabs alike, must enjoy equal rights.[44]

Indeed, under the guidance of the Defense Minister, the West
Bank and the Gaza Strip were economically integrated while
remaining administratively separate. At the same time, by adopt-
ing the "open bridges" policy, the Israeli government under the
influence of Dayan left the door open for Jordanian partnership in
governing the territories.

When Menachem Begin came to power, he in effect adopted
most of Dayan's principles. The autonomy plan which emerged
following Sadat's visit to Jerusalem, despite its vagueness on certain issues, incorporated most of the Foreign Minister's ideas, with
two significant differences. First, Begin, unlike Dayan, presented
his plan in a more or less comprehensive manner, including structural and legal elements. Second, while Dayan saw Jordan as the
main partner with whom Israel would share power, in Begin's
plan the role for Jordan was diminished and that of the Palestinian
Arabs upgraded. The institution of an administrative council, as
Begin suggested in his autonomy plan, meant a functional compromise between Israel and the Palestinian Arabs. Or, as Begin
stated when explaining paragraph 11 of his plan which gives
Israel authority over the maintenance of security, "for the Palestinian Arabs, administrative rule; and for the Palestinian Jews, real
security."[45]

Returning to the equilibrium model, both the Dayan approach
and the autonomy plan can be tailored on this framework. They
both accept the existence of the two factors, irritation and tempta-

tion. Their approach differs from that of the Allon Plan in that they propose to substitute territorial concessions in the West Bank and the Gaza Strip with powersharing. While the Allon Plan is guided by the principles of a purely territorial-state solution, the latter plan contains within it elements of shared rule.

To a certain extent, the Dayan-Begin approach can be perceived as symmetrical to that of the American-Egyptian position. The latter suggests reducing Arab irritation by an almost total withdrawal to pre-1967 borders (including the establishment of a Palestinian entity) and reducing the temptation curve by non-territorial elements. The current Israeli government emphasizes the temptation factor and, in order to reduce the irritation factor, it proposes to create a limited Palestinian entity with which it will share power. In terms of our framework, while the Americans want to move the temptation curve towards the left, the Begin government proposes to move it towards the right.

Summary and Conclusions

In the first part of this essay, we have analyzed the process that led to territorial partition of Palestine. Three main factors were responsible for this outcome: the extremism of the Palestinian Arabs who objected to any co-existence with the Jews, the interests of the great powers, and finally the interests of two moderate groups—the Hashemites in the Arab camp and the statists in the Zionist camp—who were able to compromise and satisfy their minimal aspirations. This partition, which was probably a necessary condition for the founding of the State of Israel, collapsed in 1967 partly, at least, because of the geo-strategic disadvantages that were inherent in the 1949 armistice lines and which emerged in the June 1967 crisis. But the new ceasefire lines which Israel achieved in that war did not promote stability and, in fact, resulted in an increase in the rate of the outbreak of violence and war. Thus, the geo-strategic dilemma facing Israel since 1967, analyzed in the second part of this essay, was that of determining new borders since neither the present borders nor the previous ones could promote stability between Israel and her neighbors.

In any discussion of the future of the territories, most objective analysts would have to accept that a clear-cut extreme solution is inconceivable. Israel cannot afford a total withdrawal to the pre-1967 borders either in the West Bank or the Gaza Strip because of strategic reasons. Even if we discount domestic political factors —and they are important in any state, particularly democratic ones—Israel cannot permit the return of these territories to full Arab sovereignty. Such an act would imply the possiblility that large Arab forces would be introduced into these areas, thus threatening the heavily populated urban centers of Israel, or the shelling of these strategic centers by terrorists from these areas. At the same time, most sober Israeli leaders also recognize that full

integration of these territories into Israel is impossible for international and demographic reasons. The direct result of this dilemma
is that the Jewish state must accept some sort of compromise.

Having accepted these realities, the various possibilities of
compromise can be translated into two possible alternatives: a
territorial compromise, or a compromise over political control of
these areas. The first solution implies a new partition of Palestine
(Eretz Israel) in continuation of the process whose origins can be
traced to the Peel Commission of 1937 and which was implemented in 1948. The second alternative implies a new framework
of powersharing without a repartition of the land of Israel. In practical terms, the first option can be identified with the Allon Plan and
the general outline for peace advocated by the Labor Party in
Israel, while the autonomy plan of the Likud Party is an outgrowth
of the second alternative.

If one examines the history of the Arab-Israeli conflict, several
conclusions can be drawn with regard to the two competing
options described above. First, it is clear that partition was a major
vehicle in the establishment of the State of Israel. On the other
hand, it is by now clear that partition was also responsible in several respects for the outbreak of three wars between 1948 and
1967. Second, partition also contributed to the insulation of the
Arabs and the Jews from each other and widened the psychological and cultural gaps between the two peoples. To be sure, the
incorporation of a million Arabs as as result of the Six-Day War did
not overcome the hostility of the Arabs to the Jews. Yet one would
have to admit that communication between the two camps has
increased since the 1967 war. Third, even if repartition along the
lines of territorial compromise may be satisfying to Israel from a
strategic and demographic point of view, the Arab states do not
want to hear of such an arrangement.

That the autonomy plan of Prime Minister Menachem Begin
involves a certain degree of powersharing is undebatable by definition. The main political problem so far is that only one Arab country— Egypt—is ready to accept it overtly and only as a temporary
solution on the road to total Israeli withdrawal. But there are other
problems in this approach and these are rooted in the cultural-
political background of the nations of the region. The Middle East
so far has been rather inhospitable to federal principles.[46] Furthermore, the countries of the Third World in general, to which almost
all of the states of the Middle East belong, are very sensitive to
questions which involve limited or divided sovereignty. Because
of their newly achieved independence, they cherish the concept
of sovereignty as one of their most worthwhile attainments.[47] A
scheme of divided powers and limited independence which is
basic to various Western systems of government would encounter opposition in this part of the world.

In order for a powersharing solution to succeed, the peoples
involved in the conflict will first have to realize that, in an era of

economic and strategic interdependence, the pure nation-state model has lost much of its sanctity. They will have to recognize, as the Europeans have learned after many centuries of bloodshed, that shared-rule arrangements and transnational cooperation may bring with them economic prosperity instead of recurrent wars.

Notes

Historical aspects of this paper were originally published in French. See Shmuel Sandler,"Historique du Conflict israelo-arabe," *Les Cahiers du Federalisme* 5 (Janvier-Mars, 1979); 13-26.

1. On the subject of powersharing and related material see the following literature published by the Jerusalem Institute for Federal Studies (JIFS): Daniel J. Elazar, "The Ends of Federalism." *JIFS Papers*, No. 1 (January, 1978); Daniel J. Elazar and Ira Sharkansky, "Alternative Federal Solutions to the Problem of the Adminstered Territories," *JIFS Papaers*, No. 2 (January, 1978); Daniel J. Elazar, "Arrangements for Self-Rule and Autonomy in Various Countries of the World: A Preliminary Inventory," *JIFS Papers*, No. 3 (November, 1978); Daniel J. Elazar and Shmuel Sandler, "A Plan for Joint Rule of the Territories," *JIFS Papers*, No. 4 (July, 1978). See also Gabriel Ben-Dor, "Federalism in the Arab World," *JIFS Working Paper* No. 1 (January, 1978). On Israeli public opinion regarding the territories, see Louis Guttman, "The Israel Public, Peace and Territory: The Impact of the Sadat Initiative," *JIFS Reports*, No 1 (January, 1978).

2. Bernard Lewis, *The Middle East and the West* (Tel Aviv: Maarachot, 1970), ch. 4, in Hebrew. Regarding the birth of the Arab national movement see: George Antonius, *The Arab Awakening: The Story of the Arab National Movement* (New York: Capricorn Books, 1965), p. 54.

3. Christopher Sykes, *Cross Roads to Israel* (London: The New English Library, 1975), pp. 18-19.

4. For a discussion of the attitude of Arab Palestinians toward Jews prior to the Balfour Declaration see Nevill Mandel, "Turks, Arabs and Jewish Immigration into Palestine, 1882-1914," *St Antony's Papers, No. 17. Middle Eastern Affairs No.4*, ed. by Albert Hourani (London: Oxford University Press, 1965), pp. 83-84 And Yehoshua Porat, *The Emergence of the Palestinian-Arab National Movement 1918-1829* (Jerusalem: Hebrew University, 1971), pp. 18-19, in Hebrew.

5. Sykes, *op. cit.*, p. 39.

6. *Ibid.*, p. 40.

7. For an elaborate discussion of this subject see: Porat, op. cit., ch. 2.

8. Sykes, *op. cit.*, p. 41.

9. See Winston Churchill's speech in the British Parliament: Great Britain, House of Commons, *Parliamentary Debates* (London, 1921), Ser, V. Vol. 143, pp. 163-170.

10 Sykes, *op. cit.*, p. 55.

11. See Churchill's speech in Parliament defending the agreement: House of Commons, *Parliamentary Debates*, Ser. V. Vol. 143, col. 289.

12. Sykes, *op. cit.*, p. 56.

13. Robert John and Sami Hadawi, *The Palestine Diary* (New York: New World Press, 1972), p. 186.

14. *Ibid.*, p. 207.

15. Sykes, op. cit., p. 134.

16. Quoted in Ahron Cohen, *Israel and the Arab World* (New York: Funk and Wagnalls, 1970), p. 192.

17. Amin Abdullah Mahmoud, *King Abdullah and Palestine*. A dissertation submitted to the Graduate School of Georgetown University (Washington, D.C.: 1972), pp. 46–53.

18. Esco Foundation for Palestine, *Palestine* (New Haven: Yale University Press, 1947), [New York: Kraus Reprint Co., 1970], p. 743.

19. For a broad analysis of the national idea and its supporters see Susan Lee Hattis, *The Bi-National Idea in Palestine During Mandatory Times* (Tel Aviv: Shimona Publishing Company, 1970), pp. 38–77.

20. *Ibid.*, pp. 76–77.

21. J.C. Hurewitz, *The Struggle for Palestine* (New York: Greenwood Press, 1968), pp. 67–72.

22. *Ibid.*, pp. 73–74.

23. *Ibid.*, p. 74.

24. Sykes, *op. cit.*, pp. 184–186.

25. Mahmoud, *op. cit.*, p. 73.

26. Hurewitz, *op. cit.*, pp. 162–163. See also Sykes, *op. cit.*, pp. 150–151.

27. Hurewitz, *op. cit.*, p. 204.

28. For details of the Morrison-Grady Plan and the Jewish Agency's reaction see *ibid.*, pp. 157–182.

29. *Ibid.*, pp. 296–298.

30. For a detailed examination of the negotiations between Abdullah and the Israelis, see Mahmoud, *op. cit.*, pp. 90–126.

31. David Ben Gurion, *The Restored State of Israel* (Tel Aviv: Am Oved, 1969), p. 73. For the relationship between ideology and the political attitude of the various parties, see Dan Horowitz and Moshe Lissak, *The Origins of the Israeli Polity* (Tel Aviv: Am Oved, 1977), Hebrew, pp. 195–196. See also the reaction of the various party newspapers: the Revisionist *Ha-Mashqif* of September 2, 1947 rejected the idea of false independence in a toy state; and the binationalist *Mishmar*, same date, objected to both the majority and minority proposals. In Hurewitz, *op. cit.*, p. 359.

32. On the cooperation regarding Jerusalem see: Michael Brecher, *Decisions in Israel's Foreign Policy* (London: Oxford University Press, 1974), p. 10. Regarding the Jordan-Yarmuk River system, see *ibid.*, p. 224.

33. For details on the Allon Plan see Yigal Allon, "Israel: The Case for Defensible Borders," *Foreign Affairs*, 55 (October, 1976), pp. 38–53.

34. Several Israeli leaders have confirmed this information on different occasions.

35. For further analysis of Israel's vulnerability in the pre-1967 borders see Dan Horowitz, "Israel's Concept of Defensible Borders," *Jerusalem Papers*, No. 16, 1975, pp. 9–13. For a general analysis of the relationship between geography and the balance of power see: Steven J. Rosen, "Military Geography and the Military Balance in the Arab-Israeli Conflict," *Jerusalem Papers*, No. 21, 1977.

36. Allon, *op. cit.*, p. 40.

37. Theodore Draper, *Israel and World Politics* (New York: Viking Press, 1968), pp. 96–97.

38. Allon, *op. cit.*, p. 44.

39. *Ibid.*

40. *Ibid.*, p. 41.

41. *Ibid.*, p. 43.

42. See for instance an interview with Alfred Atherton in the *Jerusalem Post Magazine*, April 6, 1979, pp. 6–7, in which he confirms the American position regarding the final borders.

43. See, for instance, Sadat's interview with Eric Rouleau, reprinted from *Le Monde* in *Survival*, March/April, 1975, p. 84.

44. Gidon Gottlieb, "The Future of Palestine—Eretz Israel," in Gregory Henderson *et al.*, *Divided Nations in a Divided World* (New York: David

McKay Co., 1974), p. 383.

45. *The Jerusalem Post*, December 29, 1977, p. 4.

46. For a broader discussion on this subject see: Daniel J. Elazar, "Options. Problems and Possibilities in Light of the Current Situation," in Daniel J. Elazar, ed., *Self Rule/Shared Rule, Federal Solution to the Middle East Conflict* (Ramat-Gan: Turtledove Publishing, 1979), p. 4; and Gabriel Ben-Dor, "The Situation in the Arab World," *ibid.*, pp. 70–71.

47. On this problem see: Ahmed Sheikh, *International Law and International Behaviour* (New York: John Wiley & Sons, 1974), p. 247.

Home Rule or Occupation?
A Discussion

Daniel Elazar: The approach General Vardi presented to us was the Israeli doctrine of minimum coercion–maximum consent in the military government's administering of the territories. What emerges is a continuum between a maximum of self-rule for religion and culture at one end to the minimum amount of self-rule in matters of legislation at the other end, with judicial and administrative powers somewhere in the middle. Professor Nakhleh responded by giving the apparently very different perceptions of West Bank mayors.

I was struck by two points, which seem at first glance contradictory but may not be. As a veteran student of municipal affairs, I can attest to the fact that one commonly hears mayors complaining about external authorities, no matter who they are. This is the way of mayors all over the world. It must be, since gaining external support is a standard problem for local authorities these days. Beyond that, I sensed a narrowing down to a real issue of lands —that the bulk of the feeling of limitations has to do with control over lands, with planning and zoning which have to do with control over lands, with the construction of new housing, which has to do with control over lands. Perhaps this focus would help us.

Finally, Mr. Drori has suggested that, at least with regard to the judicial and administrative dimensions in this continuum, there has been an element of sharing. Once, in a private conversation, he suggested to me that some dimension of sharing had been built into the framework that was created in the past 12 years, at least with regard to judicial and administrative functions. This may be of further interest as we go forward to create some creative ambiguity and shared powers in the autonomy plan.

Robert Pranger: Mr. Drori, were you representing in any way what would be the official Israeli position when you defined inhabitants of the West Bank and Gaza to mean everyone living there, whether in Jewish settlements or in Arab towns? As I understand it in the Camp David accord, in the U.S. view of the language, "the inhabitants" refers to Arabs in the. West Bank and Gaza, on the grounds that, because they have no citizenship you call them something. Those Jews living in the West Bank and Gaza are Israeli citizens, and that language was deliberately drafted to exclude precisely what you are suggesting is the meaning. Now, if this is the position of the Government of Israel, then I can only say that there is going to be a very stormy session ahead on this issue of settlers meeting and deciding their own fate under the accord.

Now, either you are not really presenting the language as the Government of Israel understands it, but simply in terms of its face value, or there is a difference of opinion as to what the language means. But I know, or at least I think I know, that the Department of State was very clear in the way that language was drafted, that it did not include Israeli settlers. Now you might want to comment on that.

Gabriel Ben-Dor: I had the feeling during this morning's discussion that we may have missed part of the point by mistreating the whole issue of autonomy. If I read the situation correctly, autonomy was not really intended either to work very effectively, nor was it intended to be the midwife of the next stage. I think we are reading too much into it. I think it was intended to be Sadat's and Begin's way of saying, "We agree on the Egyptian-Israeli part. We disagree, but we agree to disagree, on the Palestinian part. Let's not do anything which will unsettle the situation for a long time. Let's make some minor incremental improvements which will make it look good to the others but not try to resolve the issue at this stage." So I think that this exercise of looking into the exact language, looking into Article 3, 4, 5, 6, and how they contradict each other, and what they mean juridically, may be really overdoing it.

The question is not whether the text is to be torn apart easily, but whether the political framework will hold or not. And—I think this is a very crucial point—to see in what political context the whole exercise takes place. The idea of creative ambiguity here is precisely that, by creating new rules for the game in the Middle East, solutions will emerge in five years' time which are not yet discernible. We will have a new reality created by peace gaining ground and taking off. This is one point. The second one is directed to Professor Nakhleh. It is a methodological point. You based the vast majority of your conclusions on interviews. I want to ask you something about the methodology of these interviews, because interviewing people under such constraints is an extremely difficult task. Some of us have tried to do it and found that a very great deal depends on how you pick your sample, how you present the questions, and so forth.

To give you just one example, five years ago exactly I participated in a conference in which a bright young professor from the University of Pennsylvania by the name of William Quandt presented all kinds of ideas about the Palestinians. I asked him, "This sounds very good, but how do you know the Palestinians will buy it?" He said, "They will have to buy it, because the way it will be presented to them is either this or nothing, and then I am going to interview them."

With this kind of attitude, apparently you can get very far in diplomacy. Whether you can from the scientific point of view I do not know. But a great deal really depends on whether you ask people, "What do do you think is the best solution for the Palestinian problem," or "Who optimally represents the Palestinian cause in the most trustworthy manner"—or if you say to them, "Look, there is a Middle East, and there are 18 Arab states, and there is Israel, and there is the United States, and there is a whole political dynamic moving, and within this huge framework in which you have a certain freedom to maneuver you have two or three options," and then ask them which they pick; this is an entirely different business.

Finally, like Professor Elazar, I was struck by the difference between the presentations of Professor Nakhleh and General Vardi. Of course, if General Vardi's presentation was correct as perceived by the inhabitants, then Professor Nakhleh's paper should have been entirely different. The General really presented the image of a relatively benign military occupation, exercising minimum coercion. But if Professor Nakhleh is correct, and there is no reason to presume that he is not, then it is not seen that way by the inhabitants.

How do you make policy when you do not have the right kind of feedback? We are all assuming that we are running a very liberal, benign kind of military occupation, but the people who are ruled by that particular regime do not think so. And therefore, we may have two choices. If we want to be really benign, we have to do something else. Or, since we cannot get their good will and recognition, we might as well do other things that we really want. The whole question is policy making without feedback.

Don Peretz: I have been involved in this kind of interviewing in the West Bank for eleven years now and I can say that both General Vardi and Professor Nakhleh's remarks might be true, so that I cannot criticize what they say. They are all true. But the question is now how to get out of this dilemma and also the dilemmas of the very ambiguous legal status in the future. Therefore,I want to ask Professor Nakhleh especially if, in his interviews, he did not also encounter the idea of a confederative solution. If the West Bank, after this transition period, will become a full-fledged member state in a confederation with Israel, I believe that the legal status and all the difficulties that were enumerated here would find a much easier solution.

Then, too, the asssumption of Israel and Egypt that they should deal with the future of the West Bank and Gaza is, I think, the same as saying that we want the interference of the big powers in our affairs. People do not want other people to decide their fate, and therefore, I think this must be taken into consideration too.

Joseph Abileah: Since Egypt never had any territorial or legal claims to the West Bank, what is the legal basis for Egypt's participation in the autonomy arrangements? Why should an agree-ment reached between Israel and Egypt pertaining to autonomy on the West Bank have any more legal validity under international law than, say, an agreement between Jordan, the former legal trustee of the area, and Britain, a former legal trustee, and the Palestine Liberation Organization, which is recognized by the Uni-ted Nations and a number of other international entities as the sole legitimate representative of the Palestinians?

Yosef Goell: Perhaps by expressing agreement, as I do, with Pro-fessor Nakhleh's statement that no real improvements are possi-ble under a system of occupation, a good part of the rest of the problems that have come up during the course of the morning fall away, because many of them are are simply insoluble given the situation of occupation, and that returns us to the basic political problem.

I would also note the trouble I have with "benign occupation," although I use the term quite frequently myself. Benign occupa-tion, of course, is a contradiction in terms, like military justice, or even military music. I think part of the difference between General Vardi and Professor Nakhleh has to do with the difference between intent, on the one hand, and perception by the popula-tion, on the other.

Professor Nakhleh, there are many things that you say with which I agree. There are quite a number of things that I would tend to dispute. One thing bothers me in regard to either your own credibility or, I would suspect, the credibility of the people you interviewed. If I took notes correctly here, you reported their per-ception of the occupation's economic policy as being detrimental to the population. I would suggest that simply the raw statistics on the West Bank, regardless of intention, regardless of perception, are such that, if any West Bank leader claims that the economic policy has beeen detrimental to their population, everything they say is not very credible.

General Vardi, assuming the benign intent of the occupation, would you be able to assess the effectiveness of such a policy, even at the present time, in trying to get the Palestinian population to cooperate with an autonomy idea or with some idea of self-government alongside Israel? Could you assess, for example, the effect of the open bridges policy, or of Israel's imposing on the West Bank what in our sense was a more democratic electoral system? Could you also, in this context, consider the possibility of an opposite policy, such as closing the open bridges, preventing money coming from Saudi Arabia and the oil states to finance the West Bank? Would that lead, in your opinion, to an uprising on the West Bank, or would it, perhaps, lead to a sense of greater pres-sure towards cooperation with the Israeli intention?

I did not know how to interpret one of Professor Nakhleh's final statements in speaking of the West Bank leadership—and I assume he included here the Gaza district, too. He said that the strength of their clinging to the PLO was in inverse proportion to the readiness of the U.S. and Israel to speak with them. Perhaps you would interpret what you meant by that. Had we made more overtures, would there be a readiness on the part of the indigenous leadership to part ways with the PLO leadership, or is that not correct?

Pinhas Rosenbluth: General Vardi, the military allowed and encouraged the inhabitants to run their own affairs. As far as I know, political activities during most of those years were not allowed. Can you define the term, "to run their own affairs" without political activity?

What is the difference between what you described here and the plans of Begin and his ministers? I suppose that it is more a matter of the details, which are much more restrictive than what you described as the policy of the last years.

Professor Nakhleh, when you based your conclusions mainly on the interviews, did you also discuss with them the Israeli point of view, the wider issue of security? Did you raise this, and what was the reaction of the inhabitants?

Ilan Greilshammer: What exactly has been the process of decision making on the West Bank and Gaza, and was there, in your opinion, a real continuity in the policies followed by the different governments—Eshkol, Meir, Rabin and Begin—with regard to the objectives and the implementations? Or, on the contrary, was there a broken line made up of shocks and ruptures?

General Vardi repeated several times, "we, the Israeli government," or "the Israeli military administration" or "authority"; which opinions or external advisors do the Israeli government accept? Did they ask the opinion of Israeli intellectuals? Arabists? Political scientists? Sociologists? Or other groups or institutes of research in Israel? Or, on the contrary, did the different governments choose the options alone or only with the advice of a military think team?

Hillel Frisch: I would be interested to know what proposals were made by Arab mayors at various stages about the regionalism that they sought. I would also like to know why the military government, while possibly recognizing the need for regionalism, attempted to resurrect once again a centralized form of government in the form of the Mukhazim and not look at possible Israeli solutions based on regionalism and set them up in the West Bank? I would like to know the relationship between the decisions taken on regionalism and their importance for political developments on the West Bank.

Amiel Ungar: We assume that there was a basic coordinating policy between the political sphere and the administration of the territories. I want to ask General Vardi if the policy was formulated simply because it meant good administration, or if it was intended to conform to the political vision of an ultimate settlement?

Leonard Binder: I gather from the remarks that have been made that the regime in the occupied territories has been characterized by a good deal of external influence, and this has resulted in stagnation rather than change because of the regional context of constraint. The elites on the West Bank have responded with a certain policy of non-commitment. The autonomy talks seem likely to break this stagnation. They offer a number of possible solutions. I have listed six—a Jordanian solution, a Syrian solution, a PLO solution, a solution which includes autonomy and sovereignty, a solution of autonomy without sovereignty, and a solution which is based upon personal but not territorial arrangements, with citizenship in various states that already exist.

It seems to me that the autonomy negotiations will proceed in the light of these possible solutions, but they may also respond to shorter term pressures toward goals that will interest the Israelis and the Egyptians. I have a number of these to suggest. One, the most obvious, is to relieve the Egyptian problem of isolation. The second is to respond to the Lebanese situation. The third is to respond to a possible Syrian and Iraqi unification. The fourth, to attempt to influence Saudi Arabian policy. And the fifth, to respond to possible regime changes in Iran as the situation there settles down.

As I think about this larger political context, it seems to me that any autonomy arrangements that are decided upon are likely to be a rather crude instrument responding to these challenges, and at the same time a guide through this rather difficult immediate situation towards some ultimate solutions.

Don Peretz: If the land issue is so crucial, not only in the legal sense but in the emotional sense, is there any provision for arbitrating differences between the authorities and those who feel that decisions taken pertaining to land are not appropriate?

General Vardi: This audience has benefited from two views. I had the feeling, though, that Professor Nakhleh in his research only heard one view, that of the mayors of the West Bank. I am certain that in continuing his research he will listen to the other side, the Israeli side.

In my address, I tried as far as possible to confine myself to facts, to the experience of the military government, not to views and opinions. If I understood well, Professor Nakhleh mainly based his work on the views of the mayors which are not necessarily facts. Now to some of the facts themselves. In any system of government, there can hardly ever be a situation in which you can, from moment to moment, give orders or directions. I mentioned already that our policy was not to intervene and that the mayors had complete freedom to do whatever they wished in running the municipalities. And they have done so.

Of course, they had to get some approvals, according to the law: for budget expenditures, for the annual budget, and so forth. This is exactly what the Jordanian authorities did before 1967, and we did not hand over to them whatever was the government's responsibility. We functioned as any government usually does, but did not intervene in the daily running of the municipalities.

There are certainly many complaints from the mayors and from the population about maladministration, about the fact that the budget is small, that there is not enough development, and so forth. They are voiced every day. And this is the way it works everywhere. But this is not intervention in affairs that are run by the municipality.

Professor Nakhleh cited the officer in charge of "Interior" as the one who controls the daily business of the municipalities. In this office there are only four Israelis—the officer and two or three assistants—so that to interfere daily in the working of the 23 municipalities and tens of village councils is humanly impossible. Even if we had intended to interfere, it would have been impossible. We have only three or four Israeli officers in charge of interior affairs precisely because we have no no such intentions.

There were, on the contrary, complaints that it took a long time to approve the annual budgets of the municipal councils because the staff that had to approve it—the Israelis and the local staff as well—was too small. The demand in fact was that we should increase the staff.

Now to town planning. Under Jordanian rule, the Mukhtasaret was in charge of town building and planning. Under the Israeli administration, the mayor is head of the town planning committee which consists of the town counsellors. The mayor and the committee are the licensing authority for construction of houses within the limits of the town. There is no other authority within the limits of the town.

I mentioned already that most of the towns have extended their limits and their jurisdiction, some of them by 50 to 70 percent or even twice the original jurisdiction of the town. This has happened with our confirmation.

But this is not the subject of the discussion here. We are dealing with the question of self-rule and self-government and not with questions of economic development, raising the standard of living of the population, raising personal income, development of industries and housing and the like. On this I am not going to quote statistics; they speak for themselves. The rise in the standard of living and the gross national income was much higher in the West Bank in this period than in Jordan itself due to Israel's policy of economic development. The standard of living rose fourfold in twelve years. In many aspects of the life of the individual and of the economy of the territory, things are much better. We know, for instance, that the five thousand workers who live in the El Arish areas, now back in Egypt, have a problem. They have a problem because the wages in Israel are much higher than those that they will get in Egypt. Of course, on the other hand, the prices are also lower. Still, they will have a problem adjusting to a lower income.

On the question of zoning, Professor Nakhleh mentioned the Supreme Council for Planning. It was a very good idea, and it was even put into law, but unfortunately it was not implemented for various reasons. It is also true that we have used land for Israeli settlements. But most of the land that we used was Jordanian government land, mainly in the Jordan Valley and in other places. We were very strict in not expropriating private lands from individuals. For example, if you have followed the press, there is a dispute over 200 acres not far from Nablus which is private property. On the one hand, there is a decision to expropriate it. On the other hand, there is an appeal by the Minister of Defense to the government not to do it (*Editor's note*: The Israeli Supreme Court subsequently ruled against the expropriation and the lands were restored to their owners). In this respect we have been very cautious.

Mayors meet socially whenever they wish. There is freedom of movement, not only between Jordan and the territories, and Israel and the territories, but within the territories as well. It is true that on certain occasions we did not allow meetings of mayors which the mayors themselves informed us were intended as political gatherings having nothing to do with municipal affairs. Sometimes they tried to describe these meetings as dinner parties or luncheons when the purpose was political. In those cases, we did not allow it, because usually such meetings, with or without permission, were devoted to abusing the military government, support of the PLO, or similar activities.

From the beginning, our policy was, if I may paraphrase Professor Elazar, a maximum of self rule with a minimum of coercion. It was our intended policy to extend self-rule to the degree that the population was ready to take over, but if they were unwilling, we did not coerce them to accept.

The population can freely criticize the military government, can express their political views—I am not speaking about political *activities*, but about expression of views—they enjoy complete freedom of speech. They can say whatever they wish, and very unpleasant things are said of Israel and of the military government. We are proud that under the circumstances we allow freedom of speech and freedom of movement to such an extent. Unfortunately, the Arab inhabitants are not as free regarding their relationship with the surrounding Arab world, because there violence is exerted. Whoever tries to voice a different opinion is subject to threats, violence and extreme measures.

I already told you that in this triangle of Jordan, the PLO, and

Israel we have the upper hand. Still, the population tends to look back over their shoulders and to see first what will be the reaction of Jordan and of the PLO regarding the West Bank, or Egypt regarding the Gaza Strip. And they have done so very easily. Jordanian officials come into the West Bank through the open bridges and give instructions on the spot. The leaders go to Jordan, Egypt and Beirut to ask advice or permission with regard to any move that was not within the framework of the strict status quo as established since 1967.

As to the Jordanian law, in those instances in which we have tried to reform it, as in the case of the election law, we were criticized from both sides, even when our reforms were expressly for the benefit of the population and its development. The Israeli High Court of Justice held otherwise. Justice Haim Cohen, in his dissenting opinion, claimed that the military government, according to international law, should not do anything to change the existing laws, even for the benefit of the population. In his opinion, what we should do is to "freeze" the situation as it was on the 7th of June, 1967. The majority of the Court decided otherwise, and we have since been acting accordingly, but very cautiously.

Whenever we have tried to reform anything, one side would accuse us of tampering with the local law, while the other attacked us for maintaining outdated, archaic laws. When we were about to reform the law regarding the franchise for women—and that was after Jordan had already extended the franchise to women in elections to parliament only (not municipal elections), we consulted the mayors and other leaders and most of them objected. When we mentioned the reform in Jordan, they based their objection on the fact that in Jordan's elections the law has not yet been reformed. There are many other similar examples.

The question has been raised about our intent in construing this policy of self-rule. In the first place, what drives every nation is the best interests of the given nation. And we acted in the best interests of Israel. Israel's best interest is to establish coexistence with the local population, to live peacefully together. This is why we implemented the open bridges policy, although it jeopardizes our security each and every day. From the point of view of security, the proper policy would have been to close the borders. Then it would have been more difficult to smuggle in explosives and other weapons to kill people in Jerusalem or in Netanya or Petach Tikva or in Tel Aviv. But we have taken this risk. For the same reasons we opened the borders to Israel, notwithstanding security. This is why we never closed the borders and the linkages even when terrorist outrages were committed.

Our policy of granting more self-government was in this context. As long as security was not impaired, we did not want to intervene in their internal affairs. And though the circumstances were not favorable, by and large we have been able to implement this policy, at least from our point of view.

Has this policy influenced the population to accept certain kinds of solutions in the future? If we are speaking about the autonomy plans laid out in the Camp David agreement, I do not think that at present we have a partner among the population to talk with about autonomy. The reason for this is not because some of the leadership in the population would not have liked to discuss it. The true reason is that they cannot formulate their own view about their own future. This does not mean that a certain part of the population does not adhere to the PLO. They do. But they are not free to voice their true feelings, not only because they are under military occupation. Some of us in Israel were of the opinion that if the borders were closed and the population would have known that they have to live only with Israel, that their political attitude might have been different. But since this was not our policy, this option has not had a chance to be tested.

Bearing in mind the circumstances and the environment, the population of the West Bank as well as of the Gaza Strip cannot formulate a policy of their own free will. Professor Binder asked to what extent the population is sensitive or responds to what happens generally in the Middle East, and is influenced by developments in the area. We have observed the population every day in an effort to find out their reaction to a variety of events, their feelings and opinions and changes in them. What I have noticed over a very long period is that in the early seventies, the solution from their point of view was still the return of the West Bank to Jordan, not the PLO solution. Even more recently, whenever Jordan's esteem rose in the Arab world, we noticed a pro-Jordanian shift in public opinion. Beginning in 1974 when the PLO became more prominent, we saw the shift in public opinion towards the PLO. During these years, there was always this kind of movement, pro-Jordan, pro-PLO, again pro-Jordan, and again pro-PLO. One may speculate that if Jordan would join the peace process now, then again there would be a shift, at least of a considerable part, if not the major part of public opinion, towards solutions within the framework of the recent agreements.

Now to policy and feedback. We in the military government have our own feedback. We have a constant dialogue with the leaders, with the intellectuals, with people from every stratum of society. What is expressed publicly is not always the real and true opinion. Usually the real opinion is less critical than when it is exposed in public. We always know exactly what will be expressed publicly, whatever the case may be. Had the military government been an ideal government, which is of course impossible, I do not presume that anybody would have admitted it, even if he thought so. I heard from Professor Nakhleh that under military occupation it is impossible for there to be any improvement. There *can* be improvements, for example economic improvements —you cited the statistics—but not in all fields. I am certain that in the view of the population which wants and desires to determine

its own future, a military government *per se* is not an improvement, and it cannot be an improvement. Any military government,
benign or not benign, cannot be.

I would like to tell you of an episode that may throw some light
on the subject. Once, when I was Military Commander of Judea
and Samaria, a well-known foreign correspondent came to interview me. He told me that he came directly from an interview with
a certain mayor who was known for his extreme anti-Israel opinions. I won't mention his name. Incidentally, present at the interview was the district military commander. The correspondent told
me that the mayor started a tirade against the military government
and its abuses. He presented his severe complaints, explaining in
detail all the vices of the military government—and among them
he complained about alleged limitations on freedom of speech. At
this point, the correspondent asked him, "Aren't you afraid to tell
me all this in front of the military government?" The mayor replied,
"What? I am afraid of him? I tell this to everybody, I say it on the
radio. I say it on the television. I am not afraid to say whatever I
wish. I can speak and say anything." This is the usual dissonance
between what sometimes appears as the publicly expressed
view and the facts of life under the military government.

That does not mean that I think that everything is nice and fine
under the military government. I can specify many discrepancies,
but let us keep a sense of proportion.

Emile Nakhleh: I should like first of all to thank Professor Dan
Elazar for this great opportunity. This is one of those rare times in
which the issues of security and the issue of military occupation
have been discussed in public at such a conference. I am grateful
to be invited.

Secondly, I would like to thank you for this very calm reaction
to indeed very provocative statements, particularly since such
statements are made by a Palestinian—that makes it even harder
a pill to swallow.

My personal views were not expressed in this presentation
today, contrary to the misperception. The views I expressed were
the views of those interviewed. I would be very happy to share my
own views with you. I do support the peace process. I do see a
positive dimension to it, even though I have some questions. I
think this is a fantastic opportunity. I wish Palestinians were
involved, and I wish they would get involved. I think the momentum of peace can get underway if it is done right.

I do not throw bombs. Nor do I believe in the throwing of
bombs. I do believe that the United States has a role to play, and I
support that role. I do believe that no independent entity or state
can come into being right away, and when such a state does
come into being, I believe that it will have to have links with its
neighbors—economic linkages and hopefully political linkages,
particularly with Israel and Jordan. But I do not believe such a state

can operate by itself in a vacuum either, isolated from either its contiguous neighbors or the region, or even the international community.

I believe that such a state, if it comes into being under certain conditions, would be viable. It would be responsible. We have at least a hundred examples in the world in which states that arose out of conflict became supposedly responsible. I offer Israel as a case in point. I really do believe that if peace is going to come about, it is going to come about as a result of a dialogue.

The second point I want to make here is about the confusion that arose over my presentation. I am not surprised because it is a summary of my study which you have not read. The study is very, very highly documented. General Vardi's response gave me the idea that perhaps the terms I used were not clear. I used the terms "ubiquity" and "pervasiveness." Ubiquity and pervasiveness, do not mean, in my mind, that there is a daily physical presence around the corner. The principal problem is that military rule is based upon force instead of being rule based on legitimate authority.

When I started my research I really did not know much about the West Bank. I started in Summer 1977 and then I went back regularly. Every time I heard something about, "Oh, the occupation is bad," or this, that, or the other thing, I asked for examples. I have collected plenty of evidence to substantiate those statements. And as I tell you in my report, I did not make one statement that was not based on evidence that I collected, in economics, in housing, in land, in municipal government, and so on. Secondly, the conclusions were not just based on interviews. I have the documents from two budgets, detailed operating budgets, and the two military decrees relating to those budgets. The methodology and the issues that were raised are explained in the beginning. Therefore, the report, I think, is more than just fiction and opinion.

Now, the first point that Professor Elazar raised I think is correct, namely that the basic issue is land and all the issues that are related to land—water, housing, development, transportation, roads—the infrastructure that deals with land. In addition to that, there are very real problems that involve economic development, regional planning, cooperation with the neighbors, commerce, borrowing money, agricultural policy—there are many other areas. I truly wish the picture was as pretty as the General presented it. It isn't.

Let me re-emphasize that the study was not a political study. Actually, these were some of the conclusions that were drawn based on these interviews. The original idea was to go in there and deal with the essentially non-political issues, issues that would have to be faced regardless of the regime. I used several terms interchangeably on purpose. I did not say "a state." I used "state," "entity," "post-occupation regime," "transitional regime." In terms of the research, I was not really interested in any specific type of state, entity, or regime that the inhabitants ought to create. I have assumed that whatever political arrangement was going to be worked out, it would have to deal with these issues.

Therefore, I went there to examine the issues and to examine the institutions that are dealing with these issues and how they could improve their role in dealing with these issues in the post-occupation regime, until a national authority is established.

As for the constraints, I did not really go in there with a Jack Anderson idea to dig up every piece of dirt. I went in there to examine the constraints under which these institutions operated in the area of those issues in which I was interested.

The point I made about the ubiquity of the occupation in economic policy did not deny the fact that personal income did go up. I have available to me statistics of the administered territories and I conducted extensive interviews with Arieh Bregman, the authority on the subject. I do not deal with the numbers of workers who are working in Israel except in passing. As a matter of fact, I did refer to it as one of the problems that a post-occupation regime will have to address.

What I was talking about are other kinds of issues. A citrus grower in Gaza, for instance, cannot dig a well without the military government's approval. He cannot transport his products from Gaza to the East Bank except in trucks approved by the military government. He cannot open up new fields without the approval of the military governor. This is what I meant by ubiquitousness, a system. I think this is best illustrated in the settlements question. Without the presence of the occupation as a system, the settlements question would not be all that important. The settlements as part of an extension of that system are built on lands taken under the guise of security. We are not surprised by the term "security." You hear about security in many states; even at the time of Watergate, Mr. Nixon was asked to turn over some documents, and he said that for the sake of national security he would not do so.

The point I am making is that land is taken in the name of security, a settlement is established in the name of security, water is taken in the name of security and guarded in the name of security, all to make possible civilian settlements. Were this to happen outside the context of the military government as a system, then those settlements, the people there, would have to negotiate with their neighbors. They would say, "We have to have water. We have to have roads." Fine. No problem there. But I cited these examples as an indication of the ubiquity of the occupation.

With regard to the PLO, there is a direct relationship between Israel's denial of the PLO and of the Palestinians' adherence to it. I did not focus in on any one leader. I did not focus in on any one specific group. I did not focus in on any specific elite within that leadership. Basically, my position here is in line with the point that Professor Weiner made in his presentation, that so far the PLO is the only leadership available, regardless of whether you like it or not. We have not seen any alternative or counter-leadership develop for twelve years. All the research questions and interviews have pointed to that. It is the only leadership there.

About the question of security, yes, the question was raised. And I was surprised, really, at the reaction in two ways. One was the level of moderation, in other words their understanding of Israeli security needs, and second, the level of sophistication concerning that question. These West Bank leaders distinguish between two parallel Israeli positions vis-a-vis the territories. One is the ideological or the Begin position, if you will, the Eretz Israel position. They distinguish that from the other position, the security position, that Israel's view on the West Bank is dictated by security. In my interviews, they do not deny the right of Israel to act on behalf of its own security, as they would expect to do in their own entity. They accept that right in the larger context that has to be worked out as well. That would have to be worked out in any agreement or treaty that is going to be produced.

With regard to regional arrangements, they do realize that any arrangement would have to include real linkages with their neighbors. As for the question of regional links within the territories, several mayors raised the point—and General Vardi has also—that they were not allowed to meet politically. It is very difficult, you know, to be under occupation and talk only about the weather. Yet regional planning is necessary; you cannot expect a little town to establish its own industrial zone without cooperation with neighboring towns. That is the issue that they specifically referred to and specifically indicated that they could not do.

The question was raised about the Palestinians as one nation. What I meant by that is that really no arrangement ultimately can work with only the approval of the Palestinians on the West Bank and Gaza and not the other Palestinians. That is what they meant by the statement, that there also has to be some role for the Palestinians outside in the arrangement. They were talking about the West Bank and Gaza; they did not really deal with the Israeli Arabs at all.

One last point. I will just complete the circle by saying that, personally, I really do not believe that a peace arrangement will endure without the cooperation of the Palestinians in the West Bank and Gaza. And I do not mean token cooperation. I do not mean Uncle Ahmeds or Uncle Toms. I mean real cooperation. They know it. They see it. And I think this ought to be the purpose of all of our efforts. If we all reach that point and can really bring about real Palestinian cooperation, we will have covered half the way.

Moshe Drori: As Emile Nakhleh said, there should either be open borders or there should be no borders at all between Israel and the autonomous areas in order that free access for goods, workers, and tourism be maintained. For example, the autonomy authority should not have separate policies as to who will or will not enter the autonomous areas. Today, the road from Jerusalem to Tiberias runs close to the autonomy borders, the Judea and Samaria area. Of course, no one is suggesting that it would be closed after the autonomy regime is inaugurated. There should also be one united customs policy, because if the Jordan bridges will be open and the autonomy authority can make its own customs policy, it could affect all the markets in Israel as well as in Judea and Samaria. Here again, I think, that there should be coordination between the Israeli and the autonomy authorities. Israeli supervision of imports and exports is necessary from the economic point of view, but it is also necessary from the security point of view. Professor Nakhleh said that the security regulations regarding what trucks can deliver oranges from Gaza to the East Bank represent a way of interfering with the population. But this is not a Nixon-like abuse of the security argument because the struggle between Israeli security and the PLO over the PLO's attempts to deliver munitions and other bombs through these open bridges is a very real one. If they were not supervised by the Israeli authorities, the consequences can be easily imagined.

Although the green line should be abolished between Israel and the autonomy area, there should be exact borderlines between the powers of any department of the administrative council and the Israeli authorities. Take the example of the Health Department. If we say that all the authorities of the Ministry of Health under Jordanian law will be transferred to the. Health Department or the Administrative Council, they could say that, because there is disease, they are now closing the border and not allowing anyone to come to Israel for a day, for a month, for two months. You know what the impact would be on the labor market, agriculture, or any industry if the border were to be closed and no one of the 70,000 employees from Judea, Samaria and Gaza would be allowed to come to Israel. It can be done on very innocent grounds, so even those simple powers should be very exact, as one can easily perceive what would be the consequences of absolute power were it given to the autonomy authorities. Coordination is very, very necessary.

If we are looking into the words themselves, the word "inhabitants" can be interpreted in at least two basic ways. First, as you have said, because there was a question of citizenship, it was the one key word which could include all the Arabs. But the other interpretation, that it applies to everyone who inhabits this area, can also be accepted without any hesitation. Therefore, if there are two interpretations, one can adopt whichever one feels is necessary.

I, myself, do not have any official status; I am a private citizen. But I feel that the interpretation including the Israeli population in the settlements is stronger. If there should be a discussion about the final status of the areas, and the Israeli settlements are there, why should they not have the same rights as the Arab residents? If there are discussions about the final status of the territories on the basis of the principle of self-determination, and everyone has the right to express his desires about what will be his future, why deny the Jews what is granted to the Arabs?

As you know, the last paragraph of the Peace Treaty said that if there is a misunderstanding, the English version is to prevail. But this is in the Peace Treaty and not in the Camp David agreement. The Camp David agreement was signed only in English as far as I know. It was submitted to the Knesset in Hebrew, and there was a question whether that translation was accurate—indeed, that is an understatement.

Don Peretz made an important point when he asked whether all these negotiations about autonomy are necessary, because Egypt has no rights in Judea or Samaria. It is better to negotiate with the real parties; he mentioned some alternatives—Jordan, the inhabitants, and the PLO. One can think that one party is better than another, but now I want to explain from the legal and historical points of view what has been done here. The Israelis and the Egyptians have signed an agreement. From a legal point of view it is the same as if Israel had signed an agreement with Greece or with England or with the United States and the three together would negotiate about what would be somewhere else. On one hand, Israel is obliged to fulfill what has been decided by this agreement but, on the other, the negotiation itself is not binding. The treaty does not compel the Palestinians, it does not compel the residents of Judea and Samaria to accept the results of the negotiations or to participate in them. It has only one purpose, that Israel should fulfill its obligations according to the Camp David agreement.

If one looks at this subject from the linkage point of view, there is an inverse linkage. Because there are two agreements that are connected and were signed on the same day—one, that Israel will fulfill its obligation according to the Camp David agreement and will negotiate with Egypt; and two, that the Palestinians will be allowed to participate if they wish. Once Israel and Egypt have reached an agreement, Israel, from the legal point of view, has done all that she was asked to do according to the Camp David agreement.

Then there is the question as to whether this agreement can be implemented. But this is an irrelevant question from the Israeli point of view, because there was an agreement to negotiate and then to sign the results. If the Palestinians do not accept those results, from Israel's point of view she has done whatever she was asked to do. From the legal point of view, no one can accuse Israel of not fulfilling the obligations between her and Egypt according to the two Camp David agreements. This is the legal answer to this question, but as I said earlier, of course, to implement autonomy, there must be cooperation on the part of the inhabitants.

Nafez Nazzal: I want to address myself to four issues that were mentioned, specifically: the economic conditions; cultural, educational, and religious freedom in the occupied territories; the Israeli settlements and Palestinian-Israeli co-existence; and finally, autonomy.

We have a very popular Palestinian proverb which says that hearing about a situation is nothing compared with being an eye witness to it, to say nothing about having to live it. And this is our situation.

I am not worried about being too scientific. I just look at the situation as humanly as possible, without being too theoretical. Let us look at the question of economic conditions in the West Bank. I am not very easily misled by statistics that are given about the economic conditions in the West Bank because, although the standard of living in the West Bank has risen since 1967, this is as far as a comparison with the situation that existed in 1967 goes. Since 1967, of course, economically we are better off. But let us not forget that other regions in the Arab countries, specifically the East Bank of Jordan, are also very highly developed. A recent study concerning the East Bank and the West Bank standards of living shows that since 1967, the growth in the standard of living in the East Bank was 4.5% higher than that of the West Bank.

The economic relations between the West Bank and Israel today are based on two characteristics which I think you must be familiar with. The first is a growth of a market for Israeli commodities in the occupied territories, and the second is a growth of a market for unskilled Arab workers in Israel. What does this mean to us?

As far as we are concerned, since 1967 this means that the West Bank became totally dependent on the Israeli economy and imports. At present, the West Bank and Gaza are Israel's second largest export market after the United States, ahead of Great Britain and West Germany. The West Bank and Gaza today import about 90% of their needs from Israel. We find ourselves a captive market for Israeli industrial products.

As far as workers are concerned, we are being robbed of 50% of our active population. And our workers, as you know, are confined to heavy, unskilled jobs. This means that the occupied territories today are being robbed of their skilled and technical workers. Many skilled Palestinians, educated Palestinians are finding it very difficult to stay and are leaving.

My point is, let us not compare economic conditions as of 1967 without looking at the other parts of the Arab world. If we had been under Jordan, we could also have enjoyed the developments that are taking place in the Arab countries today.

Now, as far as cultural, educational, and religious freedom are concerned, I think you should know that all our professionals in

the occupied territories do not totally depend on their own professions. I disagree with General Vardi that we have the right to carry
on with our lives, because the military government can deprive
individuals as well as institutions of the right to carry on with their
business under the pretext of security, whatever that means.

Birzeit University is closed because of security. The villagers of
Birzeit are not allowed to leave the country because of security.
Telephone services are cut off from Birzeit because of security.
Collective punishments are levied because of security. Khalhoul
was under curfew for two weeks because of security. This collective punishment, under the pretext of security, is overdoing it, to
say the least.

Also, you must be reminded that our native language is
Arabic, but please bear in mind that all signs, all bills, all communications are in Hebrew, and we do not speak Hebrew. We are
forced to go and translate all these documents—traffic tickets,
fines, and what have you—which are in Hebrew. So far as the
question of language is concerned, this is not freedom.

With respect to the Israeli settlements, I do not agree that settlements have been established only on Jordanian property. I would
like to remind you that there is a difference between public property and miri land. As far as the Israelis are concerned, miri land in
Israel is considered private property, but miri land in the occupied
territories is considered to be public property. So under the pretext
of using public property, most settlements are being established.
And I do not have to go into cases.

Under Jordanian law, too, miri land is private property. The
Israeli law today interprets miri lands as public property, therefore
they can confiscate it and establish settlements. When we are
talking about settlements, our concern is not only with land. Our
concern is with power. Settlements in the occupied territories
represent power against us. These settlements have been established under a military occupation, and the basis for the existence
of the settlements is security. I think the war of 1973 proved that
settlements, at least in the Golan, were a burden to the Israeli army
and not the contrary. A settlement near Beit El, surrounded by
Arabs and Arab land, does not seem to me to offer such security
for the State of Israel. Here we have to be very careful about settlements that have been established in the occupied territories since
1967, and settlements that were established in Israel during the
Mandate period.

Now, regarding coexistence, General Vardi said very proudly
that the Israelis have established a coexistence with the Palestinians. I think you must know that this coexistence is not based on
mutual respect. It is based on fear. Such coexistence is artificial,
and soon it will be eliminated.

I am not so impressed with the open bridges policies. Let's
face it, the policy of open bridges is for Israeli interests. First of all,
the open bridges policy diverts the Arab communities in the West

Bank towards the East Bank, because the Israelis have two things to do as far as we are concerned. One is to integrate us, to make us part of Israel, which, of course, they do not want to do. There would be too many Arabs in a Jewish state. The second is to create a diversion whereby we will be in Eretz Israel but detached from it.

This is very much related to the policy of workers. Arab workers are being taken in buses in the morning to the so-called green line, and then they are driven back at the end of the day to their villages to prevent integration. What is really the essence of occupation? The essence of the occupation is its irrationality. An elaborate and intricate machine has been set up to serve ends for which no sensible, practical, or moral justification exists. The machine perpetuates the ends and gives them substance. The whole thing has become a runaway process that controls everybody involved in it, including the people who think they are controlling the process. What this means, of course, is that the situation robs everyone of the basic capacity for logical decision-making and ethical choice.

Finally, about autonomy. I was one of those who was almost ready to consider autonomy for the West Bank. But having heard people here talking about it confirms the Palestinians' fears that what we are about to negotiate already exists. If I am to believe that we have autonomy, as General Vardi stated, why should I be bothered to go through five years of negotiations in order to achieve what we already have? And this is precisely the whole argument. If we have an autonomous region, then what are we negotiating? What are we discussing?

I hope you understand what I am saying, because all of the Israelis that I know tell us this is a chance of a lifetime. "Your history is associated with rejecting everything. Please accept it." And I come here, and I hear that we already have it. So it only confirms the Palestinians' fear and rejection of what is being offered.

General Vardi: I think that the points raised by Professor Nazzal are part of mutual coexistence, discussing and talking with each other. I do not agree with most of the points, but since I am already quite experienced in such discussions, I know that they do not lend themselves to agreement. Each party consults its own figures, its own statistics, although I was quite glad to hear that the Jordanian government published our statistics regarding the West Bank.

Nafez Nazzal: This was a study made by the Department of Economics at Birzeit University, and it was not done to compare the standard of living here and there. The faculty members were asking for a raise and then they told us we had to send a team to Jordan to talk about the whole situation.

General Vardi: Professor Nazzal must remember that Birzeit University was established as a university—not as an institute, but as a university—under the military government. The university in Bethlehem, which previously did not exist, was also established under the military government, as was the recently founded Kuliat Nadjah University in Nablus. There are now three universities in the West Bank, all developed under the military government.

I want to tell you that at the time that I was military governor, I did not know what program of studies was being taught in Birzeit University, although we know that a lot of the PLO theories were being taught. But Birzeit University was not closed for this reason. I had long discussions at the time with the late Dr. Mussa Nasser, with whom we had very amicable relations, who was the founder of the institution over sixty years ago. And later I also met with his son and with Professor Barrankie as well, who is the present Dean. And always the discussion turned to this subject.

I used to tell him, "Please do one thing. Please study. Do what you claim to do—teach. Don't be involved in public disorder." He said, "I can't control the students." And these discussions went on twice, and ten and fifteen times without results, and then I was the one who approved—in 1974—the closing of the University for 15 or 20 days. The University of Birzeit was closed, not because of what was being taught there, but only because of the students' involvement in very serious public disorders and violence. And when I came to Dr. Nasser at the time, he said, "I can't control the students. I am sorry."

Closing of universities is not the object of the military government. In well-known democracies, when in their own universities there was public disorder, they were closed, and for long periods. Cairo University was closed for three months, if not more. So I do not think that with these examples you can challenge what I asserted in my presentation, your independence in education. And not only you, the government schools, the other universities, private schools and UNRRWA schools.

Now regarding the economy, I was very glad to hear that you, too, agree that there was development and economic growth. You have said it, so I will not comment on this. I would be very glad to see those statistics that show that in Jordan the standard of living has been raised above the standard of living in the West Bank. I know that it is the opposite, but this is a matter of statistics. So we do not have to argue about this.

Regarding unskilled labor, I wonder if you know that under the Israeli military government at least 15 schools for vocational training run by your own instructors were opened throughout the West Bank. We just finance them. In 1976 there were already 7,000 graduates who had become skilled workers, technicians, and the like. Most of them may work in Israel. Others work in the West Bank.

I cannot accept your statement that we have robbed you of your labor, because nobody coerces any worker to come to work in Israel. He comes voluntarily to work in Israel, in fact he demands to be allowed to work in Israel. You can say that we have created conditions whereby he demands it, but you cannot say that we coerce them to come and work in Israel. A considerable number of those who work in Israel are farmers, not laborers *per se*. They cultivate their farms and at the same time members of their families work in Israel to earn additional income.

It is true that most of the imports come from Israel. If not from Israel, they would have had to come through Jordan, because you do not produce everything that you need. And since the standard of living has been raised, private consumption has risen. This is why import of special commodities increases all the time.

You spoke about the pretext of security. I think that when we act, we act on genuine security matters. This is not a pretext. I have already said that we sometimes jeopardize security. For instance, we license or authorize each truck from the Gaza Strip that has to go to Jordan and then to Kuwait with citrus. We also license the trucks that go from the West Bank, and only for one reason, because on many occasions explosives were smuggled in those trucks. So we check them when they go out and when they come in. We have no other choice.

What of the wells in the Gaza Strip? There is a very serious problem of water salination in the Gaza Strip because of extreme utilization by the orange-growers. In order not to impair the whole produce of the groves, the military government has decided that any new plantations have to be licensed. Everybody wants to plant new groves because the prices are very good, and the exports to the east are very good. Therefore we have to license them, otherwise there is a danger to the whole citrus industry, one of the most important in the Gaza Strip economy.

I am specifying this in detail because otherwise you get a distorted point of view, and you do not have the whole picture. But you have to know one thing. The Israeli settlements in Rafiah get their water from the Israeli pipelines, from the Yarkon River, not from the Gaza Strip. In the Gaza Strip there are three Israeli settlements; two of them are military settlements that use local water only for drinking, so you cannot blame the Israeli settlements there for the salination of the water.

Regarding the Arabic language, I do not know if it is always adhered to, but there is a permanent order which I know is implemented that each letter from the military government has to be accompanied by an official Arabic translation. To the best of my knowledge, this is complied with. There were some cases which came to my attention in which it was not, and I dealt with them. However this is our policy regarding language. Nobody can claim that we impose the Hebrew language on the Arab population.

Regarding the open bridges, what came out of what you said was actually a suggestion that we should close the bridges. You don't suggest it? Thank you.

Now regarding settlements and security. I do not suppose that you want to take our advice regarding, let's say, the security of Jordan. On the other hand, you are trying to advise us as to what are the best interests of our own security. We alone can determine that, and we think that settlements are part of the security arrangements. Now, of course, you may say that you differ, but this is our opinion.

Regarding types of land, we have only taken the land that was in the physical custody of the Jordanian government, and where our custodian has taken over. These are the lands that we consider to be government land, just as did the Jordanians. The settlements in the Jordan Valley and in other places are mainly on this land. Those government lands amount to about 700,000 dunam (175,000 acres).

Fear or no fear, there is a certain amount of coexistence as you yourself have admitted. By the way, I did not say there is much. Still, in spite of everything—security, public disorder, demonstrations—there is a better understanding between us, and at least we know each other better. We talk, we discuss, and we agree or do not agree to differ in our opinions. I think that this is important to the goal of establishing peace some time in the future.

In my presentation, I tried to show to what extent there already exists the nucleus of self-government on the West Bank, and even more. As to the question of autonomy, I did not claim that autonomy in the sense proposed exists now. I spoke about self-management of local affairs, of local government, of self-rule, even in the sense of participation of the local population in running its own affairs, elections to the municipalities, and so forth. I think that autonomy is something entirely different. We tried to bring about autonomy in that sense as well. I reminded you that in 1968 we tried to establish an overall executive with powers and authority. I am sorry this was refused then and later on as well.

Leonard Binder: Really one could say that facts have been created for twelve years which give Israel a certain position to say that the situation has changed—we're there and the others are there. Now we want some kind of partnership, a decision to live together in the territories, not for Israel simply to pull back. Obviously the Palestinians, as we have heard, totally reject this idea, as do most other Arabs.

Why doesn't Israel simply recognize the Palestinians as a nation, or a community with power theoretically equal to Israel's in order to legitimize Israel's own claim to having a partnership in the West Bank? This would involve, therefore, two partners.

It seems to me that at this point in time the Israeli position is to ask to be a partner in a situation in which most people are rejecting it as the partner; and it in turn is rejecting the Palestinians as a national partner. And, of course, with the nation comes a government. It is not unusual that some nations still to be born have movements rather than capitals.

But somehow, in listening to this notion of partnership and shared rule, I am not so sure what the concept of sharing is. On the one hand, there is a dominant military force asserting its historical claim as well as its security needs. And on the other hand, there is a force which has no power and which is rejecting this assertion. Somehow there is a lack of parity between the two communities. It would seem to me that one would somehow have to create some sort of a situation in which, in fact, there were two equals talking, theoretically, if not literally.

I was struck by some things Dr. Sandler said. I think he was setting forth Israeli claims to territory in terms other than security. He is saying that Israel, in essence, has the same historical right to the West Bank and Gaza that the Palestinian residents there do.

I think that today to most of the Arab world and, indeed, even to the United States, Israel's assertion of rights seems in fact to be based on superior force more than on any kind of actual relationship that it has in terms of a community relating to the other community. So I found myself really interested in the idea that in a sense Israel may have to create a partner for itself.

Gabriel Ben-Dor: I think there are three ideas we are discussing. One is what Professor Pranger chose to label "parity." I choose to label it "symmetry," and in some of my previous work on federalism and federal solutions, I have discussed it with Professor Elazar at length several times. I found that in the Third World, and in the Middle East in particular, a certain amount of symmetry between the partners is necessary to make federal solutions work.

Now, reading Dr. Sandler's very eloquent exposition of the historical argument in the Zionist camp about the binational solution, my feeling is that the binational solution, among others, was rejected for the main reason that it was put forward in a situation of lack of symmetry. A perpetual Arab majority would have been guaranteed, thus preventing the development of full-fledged Jewish statehood. Therefore, it was rejected by the Jews, because it would have perpetuated an Arab majority.

Now we are offering, however generously and magnanimously, a type of federalism to the Palestinians in which we are three million and they are a million and a half, in which we have the superior military might, economic infrastructure, higher level of technology, education, and so forth. And my feeling is that, among the many reasons why they reject it, they are afraid that this will perpetuate their inferior status, inferior in a purely quantitative sense.

Then, too, when you speak about federalism between Israel, say, in the pre-1967 boundaries and Judea and Samaria, you also have to know that if we want to share sovereignty over Nablus, that means we have to share sovereignty over Tel Aviv and Haifa, not to mention Jerusalem. The question is, do we have that kind of symmetry in mind? Are we prepared for it? Have we really thought it over? I don't know whether that goes along with your notion of parity—I call it symmetry.

I find that only in one case in the Middle East has federalism worked, and the secret of why it worked there and not elsewhere was symmetry. The case is the United Arab Emirates. I do not know whether you agree with this analysis, but I think that, if the Abu Dabi-Dubai balance of power did not exist, the UAE would have broken down a long time ago. So the issue of symmetry seems to me very crucial.

Second is the issue of security. The territorial dimension of security is very important but it is only one dimension. The whole point should be that one can have various trade-offs between territory and other things—weapons technology, levels of armed forces, manpower, preparedness, motivation and the like—not to mention the political relationships with the possible opponents.

The same goes for temptation, though. You showed us a temptation curve, and in this curve your only reason for the Arabs being tempted to attack Israel is its size, or their proximity to the whole area of the country. But there have been many other reasons for the Arabs wanting to attack. We have to take into account more variables. That will spoil the elegance of the curve, but it will make the picture richer.

Yehezkel Dror: I think that any partnership or shared rule must be based on the parity system, otherwise we will not solve two great problems—free immigration and the return of the refugees. One group of citizens will always be afraid of the other group. If we want to create a sharing system, we must have parity in order to solve these two problems.

Also, we must go beyond the claims of historical rights. We Jews have our home rights here, and the Arabs have their home rights. We must find a way to share this common homeland. This is what we have to discuss, and the political scientists have to find the formula for us to share this homeland. Security for me is the friendship of my neighbor.

Myron Weiner: I think that language affects the way we think about things. I wonder if our thinking wouldn't be clarified if, instead of using the word "rights," we use the word "interests" or "claims." Our whole thinking about demands would be quite different if we didn't use the word "rights."

Daniel Elazar: There are various kinds of symmetries. For example, in some cases there are symmetries of size or symmetries of power, along with asymmetries of interests. I think that in many cases we may have asymmetries of power and symmetries of interest which function in the same way. Something must be symmetrical in any bargain, not only federal bargains.

It is much easier to talk about "interests" or "claims" than "rights," but my guess is that in any situation it is possible to get to the point of talking about interests only after rights are established. Look at the United States, where the term "interests" is most widespread. "Interests" became a usable term in American politics only after the American Revolution was completed, when the right of the Americans to create a polity of their own with their own framework was clearly established. Then, prior to the Civil War, the slavery issue reintroduced the question of rights. People talked about the "rights" of the various parties—the states, the slaves—not simply their interests, and for obvious reasons. Once the rights issues of the Civil War were settled, then it was possible to talk about "interests" again. However, when American blacks were finally able to assert their claims as U.S. citizens, they, too, put the discussion on a "rights" footing and properly so. I think it would be nice if we could talk only about "interests" in any conflict, but I am not certain that that is always possible until certain rights are sufficiently accepted by the various parties to the conflict.

Yehezkel Dror: If there were a metaphysical entity providing a foolproof energy barrier around Israel through which one could only move with an Israeli stamp, in other words, some form of total security, and the price for the barrier was to leave the West Bank—I am not speaking about Jerusalem—I think that the large majority of Israelis would accept it. If anyone can engineer such a barrier, please let us know, but I believe there is no such thing in the world. There is a consensus that security is a main component of the goal and values set by Israeli policy-making. If the security problem is solved, other things will become clearer and easier.

The term "symmetry" as such has no appeal to me. Neither do I reject it. It is a multi-dimensional business. I am very sorry that there is no symmetry between the Arab countries and Israel, either in petrol-dollars or in population. In any case, some variables are asymmetric. So the question of what symmetry is constitutes another problem. To put it into real political terms, if assymetry is to my advantage, I will reinforce it, not weaken it. In other words, I need an argument that at this stage of the game Israel's recognizing the Palestinians, whatever that may mean in the political sense, is advantageous. I am not sure whether that recognition *a priori* will make bargaining easier. I really doubt it. I personally do not reject such a move *a priori*. For me it is a cost-benefit question, an apolitical question. There may be circumstances where I will regard it in our interests to do it, and then I will say: Let's do it. It is not closed forever.

At present, however, such a move would not be beneficial. I am sorry to say this, but I am not sure that there may not be another war in the Middle East, and then this movement may be destroyed. I do not want war but it may happen. Then, recognizing the Palestinians may make matters more difficult for us.

Next, it may well be that at a certain stage the preferable solution from the Israeli point of view will be a deal with Jordan, whether the Palestinians like it or not. And we would make it difficult for ourselves by legitimizing a move which is very difficult to reverse.

With regard to a Palestinian state, there are two predictions from a socio-political dynamic point of view. One set of predictions suggests that no national movement has become quiet without a state. Therefore, if the Palestinians get a state, never mind how small and unviable, they will be busy with their internal politics and will forget their ambitions or their ideologies abroad. There is a logical fallacy in this. The second prediction says that, if they have a state, it will be a basis for further expansions. One cannot say with high probability that this will happen. If there is uncertainty, however, I prefer a maximalist strategy; I do not want the risk. I am ready to give up the hope in order not to have the risk.

Robert Pranger: You insist that it is in Israel's interest to maximize asymmetry?

Yehezkel Dror: At this point, yes.

Robert Pranger: It may be in Israel's interest to court the favor of the United States. Well, those are two interdependent decisions, and they are both present now. So therefore, in terms of your argument, it is not necessarily in Israel's national interest now to maximize asymmetry.

You hold the United States constant, and you are holding all other independent variables constant. I thought you were the one who argued that this was a multi-variant analysis. And all of a sudden we are down to maximizing an asymmetry between Israel and the West Bank. I do not consider that to be an adequate political analysis.

Yehezkel Dror: You brought up the United States, rightly so, and you make the assumption that Israel-United States relations necessarily depend on Israel's recognizing the Palestinians. I do not think that this is the situation.

Robert Pranger: I didn't quite say that. I said that Israel-U.S. relations depend on Israel not maximizing asymmetry. I didn't say they depend on recognizing the Palestinians.

Yehezkel Dror: I am not sure what the United States would mean by maximizing the asymmetry. Also, from the Israeli point of view, I think, well, how shall I put it carefully without being able to elaborate on it? Israel will not do what the United States likes under all conditions. I do not expect morally that we can always do what we like, but we have the right to apply cost-benefits to each case.

Shmuel Sandler: Why don't we recognize the Palestinians in order to legitimize partnership? If one looks at the history of the conflict and the history of the three sides—Israel, the Palestinians, and the Hashemites—one sees that the Palestinians from the beginning rejected both of the two solutions that existed, power-sharing and partition.

The only Arab party that did not reject them was the Hashem-ite camp, because of their own interests. Abdullah had a dream of a greater Syria as his ultimate goal, but in the interim they were the only party with whom we could sort of talk, even if it was only by tacit bargaining.

So what happens here is that, if we recognize the Palestinians, we may close the door to a deal with Jordan. Why should we do it, and with a side which always rejected any compromise? After 70 years of conflict, you come and ask me, "Well, for your own good, just recognize the Palestinians." But the history of the conflict teaches me another lesson. I know from the history of the conflict that the Hashemites, in order, I would say, to sell out the Palestini-ans, did deal with us. I do not say that they did it for humane reasons. They had their interests, we had our interests, and that is how partition came into effect.

At this point, we have the historical evidence showing that the PLO does not want to make the first move. They do not want to make the first move not only towards recognizing Israel, but even towards accepting U.N. Resolution 242, which does not even men-tion Israel. If I were a Palestinian, I would do it, just say "I recognize 242." What does 242 say? All the states in the region have a right to exist. "But Israel is not a state"—that is how I could get out of this whole dilemma. But even that they are not ready to recognize.

Now, about parity or power-sharing, I agree with Ben-Dor. This was always a problem. When one side was a majority, the other side was not. You cannot today come to another side and say, "Well, in order to solve our problem, I am going to make us sym-metrical." States do not behave like that. States do not voluntarily reduce their power in order to become symmetrical. No state ever did it.

Ilan Greilsammer: There is no doubt that it is hard to find a com-mon denominator in this discussion. However, it seems to me that there are some elements which arose either explicitly or implicitly from the bulk of our debates, namely the concepts of partnership, dialogue, links, and cooperation.

A number of participants in this symposium have criticized the Israeli administration for not having been able to promote a part-nership with the inhabitants of the territories which will be subject to the autonomy process. Several of these participants, when speaking about this future process, have stressed the fact that it should be based upon partnership structures, deep cooperation between Jews and Arabs, Israelis and Palestinians, between the autonomous institutions which will be established in the West Bank and in Gaza and the Israeli governmental institutions.

We have reviewed at least three points in this regard—the discrepancy between the expectations of the Israeli government and those of the West Bank inhabitants as regards their future; the problem of guarantees for Israeli security; and the obligation of policy planning for the process of autonomy. As Secretary of the Jerusalem Institute for Federal Studies, I think I can say that what we believe at the Institute is that these problems could be solved in accordance with two basic principles: first, respect for everyone's identity and his right of self-administration. Second, cooperation or partnership should be extended at all levels, for example, through common agencies and joint projects.

These two principles, self-administration and cooperation, are the very essence of federalist or quasi-federalist solutions. We all know that solutions of this type have already been applied in various parts of the world in order to resolve conflicts, including serious ones. I would hope that this appeal for federalist solutions will become concrete within the next weeks or months.

Part Four
Directions

Sharing the Land: The Only Realistic Option

Yehudah Ben Meir

Implementing the Israeli-Egyptian Peace

I certainly would not be in a position to try to predict with any degree of accuracy what will be next, not even with what scientists call an educated guess. Indeed, I think that next is not only a continuation of what has happened until now, but also represents a totally new step in dealing with new issues. It is very hard to predict exactly how the negotiations which we face will develop in the future, but we in the Middle East expect progress in the next year in two different areas. In the first area, Egypt-Israel relationships, I would say that development has been prescribed at least for the next three years along the lines set forth in the peace treaty between Egypt and Israel. Whether matters will develop as they are supposed to is another question. But we know that there is a clear delineation of the movement toward normalization between Israel and Egypt. I am sure all of you are familiar with the peace treaty and all its annexes with dates and timetables for normalization. It may be quickened or may not be quickened, but there is a timetable.

There are three stages to this normalization process. In the first stage, the first nine months, all the obligations are upon Israel, with one exception. The obligations which Israel has taken upon itself are to withdraw in nine months to the line specified as the interim El Arish–Ras Muhammed line. The only concrete obligation demanded of Egypt, which Egypt has already fulfilled, is to enable free Israeli shipping through the Suez Canal. Egypt's claim to prevent Israeli shipping through the Suez Canal was based on the existence of a state of war between Israel and Egypt. Article 1 of the treaty declares that the state of war between the Arab Republic of Egypt and Israel has ceased to exist and peace is established

279

between them; therefore, free shipping through the canal is Israel's right. Israeli merchant vessels began to pass through the canal about a week after the instruments of ratification were exchanged and Israeli naval vessels began to pass through at the end of May.

Then comes the part which may present difficulties for either side; the obligations of normalization of relationships. At the conclusion of the nine months when Israeli forces reach the interim line, Egypt must open its borders; this is stated specifically in the treaty. There must be free intercourse of people, of goods, through open borders. In effect Egypt has committed itself to relate to Israel regarding posts, telecommunications and transportation, movement of people and goods, as she relates to any other nation within the various multilateral national agreements which exist. One month following the interim withdrawal, Egypt must establish a diplomatic legation in Israel at the head of which will be a resident ambassador. Egypt must also accept such an Israeli delegation in Egypt. Within five months after that, negotiations must begin between Israel and Egypt for the conclusion of various economic and trade agreements as well as many other steps required by the treaty, such as opening and improving roads connecting the two countries and reconstructing the rail link between Israel and Egypt through Sinai. All this is specified in the cultural annex of the treaty.

Three years later, after all this is supposed to be well under way, Israel has to fulfill the third stage. The obligation is upon Israel to withdraw its forces to the previous international border, which is now recognized by the treaty as the final and permanent boundary between Israel and Egypt.

Now whether or not things will develop along these lines is an open question. My personal opinion at the moment is that so far things are developing along lines which I would consider favorable and good. I certainly would hope that all the obligations and all the features of the treaty will be fulfilled equally.

I can foresee no substantial difficulties in the developing of the relationship between Israel and Egypt along the lines formulated by the treaty. I see no specific problem developing now, in nine months, in a year, in a year and a half. I see no difficulty that will prevent both sides from concluding cultural, economic and other such agreements which could not easily be resolved. In my opinion it is very important to prove that we can give life to this peace treaty and give life to the peace relationship between Israel and Egypt.

Negotiating Autonomy

The second dimension which lies ahead of us is the negotiation with regard to autonomy for the inhabitants of the administered territories which began on May 25, 1979, in Beersheba. These negotiations are based to a certain degree on the Camp David agreement. Technically they are based on the letter attached to the peace treaty, the joint letter signed by Israel and Egypt. It commits the parties to begin the negotiations referred to in the Camp David agreement one month after the ratification of the treaty, and they began exactly one month to the day. The goal was to engage in negotiations continuously, in good faith, to conclude them within a year, and, after they are concluded, to hold elections as expeditiously as possible. There is no timetable given for the elections after the agreement. First of all, it is clear that the elections have to be held after agreement is reached on all the outstanding issues. This is stated clearly in the letter. No timetable is given for these elections except for the term "as expeditiously as possible" which anyone can interpret as he feels. The only explicit requirement is that one month after elections are held the elected body will begin to function.

I do not want to go into the question, which is of course a genuine question, as to what relationships there are between the Israel-Egypt peace treaty and elections in the territories. I do not claim for one minute that there is no relationship; what I want to say is that in the best opinion which I think exists there is no legal relationship between the two. There is not one word in the treaty of peace signed between Egypt and Israel which in any way links them. This does not mean that politically there is no linkage. Only time will tell to what degree the implementation of the various parts of the peace treaty may be linked to the question of negotiations on the second issue.

Turning to the second issue, the autonomy plan, what is the position of the National Religious Party and of the government as a whole on autonomy? What are we trying to achieve, and how do we view the main questions of autonomy?

I think that the problem of Judea and Samaria—when I say "Judea and Samaria" Gaza is included just to make it shorter and save time—is unique. The Jerusalem Institute has inventoried the various examples of different solutions to questions of autonomy. Each example is nevertheless unique. In my opinion, the question of the Arab Palestinians living in Judea and Samaria is a unique

question, because of the unique relationship existing in this area. Therefore, it must have a unique solution. There may be a specific example that is comparable to which we can turn but, even if there is no precedent, I do not see this as in any way a drawback which cannot be overcome. Precedent is the great enemy of advancement and of innovation. One simply has to be able to apply human skills to try to find the unique solution.

I am sure everyone is aware of the central problem of Judaea, Samaria and Gaza, the relationship that Israel has to this area, versus the fact that are in it 1,050,000 Arabs who do not want to be part of a Jewish state. Therefore, as I see it, there are four possible solutions. The Arab solution is that all this area ought to be returned to the Arabs. In my opinion, Israel cannot, should not, and will not agree to a solution which involves the restoration of the borders of June, 1967, and the complete cutting off of these areas from Israel and the Jewish people. We oppose this for historical reasons, for security reasons, and for many other reasons.

In my opinion, this is a correct and just stand. I think it reflects the consensus of the vast majority of Israelis who are not ready to accept the Arab proposal of total withdrawal of Israel from all these areas. I certainly would do everything I can not to have it accepted, because I feel it undermines the very future and security and rights of the people of Israel and the Jewish people.

Another solution, the opposite of the first, is to incorporate Judea, Samaria and Gaza as part of Israel and to give Israeli citizenship to all those inhabitants who want it. In my opinion, this solution is not viable politically. Again I do not want to go into the merits of the case. I think it would be the most just solution, if we could work in our world on the basis of absolute justice, and I am ready to explain why I think so. But I am convinced that it is not a politically viable solution. I do not think that we can achieve an agreement with the Arab states surrounding us on this basis, and I do not think we can reach a *modus vivendi* with countries such as the United States with which we have to live. That is why, to the best of my knowledge, no government and no significant political party—including the NRP and the Likud—ever suggested in its platform the unilateral annexation of Judea and Samaria.

In the national unity government of 1967, of which Mr. Begin was a member, he did not suggest the annexation of Judea and Samaria. On the contrary, the only annexation was that of East Jerusalem to West Jerusalem, and it was unanimously approved by the Cabinet. There were those who suggested that the area of Jerusalem be enlarged to include Bethlehem. (By the way, the Arabs in Bethlehem were the ones who requested inclusion in the annexation at that time.) Mr. Begin, in my opinion correctly, was opposed to it, because, he said, if we do so, we will already have made it clear that we do not have any claims to the rest of Judea and Samaria. If we just annex East Jerusalem, it is clear that we are just reuniting Jerusalem as a city and the question of Judea and Samaria will be left for negotiation. Begin also realized that total annexation is not viable. Thus, we are left with two possible compromise solutions.

One is the solution which the Labor Alignment has championed from the beginning, a territorial partition of Judea and Samaria along the lines of the Allon Plan., Those areas which have great security importance and which also are not heavily populated by the Arabs will be annexted to Israel. Other parts will become part and parcel of an Arab political entity whose character will be determined in the negotiations. This is one possibility.

In my opinion, this proposal has several merits, but I do not feel at the moment that it is politically acceptable. So far we have not found any country in the Arab world, including Egypt with whom we now have a peace treaty, which has been willing in any way to accept this solution. If any Arab leader would be ready to discuss it seriously, I think there is room for Israel to examine it as a possibility. But at the moment I do not think it is a viable solution, nor do I think it is the best one.

The fourth possibility is what is called a political solution in Judea, Samaria and Gaza. It is not based on partition of land, but rather on a division of authority, a division of rights and of functions within the territories. A political solution first of all involves two things in a negative sense and a number of things in a positive sense. In the negative sense, when I say a political solution through division, it clearly means that Israel will not exercise sole sovereignty over Judea and Samaria. If Israel did exercise sovereignty, there would not be a proper division of functions. Nor will any Arab entity, independent or part of another Arab entity, exercise sole sovereignty over the area. This clearly is what a political division means. It can have no other meaning. If one side is going to exercise full sovereignty over this area, there would not be a political division or a political solution.

The essence of the fourth solution is that neither side exercises full and complete sovereignty over this area, but we have some type of joint sovereignty in which we have a division of functions. Now, in my opinion, if there will be good will on all sides, I think we can arrange such a solution. This is the essence of the government's position on autonomy, which I think is a just and correct one. Whether it will be accepted or not is another question.

At the moment, we are dealing with a transitional solution. The Camp David agreement stipulates no effective guidelines for the permanent solution. In my opinion, however, the permanent solution has to be some further development of the interim solution. The principle, now or five years from now, has to be that both communities—the Arab community and and the Jewish community living in Judea, Samaria and Gaza, with Israel having a vital interest in the territories for reasons of security and Jewish settlement rights—have to divide their functions between themselves.

The Arab population of Judea and Samaria will enjoy full and complete rights to run its own life in every way and to be solely responsible for the development of its own society. The Jewish population in Judea and Samaria will enjoy, of course, its own right to develop its own life and be responsible for its own future, with Israel guaranteeing that this division will be viable.

In other words, Israel is the only factor at the moment. Anyone who is clearly objective has to admit this, that Israel is the only power at the moment which is in a position to guarantee this solution, at least for the foreseeable future. Not only would the Palestinians be unable to guarantee it, but neither would Jordan. I do not think, for instance, that Jordan would even be able to sustain a solution whereby Judea and Samaria would be part of Jordan. That, in my opinion, is why King Hussein is not at all interested in joining the negotiations, because he has nothing to gain. Even if tomorrow Israel would give him Samaria and Judea on a golden platter, he probably could not hold on to them more than two or three days at the best. The price he would have to pay would be far to great. Therefore, to repeat, the only factor which can guarantee such a joint solution is Israel.

This, in summary, then, is the essence of the autonomy plan: that through free elections and institutions the Arabs living in Judea, Samaria and Gaza will be in charge of their day-to-day lives. Side by side with them, the Jews will have the right and the ability to live in settlements and be responsible for running their own lives. The ultimate responsibility, which mainly involves the security question, will lie with Israel. Israel will have the ability through its forces to guarantee this solution and to divide the functions, the responsibilities, and the authority between the two communities in the area. I do not think that the Palestinians, even those who want such an arrangement—and there may be come who would—are capable of upholding it; the Jewish community in Judea and Samaria is also not capable of upholding it. Nor is any foreign power, Arab or otherwise, capable of upholding it. The political reality is that the only power which can do it is Israel. This, the security issue, is what is behind Israel's position regarding the source of authority for the autonomy plan. For a few years, Israel must guarantee that this solution be given a chance to prove itself, and afterwards, if it works, then we will see what will happen.

What happens next? We all see the problems involved in making this arrangement work. Therefore, I do not exclude the possibility that Egypt will suggest trying to work out this scheme in the Gaza District first to see how it will work, with the clear understanding that the model which we develop for the Gaza Strip has to be the model which would be applicable tomorrow to Judea and Samaria. I am not suggesting different models, but I am suggesting the possibility of different timetables. It may even be beneficial to try to work out this model first on a much smaller scale and later on try to effectuate it in Judea and Samaria. This is not the position of the Israeli government, but I have reason to believe that if this suggestion were to be put forth by Egypt or by the United States, that it would not be rejected by Israel. It would definitely be worthwhile examining.

The Virtues of Repartition
Dan Horowitz

The topic before us is whether or not autonomy, or some similar form of government, can be made to work either as a temporary settlement, or a permanent one. I have studied this issue in the general framework of comparative politics. In my view, the relations between communities within such systems are bound to become like international relations rather than internal ones, even within the same political system. Consequently, such systems are most unstable, vulnerable to changes in the balance of power between the different communities, and very likely to end up in either partition, or if there is no territorial basis for partition, in civil war which ends in partition after a transfer of populations. Wherever partition is possible, it is always the preferable solution to reduce tension and reduce friction among the various communities.

Now, turning to the solution presented to us by Dr. Ben Meir, I would question whether it is really more viable than than the other three solutions he rejected. If we speak in terms of viability, I would say that the only solution which is politically viable is a withdrawal of Israeli sovereignty, not the Israeli military presence—and this is an important distinction—to something very close to the 1949 armistice lines, usually referred to as the June 1967 lines. This is the only solution which is politically viable and which may lead to a permanent peace rather than a transitional solution. Any solution which does not include a withdrawal of sovereignty would be temporary. Any solution which would be based on division of government or division of authority can survive for several years and can even serve as a point of departure for further development, but it cannot become a permanent solution. I would claim in addition that the whole debate on autonomy is not actually a debate on the temporary settlement, but on what temporary settlement we want in the light of the need to transform it in the future into a permanent solution. Therefore, what must be discussed is not the autonomy so much as it is the kind of solution which has to evolve out of the autonomy.

In this context, I regard the kind of autonomy suggested by Dr. Ben Meir as not viable, in fact, as likely to lead to the failure of the negotiations and to the collapse of the whole peace initiative, whether there is a formal linkage with Egypt or not. Nothing can prevent Sadat, after making the first steps towards normalization and after getting back all of Sinai in three years to refuse to make any further advances. Thus the process would actually end in an

285

interim settlement, but not an interim settlement along the existing lines, not an interim settlement along the El Arish–Ras Muhammad line, but an interim settlement along the international border. This would be a return, not only to the pre-1967 borders, but also basically to the pre-1967 situation. If we want to prevent this from happening, then we have to contrive an autonomy scheme that could be developed into a viable, sensible, permanent solution.

There are three basic reasons why the government's autonomy solution does not seem viable to me. First of all, I do not believe that it is acceptable to any other party; it is not even acceptable to Sadat, who is the most moderate among the Arabs. But this is less important than the second consideration, that the autonomy plan is not acceptable to world public opinion and to American public opinion. No American government has ever accepted basic changes in the pre-1967 war borders because it goes against their conception of the international order. Both the Americans and the Soviets have a strong interest in preventing changes of borders through wars carried out by small client countries. This would undermine their attempts to control international relations, to control what is happening in the world. Such border changes could result in a sabotage of the game of international relations as they play it. That is extremely dangerous to the big powers and might drive them into, if not a military confrontation, at least a political confrontation. Therefore, I do not believe that there will be international legitimization of any changes in the 1967 borders, in terms of sovereignty. If, then, we view autonomy as the only viable solution, we must be ready to accept a continuation of the conflict without U.S. backing and a state of belligerency between Israel and the Arab countries, including Egypt, sooner or later.

If this last point—the return of Egypt to the ranks of the confrontation states—is correct politically, then we have the choice of whether to accept it or to reject it. This is the only solution that might bring about peace, and if we do not accept it, we have to remember that we are not only opting for the continuation of the conflict, but ultimately for the continuation of the conflict without the backing of the United States, and without the backing of public opinion in the West. In fact, the choice is clear. I have only one condition; I would accept Israel's withdrawal to the 1967 borders if Israeli defense requirements are met.

Israel's security problem is that the West Bank, unlike Sinai and, to a certain extent, also unlike the Golan Heights, is a threat to Israel's basic security, not only security against terrorism. A well-equipped Arab military contingent on the West Bank possessing offensive weapons and such defensive weapons as ground-to-air missiles can prevent any Israeli aircraft from taking off from any Israeli airfield. The basic security interest of Israel is to prevent such a situation. This means that a necessary precondition for Israel's accepting any withdrawal solution is that the West Bank should be demilitarized.

The problem is, what are the guarantees for demilitarizing the West Bank. I believe that only Israel itself can provide those guarantees; no international nor even American guarantees are viable in this case. And the only guarantees that Israel can rely on are guarantees based on Israel's capacity to defend itself. If this assumption is correct, then there is a need for some kind of Israeli military presence in the West Bank. In other words, the security problem has to be divorced from the sovereignty problem. The territory should be returned to Arab sovereignty, but the complete withdrawal of Israeli sovereignty should not also involve a withdrawal of an Israeli military presence.

Is this solution viable? I believe it is, and I have clear reasons to believe it. The first is that Sadat himself hinted in this direction in his speech. He spoke about the legitimate security interests of Israel, and left matters open to move in this direction. Several American leaders, among them Secretary of Defense Brown, have also expressed this view in one way or another, so it also seems to be acceptable to the Americans. And in the Camp David agreements themselves, there is a paragraph which speaks about the Israeli army withdrawing to certain specified areas in the West Bank. I believe Israel should insist on defining these specified areas in the interim settlement and gaining agreement for their continued maintenance in the future. After the period of autonomy, Israel should maintain a military presence in those areas which control or dominate the main routes leading from the East to the West Bank. This is something along the lines of the Allon Plan, but on a narrower scale and without annexation. It is accepting the military basis of the Allon Plan but without the change of sovereignty involved in it. This, I believe, can be achieved, but if it cannot be achieved, then Israel should not sign any peace treaty involving the West Bank and must take the risk of having the whole peace initiative collapse. Security is, in my view, the only condition that is really vital to Israel; it is a condition which we have to insist on fully. It is also the only condition which can be accepted, or whose rationale can be accepted by other powers and by world public opinion.

In translating the Camp David agreements, the present government changed the English terms "West Bank and Gaza" into loaded terms like "Judea," "Samaria" and "Gaza District." The "legitimate rights of the Palestinians" became "the legitimate rights of the Arabs of Israel." I do not think that we have changed the spirit of the agreement by these translations. I believe, too, that Sadat will have a strong point if he claims that the concept of autonomy presented here by Dr. Ben Meir is not compatible with the wording or the spirit of the Camp David agreement. Therefore, if Israel does not make a more positive proposal than that we heard today, the onus of failure will fall on us. I think, moreover, that Sadat's position will have the full support both of the United

States and of Western public opinion, and, therefore, I do not see how this autonomy proposal can be presented to us as viable.

The Autonomy:
Some Considerations

Daniel J. Elazar

As we approach negotiations on autonomy, no one has been able to ascertain whether or not Israel has a clear plan in mind to present as the basis for those negotiations. At best, we have some agreed upon guidelines, namely that the autonomy should be extended to people, not territory; that Israel must maintain sufficient control over security matters, water and other essentials that directly affect its safety and the lives of Israeli settlers in the administered territories; and that the right of Jewish settlement remain open. On these points there is such general agreement that they form a consensual basis within the Israeli government, but they do not constitute a plan. For example, even assuming that Israel is successful in securing endorsement of its stand that autonomy falls upon people rather than territories, still there are territories predominantly Arab in population, including most of the duly constituted municipalities in Judea, Samaria and the Gaza region. One assumes that some relationship between people and territory will be worked out so that the people in those territories will implement the autonomy within them. Thus, though the principle is a valid one, it is not automatically self-executing.

This observer is convinced that Prime Minister Begin has a clear plan in his own mind. Until such time as he does present his plan, most of the discussions on the matter will have to be confined to generalities. Nevertheless, there are certain basics which can be considered regarding the autonomy and the debate that inevitably surrounds it.

There is no need to review the political and military reasons why Israel is seeking a solution that does not involve its withdrawal from the administered territories and which remain central. But beyond those reasons there are others which also reinforce the necessity to reach an accommodation based upon some combination of self-rule and shared rule in the territories in the interests of both Israelis and Palestinian Arabs. These reasons lie in the changed circumstances of settlement and economic and technological development in which we all find ourselves.

In many respects, the Zionist enterprise was an extension of the great frontier of the Western world and the expansion of settlement on the Western model into new territories.[1] Like other examples of that great frontier, the first Zionist settlements were principally rural in character, self-contained rural agricultural com-

289

munities with a minimum of urban development designed to provide them with the necessary commercial infrastructure (plus, in the Zionist case, urban settlement for non-economic reasons—either religious, as in the case of Jerusalem, or national—which need not be spelled out here). The very self-contained nature of these first settlements meant that it was possible to establish a Zionist presence in various points around the country without particularly interfering with the Arab presence in any direct sense. Indeed, much of the land was substantially empty and even unwanted by the Arabs because of its inferior character so that Jewish settlements did not even displace Arab populations, except in marginal cases. Links between settlements were at most a matter of security whereby a number of small settlements would be built adjacent to one another so as to create a complex that would be self-sustaining, particularly from a security point of view.

With the establishment of the state, and the coming of the mass migration, Israel began to industrialize on a serious basis and thereby moved onto a second frontier stage which also had its parallel in other new societies, namely that of the urban-industrial frontier. Industrialization involved urbanization, and the cutting edge of development was to be found in the building of cities, either entirely new ones or the transformation of settlements founded as agricultural villages into large cities based upon industry. For the most part, these cities were also self-contained, or at least functioned in self-contained clusters.

In order to benefit from the urban-industrial frontier, people had to migrate to a city or to one of the small complexes of cities, such as the Dan region (metropolitan Tel Aviv), and find work there. Dependent as they were on a public transportation system utilizing a very modest road network, people could not expect to travel far to their places of work but sought to be as close as possible to them. At the same time, industry and agriculture remained predominantly separate, with the rural sector continuing to expand on the basis of agricultural development.

Then, in the latter years of the 1960s, approximately coincident but not as a result of the Six-Day War, Israel began to move onto the next stage of development that has been characteristic of the Western world and particularly of the frontier societies within it, namely metropolitanization or, more precisely, onto the metropolitan-technological frontier.[2] Metropolitanization involved, on one hand, a transformation of simple industrialization through the application of sophisticated new technologies plus a concomitant transformation of patterns of settlement based upon new systems of transportation and communication. The earlier unity of place of residence and place of work began to disappear as the possibility of moving quickly across substantial distances on a daily basis became real. So, for example, during the days of the urban frontier, Israeli Arabs living in the Galilee had to forego involvement in the industrialization process because their villages did not attract industry, or move to Jewish cities away from their own cultural frameworks and live lonely lives in order to achieve greater economic advantage. With the coming of metropolitanization, the same Arabs could remain residents of their villages and take a bus to some destination in the Haifa Bay metropolitan region to work in the morning and then back again at night without being unduly burdened as a result.

Not only were residential possibilities decentralized but so, too, were places of work. Increasingly, the industrial base became regional, spread throughout the emerging metropolitan areas rather than concentrated in one place. Israel always had a tendency in this direction and the metropolitanization process simply accelerated it.

Israel's urbanization and metropolitanization began along the coast in the Dan and Haifa Bay regions.[3] Jerusalem, whose urban development had always taken a very different turn, never really entered the urban-industrial frontier because at the time it was cut off at the end of the Jerusalem corridor surrounded by territory under Arab rule. Then came the Six-Day War and suddenly Jerusalem was reunited with its potential hinterland, precisely at the time that metropolitanization was beginning to engulf the country. In the ensuing decade, Jerusalem not only gained strength as a focus for Jewish developmental activities related to servicing the metropolitan frontier, such as higher education, government, and other public sector activities, but also was reintegrated with a hinterland in Judea and Samaria that was increasingly drawn toward it. From an agricultural point of view, the region from Hebron on the south to Nablus on the north, Jericho on the east and Bet Shemesh on the west, became a single market with produce flowing into Jerusalem daily from every part of it. Jerusalem, in turn, became a magnet for employing the residents of the mountain ridge along the same axis, particularly as development of its Jewish sections required more hands for building, a need met principally by the Arab population. Some of these new workers moved to the city, others remained in their native towns and villages and commuted, utilizing the improved transportation facilities of the post-1967 years. Thus the country acquired a third metropolitan region, only this one embraced both Jewish and Arab nodes and united them into a single economic framework whose prosperity rested upon this mutual interaction.

This new development, as much as any security or other considerations, makes a return to partition an atavistic step. One is tempted to say that such a return is no longer feasible except that history has shown that politics can overrule economics even in such circumstances. Jerusalem could be cut off at the end of a corridor again and returned to the peripheries of Israel. The Arab areas around the city could be cut off from their natural focal point if political decisions are made to that effect. But in such a case everybody would suffer; not only the individuals who would lose their only significant opportunities for employment but the two peoples as peoples would lose a major opportunity for economic and social development enhancing their prosperity which has been the result of the reconnection since 1967.[4]

Thus there should be a major interest on the part of both parties to work out a political arrangement that will recognize the unity of the country even as it provides for maximum self-government for its peoples combined with shared rule where necessary. The autonomy plan offers the beginning of a possibility for doing just that, if it is properly developed.

Think of some of the possibilities. Jerusalem by its very nature does not lend itself to becoming a major industrial center. Indeed there are many reasons why the city and its environs have escaped the impact of industrialization so as to preserve Jerusalem's special character. Prior to the metropolitan frontier, this, in effect, doomed Jerusalem to being a backwater and its region to suffering from lack of development. One of the characteristics of the metropolitan frontier, however, is that other nodes in the metroplitan region can industrialize to everyone's benefit without damaging Jerusalem's special character.

On the metropolitan frontier, education itself becomes a major industry, a means of developing a population that is equipped to participate in the sophisticated socio-economic systems of the metropolitan era. Jerusalem is ideally suited to be a major educational center. Indeed, education is one of the functions that is most appropriate to the city, given its historic role.

Jewish Jerusalem has already become the educational center of the Jewish people, through the Hebrew University, its many yeshivot, and, increasingly, through the technical colleges sponsored by the Orthodox community and social and humanistic research institutes of various kinds. There are, in addition, many renowned Christian-sponsored institutions for Bible and theological study. While no similar development has taken place in Arab Jerusalem, the beginnings of serious institutions of higher education serving the Arab population are to be found in Birzeit and Bethlehem. Only peace will enable those institutions to develop further. United within a common metropolitan region, they will add an additional dimension to Jerusalem's position on the world's educational map. Together, these institutional complexes can put Jerusalem in the forefront as a world educational center. But it is precisely the ability to concentrate a number of separate institutions, each maintaining its separate identity in every respect, but within close proximity to one another so that synergism can play its role, that will make the difference. This indeed is the essence of the metropolitan frontier—separate but synergistic—and is the way in which other great educational centers in the world have become what they have become.

Much of the discussion regarding the autonomy has revolved

around whether it should fall on persons or territories. In fact, its success depends upon how it combines the governance of peoples and territories, for there cannot be governance of one without the other. It is clear that the emphasis in the autonomy will be on peoples but it will be necessary to govern those peoples in their territories. At the very least, for the foreseeable future, there will be clearly separate Arab and Jewish cities and villages.

Thus it will not only be possible but probably necessary to link particular local jurisdictions either with the Arab oriented autonomy or with the Jewish dominated State of Israel. This, indeed, is the direction in which things have developed informally since 1967. In local government matters, Arab municipalities and villages already have almost complete self-rule in local matters, while Israeli settlements began with internal self-rule and have recently been organized into regional councils or given more clear-cut municipal status under Israeli law so that they can formally exercise those self-same powers.

The importance of these local organs should not be minimized. In an age and region where the focus tends to be on national governments and international relations, it is far too easy to minimize the importance of local self-government. Jews with good historical memories will know how the local Jewish community became the focal point for Jewish self-government and the maintenance of a Jewish corporate identity throughout the long years of the exile in very meaningful ways. Similarly, it can truthfully be said that the Palestinian Arabs have never had so much self-government as they have had since 1967 under the Israeli policy of maximizing local self-rule through Arab municipalities.

This is not to suggest that the Palestinian Arabs would be satisfied with a simple continuation of that arrangement. There are certain areas of self-government which are closed to them, some of which are substantively important and others symbolically necessary. Be that as it may, the possibilities of building an appropriate combination for governing people with some local territorial base is a real one that offers many advantages.

Beyond that, there is the question of supralocal organization. The original Begin plan talked about a single administrative council for the Palestinian Arab people. Others in Israel and Egypt thought that it might be best to organize supralocal institutions on a regional basis. Whatever the final arrangements, there is enough experience around the world and, for that matter, in the territories themselves, with regard to the mechanisms for autonomy to develop proper substitutions for its implementation. For example, all the tools are available and much has already been done to establish a legal basis for an arrangement in which persons take precedence over territory in determining who belongs where legally. There are nearly 100 models of diversity of jurisdiction arrangements, mixed governments, power-sharing and the like presently in operation around the world from which to draw, not to speak of the highly significant and in the end most important fact that there are twelve years experience behind us of *de facto* autonomy in the territories. The problems that often are presented as the most difficult in fact can be overcome technically without any particular inventiveness.

More important by far are the political barriers to implementing autonomy. For, in the last analysis, it is a political problem, not a legal or technical one. As a political problem it can only be solved when the parties perceive a political advantage in solving it.

What does the autonomy offer for the various parties in the long run? Needless to say, this is the crucial test and the plan's most useful contribution to creating movement toward a full and comprehensive settlement. It is here that the differences between the territorial compromise approach and the autonomy plan become most apparent. In the case of the former, the first step is also the final one, that is to say, a refusal to agree upon a territorial compromise offers no possibility for going any further, while agreement requires a decision on the final territorial arrangement now. In the case of the autonomy plan, a "no" would also close the doors to movement while a "yes" does not require a final solution immediately but, rather, creates a framework for movement that could lead in any number of directions.

Take what is for Israel the worst possible case, namely the creation of a Palestinian state. If things came to that pass as a result of the autonomy, they are likely to come to that pass whatever Israel does. That is to say, it will be because the overwhelming pressures of the Arab states plus the rest of the world will prove irresistible in one way or another. Under such circumstances, the autonomy could provide a basis for learning to live together in such a way that a Palestinian state would be neutralized as a threat and change its direction toward a more pacific approach to coexistence. Moreover, sufficient linkages between the two states could be developed and institutionalized so as to provide greater security for Israel even with this worst possible scenario.

On the other hand, take the worst possible case from the Palestinian Arabs' perspective, namely full absorption of the territories into Israel. Even under such circumstances, absorption could only take place in a way that continued the autonomy framework as long as the Arabs wanted it, thereby securing their status as an entity no matter what. In essence, if the autonomy works at all, it could prevent excessive damage to either side in either of the worst case situations.

More than that, however, the autonomy offers the possibility of building toward cases which may be mutually satisfactory for all parties, even if they offer less to any one of them than they would prefer. One such possibility is a renewed linkage with the Arab state on the east bank of the Jordan, either Jordan as it is presently constituted (which is already a Palestinian state demographically) or a Palestinian-dominated state east of the river which is likely to be the case in the long run. Such a linkage could take the form of a repartition with arrangements for a common market and other forms of mutual control over functions of mutual concern or a condominium in which shared rule over the territories by a Jewish and an Arab state, each of which preserves exclusive rule within its core territory. With or without the East Bank connection, it might be that some form of confederation or economic community would develop, linking the Palestinian and Israeli polities in lasting yet limited ways. Each of the options, in a number of variations, remains open, so that the plan is a very flexible one that allows the development of a peace process and a process of accommodation rather than foreclosing options at the outset.

What we have confronting us is an effort to come to grips with a situation in which two energetic peoples with certain fundamental interests that are diametrically opposed, are fated to share the same land. Somehow they must find sufficient common interest upon which to build a basis for a settlement. To say that this may seem well-nigh impossible is not enough. Sixty years of conflict including four full-scale wars have shown the improvidence of continuing on a collision course. In human history, peoples often continue to be improvident but it is not necessary for them to be so.

In the language of contemporary international relations, there are both symmetrical and asymmetrical elements in the relationship between Israel and the Palestinians. In some ways, the Palestinians are becoming the Jews of the Arab world. Their diaspora is spread throughout that world and increasingly plays the kind of role within each of the Arab states that the Jewish diaspora communities traditionally have played in the Christian and Muslim worlds. In both cases, the peoples, wherever they live, look to their original homeland as a focal point in their lives, even if they do not intend to live there, and are willing to supply it with resources and to exert political and other forms of influence as necessary to protect or secure what they perceive to be their homeland's interests.

These symmetries are becoming widely recognized. At the same time, they should not obscure the asymmetrical aspects of the relationship. The Palestinian Arabs remain Arabs, that is to say, their relationship to the Arab world is one of kinship, even if it is a kinship that sometimes is less recognized in practical policy matters than the Palestinians would like. Whatever their difficulties outside of Palestine, they have a score of other Arab states which share the same language, religion, and culture. They even have a state—Jordan—which has always been considered a part of their claimed homeland and in which they form a demographic majority. The Jews, on the other hand, may have a more widespread diaspora which feels at home in other parts of the world, but as Jews they have only one possibility for a homeland in which their own language and religion, culture and ways form the basis of its society and polity. Moreover, no one has tried to exterminate the

Palestinians. The Jews have not only undergone centuries of persecution, at times bordering on extermination, but came close to being exterminated in our own time and have been subject to further extermination efforts on the part of their immediate neighbors.

Finally, the Palestinian Arabs may indeed be on the way to becoming a separate people as well as a separate "public"—a group with long term shared interests—within the Arab world. It is too early to determine whether that is indeed the case. The Jews, on the other hand, are the most ancient of peoples, a nation whose history stretches back to the early eons of civilization and which has tenaciously preserved its peoplehood and its national identity under the most adverse conditions for thousands of years. I will not dwell here on the special character of the Jews as a people or their civilization as a world civilization, a phenomenon which has no parallel.

Both the symmetries and the asymmetries must be taken into consideration as a relationship is developed and the peace process advanced. This process is not a matter of one round of negotiations or one final decision at this point, but it can be initiated. The autonomy plan, with all of its risks and perhaps precisely because it is so risky, offers a real opportunity to make that beginning. What this leads to is a requirement on the part of the principals to think in different directions which are not even radically new anymore, but do require a certain amount of openness to change. Israel has come to the point where it must recognize the Palestinians, or the Palestinian Arabs—the terminology is not that important—at least as a public in the classic use of the term, that is to say as an entity that has a certain longstanding collective interest. As the neighboring public, they must be dealt into whatever agreement comes out in the end. There has to be a significant dimension of mutual consent to it.

Second, Israel must, in planning its negotiations for the autonomy, move toward more viable sharing arrangements, not simply a functional division on Israel's terms. It requires some division and some sharing of functions and it must include sharing in crucial matters, as well as in peripheral ones. In other words, it is not enough simply to say, "This is what we want to keep for ourselves; everything else we can either give away or share." There has to be some willingness to initiate a process that at least will increase sharing in the future as relationships develop.

Third, Israel should reassess the Hashemite option. For a long time and for good reason, it was Israeli policy to depend upon a tacit alliance with the Hashemite elements in Jordan, namely King Hussein and his supporters, to maintain a kind of security community in the Land of Israel/Palestine. The reasoning was that the most hostile element was the population living in the territory between them and that this hostile element could be kept in its place if there were this security community. Whether or not this option remains viable in the long run is now open to question. On several occasions, Hussein has suggested to Israel that it return all the territories to Jordan, including east Jerusalem, and he, in turn, will guarantee that the Palestinians are suppressed. Does it make sense for Israel to rely on such an arrangement whereby Hussein and the Hashemites repress the Palestinians in order to maintain peace here. I think not. Even if we could work out some repartition arrangement, returning some of the areas to Jordan on the grounds that Jordan would then keep the lid on, I do not think that is in the long term interests of Israel anymore. It may have been in the past but the Palestinians have developed beyond that. Therefore, I think that Israel has to reassess the Hashemite option.

As for the Palestinians, those who have not already done so, must reconcile themselves to the permanent fact of the State of Israel. Second, they must reconcile themselves to a continued Jewish presence in the territories, including settlements and other measures. That is as much a *sine qua non* to future progress as the points made above with regard to Israel. Beyond that, they must reconcile themselves to shared rule west of the Jordan River. This leaves options open for them east of the Jordan which we might want to discuss later on.

Finally, they must recognize the role that Israel now plays in preserving their collective interests vis-a-vis other elements in the Arab world—the Hashemites and maybe Syria. That is to say, just as Israel, by its presence, for a long time protected Jordan against the designs of others, it now protects the Palestinians. In light of the Hashemite interest in repressing separate Palestinian interests, Israel's role in the territories serves and could continue to serve as a way of protecting the Palestinians against their own brothers to the extent they want to maintain themselves as a public or as a separate community, maybe even some day as a people.

Finally, Jordan must reconcile itself to the Jewish presence and shared rule if it wants to be part of the game. Ultimately its leaders are going to have to reconcile themselves to a greater Palestinian role in Jordan itself. This is a less attractive proposition for the Hashemite Kingdom, but I do not know whether any of us really have to worry anymore about the health of Jordan. That is now Jordan's lookout. By detaching himself from the negotiations, Hussein has relieved Israel of that responsibility.

For each party, the foregoing involves changes in direction. In a sense the trick of learning from history is not simply to learn precedents, but to learn when historical lines of development change direction, so that we do not end up politically refighting the last war.

Notes

1. For an elaboration of the thesis presented here, see Daniel J. Elazar, *Israel: From Ideological to Territorial Democracy* (New York: General Learning Press, 1971).

2. The invention of the internal combustion engine, which led to automotive transportation in its various forms, brought about a major transformation in the way in which people could move from place to place and transformed the compact relationships of the agricultural village and the center-periphery relationships of the industrial city into matrix relationships. People came to live in grids or networks which allowed them to go in every which way to satisfy their various needs and desires. The changes brought about by the development of the telephone, radio, and television made possible communication across long distances and through very complex grids that did not require physical proximity or fixed and limited axes. These technological changes brought with them substantial changes in the pattern of human settlement around the world. Urbanization gave way to metropolitanization— large regions of relatively low density built around scattered settlements with a high level of economic interdependence. This transformation began in the developed parts of North America and Western Europe some time around the end of World War I or shortly thereafter and became the dominant form of socioeconomic organization in those developed parts of the world after World War II.

3. The shift in the Dan Region can be marked by the beginning of the decline of the population of Tel Aviv in favor of the population growth of outlying cities about 1962. The transfer of the locus of the key new industrial developments began shortly thereafter. The Israel Aircraft Industries, which is the principal industrial complex of Israel and the largest single industrial employer in the Middle East, is located near Lod Airport, which is on the eastern periphery of the Dan metropolitan region. It is served by workers who come from all parts of the region—Rishon Le-Zion and Rehovot in the south Petach Tikva to the north, Herzliya to the northwest, and so on. The IAI is not a major source of jobs for Ramle and Lod despite their closer proximity because few skilled workers and professionals choose to live in those cities. The relocation of the diamond exchange in Ramat Gan instead of Tel Aviv is typical of another kind of movement from the center to a new site better located from a metropolitan perspective.

4. Significantly, the Etzion Bloc and Maale Edumim settlements on the West Bank were built with the metropolitan region in mind and are integral parts of it. The Gush Emunim settlements go even a step further, anticipating the next frontier stage (now emerging in North America and Europe) based on the integration of "urban" and "rural" areas an functions through cybernetics.

American Policy for Peace in the Middle East: What Next?

Robert J. Pranger

The expression "What next?" can have a somewhat cautious as well as neutral meaning. For example, after ten years of frenetic American activity in achieving peace in the Middle East, what can we expect next? What surprises are in store for the region and the world? What new *tour de force* lies hidden in the White House? What novel twist? What traumatic initiative? These questions are no doubt of concern in Israel; perhaps a mood has emerged since the signing of the Israeli-Egyptian peace that things should cool off, that the really tough problems ahead should be postponed, or that it is time to simply stop the peace process and let matters take their own course. Certain American politicians may have the same feeling after the spectacular days of Camp David and the Washington festivities. Some Egyptian officials may wish to turn their attention to more pressing domestic issues.

What will be next in the drama of Middle East peace? The answer seems both simple and complex: the historical road to peace in the Middle East has not ended, for beyond Sinai lies the West Bank and Gaza in both geographic and historical terms. In other words, history has not stopped with the summits of 1978 and 1979, it has simply changed course in the Middle East from the relatively easy problems between Israel and Egypt to the nearly intractable issues between Israel and the Arab world—the Palestinians and Jerusalem.

I

Whether one applauds the accord between Egypt and Israel, as I do, or deplores its existence as many Arabs do is relatively unimportant in answering the question, "What next?" History will not go away, whatever the verdict on Camp David. Military realities which cannot be avoided will persist—Israel's superiority and its occupation of territory the Arabs claim as their own. There will continue stubborn political realities of a near-unanimous Arab policy that Israel must totally withdraw from the areas it occupied in 1967, including parts of Jerusalem, before peace is possible. There will remain the human challenge of over one million stateless Palestinians supported by their own diaspora. Finally, no end is in sight for the economic dependency of the industrialized West on the Arab oil producing nations.

Beyond Camp David lies the same Middle East situation found before Camp David, save for the notable defection of Egypt from this history. In my estimation this is how the future should be viewed: Egypt has left the center of the Arab-Israeli struggle, but has not transformed it. Surely a critical partner in this protracted conflict has now vacated its prominent place on Israel's western flank, but other Arab states seem more dedicated than ever to making up the difference. What next? The answer to this question is more hard work to bring an end to violence between Israel and the Arab world before this violence brings an end to the combatants themselves.

This does not mean that the Israel-Egyptian step has been unimportant in controlling conflict in the Middle East. By effectively removing one front of potential warfare from Israel, the 1979 treaty has probably diminished the likelihood of full-scale war in the Middle East. Yet, the treaty is only a step toward some undetermined end. It has not terminated the struggle over Israel's legitimacy, because it has failed to account for the force that Egypt itself once represented, the Arab world's belief, reinforced by the 1967 war, that Israel represents a colonial intrusion in its midst, forced into the Eastern Mediterranean by Western imperialism. Camp David was, after all, held under the auspices of the leader of the Western capitalist world, the United States. Nasser's Egypt was accepted as leader by many Arabs because it was the most powerful expression of Arab animosity against Israel and the West. Similarly, Sadat could lead only so long as he took on Nasser's mantle of unrelenting animosity to an alien Zionist presence in the Eastern Mediterranean supported by American power. In rejecting the Nasser vision, Sadat lost whatever claim he had to genuine Arab identity in relations with Israel. The step taken by Sadat may have temporarily impoverished Arab military might, but it did not diminish Arab anger. Sadat could only speak for the Arabs as long as he led them in battle against Israel. The peace treaty he signed with Prime Minister Begin is not the first step in a process of reconciliation between Arabs and Israelis; it marks instead Egypt's defection from the Arab world.

II

One may be tempted into various explanations for the determined unity of Arab sentiment against the Camp David accords, the Israeli-Egyptian peace, and President Sadat's policies. Does it not seem likely that Arab identity has become so tenuous a thing that the common enemy, Israel, represents its only focus? Are not Arabs clinging to this negativity for fear that anything more positive will paradoxically prove vacuous? Various students of the Middle East have pointed to such an identity crisis in the Arab world, always focusing its frustrations on Israel, at times from anger and at times out of inferiority.

Amateur psychology is too dangerous a game to play in international politics. No Arab leader suffers from lack of pride. Quite the contrary, the Arab world is absorbed in its own hubris, dating back to Muhammad and before, that it represents the quintessence of human spirit and the epitome of civilized existence. This is why the Arab world is so proudly urban, so enthralled by spoken and written language, so absorbed in complex historical equations. In Baghdad and Riyadh the explanations for Israel's power and Egypt's defection are quite sophisticated, and this reasoning is enhanced by the Camp David spectacle of the world's leading Western power, which trumpets its friendship for the Arabs, presiding over the dismemberment of Arab unity against Israel. Imperialism from Europe—and now the United States—has always divided and conquered the Middle East, Arabs argue, and this is why they must, in turn, practice balance of power in their own relations with the Great Powers. Play the United States off against the Soviet Union and vice versa. Ally oneself with certain powers in NATO against the Americans. And above all retain a balance of outside power on one's own side against Israel and the United States in order to prevent this alliance from gaining hegemony in the Middle East. Every Arab, including Sadat, asserts that Israel's might has been underwritten by the United States. Whether conservative or radical, every Arab must be suspicious of Washington's favors since the United States will never desert Israel. Camp David only reinforces this vision in the minds of all the Arab states and the Palestinians, including Egypt for reasons quite different from the others. Sadat took the Arab stereotype of American bias toward Israel and worked it to his own advantage by joining his fate with that of Israel.

As some are tempted to play psychology with very serious national differences in international politics, so some hold that the Arabs see images having little relation to reality. The Arab view of Israel may be yet another instance of international perception colored by stereotypes. A strong argument has been made on behalf of the Camp David accords, for instance, that through direct and bilateral negotiations Egypt has been returned its territories lost to Israel in 1967. In turn, Israel has proved to be a good, if somewhat demanding, partner in serious diplomatic relations with an Arab state. Surely Arab perceptions cannot fail to be impressed by benefits that far outweigh costs in direct negotiations with Israel. To put it very simply, Arab myths about Israeli perfidy and American collusion have been dashed by the evidence of a generous peace, or so it has been argued. Indeed, one could argue that for this very reason the Arabs will cling to misperceptions for fear of admitting that they were mistaken all along. Zionism is not some voracious tiger, this position would maintain, but a legitimate nationalist movement that can safely be allowed to co-exist in the Middle East with Arabism. The problem after Camp David, then, will be to turn the other Arabs toward practical peace-making with Israel on the strength of the Egyptian example. Perhaps Jordan should come forth first, lured by promises of a share of the West Bank, followed by Syria with some prospect on the Golan. Saudi Arabian support should be courted by the United States some would say.

Tangible power, however, not perception, was the primary force at work in achieving the Camp David accords. Played among mature adults and nations armed with sophisticated weapons, politics is not a matter of exorcising fantasy and installing reality through some kind of international therapy session. The stakes are profound, the results irreversible, and the wagers made in forms of power and force. Camp David was organized under the aegis and ever-watchful eye of the world's greatest power, the United States. It was managed by a president whose political reputation depended on it. Partners to the negotiation possessed the Middle East's two strongest military organizations. The results were consummated in a city notoriously impressed by great deeds and notably unimpressed by academic theories. The answer to what is next in Middle East peace, therefore, can be found in the Camp David emphasis on the potential of political power to bring about profound historical change: on its own initiative, with the powerful support of the United States, Egypt has defected from the unanimous Arab rejection of Israel as a trustworthy diplomatic partner. Egypt's defection from this principle was signalled by Sadat's decision to negotiate *directly* with Israel for a settlement. Will other Arab states or the Palestinians spontaneously follow Egypt's example? This is the really important issue underlying the question of "what next?" in the Middle East. Two corollary issues are obvious. Will the United States be able to use its vast power to secure more such defections? And *should* the United States do so?

III

The Arab world is aware of the significance of Egypt's actions at Camp David. Egypt has defected from the ultimate principle of Arab solidarity against Israel which says that the latter is untrustworthy as a partner in diplomatic relations under conditions present in the Middle East since 1967 and perhaps even under circumstances of complete Israeli withdrawal from areas it has occupied. Since Sadat has unilaterally declared himself against this principle by directly negotiating for peace with Begin, Egypt must be cast out of the Arab world in both symbolic and tangible terms. Hence, Arab states have cut their diplomatic ties with Cairo and have withdrawn their assistance. Some have even pushed for Egypt's symbolic expulsion from the Islamic world by excluding it from a recent Islamic foreign ministers' meeting in Morocco. In other words, Sadat's defection comes in relation to a negative not positive source of Arab unity. By emphasizing tangible issues at stake between himself and Israel, and by considering optional peace plans in direct negotiations, Sadat has violated the Arab principle of negativity toward Israel. The severity of Arab reaction may indicate, however, that such a negative principle can maintain itself only as long as it has both external and internal validity. When one partner defects, the principle loses some of its potency as surely as if the external focus of solidarity changed in some revolutionary way. It can be argued in the case of the Camp David accords that Egypt's defection from Arab solidarity against Israel will prove a much more important source of change in Arab perceptions of Israel than anything Israel could possibly do to cause this change.

The Sadat initiative in coming to Jerusalem in 1977 became a dramatic instance when Egypt converted its negative principle of relations with Israel into a positive principle. This was not the result of divide-and-conquer strategies in the West, but was apparently spontaneous. It obviously signified a profound reassessment of Israel by Egyptians. More importantly, however, the change was Arab-initiated and this explains the severe disruption in the Arab world because of it. Had the shift been inspired in the United States, it could have been explained in the usual terms of Western betrayal. Had this been somehow triggered by an overt Israeli act, it could have been seen as gullibility on Sadat's part. While both betrayal and gullibility have been alleged by some Arabs, the fact remains that the deed performed by Sadat in 1977 and then institutionalized in 1978 and 1979 was disconcerting enough to mark a profound change in the historical path of Arab-Israel relations. Yet, while this path has been radically changed, its direction is still undetermined. What has been established is a positive principle of direct relations between Israel and the Arab world as well as a negative one. Now two principles compete. Perhaps this competition will extend to the question of what determines Arab solidarity in relations with Israel. How can this positive principle be extended without becoming identified too closely with betrayal and gullibility in action as well as words?

What I would like to explore a little more fully is how one might encourage the principle of positive spontaneity in Arab-Israeli relations developed by President Sadat since the fall of 1977. It is necessary to keep this discussion on the plane of principle, because it is likely that future path of peace in the Middle East will deviate in certain respects from the Camp David approach. For example, it is hard to imagine an American president placing himself between Arafat and Begin at Camp David in quite the same way Carter did with Sadat and Begin. What is important to encourage, however, is the possibility of more spontaneous gestures in the peace process, focusing in the future on the West Bank, Gaza and Jerusalem. In other words, space and time must be provided for the possibility (not probability) of expanded operation of the principle of positive spontaneity.

Turning first to the question of space, it is important that the spatial arrangements for encouragement of direct negotiations be political ones. By this is meant that the peace process take place within governmental institutions and between them so that conflicting interests may be resolved authoritatively to the satisfaction of the national states involved. One can sacrcely argue with ingenious efforts at Arab-Israeli dialogue outside formal governmental institutions, since such efforts will probably help shape a favorable environment for positive negotiations. But the question also remains as to how one translates such dialogue into the heady atmosphere of partisan politics (domestic and international) so that the principles of openness and justice can be made public policy.

From the above perspective, it seems evident to me that political arrangements for shared rule on the West Bank and in Gaza, backed by the authority of established governments in the region, provide the most promising spatial organization for encouraging positive spontaneity in the peace process. Governmental institutions of the kind suggested by Daniel Elazar seem ideally suited for this purpose.

Spontaneity involves openness, however, a freedom of action that may be quite indeterminate. This brings us to the second question of temporal arrangements for the principle of positive spontaneity. There must be time for negotiations between Palestinian Arabs and Israelis to take place, but this time must have certain features. First, a sense of urgency should be present with a timetable that creates excitement and desire for movement from negative to positive ways of dealing with conflict. Such a timetable might have deadlines but no preconditions. Second, the feeling of intimidation or imposed solution should be, as much as possible, eliminated. This applies to both outside pressure and internal constraint. Obviously, the idea of an imposed settlement from the Great Powers runs counter to the idea of positive spontaneity—a matter about which Israel has special concerns. At the same time, however, internal imposition should be avoided as much as possible too—a matter about which Palestinians have great fear in dealing with Israel. The latter concern relates, of course, to the continued presence of military occupation authority as distinguished from military authorities charged with Israel's security.

Space and time are needed for a peace settlement that will bring justice and security to Israel and the Palestinians. Such space and time, however, must comprise special forms—institutional arrangements flexible enough to encourage positive spontaneity and temporal arrangements that eliminate the feeling of intimidation. As Hannah Arendt noted in her analysis of violence, power which sustains community does *not* flow from the barrel of a gun, whether one is speaking of international or domestic policies.

Returning to the example of President Sadat, the space and

time he envisaged for constructive negotiations with Israel were highly indeterminate when he first announced his intention to go to Jerusalem. Where the negotiations would take place and what would be their substance and pace were left quite open. He surely avoided most standard institutions such as the United Nations. And it is difficult to imagine that his initiative would ever have taken place under Israeli threat or American prodding. A similar spirit must pervade the next phase of the Middle East process where negotiations will take place to bring peace to Israeli-Palestinian relations in the West Bank and Gaza. Beyond this, of course, lies the question of Jerusalem. It is important to pile prece-dent on precedent in order to sustain the principle of positive spon-taneity in the quest for peace in the Middle East.

IV

Then what is next for American policy in the Middle East? It is essential to start where the peace treaty between Egypt and Israel has left off, the reality of an American commitment to see through to its conclusion a just and safe peace for the West Bank and Gaza. This American role has grown out of the involvement of the United States in support of Sadat's initiative, once it was announced, and in full cooperation with Israel to encourage a realistic peace accord. Yet, the process ought not to stop in Sinai, but should spread to the West Bank. Unless this takes place, American credi-bility in the Arab world, already severely strained by the peace treaty between Egypt and Israel, will be totally destroyed. This cannot be to the advantage of either Egypt or Israel.

It is difficult, nevertheless, to see how the heady atmosphere of Camp David summit and its aftermath can bring about an ade-quate peace settlement between Israel and Palestinians. Already it is clear that the American role in these negotiations will take place under the aegis of a special ambassador, though it may be the case that more dramatic efforts will take place in the future. Drama at this point, however, would be premature. Space and time, in the special ways discussed above, should be provided, and in this effort the United States can play a highly constructive, if unobtrusive, role.

In the near future, the major American role for encouraging positive spontaneity in West Bank negotiations should focus on the dimension of time rather than space. Some organizational arrangements are already provided in the Egyptian-Israeli treaty as well as a rudimentary timetable. At the same time this confer-ence is meeting Egyptian and Israeli negotiators have gathered to begin the complex process toward settlement of the Israeli-Palestinian struggle, with the interested participation of the United States in insuring that this process continues. Daniel Elazar's "shared-rule" formulations would establish an elaborate condomi-nium for Israel, Jordan and the Palestinians within which they could build workable institutional arrangements. As Emile Nak-hleh points out, there is already a complete structure of Arab institutions. What the United States can provide, over the course of settling disparate claims to the West Bank and Gaza, is a guarantee that this settlement will be free from intimidation in both external and internal terms.

In external terms, the United States will no doubt take steps to insure that outside powers will not seek to intervene in the process of settlement, whatever views these powers hold about the nature of the Camp David accords themselves. Of great interest will be the role the Soviet Union might play. One doubts that the U.S.S.R. will join the process of encouraging positive spontaneity along the lines mapped by President Sadat and Prime Minister Begin. What is of extreme importance is that the Soviet Union be discouraged from working deliberately to destroy opportunities for such spontaneity to take place. A combination of American inducements could be helpful. As usual, American protection of its policies will also require more forceful measures ranging from general deterrence to contingency planning for special crises.

As for the other Arab states, it is premature for the United States to pressure those who reject the Camp David formula into cooperating. It would be better to encourage the Palestinians, who have no national institutions, to work for their own nationhood than to press other Arab countries to support the peace process in the near future. Efforts to entice Jordan and Saudi Arabia into the Camp Davod framework might wait until some progress is reported on Palestinian involvement in settling their own fate. Meanwhile, the United States should work to prevent outside interference by various Arab powers.

An equally important American role should be played in encouraging the relaxation of internal pressures on Palestinian Arabs on the West Bank and in Gaza. Such pressures are likely to come from two sources—the strong presence of the Palestine Liberation Organization and Israeli occupation authorities. Regarding the PLO, it would be extremely desirable, in my judgment, were there some kind of orderly communication between it and the United States government. Much as American representation in Arab countries with whom Israel has no formal ties has proved an invaluable resource for the direct presentation of Israel's policies without ideological interpretation, so such contacts with the PLO, *now that the peace process has moved to its Palestinian phase,* could help encourage and protect Palestinians involved with peace negotiations. Indeed, through American auspices, Palestinian positions, including the views of the PLO, could be more objectively transmitted to Israel—and vice versa—than is now the case.

Turning to Israeli occupation authorities, it is important, in my estimation, to de-emphasize military government on the West Bank and in Gaza to the maximum feasible extent. Here the United States should use its influence with Israel to achieve a freer environment for economic and political activity among Palestinians. This would apply to schools, including colleges and universities, as well as to local governing bodies. The most visible forms of military rule should everywhere be abolished or sharply curtailed. Finally, intimidation of all sorts, by public and private groups, should be prohibited. Spontaneity will more likely be negative than positive as long as the symbols and realities of occupation remain highly visible.

V

In conclusion, the Sadat initiative replaced the principle of negativity toward Israel in Egypt's policy with something more positive and spontaneous. This principle of positive spontaneity should be kept alive in negotiations concerning the future of the West Bank and Gaza. To accomplish this, space and time must be provided for the possibility of expanded operation for positive spontaneity. Political arrangements for shared rule on the West Bank and Gaza, backed by the authority of established governments in the region, provide the most promising spatial organization for encouraging this principle.

From a temporal perspective, a sense of urgency should be present with a timetable that creates excitement and desire for movement from negative to positive ways of settling the disputes between parties to the negotiations. Equally important during the course of negotiations, however, the feeling of intimidation or imposed solution should be, as much as possible, eliminated. This applies to both outside pressure and internal constraints. Israel seems more fearful of external intervention in the West Bank and Gaza from the United States, the Soviet Union, and various Arab powers including the PLO. Palestinians, on the other hand, have great doubts about dealing with Israel because of the latter's military control over the territory over dispute. This control by armed force involves governmental authority as well as security.

America's future role, to insure that positive spontaneity will have a chance during the peace process after the treaty between Egypt and Israel, would seem especially necessary to guarantee that temporal arrangements will curtail undue harassment from external or internal sources. Externally, the chief problem will be the Soviet Union and Arab states opposed to the Camp David approach. With the U.S.S.R., the United States can provide both positive incentives not to interfere and deterrence measures. As for Arab nations opposed to the Camp David approach, it is better not to pressure them into cooperating at this time. Internally, the problems of safeguarding the peace process from excessive intimidation are twofold, relating to both the PLO and Israel's occupation authorities. It is my belief that now is the time for the United States to develop more orderly relations with the PLO. Communications between Palestinians and Israelis, *in political terms*, could be greatly improved if the United States had its own direct ties with the PLO. As for Israel's military government, the United States should urge that various stringent measures imposed on residents of the West Bank and Gaza be relaxed and that the most visible forms of military rule everywhere be abolished or sharply curtailed. Spontaneity will more likely be negative than positive as long as the symbols and realities of occupation remain highly visible.

What next? Hopefully, the answer to this question will be that the same principle of positive spontaneity used by President Sadat, Prime Minister Begin and President Carter for the treaty between Egypt and Israel will operate during the next phases of the peace process—for the West Bank and Gaza and Jerusalem. Those who have negotiated this treaty should now make sure that the flexibility and spontaneity underlying it will continue. This is a heavy responsibility for those who are parties to the Camp David accords and for those who are not. Surely the United States will have a special role to play in guaranteeing that positive spontaneity has a chance to operate as effectively in matters important to Palestinians and Israelis in the next phase of the Camp David framework as it did in the case of negotiations between Egypt and Israel for their treaty.

Whither Autonomy?
A Discussion

Yehudah Ben Meir: Regarding Dr. Pranger's discussion of spontaneous contact with Arabs, Israel today has extensive communication and contracts with all the leaders of the Arab community and all the varieties of Arab public opinion throughout the West Bank and Gaza. Paradoxically, by the way, those contacts were made possible by the Israeli occupation of the areas. Before that, we had little if any contact with any Arab public opinion. As a result, we have a far better knowledge of the opinions, desires, and point of view of the Arabs, and they have gotten, I would hope, to know us much better. Perhaps as a result, some of the previous stereotypes regarding the Israelis have been demolished in their eyes.

Unfortunately, all of these extensive contacts at the highest levels over the past twelve years have so far failed to bring us any closer to a mutually acceptable solution. Dr. Pranger suggested that we must move toward contact with the PLO. I don't think this is at all relevant to the issue. If we have so far failed to reach a mutually acceptable solution with the Arabs in the territories, it is not because we don't have contacts with some other party but because so far the problems are grave and it is not that easy to reach a solution.

I think one should not confuse viability with one side's position. What Professor Horowitz has suggested here in effect is to accept the Arab position and to transfer the entire West Bank to Arab sovereignty. This is the first option which I mentioned, which in my opinion is totally unviable. I always find it hard to understand why a solution which is not acceptable to the Arabs is therefore termed "unviable," but why a solution which is to the same extent totally unacceptable to the vast majority of Israelis becomes "viable." This is a one-sided approach with which I do not agree. I would certainly caution Israel against accepting such a position because I think that it would quickly lead us to very dire consequences. So viability must be examined on other levels such as those Professor Elazar mentioned.

The concept of an Israeli military presence on the soil of a sovereign Arab state, which was suggested here by Professor Horowitz, is not only abhorrent to me, but is totally unviable in my opinion and, in fact, borders on the ridiculous. It wouldn't last for one year. Sadat, for instance, is not willing under any circumstances to permit any American presence, not to mention Israeli presence, on his soil, as I understand him.

309

I met recently with two U.S. Senators who are here examining the question of aid to Israel. They had visited the Etzion and Eitan bases and were very concerned, rightfully so, that these two bases are going to go to total waste, because Israel will leave them but Egypt is not permitted by the treaty to use them for any military purpose whatsoever. They raised the question, why can't the United States have some presence there? They themselves know that the problem lies with Sadat. They are going to take it up with him. I can guarantee that they will receive a negative answer. So, too, the concept of having an Israeli military presence on sovereign Arab soil makes absolutely no sense. "Israeli go home" will come much quicker than "Yankee go home" came in Panama.

I also do not think that demilitarization of the West Bank is any viable solution, because it is something which doesn't exist. You cannot demilitarize a heavily populated area. You can demilitarize the Sinai desert, because there it makes sense for two reasons: first of all, you don't need the military there, because you don't have to police the sand; second, you can inspect it easily and detect military movements. When one speaks about as small an area as the West Bank and Gaza where there are one million Arabs, a seething population, there is bound to be a great deal of incitement. Even if we reach an agreement, there are sure to be those who will not accept it. Major upheavals, terrorism all over the area—how is anyone going to control such an area when it is totally demilitarized? We know how Hussein controls the east bank of the Jordan, with the military. How is he, or anyone else, going to control the West Bank without its just totally breaking apart at the seams? Besides, the area simply cannot be inspected, so demilitarization makes no sense.

I want to add two small comments as a matter of fact—first of all, regarding the relocation of Israeli forces on the West Bank. There are many aspects of the Camp David agreement where it stipulates that agreement must be reached. This is not the case regarding redeployment of Israeli forces. At Camp David this issue was argued at great length. The agreement specifies that there will be a withdrawal of Israeli armed forces on the West Bank and that they will be redeployed in "specified security locations." I don't think that anyone claims that this question is a matter for negotiation or agreement. According to the Camp David agreement—and I haven't even heard an American say otherwise—this is a matter for unilateral Israeli decision. The degree of withdrawal and the locations must be specified, but they have to be specified by Israel and not by any mutual agreement. Even in the joint letter, no negotiation is called for on this issue. On all other issues, yes, but not on this one.

Regarding the Sinai agreement, which some say threatens to become an interim agreement if the autonomy scheme doesn't work out: first of all, I would say that it is neither necessary nor inevitable that Egypt will go back on the peace agreement, even if agreement is not reached regarding Judea and Samaria. I don't say it won't but I don't think we should assume it as axiomatic. And if she does go back on the peace agreement, the question is to what degree. Will she say, "We cannot have normalization, but the state of war nevertheless has been abolished," or will she say, "Tomorrow we're going to war." There are a variety of possibilities. But even if she does do this four years from now, after we have reached the international border, after diplomatic relations and commercial relations and the whole gamut of exchanges between the peoples of Israel and Egypt have been established, and one morning Sadat gets up and says, "I will abolish it all," we still have not returned to the situation of 1967. There is a signed agreement stipulating demilitarized areas. If Egypt clearly breaks this agreement, then naturally Israel has options which it can take. In fact, Israel even has an agreement with the United States to support her in taking these options. Certainly no one can question that for Egypt to break the demilitarization provisions of the treaty and move her forces forward toward the international border is a clear violation of the agreement.

I think I agree with everything Professor Elazar said. At least for me, he demonstrated remarkably well that, not only are options one and three inimical to Israeli interests, but they are harmful to the Arab inhabitants as well. This is an important point. I think that Israel has definitely recognized the Palestinian Arabs as a public with a collective interest; I accept it exactly as you defined it.

I fully agree with you, too, that we should re-examine our policy regarding the Hashemite Kingdom, not only regarding its position on the West Bank, but also on the East Bank. You alluded to Israel's protection of Hashemite rule in Jordan which, in my opinion has ceased to serve Israeli interests. Since Hussein has not found it necessary to join the negotiations, we do not have any moral responsibility to protect him or his kingdom. We can act differently if we see a change as being in our interests, which I tend to think we might after proper reexamination.

Robert Pranger: I think it would be useful first to give my impression of U.S. policy in the Middle East. I think the experience of the United States in 1969 and the first year of the Nixon administration is illustrative of some of the problems which lie ahead in terms of the Middle East peace process. Frankly, in 1969 the United States' Middle East policy was in a shambles caused by decisions not made by the United States but by Israel in June 1967. Great attention was required on the part of the United States in order to repair its relations with the Arab world.

These relations have been considered crucial by every American president and secretary of state since World War II. The United States must have unimpaired access, complete communication, and, indeed, preferred treatment in all major Arab capitals in the Middle East. In 1969, we were without diplomatic relations in some of those key countries and experiencing the extreme wrath of some of the others.

In 1969, therefore, the United States launched what became a series of peace initiatives in the Middle East, beginning with full-fledged negotiations with the Soviet Union between Joseph Sisco and Anatoli Dobrinin, an option, incidentally, which the United States has never given up as a possible approach to the Middle East problem.

The opening to the Russians having failed, after a certain amount of time the Rogers Plan was announced. The plan caused a great furor, but the net result of it—using some carrots and some sticks in the form of new F-4 deals and so on—was the August 1970 ceasefire.

From then on out, although the United States continued to make initiatives, quite frankly, the major initiative for peace in the Middle East passed into Arab hands. In my estimation, all of the major breakthroughs for peace in the Middle East since then have been Mr. Sadat's; first there was his decision to go to war in October 1973, in dismay at U.S. policy, and then, of course, his now famous initiative in 1977.

The point I am making is that, historically, U.S. politics in the Middle East are quite wide-ranging. On the strategic side, they require, for example, that we maintain complete access in the Persian Gulf, that we maintain complete control of the Southern European flank for NATO purposes, that we have unimpeded access to the Mediterranean for security reasons including Israel's security, and that the approaches from the south through the Indian Ocean and the Red Sea be kept clear. For all this, we obviously need military power, but above all we need political access.

The U.S. economy, whose GNP is now over two trillion dollars, over $6,000 a year per capita, requires enormous fueling, literally, too, through the world oil market. U.S. citizens demand this. A propos of this, I recommend reading the debate which the Senate held for some eight straight hours on the sale of American F-15s to Saudi Arabia. In that debate, which was carried by some ten votes in favor of the sale, the full range of considerations of American interests in the Middle East were laid out by the Senate itself. All Senators except one or two were there, and it makes for interesting reading. It is also relevant, I think, to the question of the future of the accords on the West Bank. That is to say, the United States position on this subject will certainly take into account its wider Arab interests beyond Egypt, and this will perhaps mean some differences in points of view, to put it mildly.

Now, basically, there are two forms of peace negotiations which have been tried in the Middle East. The first form has been through American mediation, and it has been standard U.S. policy to pursue this approach, which we may term indirect negotiations between the Arabs and Israel. In these initiatives, the United States has taken the lead for reasons of its own national interests and its friendship to peoples in the Middle East.

The second approach, which was always the more remote option, requires spontaneous initiative; that is direct negotiations. There is no logic in Arab-Israeli relations or in the history of these relations that requires this kind of direct negotiations. I was not talking about contacts between Arabs and Israelis, and surely not about contacts at the point of a gun. This is not the kind of contact which establishes the sort of direct negotiations which Sadat, having initiated the war in October 1973, felt he was in a position to initiate on his own, as an equal to Israel.

Now, my feeling is that if direct negotiations do not take place out here, indirect negotiations will still take place, and U.S. policy is clear on this. Furthermore, given the cost of the Egyptian-Israeli settlement to the United States—about which there is considerable debate as to the exact price tag, but in which Congress is keenly interested—there will probably be a good deal of interest in Congress itself that somehow the Camp David accords will move back into some kind of indirect negotiations. This, I think, is really the range of the options, direct or indirect.

Professor Horowitz raised an interesting point relating to the balance of relations between the United States and the Soviet Union. It is not likely that either the United States or the Soviet Union wants the situation after Camp David to reach a flash point in a confrontation between the two. There has always been what might be called half an option beyond indirect negotiations, which is negotiations between the U.S. and the Soviet Union: "the Geneva formula." I can only say that, from my reading of current American policy, all two-and-a-half options are open. I think the most productive forms of negotiations are direct talks. But direct talks and negotiations are obviously not part of the actual logic of Arab-Israeli relations at all, but tend to be illogical. They tend to appear in moments of enthusiasm, when there seems to be the right kind of national leadership available, or in gratuitous historical circumstances.

With regard to the West Bank situation, I would not expect under the current relationship between Israel and the West Bankers for there ever to come forth an Arab leader to negotiate, either individually or collectively in the Sadat fashion. I was examining ways, therefore, by which that kind of encouragement could be undertaken. Otherwise I suspect that the future course of these negotiations will include a very strong U.S. role, and they will revert to the indirect negotiation formula.

Dan Horowitz: I want to reply to some of Dr. Ben Meir's criticisms of what I said. The first problem is the problem of viability. I didn't say that the solution I advocate is viable only because the other side doesn't accept another solution. I maintain that according to the rules of the game of international politics and in view of world public opinion, it is the only solution that will get any legitimation.

The only borders which have a chance to get international legitimation and international support are the 1949 armistice borders,
which are the pre-1967 war borders. Western public opinion and
every American president, including Lyndon Johnson in the Rusk
proposals and Richard Nixon in the Rogers Plan, re-emphasized
this. On the other hand, the Soviet Union has never accepted the
position of the PLO but has affirmed the right of Israel to exist
within those borders. It is not accidental that this is the political
consensus of the world, and Israel will not get any support if she
insists on defying it. This is the main reason for returning to the
status quo ante, because it *is status quo ante*. and not because it
has anything in itself that justifies it. The problem is that the return
to the *status quo ante* is the only course of action which has international legitimacy. From this point of view, we have very little
chance to convince even our best friends that any requirement
that is not purely a security requirement would become
acceptable.

The second problem is that of an Israeli military presence on
Arab sovereign territory. I don't believe that there is any logic in an
argument that says that the Arabs or the Americans or whoever
wouldn't accept a denial of full military control for the Arabs over
the whole territory, but would accept the denial of both military
control and sovereignty. This doesn't make sense. What Dr. Ben
Meir suggests includes what I suggest but requires greater concessions on their side. I don't think that either for the other party, for
neutral parties like the United States, or for outside parties that his
solution will be more acceptable than mine. If none of them is
viable or acceptable, and that is quite possible, then we may have
to accept the fact that the whole initiative will collapse.

I don't think that it is useful to center our efforts on the question
of how to induce maximum Arab participation in the negotiations.
The problems are too complicated, and too many issues that will
decide the future of the Middle East for a long time are involved in
the issue for us to accept this kind of short-term consideration. I
don't think that Israel should do so, although, as you have seen, I
am for far-reaching concessions. The reasoning behind these concessions should not be how to induce maximum Arab participation in the negotiations.

Now to the point about demilitarization. By demilitarization, I
do not mean demilitarization with regard to rifles, submachine
guns and armored cars. I mean demilitarization with regard to
tank forces, heavy artillery, military airfields, and ground-to-air missiles, which can be guaranteed. Such weapons are not needed to
suppress riots in the streets. This is the kind of demilitarization I
mean.

I think that I accept everything Professor Elazar said, but in the
end it comes to a new kind of paternalism. "We are improving
your position. We are improving your welfare." The fact is that in
our world, when there is a contradiction between economic wel-

fare and nationalist primordial sentiments, in most cases nationalist primordial sentiments prevail. And nationalist primordial sentiments include a demand for self-determination. We have to live with this fact of life.

Daniel Elazar: I have no doubt that primordial sentiments can win out, but I still believe that there are thresholds of political satisfaction that make it possible to change the direction of those primordial sentiments. What I am suggesting is certainly far from paternalism. If it were paternalism, I think it would be doomed from the first without any question. I am not suggesting that the Jews unilaterally brought benefits to this new metropolitan region and the Arabs simply received the benefits. Far from it. I think that it is a mutual benefit which is in its early stages and can develop. To date each group has benefitted in a different way, but so far each group has benefitted proportionately on a more or less equal basis.

As far as security is concerned, I think that almost all Israelis are agreed on the necessity for an Israeli security presence in the territories, no matter what. My own feeling is that a security presence without a larger relationship would simply be a provocation. The worst thing in the world would be to put the Israeli army in camps on the West Bank. It would not serve the security interests of Israel, which require, after all, mobile patrols and the like, while at the same time it would be a constant target for any Palestinians who would say that such an arrangement interferes with their sovereignty. If there are going to be security arrangements, I think they have to be of other kinds altogether, and that means a different framework.

Yehoshua Arieli: It seems to me that the solution which Dr. Ben Meir described as best is the one which has been accepted by treaty as a transitional solution. I speak about autonomy. Solutions one, two, and three which you described are relevant only if you speak about the period after the transition period.

Now, I assume that Dr. Ben Meir thinks that the fourth solution should be the permanent solution, in spite of the fact that the government coalition to which you belong made it very clear that Israel will claim sovereignty over and will incorporate Judea, Samaria and the Gaza district after the transition period is finished. I would like you to take a stand on that, because you actually excluded that possibility in your first solution.

Then I would like to ask you what you mean when you say that a fourth solution really does not include sovereignty, that its advantage is that there is no sovereignty over the West Bank and the Gaza Strip. Actually, sovereignty cannot be divided. There can be a governmental structure in which the sovereignty is divided by some federal act, but then this isn't a case of divided sovereignty. The federal government of the United States considers only one source of sovereignty which is the people, but neither the federal nor the state governments are sovereign. There is only one classical definition of what sovereignty means as to a territory and a society, which is that it is the source of all legitimate political authority.

Now, take that definition and then take Israel's interpretation of the Camp David agreement as it was stated officially or unofficially in the 22 points. That document says that the military government is the source of sovereignty and that beyond that Israel will retain not only security, but, apart from what has been called daily life, all governmental functions. Israel, then, is sovereign, and your definition simply is inadequate to characterize what you propose as a solution, either transitory or permanent.

You and Professor Elazar have both said that past examples really cannot teach us how to work in the future. Well, I think we should learn something from past examples, at least why they worked or why they didn't work. But if we come to a point where there is no example whatsoever of what has been suggested as a plan of autonomy, at least in the Western experience, then there is a question of what was the reason behind the creation of some-thing which has no precedent. We know that autonomy solutions of very different kinds are unstable. So, it is not simply a matter of claiming that we have invented something. The task is really to analyze whether that invention has more capacity for stability or for solving problems than solutions which have been far more conventional and proved not to be stable.

Can we describe as autonomy a plan which gives sovereignty to the State of Israel and also gives Israel some very vital rights which will really determine the private life of the Palestinians, such as all the public lands and the right to settle wherever Israel decides for security reasons, and to occupy or seize private land. Is this for security reasons, or is it for other reasons which really are not going to solve problems of security, but are going to meet certain demands which may be national or may be ideological. Then to what degree are these different demands really compati-ble with what you want to achieve, namely to have a permanent solution? From that point of view, because you doubt what can be learned from the past, I would like to remind you what we can learn from the Camp David agreements.

You can say that apart from a very limited minority of a few thousand people in the country, to which I belong, the whole country was of the opinion that we would never return to the inter-national borders of 1967 with Egypt. That was the opinion of the Labor Alignment, that surely was the opinion of the Likud, that was the opinion of everybody. Yet, behold, when we signed an agreement, that whole opinion has changed. Therefore, when you say it is the almost unanimous consensus of Israel that these things should be or should not be, we have seen that it is no argument.

Now, to Professor Elazar. I am very impressed by all the scientific categories and so on which are going into your explanation of changing patterns of metropolitanization and so on, but the question is, how much is it relevant to what we are dealing with?

Quite obviously there are in Israel two patterns of changes as far as federal, socio-economic connections are concerned and the formation of centers of population and the links between the centers. One is that which has developed, you would say, from the needs, the changing patterns, and forces of economy and society, like the Tel Aviv/Dan area. God knows that neither Ben Gurion or anybody else liked the development, but it developed. The other pattern was to develop areas for political-security reasons. Now, the whole development of Jerusalem is of the second category. It is not a spontaneous development; it has been developed since 1967 by force and power for security, political, and Zionist reasons; surely it is in a very different category from what you described.

Nor could you say that the West Bank or the Gaza Strip is practically the hinterland of Jerusalem. It is not. The hinterland might be the West Bank, the East Bank, Jordan, and, by the way, also the greater part of Israel, because of its economics and employment. But surely, from that point of view, Jerusalem is still to a certain degree the head of the military government, the head of certain institutions. You definitely cannot make out that something has happened between Jerusalem, the West Bank, and the Gaza Strip which created patterns which it would be very difficult to dislocate.

Myron Weiner: It might be useful if the Jerusalem Institute for Federal Studies were to undertake research on various international limitations on sovereignty by the incorporation of restrictions on the militarization of certain areas. There are a number of international treaties which in effect restricted sovereignty by imposing demilitarization. I believe there are provisions like that in the Soviet-Finnish peace treaty. There may be others, and I think it might be useful to explore them before ruling this out as something we haven't had any experience with.

On the question of the distinction between an interim and final agreement, I think it is worth noting that the Camp David agreement specified a new procedure for moving between this present phase of negotiations and the next one. As I recall, there are two parts of that new procedure. One is that an additional party will take part in those negotiations and that additional party is specified. It will be the elected Palestinian representatives on the West Bank. They are not part of the negotiations now, but four years from now Israel will be negotiating with them, if they choose to negotiate. The second procedure is that Jordan will then be invited to join a second committee in negotiations with Israel and Egypt to discuss both the final borders—there is the presumption that they are not yet finalized—and the final security arrangements. I would wonder, then, whether, knowing that there will be new actors in the next stage, that affects current thinking about how to proceed in this phase of negotiations.

Emile Nakhleh: I think the value of this conference is twofold, perhaps a plea to rationalism in the context of international politics and a plea, as Daniel Elazar just stated, to keep all the options open at the moment. It seems, however, that while he made that comment, practically in the same breath he supported the fourth option which Dr. Ben Meir presented. I think the value of this conference is perhaps to investigate the possibilities of options that might be open in the future.

In order to do that rationally, I think we have to examine some of the independent variables that exist in this equation. The equation is to bring two sides together. One side is Israel, which is suffering from, on one hand, the frustrations of power, and, at the same time, the frustrations of dependency on the United States. This is a reality. The second side is the Palestinians who are suffering from the frustrations of impotence. The two are there. We've got to bring them together.

Now, I am not surprised by Dr. Ben Meir's presentation; his position—his party's position—is ideological in nature. I do not think it is security oriented. With due respect to his party, I am grateful that they are not a majority in the government. I do not think a solution based on the historical argument can be developed. In my view the solution that he presented, which calls for the political de-Arabization of the occupied areas, is not much different in the final analysis from the solution presented by the PLO and some other quarters calling for the de-Zionization of Israel. Both are unrealistic; both are in my judgment irrational at worst and utopian at best.

I realize in all honesty that this is a hard pill to swallow, particularly for Israel. It is a state with political and military preponderance here. But it has to swallow this pill if we are going to move from this stage to a next stage of peace. The first variable, in my judgment, is that the Palestinians exist as a people with a land. Judging by my research, I do not think any solution would be practical that aims to dissolve this relationship between the people and the land.

The second variable is that they have developed a leadership. As both Professor Weiner and Dr. Pranger stated, if the negotiations are going to get us from A to B, they must be carried on with leadership. Whether one likes the PLO or not, no counter leadership has emerged in its place.

The third is that the security of all states must be guaranteed. In my mind, no solution will work if it does not guarantee the security of Israel, or if it does not guarantee the security of the new entity. I do not believe that Sadat will try to deny this point. The fact is that any arrangement must guarantee the security of Israel. That does not necessarily mean the placement of Israeli troops on the West

Bank. Technologically we have all kinds of methods that can be used.

The fourth variable—and I think this is a hard pill to swallow too—is the U.S. role. As a student of American foreign policy, I can tell you that, whether we like it or not, the United States' role is very crucial. It is played not only in the context of American-Israeli relations, but also in the context of American-Arab, American-Islamic, and American-Soviet relations, plus American regional interests. Any denial of America's influence is not going to lead anywhere. The fact is that there is a definite change in American public opinion on this question. There is an insistence on developing a political solution, a peace solution. There is, I tell you, even a change within the Jewish community in the United States on behalf of peace. Now I realize that this dependency pill is getting harder to swallow, but it is a fact that we ought to take into consideration.

Leonard Binder: The argument for functional autonomy coupled with the geographic entanglement of population and scientistic determinism leads to the diminuition of the significance of politics. It is an argument which has a differential input for the communities involved, one of which enjoys a strong centralized political and state apparatus, and one of which has virtually no unifying political institutions or established processes. The Lebanese situation does not differ essentially from the pre-independent situation of Mandatory Palestine. The War of Independence allowed this disentanglement, and as a consequence a solution became possible, bringing certain cultural and political benefits over against certain economic losses. The settlement policy and the administration of the occupied zones has deliberately led to a reentanglement, thus rendering what was a relatively rational solution, less rational.

The technological and functional argument for linking the two zones in a single polity or under a single sovereignty assumes one of three things: that politics is coming to an end, as presumably ideology has; or that what the PLO has called for is the solution. The dilemma of Israel's security analysis after 1967 has always been how to maintain control of the West Bank and Gaza territorially without granting citizenship. The autonomy project does just this, and for anyone with a democratic moral sense, this particular solution can only be an embarrassment. Any appeal to scientism, to center-periphery theories of preordained non-political development, or to equivocal notions of modernization is a statistical effort to sidestep the fundamental political issue, the democratic theory of politics and the moral issue of whether we are willing to allow others to enjoy the same conditions of life that we enjoy.

Harold Fisch: One important issue has not been touched on so far in this discussion. I have not heard any reference to Zionism as a force which has to be reckoned with. To put it at its very simplest,

Zionism involves a connection between a people and a land. It involves a bond which makes many, many Jews—far too many to be ignored—feel that in the West Bank they seek their homeland. Now, some people may suppose that this is just an eccentric position, but whether you or I believe in it or not, it seems to me no less a fact of life than any of the other facts that have been so solemnly and academically recognized. For example, Yigal Allon, who is now associated with a somewhat minimalistic position, was the first minister to visit and encourage the Jewish settlements in Kiryat Arba and Hebron and one of the first to help build up the Jewish presence in Kfar Etzion. Recognizing the facts of life realistically, I take the view that this dimension must be regarded as just as irreversible, just as dynamic, just as much a part of the power structure, whose elimination is just as inconceivable as any of the other facts that have been mentioned.

Very little attention has been paid to the question of Jerusalem. Now, there the entire Zionist force of idealism and politics comes into play, and to many of us—too many of us to be ignored—the notion that we can go back to the situation before 1967 is simply unthinkable. Now, this may seem a wild dream and it may seem that logic and rationality will win the day, but this is not the way I read the story of Zionism. It was the wild men who believed in Zion who finally triumphed, in spite of the fact that in 1903 Uganda seemed to be the practical solution.

Pinhas Rosenbluth: I think that we cannot work out practical options or go into details here. It should be sufficient for us to work out our principles and our attitudes. As a minimum, we have to insist on our security as a basis for every option, and secondly, we have to work for the principle of self-determination for each party. We Jews came here for Zionist reasons, not to be governed by others, not to be ruled by others, but we did not come here to rule over other people and we should say it quite clearly here. I say it for political reasons, also for moral and for Jewish reasons.

I suppose the crucial point here is what is our attitude toward further settlement in Judea and Samaria and the use of state lands. This is one of the details for practical negotiation with the Palestinians. In the interim, we have to renounce all further settlement for the period of the negotiations.

It was implied here that the principle of partition is obsolete. I don't think so. Partition as a practical political solution perhaps is, but not as a principle based on the actual situation—that there are two peoples who live together side by side here. All concepts of condominium and sharing government are premature under present conditions. Today we should just do everything not to complicate matters and not to use too sophisticated, too complicated means for achieving a solution. A condominium will bring an unending series of quarrels, we will have little quarrels about everything.

We should try once more to enter into negotiations with the Jordanians on the basis of these two principles. We insist on our security as a minimum basis, and we grant far-reaching but limited self-determination to the Palestinians in such a way as to exclude political sovereignty in an additional state.

Misha Louvish: There is an autonomy plan prepared by the Israeli government. The question is, is that particular plan viable? The whole purpose of the exercise is to get peace with the Arabs, in this case with the Palestinian Arabs. Is there any possibility of its acceptance by them?

Now if you'll take just a fairly cursory look at the plan, it says that the Autonomy Council will have control over the inhabitants but not over the territory, that the state lands will be under Israeli control, that the water resources will be under Israeli control, and that Israel will reserve the right to preserve law and order. This means that Israeli soldiers will be able to go into any Arab city where there have been disorders, arrest people, and interrogate them, because otherwise you can't maintain law and order. Is this the kind of autonomy that any Arab population or any Arab leader could possibly accept?

In addition, there have been further statements made by the Israeli government, for instance, that the Green Line no longer exists. Dr. Ben Elissar was, I think, the first man to state it and Mr. Begin has repeated it. I find it extremely difficult to reconcile this statement with the very idea of autonomy. The original plan says that administrative autonomy for the residents shall be established in Judea, Samaria, and the Gaza Strip, which means that autonomy will be established in a particular territory. What is that territory? In Camp David we agreed that Judea and Samaria is synonymous with the West Bank. The West Bank is bounded on the west by the Green Line. Surely, I think it is not intended that autonomy shall apply to Israeli citizens in pre-1967 Israel. In other words, we have here a complete contradiction in terms.

It is the declared intention of the Israeli government not to leave options open, but to close the option for a Palestinian state by extensive Israeli settlement, roadbuilding, acquisition of land, and so forth. All this would create "facts" quite impossible to change at the end of the five years.

Yosef Goell: We have been speaking to a large extent of autonomy as deriving from the Camp David agreement. To a large extent, the Camp David agreement was an imposed settlement by the United States. It should be expected that both parties, Egypt and Israel, will try to wriggle out of various inconvenient aspects of the Camp David agreement. I personally view the Israeli government's autonomy proposal as one such attempt. I think there will also be such attempt on the other side, but again this falls into place if one views the Camp David agreements not as coming down from on high but as partially an imposed agreement by a superpower who is a quasi-suzerain over both of the participants in the discussion.

Part of the problem in coming to grips with what is actually going on has to do with many of our own value and intellectual biases. I certainly include myself here. Let me just mention three of them. One of them is the assumption that peace is a normal state and that all the parties to the dispute agree that peace is a desirable goal. I would suggest, without getting into too much of an argument, that for Islamic civilization peace is not necessarily a good or desirable goal. We must realize, too, that the way in which we have used the word "peace" in our discussions is pretty much a sloganeering way of using it, rather than coming to grips with what we mean by peace. I would even suggest that in regard to the United States, peace is not necessarily a central goal of American policy. I think Dr. Pranger pointed out correctly that America has interests. It certainly has a very important oil interest. It also has an emotional interest in the sustaining of Israel and therefore has a very difficult dilemma in juggling these interests.

Second of all, I think there is a bias which is very much American in this sense, but affects us, too, because so much of political science is American-centered. The assumption is that all problems are amenable to solution, if you only try hard enough. If you have not solved the problem, it is a sign that you haven't tried hard enough. May I suggest that in the present case we are dealing with the problem of squaring the circle. There is no way to square a circle, with one exception—if the circle voluntarily undergoes metamorphosis into a square. What I am suggesting here is that there is a confrontation between two different worldviews. There is the Arab worldview that Israel is a foreign body in its midst, and one of the major missions of Arab civilization in this period is the expulsion of that foreign body from its midst. On the other hand, there has more recently arisen in Israel — let me just say in shorthand — a Beginist worldview. With these two, no permanent solution is possible. What we should be dealing with are questions of how to live with such a situation in the long term.

Finally, may I suggest there is also a bias, or perhaps a misunderstanding, in reading Palestinian intentions. We attribute to Palestinian nationalism the natural tendencies of all nationalism to want to have self-determination over its own people in a given territory. I would suggest that, as far as I see, at the present time this exists as a minor element in the Palestinian movement. The major element in Palestinian identity is still the intention to expel or to destroy Israel. Therefore I would suggest that all the philophizing about what degree of self-government can we give the Palestinian Arabs as a matter of placating or attracting Palestinians to some sort of a permanent solution, will, until that circle voluntarily changes itself, simply not work.

Shmuel Sandler: A question for Dr. Pranger. An option was suggested by Daniel Elazar and Yehudah Ben Meir to take away Israel's support of King Hussein. Do you see a possibility that the United States would remove its support from King Hussein so that, if the opportunity arises, Jordan will become a Palestinian state?

The second question is to Professor Horowitz, and it is about his statement on the 1967 borders and that partition is basically what America and the great powers want. Now, isn't it true that partition came about because of the great powers' interest and that it never brought peace? Now, should we follow the American recommendation and go back to partition, knowing from previous experience that it didn't bring peace before?

Eliezer Yapu: I am completely in agreement with Professor Elazar with regard to his sharing solution, but it should also be an agreed solution. In this respect I should like to submit that there was once an agreed upon solution between us and the Arabs. It was the 1922 White Paper, and it was very much misinterpreted at certain periods in our history, such as when Winston Churchill played the same role in 1922 as Jimmy Carter in 1979. I think that document stated that the national home would not be established in the territory east of the Jordan, while it would be established west of the Jordan "in cooperation with all its inhabitants." I think that is a principle which still holds today.

The second thing is, I think the solution based on a condominium over the West Bank by Jordan and Israel is something to be studied. We have an example of condominium, the Anglo-Egyptian condominium in Sudan, which worked for 60 years. Britain was responsible for security and the Egyptians primarily for the administration.

Finally, I thought that I would hear more about the difference between an autonomy based on territory and an autonomy based on persons. Without implying that it is my position, I tried to study precedents as far as autonomy of persons is concerned. I think that the Knesset Israel (the autonomous Jewish community in Palestine under the British Mandate) which existed here was in fact an autonomy based on persons, but I don't know whether that is what you had in mind.

Gabriel Ben-Dor: I want to examine three types of dangerous fallacies which sometimes crop up in the discussion and then, of course, let the speakers respond. First, there is something which the political sociologist Reinhardt Bendix calls the fallacy of retrospective determinism, that is presuming that things had to happen the way they did because one has the right theory to explain it. He cautions us about the future, because about that we are generally uncertain. Let's not get into the futuristic fallacy, namely that we know all the options. We don't. We don't know what is viable and what is not. If somebody had said two years ago that the President of Egypt coming to the Knesset to offer peace was realistic, I think everybody would have said it's out of the question. But it happened. Let's not get into discussions that assume we know all the options and there are no others. If a scientific discussion can get away from the dêjà vu and find new options, it will make a real contribution.

A second fallacy is that we have to talk about everything and resolve everything at once. Some of the frustration expressed here by people is that we discuss the United States and the Palestinians and the 1922 White Paper. We are not here to discuss the Arab-Israeli conflict. We are here to discuss federal solutions and shared rule as applied to one particular problem, Judea-Samaria-Gaza, at this particular time in the context of the present momentum for peace. Let's try to stick to that, and let's try to remember the particular value of the federal approach, namely the recognition of irreconcilable claims and the necessity to compromise.

The third thing is the issue of time. I think we tend to assume that things will be as they have been or as they now are. Professor Weiner has cautioned us, for instance, that new actors are entering the system, and we are obligated to negotiate with them. As Dr. Ben Meir pointed out after Sadat's visit to Jerusalem, it might be a new game. Things have changed; something very dramatic has happened. Let's remember that and not get stuck with the assumption of perpetuating the conceptual status quo in our minds.

Yehudah Ben Meir: I fully concur with what Professor Ben-Dor just said; one should be cautious and careful about speaking with certainty of what can be and what cannot be and what will be, because we have seen many things come to pass that were quite unanticipated. Professor Arieli suggested that my approach was non-rational. I think one should be cautious in throwing these terms around because history and reality have shown us that what was "irrational" can become rational and what is "rational" sometimes leads to harmful things.

Professor Arieli asked about whether I saw my solution as transitional or permanent. The autonomy scheme was not conceived of at Camp David as a permanent solution. All that was said is that after agreement we will have to discuss the permanent solution. Now, regarding the declaration of Mr. Begin, the gist, I gather, is that if the Arabs will press their claims for sovereignty over Judea and Samaria, Israel will also do so by putting its claim on the table as a rightful claim. I don't think one should interpret him as saying that this in his opinion is the permanent solution under all circumstances five years from now. I don't think this is so. One could argue whether his statement is beneficial or detrimental in terms of Israel's public relations. But the gist of it is, if the Arabs raise the claim of sovereignty, Israel also has a claim; I think Israel has a just claim of sovereignty over Judea and Samaria. As a matter of fact, in my opinion it has *the* just claim. The government, however, has never at any time taken the position that we determine this as the permanent solution regarding Judea and Samaria. The government's position is that three years after the autonomy will be in operation, we will negotiate without any prior conditions on the permanent solution for this area.

Someone raised the question of security and said that it would be colonialist to have Israel responsible for security. We have to be realistic, however. No Arab force in Judea and Samaria is capable of maintaining security in that area. There are Arabs, by the way, who say that "we know that the second that the Israeli army would leave, we would be the first who would be killed." That doesn't mean they don't want the Israelis to leave. Politics and nationalism are not only stronger than economics at times, as Professor Elazar said, but are even stronger than life. But they don't deny this very fact, and anyone who is objective knows it. The idea that a police force that will be created in Judea and Samaria will be responsible for security of the entire area is also mistaken. I would remind you that Arab students in universities here in Jerusalem, Israeli citizens, refuse to participate in the guarding of their dormitories against bombs which could kill them on the grounds that they, although they are Israeli citizens, are not willing to act against their brothers. Now, take it from there and imagine how people in Nablus are going to participate in catching and judging Arab terrorists who are coming to throw bombs to kill Jews. One has to have some grasp of reality.

This does not mean that in the permanent solution there cannot be some other arrangement, more of a sharing nature, to meet the demands of security. This definitely could develop. But Israel's stipulating her control of security now is based on the realities of the situation, because nothing else can work.

The same argument applies to the question of the state lands, which Professor Weiner raised. I disagree with people who say that the government does not want to enable the Arabs of Judea and Samaria to run their lives fully. I think the desire is to have them fully run everything which has to do with themselves. But the problem is, we also have to see the motivations involved. The government's position is that the autonomy scheme calls for the Arabs to be fully responsible for their lives in all aspects, but that Jews also have a right to live and to develop their lives and their civilian presence in Judea and Samaria. Now again, in a transitional arrangement we must find the mechanism to enable this to be so. Any objective person would realize that if you give the state lands into Arab hands, you have in effect passed a total and complete death sentence on any possibility of a Jewish civilian existence in Judea and Samaria. For example, Jordanian law today provides for the death sentence for any Arab willfully selling land to a Jew, and just a week ago, a Jordanian court approved three death sentences which were passed on Arabs who sold land. So, no one can concede for a moment that if within the transitional arrangement this power is given into the hands of an Arab council, there will be any chance whatsoever of Jews living in the areas.

Now, this can change in the permanent solution after the transitional period, once certain of these problems have been resolved and life has taken on a new normalization. There certainly is room to find some better way of guaranteeing that the land can be used for all concerned, properly, equally, and proportionally. It is not that Israel wants to control the land. It is that Israel wants to prevent control of the land from being used to snuff out any Jewish existence in Judea and Samaria. The government's position is that we will do everything in our power to prevent this from happening. It is not that we want to control the land but we want to have a way of preventing the Arabs who oppose Jewish settlement from choking off the Jewish presence in the territories. At the moment, I see no other way of doing it. Any other proposal which would guarantee that the Jewish presence would not be choked off but would be able to develop fairly and properly side by side with the Arab population in my opinion would be acceptable to us. Here, then, is one example in which we see a difference between the government's transitional solution and more sharing in a permanent solution, if things develop properly.

Now turning again to the question of the source of authority. Israel does not claim that the military authority is the sovereign in the area. According to international law, when there is no sovereignty, the military occupying power enjoys certain rights and privileges. Now, here is another case; the source of authority is something which definitely could and probably would change from the transitional solution to the permanent solution, because in the transitional solution there is no peace agreement between Jordan and Israel.

Professor Weiner pointed out correctly that the Camp David agreement calls at the end of three years for a committee composed of Jordan and Israel, without Egypt, to begin negotiating of the autonomy, to conclude a peace treaty. This peace treaty of course will stipulate what will happen in the area of Judea and Samaria. Until then, however, the fact remains that Israel is the occupying authority in Judea and Samaria. And Camp David recognizes, by the way, that during the transitional period, the only military force which will be allowed in Judea and Samaria is the Israeli military force. It will be relocated and thinned out, but it will be the only military force present. At such, it has the full responsibility and authority according to international law for what goes on in that area. For the transitional period, the source of authority in the final analysis is not the military government so much as the military presence. International law says that he who exercises effective military control over the area enjoys certain responsibilities and authority. Camp David stipulates—and there is no other way of reading it—that Israel will exercise military authority in that area—not police. Strong or weak, police are not military authority. But when a peace treaty will be concluded, then the military presence will cease and there will be a permanent solution in which this can also be changed.

Professor Arieli, I did not say that my considerations are only security ones. On the contrary. In my opinion, the vast majority of the Jewish people believe that our relationship and our interest in Judea and Samaria is not purely one of security. It is a national, historical, Zionist consideration and aspiration, as Professor Fisch indicated. I find it very hard to understand why some people, as Professor Horowitz said, find it so easy to understand national sentiment on the Arab side, but not on the Jewish side. Professor Arieli says this may be true, but it is meaningless. It cannot withstand the mighty pressure of the nationalist sentiment of the Arabs. Why, then, is he not ready at the same time to take into consideration the national sentiments of the Jewish people towards their homeland, which has been their homeland for many thousands of years.

One can say these sentiments cannot be the only factor. I say this too, or else I would have accepted option number one. But to totally ignore it, and Professor Arieli does so when he says that he only considers the security aspect, is wrong. I agree with him that there are national aspirations on the Arab side, but why totally ignore the national aspirations of the Jewish people, which are also a reality? Just as one may not be able to wipe out the reality of the Arab aspirations, no one could wipe out the reality, as Professor Fisch said very well, of many, many Jews, who have been and are willing to fight and die for their national aspirations to be part of this homeland.

The national aspirations for the Jews relate to Jerusalem, to Hebron, to the Jordan. This of course is the clear difference between the present issue and the Sinai issue. Now there may have been a consensus on Sinai, true—a national consensus exists as long as it exists; when it's changed, it changes. Mr. Begin succeeded in changing the national consensus regarding Sinai. Now, whether he will want to change it on Judea and Samaria, or whether he will succeed, at the moment is a moot question. In my opinion, the answer is negative to both questions. Why do I think he won't succeed or won't want to? Because there is a tremendous difference between Sinai and Judea and Samaria. Israel's motivation to be in Sinai always was solely a security one. I don't believe that anyone went to Sinai because he thought it is Eretz Yisrael. We put up settlements in 1970, or in 1967, because of the strategic concept of a buffer zone between Gaza and Sinai, which I think was a valid strategic concept. The moment came along when the Israeli government said, we are willing to forego the strategic concept. But the Jews who went to Judea and Samaria, who went to Gush Etzion three weeks after the 1967 war, went because they saw themselves as going home. No one in Rafiah or

Ophira saw himself as coming home. Therefore the motivation is totally different and the concensus is much stronger.

Regarding Dr. Rosenbluth's comment about self-determination, I do not think there is a genuine claim on moral grounds that demands that the Arabs in Judea and Samaria enjoy self-determination, and I will explain why. The reason is that most countries in the world have minorities, and no country in the world has given them an unlimited right of self-determination. Self-determination was normally given to colonies which were thousands of miles away from the country which granted them self-determination. Great Britain certainly had no national relationship with any territory in Africa or anywhere else. This was a colonial situation. One has to be—how should I say it—wicked to claim that Israel's relationship to Judea and Samaria is based on colonial, imperialist desires, and to deny the relationship between the Jewish people and the land of Israel.

I find it hard to understand, by the way, why the 610,000 Arabs of Judea and Samaria—we'll forget Gaza for the moment—are entitled without any question to self-determination, while 500,000 Arabs living in Israel proper are not entitled to the same self-determination. I also find it hard to understand why, in the eyes of world public opinion, the Kurds in Iraq are not entitled to self-determination, and the Christians in Lebanon are not entitled to self-determination, but only the Arabs in Judea and Samaria are entitled to self-determination.

I want to make it clear that autonomy applies only to the Arabs living in Judea, Samaria, and Gaza, and clearly not to the Arabs living on the other side, because our entire negotiations were based on U.N. Resolution 242 which refers to "the areas occupied in the recent conflict," meaning 1967. There should be no question about it. What Mr. Begin meant, and therefore it is true what Mr. Louvish said, is that there clearly will be a difference between the situation in Judea and Samaria versus the situation west of the Green Line. What Mr. Begin meant to say, I believe, is that there will be no national boundary within Eretz Israel west of the river. That's what he said. Not that there will be no differences, or there will be no boundary. Clearly the Green Line will be the boundary of autonomy—you are 100 percent correct in this—but the Green Line will cease to be a national boundary.

Robert Pranger: I think that any estimation of U.S. policy which sees U.S. peace efforts as an avocation and not central to its policy is simply inadequate. It has been determined by four presidents since 1967 that there will be a "just and lasting" peace settlement in the Middle East, meaning treaties between Israel and various Arab states and an acceptance of the U.S. formula of Israeli withdrawal to the pre-1967 lines with only insubstantial modification. I know of no president who has backed away from the principle of withdrawal to the pre-1967 lines, whatever the ideological and

other kinds of forces loose in the Middle East, whose existence
obviously the United States recognizes. We have resisted Soviet
and Arab statements that Israel is sort of a transnational ideology
run amok in the Middle East, that Zionism is some kind of threat,
some loose tiger, going for the Tigris and the Euphrates and the
Nile Rivers, all of which appears in the Soviet press. On the other
hand, I hope that the problem is not considered by Israelis to be
simply a domestic political issue to be settled within the confines
of the state and not to be determined through this multilateral
peace process.

Now, under the circumstances, whatever the party distinctions within an Arab country or Israel might be, from the standpoint of U.S. interests, they are somewhat immaterial. Only once
during the course of the period since 1967 have we let go of the
peace process. We did it, I think, largely during the election in
1972. There was an argument which developed in the U.S.
government which said, "We'll arm Israel and let the Arabs come
to their senses." Immediately after the election, a senior Egyptian
official—Mr. Fahmi I think—visited the United States and was
rebuffed. There was no U.S. response to the latest Sadat proposals,
and they simply cut themselves off from us to go to war. We
learned from that, after the quadrupling of of the oil prices and
what have you, that we were going to persist in this process. One
can call it an imposed settlement, but I don't think that is particularly material, at least from the U.S. standpoint.

Recognizing that there are limitations to this, I'm just simply
stating what I think is a fairly consistent U.S. policy, and it has been
consistent throughout Democratic and Republican administrations. This policy seems to be unflagging in its zeal for the protection of U.S. interests in the Middle East. It is considered to be the
most productive for Israel's security and most productive rom the
standpoint of our relations with the Arab world. Obviously this policy has to take into account what are considered to be local realities, but not to let them become the dominant principles in the
settlement. In fact all international negotiations are based on these
considerations, that the governments who come to the negotiating table are responsible and able to keep internal politics in
check, governments able to make compromises and adjustments
and put words to paper and live up to their agreements and keep
in check their own internal political forces. And I think that is going
to be the U.S. approach to this West Bank issue.

Dan Horowitz: I am surprised at the revival of binationalism in this
country, and a very strange binationalism at that. It is an asymmetrical binationalism. It applies to the West Bank but it does not
apply to Israel proper. I want to warn Israelis that it is impossible;
that once we do away with the principle of partition and accept
the principle of binationalism, we won't be able to keep that binationalism east of the Green Line. Everyone who raises the prob-

lem about who should be the sovereign in Nablus will soon find that someone will raise the problem as to who should be the sovereign in Tel Aviv or in Jaffa, and this applies to settlements and sentiments.

There are Jewish sentiments with regard to Nablus, there are Arab sentiments with regard to Jaffa. Partition means that the Jewish sentiments and emotional links to the land will be satisfied in part of what was Palestine, and Arab sentiments will be satisfied in another part of what was Palestine. I think there will be one concession to Jewish sentiment, and this will be the situation in East Jerusalem. After a settlement, it will not be identical with the situation prior to 1967, and there will be no real Arab sovereignty of any kind in any part of Jerusalem. Something will exist, a flag, a symbolic representation, but there will be a new situation in Jerusalem which will allow Jews to both settle and move into all parts of Jerusalem. This will be the only change that I foresee.

On the West Bank there will be no organized Jewish settlements. This doesn't mean that a Jew won't be able to buy a flat in Nablus or Ramallah and live there. That means that part of the compromise would be that the control of the right to settlement would be given to the Arabs, and this means actually—and in this I agree with Dr. Ben Meir—that in the near future, until relations change, there will be no Jewish settlement. Perhaps the existing settlements will remain—though I don't think that many Jews would want to remain—but there will be no further Jewish settlement in the West Bank. This is a symmetrical situation, and this is what I mean by partition.

Once I wanted to follow the example of those who removed the stigma from the word "partition" in the past, above all Ben-Gurion and Weizmann, and now I want to remove the stigma from the 1967 borders. I want to do so because, if there will be any peace settlement, it will end up with the 1967 borders. Therefore I don't want to feel as if it is an imposed settlement, that we didn't arrive at it voluntarily, and that somehow will be able to opt out of it through some maneuvers. If it will end there, better let us come there voluntarily and get maximum benefits out of it, in particular, security benefits.

I also don't think that our interest in Eretz Israel is only a matter of security. I think that what can be achieved in the framework of such a compromise settlement is a satisfaction of the Jewish right of self-determination in 80 percent of western Palestine and a satisfaction of the Palestinian right inside Jordan or on the West Bank. It is a problem that they would have only 20 percent, although I think that this is necessary because there are other Arab countries, but there is no other Jewish country.

For these reasons I think that we much reject any solution which is not symmetrical in the sense that the same considerations will apply to Jews in the West Bank as apply to the Arabs west of the Green Line. If this is correct, then the only constraint that must be taken into consideration and the only condition for accepting such a settlement is the security problem. The security problem will persist because many of the Arabs don't yet accept the State of Israel as an accomplished fact. As long as that is the case, we need special arrangements to protect our basic security; not our day-to-day security which would be with the Arabs; they will have to be responsible for their actions, if they allow infiltration and terrorism to be carried on from the territories, the same way that Lebanon now is held responsible, and Jordan was held responsible when Jordan controlled the West Bank. There would be Israeli reprisals, perhaps even war. This is possible. But we can't solve the problem by retaining troops in the West Bank. Perhaps during the interim settlement they would accept some such arrangement, for a transitional period, but not in the long run. In this I agree with Daniel Elazar.

I'm sorry that the interim settlement suggested by the government of Israel was autonomy and not an Israeli-Jordanian condominium. Perhaps we missed the opportunity to end up with a Jordanian-Palestinian state, rather than with a Palestinian state. It is always easier for basic security to demilitarize a region of a state than to demilitarize a full state.

As for the problem of autonomy for persons versus autonomy for the land, I agree that there was a kind of personal autonomy in the Jewish community in Palestine under the British Mandate, but this was a personal autonomy that was taken by the Jews without being fully given by the British. We always considered it as temporary, as a "state in the making." And "state in the making" means that it had to end up with full independence or with a degree of sovereignty. In this sense I also accept the premise that the autonomy plan is not a state in the making, because I prefer the result to be a Jordanian-Palestinian state and not a Palestinian state. If it will be a Palestinian state, it will be partly our fault, but either way the interim settlement will lead in the end to an entity alongside Israel — not one directly linked or integrated into it.

I want to reiterate the warning that we have had to concede more and more points during the negotiations, because we didn't see things in time. I think that if we don't want to be pushed to the bitter end, to open the door to the problem of the legitimacy of what is west of the Green Line, it is in our interest to return to the partition solution as fast as possible and to emphasize the existence of a national boundary between Nablus and Tel Aviv.

Daniel Elazar: We have had some clear-cut statements of the basic Israeli division on the issue of the territories—between the partitionists and those who are looking for something, shall we say, beyond partition. Both positions, I think, have been expounded quite elegantly and more or less fully by the various proponents. Nevertheless, there are a few points which remain to be covered.

Professor Arieli suggested that the development of Jewish Jerusalem was not spontaneous, but was governmentally planned. I think that this whole country is based on an overemphasis of government activity. Government spends a lot of money and spins its wheels a lot, but it really does not achieve that much; it may even be self-defeating in many ways. When the full story is in, we will see how much of Jerusalem's recent development has been spontaneous. It was done by the Jews who moved willingly to Jerusalem, not the ones who were forced to move up because the government offices were moved. Most of the Jews who moved to this city were people who saw in Jerusalem what Dr. Ben Meir correctly suggested Jews see in the Land of Israel as a whole.

Prof. Arieli completely neglected the spontaneous movement of Arabs to Jerusalem over the last twelve years in response to new economic opportunities, a major element in my thesis. I think, then, that spontaneity accounts for much more of Jerusalem's development than was given credit.

I was obviously not including the Gaza District as part of the Jerusalem metropolitan region. Nevertheless, as a labor market and in some other respects, it is part of the coastal metropolitan belt, particularly the metropolitan region developing around Ashdod, Rehovot, and Ashkelon. Consequently, the same thesis applies to Gaza as well.

In my opinion, research into the question of the state lands would be most useful. A small working group could study how to solve this problem of state lands over which there are dual claims. This issue is even more important than the question of international restrictions on sovereignty, most of which continue to exist because of political realities, rather than because of treaty restrictions *per se.*

Emile Nakhleh's assessment that both the Israelis and the Palestinians are suffering makes a great deal of sense as far as it goes. I don't know whether it is a question of ending the suffering, because there is a certain level of suffering that we all can tolerate, but in this case it might be helpful to alleviate it to some extent. This may indeed be part of the U.S. role, provided that American efforts don't alleviate the suffering in a very one-sided way because the U.S. doesn't, or won't understand the whole picture.

Leonard Binder gave us a really elegant partitionist polemic. I would like to point out, however, that a sharing solution does not lead to the dimunition of politics, but to its enhancement. That is to say, it is designed to move away from a solution which I believe —and which Prof. Horowitz also believes even though he also endorses partition, judging by his last remarks—will lead to a continuing necessity to resort to violence, to control the border through force of arms, toward an attempt to create a politics that will offer better means of mutual control through political means.

I think that primordial ties are of great importance. Listening to Nathan Glazer the other day, I found myself quite discomfited by a view of the world that holds that it is rational to want to make money, but irrational to want to care about your brother, a view which is essential if one prefers class-based over ethnic-based politics. Given the realities of primordial ties, I would suggest that the whole future of the world lies in the ability to create a politics that can manage these conflicts in some reasonable way. We are not as close to that kind of politics as we would like to be in Eretz Israel/Palestine, but I think we are much closer to it than we were even a few years back—and I hope that we can move even closer.

It has been suggested that condominium or some other form of shared rule will lead to unending quarrels—unlike partition which brought peace and quiet. That is the problem. None of us has a suggestion that is guaranteed to bring peace and quiet. The question is under what conditions can we maximize the chances for peace and quiet.

In this regard I think that going back to the position that Yosef Goell presented is a kind of déjà vu. We can agree that all problems are not necessarily amenable to solution, but to lean on the conventional wisdom that Islamic civilization is opposed to peace, that the Arabs see Israel as a foreign body to be expelled is to define the situation in such a way that there can never be a solution. We may be forced back to those views but I think we already have gone a step beyond them. It is like saying that, if the Jews had their way all Arabs in the land of Israel would disappear or that Israel would be an island or something like that. We are at least beginning to understand that nobody is going to disappear; as much as some would want others to do so, it won't happen. I hope that we can build upon that new understanding.

No matter how optimistic we may want to be, however, I don't think a conventional federal solution will work in this situation. It should be once again stated that, when we talk about federalist solutions among ourselves, we are not talking about conventional federal solutions. I think that there is too great a gap between the parties on one level, and even a convergence of interest in preserving their respective integrities, to allow that approach to be useful. It is not the most fruitful line to pursue. One who wants what I want for a Jewish state must understand when others want something else for their state, or whatever. Hence I just don't think that federation in the American sense is the most fruitful line to pursue.

With regard to self-determination, had the Israeli government asked me, I would have said long ago that it should have endorsed the principle of self-determination, and then given it an interpretation acceptable to Israel's point of view but still well within the accepted meaning of the term, but that is a tactical answer. In my opinion, it is not one of the more useful words in the contemporary political lexicon, not because I object to self-determination, but because I work within a system in which consent is the more basic term. Self-determination sounds much too particularistic. The point that Dr. Ben-Meir raised, that virtually every country in the world has a minority which is not granted self-determination, leads me to believe that the term itself has a tactical use and little more. It was put to very good stead in the Third World revolution and will probably continue to be used in the same way. But in the practical matter of creating a politics, rather than simply a polemics of freedom, consent is a more appropriate approach, because consent is something that can be shared. It isn't so separatist, so individualistic.

I believe fully that no solution will come about unless there is a sufficient level of consent on the part of all the parties who are going to be affected by that solution. That is one lesson we should have learned from the development of modern democracy. As a democrat and a political scientist, I do not think it is realistic to believe that anybody can go back on it other than through coercive means of the kind that, as Jews, the majority in Israel would oppose even if they worked—and I have my doubts that they would. The problem, then, is to explore ways to build consent.

Gabriel Ben-Dor: I remember when I joined the Jerusalem Institute for Federal Studies in the summer of 1977, it seemed that we were pursuing some chimeras. People said we were daydreaming and so on and so forth when we spoke about federal arrangements for the future of the West Bank and Gaza at that time. Everything seemed to be frozen. And by our third annual conference, we may even be behind what the politicians are offering and what is being discussed at the highest levels of policy making. That just shows that it is not entirely certain who is really daydreaming. Are we any more detached from the dynamics of politics than the politicians are? This is the question which in this particular case has not been answered in a very clear-cut way in favor of the politicians.

Appendix 1

Self-Rule
for Palestinian Arabs, residents of Judaea, Samaria and the Gaza District which will be instituted upon the establishment of peace

The following programme was submitted by Prime Minister Begin to President Sadat, as announced by Mr. Begin in the Knesset on 28 December 1977.

1. The administration of the Military Government in Judaea, Samaria and the Gaza district will be abolished.

2. In Judaea, Samaria and the Gaza district administrative authority of the residents, by and for them, will be established.

3. The residents of Judaea, Samaria and the Gaza district will elect an Administrative Council composed of eleven members. The Administrative Council will operate in accordance with the principles laid down in this paper.

4. Any resident, 18 years old and above, without distinction of citzenship, or if stateless, will be entitled to vote in the elections to the Administrative Council.

5. Any resident whose name is included in the list of candidates for the Administrative Council and who, on the day the list is submitted, is 25 years old or above, will be entitled to be elected to the Council.

6. The Administrative Council will be elected by general, direct, personal, equal and secret ballot.

7. The period of office of the Administrative Council will be four years from the day of its election.

8. The Administrative Council will sit in Bethlehem.

10. The Administrative Council will operate the following Departments:
(a)   The Department of Education;
(b)   The Department of Religious Affairs;
(c)   The Department of Finance;
(d)   The Department of Transportation;
(e)   The Department for Construction and Housing;
(f)   The Department for Industry, Commerce and Tourism;
(g)   The Department of Agriculture;
(h)   The Department of Health;
(i)   The Department for Labour and Social Welfare;
(j)   The Department for Rehabilitation of Refugees;
(k)   The Department for the Administration of Justice and the Supervision of Local Police Forces;
and promulgate regulations relating to the operation of these Departments.

11. Security and public order in the areas of Judaea, Samaria and the Gaza district will be the responsibility of the Israeli authorities.

12. The Administrative Council will elect is own chairman.

13. The first session of the Administration Council will be convened 30 days after the publication of the election results.

14. Residents of Judaea, Samaria and the Gaza district, without distinction of citizenship, or if stateless, will be granted free choice (option) of either Israeli or Jordanian citizenship.

15. Any resident of the areas of Judaea, Samaria and the Gaza district who requests Israeli citizenship will be granted such citizenship in accordance with the citizenship law of the State.

16. Residents of Judaea, Samaria and the Gaza district who, in accordance with the right of free option, choose Israeli citizenship, will be entitled to vote for, and be elected to, the Knesset in accordance with the election law.

17. Residents of Judaea, Samaria and the Gaza district who are citizens of Jordan will elect, and be eligible for election to, the Parliament of the Hashemite Kingdom of Jordan in accordance with the election law of that country.

18. Questions arising from the vote to the Jordanian Parliament by residents of Judaea, Samaria and the Gaza district will be clarified in negotiations between Israel and Jordan.

19. A committee will be established of representatives of Israel, Jordan and the Administrative Council to examine existing legislation in Judaea, Samaria and the Gaza district, and to determine which legislation will continue in force, which will be abolished, and which will be the competence of the Administrative Council to promulgate regulations. The rulings of the committee will be adopted by unanimous decision.

20. Residents of Israel will be entitled to acquire land and settle in the areas of Judaea, Samaria and the Gaza district. Arabs, residents of Judaea, Samaria and the Gaza district who, in accordance with the free option granted them, will become Israeli citizens, will be entitled to acquire land and settle in Israel.

21. A committee will be established of representatives of Israel, Jordan and the Administrative Council to determine norms of immigration to the areas of Judaea, Samaria and the Gaza district. The committee will determine the norms whereby Arab refugees residing outside Judaea, Samaria and the Gaza district will be permitted to immigrate to these areas in reasonable numbers. The rulings of the committee will be adopted by unanimous decision.

22. Residents of Israel and residents of Judaea, Samaria and the Gaza district will be assured freedom of movement and freedom of economic activity in Israel, Judaea, Samaria and the Gaza district.

23. The Administrative Council will appoint one of its members to represent the Council before the Government of Israel for deliberation on matters of common interest, and one of its members to represent the Council before the Government of Jordan, for deliberation on matters of common interest.

24. Israel stands by its right and its claim of sovereignty to Judaea, Samaria and the Gaza district. In the knowledge that other claims exist, it proposes, for the sake of the agreement and the peace, that the question of sovereignty in these areas be left open.

25. With regard to the administration of the holy places of the three religions in Jerusalem, a special proposal will be drawn up and submitted that will include the guarantee of freedom of access to members of all the faiths to the shrines holy to them.

26. These principles will be subject to review after a five-year period.

Appendix 2

Camp David Documents

(September 17, 1978)

A. Framework for Peace in the Middle East Agreed at Camp David

Muhammad Anwar el-Sadat, President of the Arab Republic of Egypt, and Menachem Begin, Prime Minister of Israel, met with Jimmy Carter, President of the United States of America, at Camp David from September 5 to September 17, 1978, and have agreed on the following Framework for peace in the Middle East. They invite other parties to the Arab-Israeli conflict to adhere to it.

Preamble

The search for peace in the Middle East must be guided by the following:

The agreed basis for a peaceful settlement of the conflict between Israel and its neighbors is UN Security Council Resolution 242 in all its parts.

After four wars during thirty years, despite intensive human efforts, the Middle East, which is the cradle of civilization and the birthplace of three great religions, does not yet enjoy the blessings of peace. The people of the Middle East yearn for peace, so that the vast human and natural resources of the region can be turned to the pursuits of peace and so that this area can become a model for coexistence and cooperation among nations.

The historic initiative by President Sadat in visiting Jerusalem and the reception accorded to him by the Parliament, government and people of Israel, and the reciprocal visit of Prime Minister Begin to Ismailia, the peace proposals made by both leaders, as well as the warm reception of these missions by the peoples of both countries, have created an unprecedented opportunity for peace which must not be lost if this generation and future generations are to be spared the tragedies of war.

The provisions of the Charter of the United Nations and the other accepted norms of international law and legitimacy now provide accepted standards for the conduct of relations among all states.

To achieve a relationship of peace, in the spirit of Article 2 of the UN Charter, future negotiations between Israel and any neighbor prepared to negotiate peace and security with it, are necessary for the purpose of carrying out all the provisions and principles of Resolutions 242 and 338.

Peace requires respect for the sovereignty, territorial integrity and political independence of every state in the area and their right to live in peace within secure and recognized boundaries free from threats or acts of force. Progress toward that goal can accelerate movement toward a new era of reconciliation in the Middle East marked by cooperation in promoting economic development, in maintaining stability and in assuring security.

Security is enhanced by a relationship of peace and by cooperation between nations which enjoy normal relations. In addition, under the terms of peace treaties, the parties can, on the basis of reciprocity, agree to special security arrangements such as demilitarized zones, limited armaments areas, early warning stations, the presence of international forces, liaison, agreed measures for monitoring, and other arrangements that they agree are useful.

Preamble

Taking these factors into account, the parties are determined to reach a just, comprehensive and durable settlement of the Middle East conflict through the conclusion of peace treaties based on Security Council Resolutions 242 and 338 in all their parts. Their purpose is to achieve peace and good neighborly relations. They recognize that, for peace to endure, it must involve all those who have been most deeply affected by the conflict. They therefore agree that this Framework as appropriate is intended by them to constitute a basis for peace not only between Egypt and Israel, but also between Israel and each of its other neighbors which is prepared to negotiate peace with Israel on this basis. With that objective in mind, they have agreed to proceed as follows:

A. West Bank and Gaza

1. Egypt, Israel, Jordan and the representatives of the Palestinian people should participate in negotiations on the resolution of the Palestinian problem in all its aspects. To achieve that objective, negotiations relating to the West Bank and Gaza should proceed in three stages:

(A) Egypt and Israel agree that, in order to ensure a peaceful and orderly transfer of authority, and taking into account the security concerns of all the parties, there should be transitional arrangements for the West Bank and Gaza for a period not exceeding five years. In order to provide full autonomy to the inhabitants, under these arrangements, the Israeli military government and its civilian administration will be withdrawn as soon as a self-governing authority has been freely elected by the inhabitants of these areas to replace the existing military government. To negotiate the details of a transitional arrangement, the government of Jordan will be invited to join the negotiations on the basis of this framework. These new arrangements should give due consideration to both the principle of self-government by the inhabitants of these territories and to the legitimate security concerns of the parties involved.

(B) Egypt, Israel, and Jordan will agree on the modalities for establishing the elected self-governing authority in the West Bank and Gaza. The delegations of Egypt and Jordan may include Palestinians from the West Bank and Gaza or other Palestinians as mutually agreed. The parties will negotiate an agreement which will define the powers and responsibilities of the self-governing authority to be exercised in the West Bank and Gaza. A withdrawal of Israeli armed forces will take place and there will be a redeployment of the remaining Israeli forces into specified security locations. The agreement will also include arrangements for assuring internal and external security and public order. A strong local police force will be established, which may include Jordanian citizens. In addition, Israel and Jordanian forces will participate in joint patrols and in the manning of control posts to assure the security of the borders.

(C) When the self-governing authority (administrative council) in the West Bank and Gaza is established and inaugurated, the transitional period of five years will begin. As soon as possible, but not later than the third year after the beginning of the transitional period, negotiations will take place to determine the final status of the West Bank and Gaza and its relationship with its neighbors, and to conclude a peace treaty between Israel and

Jordan by the end of the transitional period. These negotiations will be conducted among Egypt, Israel, Jordan, and the elected representatives of the inhabitants of the West Bank and Gaza. Two separate but related committees will be convened, one committee, consisting of representatives of the four parties which will negotiate and agree on the final status of the West Bank and Gaza, and its relationship with its neighbors, and the second committee, consisting of representatives of Israel and representatives of Jordan to be joined by the elected representatives of the inhabitants of the West Bank and Gaza, to negotiate the peace treaty between Israel and Jordan, taking into account the agreement reached on the final status of the West Bank and Gaza. The negotiations shall be based on all the provisions and principles of UN Security Council Resolution 242. The negotiations will resolve, among other matters, the location of the boundaries and the nature of the security arrangements. The solution from the negotiations must also recognize the legitimate rights of the Palestinian people and their just requirements. In this way, the Palestinians will participate in the determination of their own future through:

(1) The negotiations among Egypt, Israel, Jordan and the representatives of the inhabitants of the West Bank and Gaza to agree on the final status of the West Bank and Gaza and other outstanding issues by the end of the transitional period.

(2) Submitting their agreement to a vote by the elected representatives of the inhabitants of the West Bank and Gaza.

(3) Providing for the elected representatives of the inhabitants of the West Bank and Gaza to decide how they shall govern themselves consistent with the provisions of their agreement.

(4) Participating, as stated above in the work of the committee negotiating the peace treaty between Israel and Jordan.

2. All necessary measures will be taken and provisions made to assure the security of Israel and its neighbors during the transitional period and beyond. To assist in providing such security, a strong local police force will be constituted by the self-governing authority. It will be composed of inhabitants of the West Bank and Gaza. The police will maintain continuing liaison on internal security matters with the designated Israeli, Jordanian and Egyptian officers.

3. During the transitional period, the representatives of Egypt, Israel, Jordan and the self-governing authority will constitute a continuing committee to decide by agreement on the modalities of admission of persons displaced from the West Bank and Gaza in 1967, together with necessary measures to prevent disruption and disorder. Other matters of common concern may also be dealt with by this committee.

4. Egypt and Israel will work with each other and with other interested parties to establish agreed procedures for a prompt, just and permanent implementation of the resolution of the refugee problem.

B. Egypt-Israel

1. Egypt and Israel undertake not to resort to the threat or the use of force to settle disputes. Any disputes shall be settled by peaceful means in accordance with the provisions of Article 33 of the Charter of the United Nations.

2. In order to achieve peace between them, the parties agreed to negotiate in good faith with a goal of concluding within three months from the signing of this Framework a peace treaty between them,

while inviting the other parties to the conflict to proceed simultaneously to negotiate and conclude similar peace treaties with a view to achieving a comprehensive peace in the area. The Framework for the Conclusion of a Peace Treaty Between Egypt and Israel will govern the peace negotiations between them. The parties will agree on the modalities and the timetable for the implementation of their obligations under the treaty.

C. *Associated Principles*

1. Egypt and Israel state that the principles and provisions described below should apply to peace treaties between Israel and each of its neighbors—Egypt, Jordan, Syria and Lebanon.

2. Signatories shall establish among themselves relationships normal to states at peace with one another. To this end, they should undertake to abide by all the provisions of the Charter of the United Nations. Steps to be taken in this respect include

(A) full recognition;

(B) abolishing economic boycotts;

(C) guaranteeing that under their jurisdiction the citizens of the other parties shall enjoy the protection of the due process of law.

3. Signatories should explore possibilities for economic development in the context of final peace treaties, with the objective of contributing to the atmosphere of peace, cooperation and friendship which is their common goal.

4. Claims Commissions may be established for the mutual settlement of all financial claims.

5. The United States shall be invited to participate in the talks on matters related to the modalities of the implementation of the agreements and working out the timetable for the carrying out of the obligations of the parties.

6. The United Nations Security Council shall be requested to endorse the peace treaties and ensure that their provisions shall not be violated. The permanent members of the Security Council shall be requested to underwrite the peace treaties and ensure respect for their provisions. They shall also be requested to conform their policies and actions with the undertakings contained in this Framework.

For the Government of the   For the Government of
Arab Republic of Egypt: Israel:

Witnessed by:
Jimmy Carter, President of the United States of America.

Text of United Nations Security Council Resolution 242 of November 22, 1967
Adopted Unanimously by the 1382nd Meeting

THE SECURITY COUNCIL

Expressing its continuing concern with the grave situation in the Middle East,

Emphasizing the inadmissibility of the acquisition of territory by war and the need to work for a just and lasting peace in which every state in the area can live in security.

Emphasizing further that all member states in their acceptance of the Charter of the United Nations have undertaken a commitment to act in accordance with Article 2 of the Charter.

1.   *Affirms* that the fulfillment of Charter principles requires the establishment of a just and lasting peace in the Middle East which should include the application of both the following principles:

     (i) Withdrawal of Israeli armed forces from territories occupied in the recent conflict;

     (ii) Termination of all claims or states of beligerency and respect for and acknowledgement of the sovereignty, territorial integrity and political independence of every state in the area and their right to live in peace within secure and recognized boundaries free from threats or acts of force;

2.   *Affirms further* the necessity

     (a) For guaranteeing freedom of navigation through international waterways in the area;

     (b) For achieving a just settlement of the refugee problem;

     (c) For guaranteeing the territorial inviolability and political independence of every state in the area, through measures including the establishment of demilitarized zones;

3.   *Requests* the Secretary General to designate a Special Representative to proceed to the Middle East to establish and maintain contacts with the states concerned in order to promote agreement and assist efforts to achieve a peaceful and accepted settlement in accordance with the provisions and principles of this resolution.

4.   *Requests* the Secretary General to report to the Security Council on the progress of the efforts of the Special Representative as soon as possible.

Text of United Nations Security Council Resolution 338
Adopted by the Security Council
at its 1747th Meeting on 21/22 October 1973

THE SECURITY COUNCIL

1. *Calls upon* all parties to the present fighting to cease all firing, and terminate all military activity immediately, no later than 12 hours after the moment of the adoption of this decision, in the positions they now occupy;

2. *Calls upon* the parties concerned to start immediately after the ceasefire the implementation of Security Council Resolution 242 (1967) in all of its parts;

3. *Decides* that, immediately and concurrently with the cease-fire, negotiations start between the parties concerned under appropriate auspices aimed at establishing a just and durable peace in the Middle East.

[September 17, 1978]

Framework for the Conclusion of a Peace Treaty Between Egypt and Israel

In order to achieve peace between them, Israel and Egypt agree to negotiate in good faith with a goal of concluding within three months of the
signing of this Framework a peace treaty between them.

It is agreed that:

The site of the negotiations will be under a United Nations flag at a
location or locations to be mutually agreed.

All of the Principles of UN Resolution 242 will apply in the resolution of
the dispute between Israel and Egypt.

Unless otherwise mutually agreed, terms of the peace treaty will be
implemented between two and three years after the peace treaty is
signed.

The following matters are agreed between the parties:

(A) the full exercise of Egyptian sovereignty up to the internationally
recognized border between Egypt and mandated Palestine;

(B) the withdrawal of Israeli armed forces from the Sinai;

(C) the use of airfields left by the Israelis near El-Arish, Rafiah, Ras
en-Naqb, and Sharm el-Sheikh for civilian purposes only, including possible commercial use by all nations;

(D) the right of free passage by ships of Israel through the Gulf of Suez
and the Suez Canal on the basis of the Constantinople Convention of 1888 applying to all nations; the Strait of Tiran and the Gulf
of Aqaba are international waterways to be open to all nations for
unimpeded and nonsuspendable freedom of navigation and
over-flight;

(E) the construction of a highway between the Sinai and Jordan near
Eilat with guaranteed free and peaceful passage by Egypt and
Jordan; and

(F) the stationing of military forces listed below.

Stationing of Forces

A. No more than one division (mechanized or infantry) of Egyptian
armed forces will be stationed within an area lying approximately 50
kilometers (km) east of the Gulf of Suez and the Suez Canal.

B. Only United Nations forces and civil police equipped with light weapons to perform normal police functions will be stationed within an
area lying west of the international border and the Gulf of Aqaba,
varying in width from 20 km to 40 km.

C. In the area within 3 km east of the international border there will be
Israeli limited military forces not to exceed four infantry battalions
and United Nations observers.

D. Border patrol units not to exceed three battalions, will supplement
the civil police in maintaining order in the area not included above.

The exact demarcation of the above areas will be as decided during
the peace negotiations.

Early warning stations may exist to insure compliance with the terms
of the agreement.

United Nations Forces Will Be Stationed:

(a) in part of the area in the Sinai lying within about 20 km of the Mediterranean Sea and adjacent to the international border, and

(b)   in the Sharm el-Sheikh area to ensure freedom of passage through the Strait of Tiran; and these forces will not be removed unless such removal is approved by the Security Council of the United Nations with a unanimous vote of the five permanent members.

After a peace treaty is signed, and after the interim withdrawal is complete, normal relations will be established between Egypt and Israel, including full recognition, including diplomatic, economic and cultural relations; termination of economic boycotts and barriers to the free movement of goods and people; and mutual protection of citizens by the due process of law.

Interim Withdrawal
Between three months and nine months after the signing of the peace treaty, all Israeli forces will withdraw east of a line extending from a point east of El-Arish to Ras Muhammad, the exact location of this line to be determined by mutual agreement.

For the Government of the   For the Government of
Arab Republic of Egypt   Israel
Witnessed by:
Jimmy Carter, President of the United States of America

Washington—following are the texts of the exchange of letters accompanying the Camp David agreements released by the White House, September 22, that dealt with the status of Jerusalem, a definition of the terms "West Bank," "Palestinians" and "Palestinian People," and a statement of willingness by Egyptian President Sadat to speak for the Arab side, if necessary, in the early stages of establishing a Palestinian self-government.

1.   Begin to Carter

September 17, 1978

Dear Mr. President,

I have the honor to inform you that during two weeks after my return home I will submit a motion before Israel's Parliament (the Knesset) to decide on the following question:

If during the negotiations to conclude a peace treaty between Israel and Egypt all outstanding issues are agreed upon, "are you in favor of the removal of the Israeli settlers from the northern and southern Sinai areas or are you in favor of keeping the aforementioned settlers in these areas?"

The vote, Mr. President, on this issue will be completely free from the usual Parliamentary Party discipline to the effect that although the coalition is being now supported by 70 members out of 120, every member of the Knesset, as I believe, both on the government and the opposition benches will be enabled to vote in accordance with his own conscience.

Sincerely yours,

Menachem Begin

2. Carter to Sadat

September 22, 1978

Dear Mr. President:

I transmit herewith a copy of a letter to me from Prime Minister Begin setting forth how he proposes to present the issue of the Sinai settlements to the Knesset for the latter's decision.

In this connection, I understand from your letter that Knesset approval to withdraw all Israeli settlers from Sinai according to a timetable within the period specified for the implementation of the peace treaty is a prerequisite to any negotiations on a peace treaty between Egypt and Israel.

Sincerely,

Jimmy Carter

Enclosure: letter from Prime Minister Begin

3. Sadat to Carter

September 17, 1978

Dear Mr. President,

In connection with the Framework for a Settlement in Sinai to be signed tonight, I would like to reaffirm the position of the Arab Republic of Egypt with respect to the settlements:

1.   All Israeli settlers must be withdrawn from Sinai according to a timetable within the period specified for the implementation of the peace treaty.

2.   Agreement by the Israeli Government and its constitutional institutions to this basic principle is therefore a prerequisite to starting peace negotiations for concluding a peace treaty.

3.   If Israel fails to meet this commitment, the "Framework" shall be void and invalid.

Sincerely,

Mohamed Anwar el-Sadat

4. Carter to Begin

September 22, 1978

Dear Mr. Prime Minister:

I have received your letter of September 17, 1978, describing how you intend to place the question of the future of Israeli settlements in Sinai before the Knesset for its decision.

Enclosed is a copy of President Sadat's letter to me on this subject.

Sincerely,

Jimmy Carter

Enclosure: letter from President Sadat

5. Sadat to Carter

September 17, 1978

Dear Mr. President,

I am writing you to reaffirm the position of the Arab Republic of Egypt with respect to Jerusalem:

1. Arab Jerusalem is an integral part of the West Bank. Legal and historical Arab rights in the city must be respected and restored.
2. Arab Jerusalem should be under Arab sovereignty.
3. The Palestinian inhabitants of Arab Jerusalem are entitled to exercise their legitimate national rights, being part of the Palestinian people in the West Bank.
4. Relevant Security Council Resolutions, particularly Resolution 242 and 267, must be applied with regard to Jerusalem. All the measures taken by Israel to alter the status of the city are null and void and should be rescinded.
5. All peoples must have free access to the city and enjoy the free exercise of worship and the right to visit and transit to the holy places without distinction or discrimination.
6. The holy places of each faith may be placed under the administration and control of their representatives.
7. Essential functions in the city should be undivided and a joint municipal council composed of an equal number of Arab and Israeli members can supervise the carrying out of these functions. In this way, the city shall be undivided.

Sincerely,

Mohamed Anwar el-Sadat

6. Begin to Carter

September 17, 1978

Dear Mr. President,

I have the honor to inform you, Mr. President, that on 28 June 1967—Israel's Parliament (the Knesset) promulgated and adopted a law to the effect: the Government is empowered by a decree to apply the law, the jurisdiction and administration of the State to any part of Eretz Israel (Land of Israel–Palestine), so stated in that decree.

On the basis of this Law, the Government of Israel decreed in July 1967 that Jerusalem is one city, indivisible, the Capital of the State of Israel.

Sincerely,

Menachem Begin

7.   Carter to Sadat

September 22, 1978

Dear Mr. President:

I have received your letter of September 17, 1978, setting forth the Egyptian position on Jerusalem. I am transmitting a copy of that letter to Prime Minister Begin for his information.

The position of the United States on Jerusalem remains as stated by Ambassador Goldberg in the United Nations General Assembly on July 14, 1967, and subsequently by Ambassador Yost in the United Nations.

Sincerely,

Jimmy Carter

8.   Sadat to Carter

September 17, 1978

Dear Mr. President,

In connection with the "Framework for Peace in the Middle East," I am writing you this letter to inform you of the position of the Arab Republic of Egypt, with respect to the implementation of the comprehensive settlement.

To ensure the implementation of the provisions related to the West Bank and Gaza and in order to safeguard the legitimate rights of the Palestinian people. Egypt will be prepared to assume the Arab role emanating from these provisions, following consultations with Jordan and the representatives of the Palestinian people.

Sincerely,

Mohamed Anwar el-Sadat

9.   Carter to Begin

September 22, 1978

Dear Mr. Prime Minister,

I hereby acknowledge that you have informed me as follows:

(A)   In each paragraph of the Agreed Framework Document the expressions "Palestinians" or "Palestinian People" are being and will be construed and understood by you as "Palestinian Arabs."

(B)   In each paragraph in which the expression "West Bank" appears, it is being, and will be, understood by the Government of Israel as "Judea and Samaria."

Sincerely,

Jimmy Carter

Appendix 3

March 26, 1979

The President,
The White House.

Dear Mr. President:

This letter confirms that Israel and Egypt have agreed as follows:

The Governments of Israel and Egypt recall that they concluded at Camp David and signed at the White House on September 17, 1978, the annexed documents entitled "A Framework for Peace in the Middle East Agreed at Camp David" and "Framework for the Conclusion of a Peace Treaty between Israel and Egypt."

For the purpose of achieving a comprehensive peace settlement in accordance with the above-mentioned Framework, Israel and Egypt will proceed with the implementation of those provisions relating to the West Bank and the Gaza Strip. They have agreed to start negotiations within a month after the exchange of the instruments of ratification of the Peace Treaty. In accordance with the "Framework for Peace in the Middle East," the Hashemite Kingdom of Jordan is invited to join the negotiations. The Delegations of Egypt and Jordan may include Palestinians from the West Bank and Gaza Strip or other Palestinians as mutually agreed. The purpose of the negotiation shall be to agree, prior to the elections, on the modalities for establishing the elected self-governing authority (administrative council), define its powers and responsibilities, and agree upon other related issues. In the even Jordan decides not to take part in the negotiations, the negotiations will be held by Israel and Egypt.

The two Governments agree to negotiate continuously and in good faith to conclude these negotiations at the earliest possible date. They also agree that the objective of the negotiations is the establishment of the self-governing authority in the West Bank and Gaza in order to provide full autonomy to the inhabitants.

Egypt and Israel set for themselves the goal of completing the negotiations within one year so that elections will be held as expeditiously as possible after agreement has been reached between the parties. The self-governing authority referred to in the "Framework for Peace in the Middle East" will be established and inaugurated within one month after it has been elected, at which time the transitional period of five years will begin. The Israeli military government and its civilian administration will be withdrawn, to be replaced by the self-governing authority, as specified in the "Framework for Peace in the Middle East." A withdrawal of Israeli armed forces will then take place and there will be a redeployment of the remaining Israeli forces into specified security locations.

This letter also confirms our understanding that the United States Government will participate fully in all stages of negotiations.

Sincerely yours,

For the Government of the
Arab Republic of Egypt:
Mohamed Anwar el-Sadat

For the Government of
Israel:
Menachem Begin

Explanatory Note

President Carter, upon receipt of the Joint Letter to him from President Sadat and Prime Minister Begin, has added to the American and Israeli copies the notation:

> I have been informed that the expression "West Bank" is understood by the Government of Israel to mean "Judea and Samaria."

This notation is in accordance with similar procedures established at Camp David.

THE JERUSALEM INSTITUTE FOR FEDERAL STUDIES

The Jerusalem Institute For Federal Studies is an independent research and educational institution established by a group of Israeli scholars in 1976 to initiate, facilitate and conduct research projects and educational programs on questions of federalism, power-sharing, cooperation and covenantal relations in general, on a comparative and inter-disciplinary basis, and to broadly disseminate the results of its work. It seeks to foster understanding of the federal idea in its various forms and the use of federal principles and practices where appropriate. The Institute is located in Jerusalem in the conviction that the land of Israel, as the birthplace of the covenant idea which is the foundation of federalism, and Jerusalem as a principal center of human aspirations for a better world, must play a significant role in so vital a human movement.

THE WORKSHOP ON FEDERAL RESPONSES
TO CURRENT POLITICAL PROBLEMS

was founded on the premise that the time has come to apply the accumulating expertise of students of the federal principle to systematic consideration of current problems of political integration with a view to generating a variety of federal options for their resolution. The sponsors of the workshop are the Senator N. M. Paterson Chair of Intergovernmental Relations at Bar-Ilan University and the Jerusalem Institute for Federal Studies. The Workshop is linked with the Center for the Study of Federalism, Philadelphia, Pennsylvania. The central activity of the Workshop is the annual Paterson Conference on Federal Responses to Current Political Problems. The first two conferences, held in 1977 and 1978 respectively, focused on "Federalism and Political Integration" and "Federal Solutions for the Israeli-Arab Conflict." In addition, meetings of the Workshop seminar are held on a periodic basis.